D1279111

Praise for Top Maui Restaurants

"This book is a treasure chest of information. This is the third edition of the book that I've purchased over the years, and each year James and Molly exceed my expectations and amaze me that they continue to seek out and find gems of restaurants on Maui. This book is more like a "Bible" than a reference book when it comes to providing valuable information, and the money that you'll save by following their advice and dining at the recommended establishments will pay for this book many times over. I'm sold on James and Molly!"

– EDWARD MENDELSOHN, WESTON, FL

"I love ur book. We just left maui and I used ur book for the second year in a row. U and your wife have the best advice."

– ALISON, SENT FROM HER VERIZON WIRELESS BLACKBERRY

"This book is one of two guidebooks to Maui that we consider a must. Unlike the free guides readily available everywhere, the authors give you the straight scoop on a whole range of restaurants. It is very easy on Maui to find terrible restaurants and leave feeling ripped off. Even the bad ones are expensive. This guide led us to several places we would not otherwise have given a second look … This wonderful, entertaining guide was worth every penny. It will be on our short list of "must brings" to Maui — unless there is a new version out."

– S. PIPER, PORTLAND, OR

"Not having visited Maui in 30 years, I had no idea where our family of four would be able to eat at reasonable prices. Given the fact that Hawaii, in general is so expensive, this wonderful book not only gave a comprehensive and entertaining review of Maui's offerings, but it was organized, thorough and easy to use as a daily guide … This book made an important part of our trip less challenging and took away the stress and frustration of trying to find nice, clean and reasonably priced restaurants. I am so very glad we purchased this book — I recommend it highly — no one should travel to Maui without it!"

– KRAIG AND DEBBIE, YORK, PA

"We just returned from Maui with a well-used copy of this book! We are VERY frequent visitors to Maui (about three times a year) … The book paid for itself the first new place we tried. James and Molly, mahalo nui loa!"

– KIMBERLY SHAW, WAILEA, HI

"We have been coming to Maui for years, and love good food. We therefore have some experience regarding the good restaurants. However, because we bought this book, we happily dined at several restaurants that we would not have otherwise frequented. Besides being accurate, the Jacobsons write in a way that is entertaining and plain fun. They are obviously devoted foodies, and their descriptions of some of the dishes that they like best are such that you can almost taste them. As anyone who has been to Maui knows, food is quite expensive over here. You can spend a great deal of money at a mediocre restaurant just as easily as at a great one. This makes the purchase price of this book (about the price of an appetizer at a good Maui restaurant) a bargain. If you like good food, and are coming over here, buy this book!"

– PAULA A. WOOD, HILTON HEAD ISLAND, SC

"I'm a resident of Maui, and think this book is great. If I decide to go out to a nice restaurant I want to know that I'm going to get what I pay for. So far I haven't been disappointed by their recommendations. Thanks for bringing honest reviews about restaurants to Maui rather than having to rely on the Menu guide."

– LAURA A. BURGER, KIHEI, HI

"Just a note to thank you for the *Top Maui Restaurants* guide. My husband I used it extensively and found some great food - your guide was very helpful. Merry Christmas and Mahalo for the guide."

– GAE SELLSTEDT, VANCOUVER, BC

"I ordered your guide on-line. It is excellent. We are from Calgary, Alberta and have been to Maui twice but not for over 10 years, so your guide will come in handy when we visit again in April."

– TERRY & SUSAN WINNITOY, CALGARY, ALBERTA

"My wife and I spend a couple months on Maui every year, and we eat out every day, so we thought we knew a lot about Maui restaurants. I even have a website of my own reviewing Maui restaurants, hotels, condos, sights and activities, so I constantly try to keep up on the latest and best Maui restaurants in all price ranges. But this book, Top Maui Restaurants, taught me much more. It helped me find out about many excellent restaurants I was not familiar with even after years of going to Maui. It helped me learn about what are the best things to order at certain restaurants. It helped me choose restaurants based on what I most wanted for any given meal based on food types, ambience, and service. Most guides to Maui restaurants just tell you the basic facts (location, type of food, and hours of operation). This book of restaurant reviews gives you all of that, plus so much more, with detailed expert evaluations and opinions. It's like the difference between looking up a restaurant in the phonebook compared to reading a full-page review of that restaurant in a local newspaper. These authors know Maui restaurants!"

– Maui Jon, Michigan

"My wife and I went to Oahu and Maui for our honeymoon and on the airplane ride there we both made our choices for which restaurants to visit. We visited one or two places a day and were pleased with all of them!! We only wish there was a book for Oahu because our trip there was disappointing every night for food, luckily we were in Maui for nearly 10 days of eating so we were able to end on a good note. We tried every level of food - from cheap eats like Guri Guri and Café O'Lei, to expensive and top-notch at Capische? and Spago. We only wish we had more time to try more places. Some places we never would have even known about with the best burgers and views and popular places where we may have gone already but wouldn't have ordered what we did without James & Molly's recommendations. All in all, phenomenal book with great picks and truly a must have for first-time Maui travelers. We'll be using it on trip #2 and if anyone we know goes this books is top on our list to let them borrow. Enjoy! Thank you James & Molly!"

– Patrick Flynn, Boston, MA

"I love the honest and artful writing style, as well as advice that is unbiased and never steers me wrong. I have found many excellent recommendations and new favorites in this book. I have also had my suspicions confirmed.... (Why did I think that meal was so average when this restaurant is supposed to be so great?). Great advice, a must have for visiting, or living on Maui if you appreciate great food!"

– DeLane

"My wife and I own two vacation rental condos in Kihei which we visit 2-3 times each year. I just bought this book as a digital download a couple of days ago and it is fantastic. I started by reviewing our favorite places as well as some expensive disappointments we have been to, and their assessments were right in line with what we thought. That has given me the trust to try their recommendations later this week and on future trips. I am buying two paperback versions to keep in our condos for our guests to use. This is a book that is fun to sit and read if you are a "foodie" who likes to read food magazines and books, or likes to watch Food Network TV shows. Since we're in Kihei we're heavy on Kihei-Wailea eating with the occasional trip to Lahaina-Ka'anapali-Kapalua, and this will be our guide to choose excellent food on those trips ... Their inexpensive-moderate restaurant recommendations are helpful, and selecting one great "cost is no object" romantic treat makes this book completely worthwhile. On our last several trips to Maui we have spent well north of $200 for dinner for two at high-end restaurants that left us completely disappointed. Ouch. It won't happen again! Buy it and enjoy!"

– Rob Meldrum,
Edmonds, WA

Top Maui

RESTAURANTS

— 2012 —

From Thrifty to Four Star

Indispensable Advice from Experts
Who Live, Play & Eat on Maui

by James Jacobson
& Molly Jacobson

with Shannon Wianecki

Published by:
Maui Media, LLC
www.MauiMedia.com

Top Maui Restaurants 2012 from Thrifty to Four Star
Indispensable Advice from Experts Who Live, Play & Eat on Maui
By James Jacobson and Molly Jacobson with Shannon Wianecki

ISBN 978-0-9752631-9-8

www.TopMauiRestaurants.com

Cover and Text Design by Dawn Lewandowski of Partners Image Coordinators • 1-877-535-1155

Author Photo Credit: Michelle Brady

Dedication

To my father, Kenneth Jacobson, who taught me
the joy of good eating and how to love with a full
heart. Those gifts inspire me today, and inspired
this book. *Ich liebe dich*.

– James Jacobson

To my aunt, Sandy Lovejoy, who taught me to
trust myself and listen deeply; to my grandmother
Ruth, whose kitchen inspires me to this day; to
my hanai mother, Rhea Barton, who taught me
to feed myself, to set big goals, and to speak my
clearest truth. I miss you all and love you very
much. Thank you for everything.

– Molly Jacobson

Finally, we dedicate this book to the joy we take
in each other, and to our marriage.

Quick Start Guide

We write this book as if we were writing for our best friends: most people read the Introduction and like it so much that they continue reading all the way through the book. (This surprises, and also pleases, us.)

Here's a quick overview of the book so you can use it with ease. Happy Eating!

Warm Aloha,
James & Molly

First:

The Table of Contents starts on page iv, and it lists every restaurant reviewed in this book as a separate "chapter." After that, you will find the Introduction, which tells you about us: who we are, and how we came to write this book. Then we give you a little insight into how we review restaurants, plus a guide to the icons used in our reviews.

Restaurant Reviews:

Restaurant reviews start on page 13 and are arranged in alphabetical order. Each review contains our thoughts and impressions about the restaurant. You'll also find handy little icons that show you special features and our star ratings "at a glance."

Top Maui Tips:

The "tips" in this section are short articles that explain what we think or how we feel about a broad range of topics related to Maui. These are our answers to the FAQ (Frequently Asked Questions) we've fielded from readers over the many years we've been writing this specialty travel guide.

Top Maui Restaurants:

We call the next section Top Maui Restaurants because it focuses exclusively on the restaurants we really like — the ones we would eat in even if this weren't our book to write. We list restaurants by food craving, location, and best bang for your buck. And then, just because we've been asked so many times, we're finally including a full list of every reviewed restaurant according to its numerical rating. The information in this section of the book does not represent our full opinion of each restaurant, but it does provide you with a culinary snapshot of Maui based on our own experiences.

Index

At the very end of the book you will find a comprehensive index that lists every single keyword we can think of, including food items, dishes, restaurant and Maui business names, and the names of key chefs on Maui.

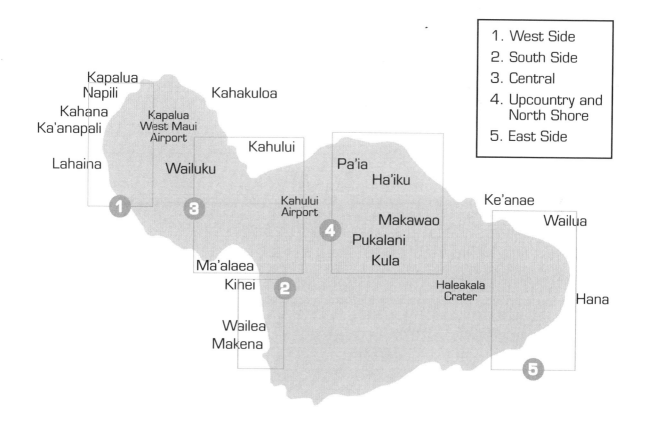

Kapalua
Napili
Kahana
Ka'anapali
Lahaina
Kapalua
West Maui
Airport
Kahakuloa
Wailuku
Kahului
Kahului
Airport
Ma'alaea
Kihei
Wailea
Makena
Pa'ia
Ha'iku
Makawao
Pukalani
Kula
Haleakala
Crater
Ke'anae
Wailua
Hana

1. West Side
2. South Side
3. Central
4. Upcountry and
   North Shore
5. East Side

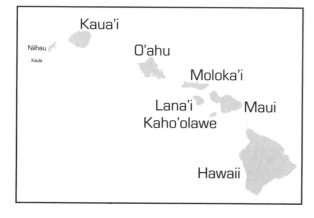

Kaua'i
Niihau
Kaula
O'ahu
Moloka'i
Lana'i
Kaho'olawe
Maui
Hawaii

Maui

Contents

C

D

E

U

V

W

Register This Book and Get Free Updates!

We want to be able to keep in touch with you throughout the year as we send out updates from our blog, www.MauiRestaurantsBlog.com.

When you register your book with our site, not only will you get **Aloha Fridays**, our (usually) weekly update on the Maui restaurant scene, but we will also send you a special "down-and-dirty" email that lists updates for this edition.

The email will list restaurants that have closed since publication, and also significant new restaurants worth your time and dollars. If our opinion of a restaurant changes significantly, we will tell you, briefly, how and why. We'll also alert you to any new food stands or Maui delicacies we think you should try while you're here. And even if you register your book months before you need to use it, you can still get this latest information by emailing customer support at cs@topmauirestaurants.com. Include the email address you used to register the book, and ask to get the latest update email.

Register your book here:

www.TopMauiRestaurants.com/2012

Introduction

This book is born of desperate necessity and soul-searing, passionate love. It has taken seven years to write, decades to research, and was inspired by a glorious Maui sunset and an unforgettable meal.

The story is so magical and romantic you might not believe it. Even my own mother can hardly believe it happened to me. But everything I'm about to tell you is true. And it could not have happened anyplace else on earth but Maui.

Several years ago James and I met on a beach on Maui. With our first glance, we were catapulted into an intense love affair. We each gasped a little in recognition of our connection; it felt downright mystical. Our hands took the initiative and reached for each other. As they intertwined for the first time, James murmured "Where have you been all my life?" (Yes, he really said that.)

I couldn't answer. I could only stare, like a wide-eyed child, then look away at the sky above his head still streaked with my first Maui sunset. The first quarter moon was already bright, and two stars popped out as his eyes twinkled.

"I don't 'like' food. I love food. If I don't love it, I don't swallow."

— Ego,
Restaurant Critic,
Ratatouille

He asked, "Are you hungry?"

I nodded; my head heavy on my suddenly weak neck. I *was* hungry. I was also struck dumb and a little dizzy. My arms tingled just above the wrist. Was my circulation cut off? But he persisted:

"Do you like sushi?"

This snapped me out of my moonstruck state. My head cleared and I spoke crisply: "No, I don't. I *love* sushi. But I have to warn you, I think most of what passes for sushi shouldn't be fed to a stray cat."

James smiled and drew me to his side. We turned and faced the distant island of Lana'i, arms wrapped around each other, pulling our quickly beating hearts close together. Watching the sky shift from pink to indigo to velvet, he said, "That's my girl. I knew you'd drift in someday." The waves crashed louder and louder until they were all I heard.

When time started again, James took me to my first Maui restaurant. Following the petite hostess in her silk kimono through a large, lusciously draped room filled with long-haired beauties and a piano player pouring honey-sweet music all over the floor was like walking into my most private dream. We were seated at a table along the rail on the wraparound lanai (porch). Two waiters immediately hustled away for our drinks.

We toasted each other, tinkling our white porcelain cups brimming with warm sake. The miso arrived, and we drank the deep, rich, hearty broth straight from the bowl. We told our life stories and held hands in between plates of fish and bowls of rice. Our fingers and our chopsticks cradled the tender pink and yellow and white morsels before delivering them to our tongues, where they quivered a little before giving up their sweet ocean flavors.

Every once in a while I pinched my thigh beneath my napkin. Was this really happening?

We stayed until the pianist had retired, other diners had departed, and the lights were dimmed. As they cleaned and stacked and cleared, the servers brought us cool water, tiny coconut creams, and refreshing green tea, assuring us that we should stay until we were ready to go. It was clear to all of us that magic was happening, and no one wanted to interrupt it.

On the drive back to the beach, heavy perfume from plumeria trees lining Wailea Ike Drive rushed through the open windows. I asked James "Is this heaven?"

He smiled and said "I think so." I had never felt so content, relaxed, and beautiful.

After we parted for the night, I called my girlfriends back on the east coast and woke them up one by one. As I giggled and swooned and stammered my way through the story of my first Maui evening, dozens of stars sprang from their places in the black sky above my car and streaked across the ridges of Haleakala in the most glorious meteor shower I'd ever witnessed.

Our *Top Maui Restaurants* review guide was conceived on that magical night, but we didn't have an inkling of it yet. Two months later, firmly established in our new love affair and still discovering the depths of our mutual passion for food, James and I were driving by "our" restaurant when we saw a "Now Closed" sign over the door.

I was shocked. How could this paragon of fabulous dining, unbelievable ambience, and stellar service have thrown in the towel?

James shook his head sadly, and a weary expression crossed his face. By this time we had eaten in several of the restaurants reviewed in this guide, and he explained carefully that each one of them — no matter how wonderful — were in imminent danger of closing due to the heavy overhead and high turnover inherent in the Maui restaurant scene. Restaurants on Maui, he explained, open and close overnight like tropical flowers. For as many superb restaurants as there are now, several times that number had failed since 1990, when he first arrived.

The following week we took a beach walk after breakfast. I noticed a beautiful restaurant practically on the sand and asked him why he hadn't suggested going there for dinner yet. He wrinkled his nose and said "It's not worth it."

I was skeptical, and pressed him. I was hungry for Italian, I said, and I wanted a special night out to celebrate our two month anniversary. According to several of my guidebooks, it was one of the best restaurants on the island. James gave up with an affectionate shrug, and we booked a table for that evening.

To my surprise and growing horror during the meal, James was right. I won't go into detail here, but will leave it to your imagination until you read the review on page 155.

After we left, I stormed "Why didn't anyone warn me?! We just spent over $200 on a meal that wasn't worth half that — at a restaurant I never would have **bothered** with in New York!"

The next day we were still talking about it, and the next, and the next. Watching my consternation grow at the "inaccuracy" and "unreliability" of tourist guides, James's author wheels started turning. The problem, he decided, was that I was relying on dining guides, not dining reviews.

What's the difference? A whole heck of a lot.

Dining Guides are primarily descriptive, and are designed to tell you the Who, What, Where, and When of a restaurant. They leave out the essential How and the crucial Why.

A Dining Review, on the other hand, is written by an actual person (or in this case, two persons joined at the hip) with actual opinions and actual (hopefully good) advice. A good review does not just *describe* the restaurant. It also helps you decide if you want to *eat* at the restaurant.

We noticed that most Maui dining guides are actually tourist guides — in other words, advertising vehicles. Relentlessly positive reviews became suspect. How could a restaurant have no flaws, whatsoever? Not possible. Or, at least, rarely possible.

Of course, many visitors turn to the internet for restaurant recommendations. We love review sites when we visit other cities — but beware when you visit a tourist area, because many reviews are written by one-time diners, not by locals who have an idea of what the restaurant offers on a consistent basis. We found this out ourselves, when we visited Kaua'i this year. If we had relied solely on internet reviews to decide where to eat, we would have missed one of the best meals we've had this year (at the Kaua'i Grill).

On a recent visit to Paris, we were steered wrong so many times by internet review sites (even those written in French by locals) that we gave up even checking. Instead, we consulted a lovingly researched book written by ... *voila!* ... a local foodie. She steered us toward the best restaurant values and — oh, heaven — the Salon Saveurs food show, which takes place twice a year, and happily, was open during our stay. It took us two days to work through the hundreds of stalls, but we ate like royalty for the next six weeks. With Clotilde's advice, we found countless other places we would have waltzed right by otherwise.

What about advice from locals? Maui is a small island, and many who live here have chosen their favorite restaurants based on their affection for the owners, rather than the quality of the food. Concierges are too often compensated for steering you towards certain restaurants. We don't take comps of any kind, and while we are all for friendship, it's what's on the plate that matters.

James and I both come from food-obsessed families and are excellent home chefs. We've eaten in the best restaurants in America, Europe, and Asia — not once or twice, but repeatedly. This past year we spent six weeks in one of the culinary capitals of the world, Paris, just to ... eat and study. They say you have to invest 10,000 hours into an activity in order to become an expert; after twenty years of dining out almost every night (and most days) we each individually passed that milestone years ago.

My aunt was a restaurant owner and nat-ural foods chef, so I grew up knowing about and eating healthy, organic food prepared to taste absolutely delicious. I started baking at the age of seven, and made all family birthday cakes, including my own. I cooked for my family when my mother returned to work, and I learned firsthand how challenging it can be to focus amidst chaos and infuse love into the food. I also learned how magical food is when you do it right, and how a good meal can pull a fractious bunch together.

Later I lived in Boston and then New York City, where I ate at the best restaurants (not necessarily always the most expensive) every single day of the week. I took cooking classes, read cookbooks from cover to cover (even though I wasn't cooking myself — I'm a perpetual student).

I've always had friends who loved good food — and my four years in New York City taught me that food can be the very best form of social entertainment. Even when I moved to Montana — not known for its high cuisine — I made a point of learning as much as possible about grass-fed beef, local produce, and the wonderfully sweet, wild-but-mild huckleberries the bears love almost as much as we do.

James's obsession with food started at his grandmother's kitchen table, at age five. He studied her cooking, trying to capture her recipes on paper. She was a French and German cook who had never written anything down, so his notes (he still has the "recipe book") include "Stir until arm grows tired," and "Pour flour into one of Grandma's hands, two of mine, until it overflows just a little." To this day he speaks in German when he makes us breakfast.

When James started his business consultancy he worked with restaurant owners so he could get complimentary meals (we have a strict anti-comp policy for our guide — much to the chagrin of our accountant). This allowed him to dine at the best restaurants in Washington, DC, where he was raised. He has taken cooking classes everywhere he's lived and traveled — including Le Cordon Bleu in Paris — picking up hundreds of techniques, ingredients, and culinary mindsets. He's even studied Ayurvedic Indian cuisine with Mother Teresa's personal chef.

Once he realized the desperate need for a genuinely insightful, useful, honest, advice-oriented Maui restaurant review, James suggested we draft a review of "our" two restaurants: the dreamy-but-closed Japanese place and the too-well-marketed-to-die-a-natural-death Italian joint.

And that's how Top Maui Restaurants was born. The more we wrote, the more we wanted to write … until soon we had over fifty reviews. We shared them with a couple of friends who were coming to Maui, and they called them "invaluable." We started selling our guide to people researching their Maui vacation online. (We still do.) Over the years the guide increased to over 200 pages. During that time, many people asked if there was a paperback book available. They didn't want to print out 200 pages from their home computers. We shook our head dismissively and said "Who needs another travel book to Maui?"

But the demand kept coming, and we finally gave in for the 2008 edition of the guide. This, the 2012 edition, is still the definitive dining review guide to Maui — and, to our continual surprise, the second best-selling guidebook to Maui.

We get mail every day from readers who have just spent time here and used this book. Their stories about the memorable meals they've had are touching and spur us to create an even better guide for each year.

To that end, we've added a new voice for this edition: Shannon Wianecki has joined us as a contributor. We've always relied on reports from foodie friends to flesh out our views on Maui restaurants — in a way, this book gives you a the opinion of about twenty Maui residents — but Shannon is the most-foodiest-of-foodies. [NB: We hate the word "foodie." But it seems to have stuck.]

Shannon very recently left her eight-year post as the Food Editor at *Maui No Ka Oi*, a magazine known for its gorgeous writing and glorious photos. She's also judged cooking competitions, hosted restaurant award dinners, and lectured on food writing. Oh, and she's waited tables in several five-star restaurants, slung espressos, and been an Indonesian short-order cook. The daughter of a French-trained pastry chef, she has been working with food in one capacity or another all her life. She's written about it for *Honolulu*, *Modern Luxury Hawaii*, *Gastronome*, and *Vacation & Travel* magazines. Her book credits include *Fodor's Hawaii*, *Fodor's Maui*, *Freedom in Your Relationship with Food*, and *Simple Ayurvedic Recipes*.

Bringing Shannon on as a formal contributor meant that we were able to keep some reviews we would normally have to cull due to lack-of-freshness. Her own experiences with each restaurant, and some of her "behind-the-scenes" knowledge, have been worked into each review. We wondered, when this project began, if Shannon's views would not mesh with ours. We shouldn't have. As she put it, "I continue to find it eerie how often I agree with your opinions on each restaurant!" Shannon has also beefed up the tips in the Top Maui Tips section.

Everyone who visits Maui feels the magic that flows through this place. It's not just paradise on earth — not just white sand beaches, endless skies, warm breezes, swaying palm trees, lush rainforests, green volcanoes, whales, dolphins, and rum drinks.

There's something else at work here. We don't want to get too woozy, but Maui can make you kind of … woozy. It's so … delicious. Like a coconut warm from the sun, cut open and spilling its milk down your throat, it's sweet. When you come here, you relax on some deeper level and life starts looking more manageable. Parts of you that may have been dormant wake up. Life looks … good.

We want you to relax on your vacation, and then relax some more. Stressing out about food — about when, where, how much, or what to eat — should not be on your agenda. Let us guide you. We write these reviews as if we were writing to our friends, and we would never recommend a place that we wouldn't send our best friend to. (In case you think we're always positive, we include some less-than-glowing reviews, especially those of places that market themselves well enough to attract your attention but are not worth your time or money.)

We write with one audience in mind: you. If the place looks dirty, we say so. If the food is overcooked, we point it out. If the dessert is brilliant, we cheer and ooh and ahh. The better the restaurant, the pickier we get.

We can usually dine anonymously, although now, of course, some of the more savvy restaurateurs recognize us. Still, we stick to our no-comping policy and refuse to take advertising from restaurants (even though some want us to). We eat out an average of eleven times every week, rotating through restaurants to update our reviews.

Our friends think we're nuts. They're happy to help by dining with us at certain places, and they report their own dining experiences back to us, but they flat out refuse to eat at many of the restaurants we have to review. And those who work with visitors get every new edition of the guide.

Why? Because the number one question they field from visitors is "Where should we eat tonight?"

You won't be asking that question. You'll be spending your time on Maui lazing by the pool, trailing your fingers in the tidal basins, or snorkeling. Thoughts of where to go to dinner may enter your mind, but they'll quickly be answered by flipping through this guide.

At least, that's our hope. After all, Maui can be magic — and we wouldn't want its romance lessened in any way.

In 2007 James and I were married on Lana'i. One day during our honeymoon, we caught a glimpse of Maui and knew we were looking at the beach on which we met those years ago. We imagined looking back through time at our former selves at that magical moment and embraced as we had then, drawing each other close and feeling each other's hearts beating with the ocean waves. We thought of our home, just one block away from that beach, and sighed with contentment and happiness.

It's our most sincere hope that you will have a magical time while you are on Maui, too. This book should help. James and I wish you shooting stars and glorious sunsets, and very, very good eating.

Warm Aloha,

Molly Jacobson

Kihei, Maui, Hawaii

December, 2011

How Reviews are Organized

There are nearly four hundred restaurants on Maui, and while we've eaten at the vast majority of them, we cannot include them all in this guide. We review nearly two hundred restaurants in this section, all of which we think are important. Restaurants are important for one of the following reasons:

1. They are restaurants we recommend.
2. They are restaurants we do *not* recommend, but have been asked about. We used to leave these restaurants out entirely (that's why we named the book *Top Maui Restaurants*) but then we received so many questions about these places that we had to include their reviews to be of service. Some of these restaurants spend a good deal on advertising, which is why so many are curious about them. In other cases, the restaurant may once have been quite good — even "Top" — but has since fallen in our estimation.

Restaurant Information

Along with the review itself, we list the:

- Street address, City, and region of the island (South Maui, West Maui, etc.)
- Nearby landmarks
- Meals (breakfast, lunch, dinner)
- Hours (accurate as of publication)
- Parking
- Phone number
- Website

Helpful Icons

There are several icons used in reviews, designed to help you get information "at a glance."

 This symbol indicates we would visit the restaurant even if we weren't reviewing it. A restaurant that has a great view and awful food cannot get this symbol, but a restaurant that serves terrific food in a dumpy location can. You will see that some "3 Star" restaurants get our Top symbol, while some "4 Star" restaurants do not.

[NB: Please don't take this symbol as a guarantee. Also, please remember that the symbol is given at publication time — and things can change. If you register your book at www.TopMauiRestaurants. com/2012 you will get our update email, which will tell you if any restaurants have been moved into or out of this category.]

 This symbol indicates the restaurant is noteworthy in some way. It may be that we love breakfast (but not dinner), or that the noodles are fantastic but the rest of the menu isn't … whatever the reason, we like them enough to recommend them for certain things. Read the review to get the full story.

If a restaurant does not have either of these symbols, assume that we do not feel strongly enough to recommend you visit.

Star Ratings

We thought long and hard before we created our 5 Star system, which incorporates five different ratings. It's very difficult to pin down a restaurant into a single Star rating. Instead, we rate on five separate categories: Food, Ambience, Service, Love, and Value. Each restaurant can earn up to five stars in each category. Then we average the scores across the five categories to come up with an Overall Star Rating. The highest possible Overall Rating is 5 Stars, but no one has earned it (yet).

Here are the categories.

Food

How good is the food, and with how much skill is it prepared? Restaurants lose points for poor ingredients, lousy recipes, unskilled prep work, and over- or under-cooked food.

Ambience

What's the restaurant itself feel and look like? Generally, this rating will reflect how upscale the restaurant is. Beach shacks may score as low as 1 Star (although a clean beach shack would get 2 Stars and one with a gorgeous view might get 5 Stars), while high end restaurants could get as many as 5 Stars. Some restaurants with gorgeous views get to keep their Five Stars even if they have other flaws in decor, because we feel the overall impression is "Wow." Restaurants lose points for dirt, being stuffy, too windy, or in poor condition.

Love

This rating reflects how much "love" we can feel in the restaurant and taste in the food. Love is hard to describe in words, because — like the emotion — love is primarily experiential: something you "know when you feel" (or in this case, taste). Remember how you felt when someone who loved you fed you something that tasted good? The feeling of being cared for and thought about is what we are trying to capture in this rating. That feeling can come through in a restaurant meal when the people in the kitchen — and when it's a really loving restaurant, in the front of the house — genuinely care about your experience. They pay attention, and they get it right.

OVERALL: **3.5** out of 5 stars

Service

How efficient, friendly, and knowledgeable is the service? (Also see the Tip on service in the Top Maui Tips section.) Restaurants lose Stars for indifferent or pretentious service (we think each is bad), slow service, and sloppiness or lack of courtesy.

Value

Is the money spent worth the experience? Most restaurant critics don't really address this in their reviews — but most restaurant critics aren't writing for people dining on Maui, the most expensive place to eat out in America (according to a 2008 AAA survey). All Maui restaurants — with just a few rare exceptions — charge at least 30% more than they could if they were on the mainland. (This is not just because we're a tourist market — it's also because rents are outrageous and food costs exorbitant.) This rating reflects how good a deal the restaurant represents when we take the previous ratings and the average cost of the restaurant into account. When we give a restaurant an average value rating — 3 stars — we mean that they give average value *for Maui*. If you see a 5 star rating, the value is extraordinary *for Maui*. A beach shack that quickly serves up bone-sucking good $5 ribs might get 5 Stars for Value, while an expensive restaurant with pretentious service and so-so food might get 3 Stars for Value (or fewer). Accordingly, an expensive restaurant with stellar service and fabulous food and ambience could easily get a value score of 5 Stars.

Overall Score

This number reflects the five other ratings, averaged.

As you start comparing restaurants to each other, you will see why our system works: there are "Top" restaurants in every price range. What is most important to recognize is everything is relative. The real value in this scoring system appears only when you compare restaurants to one another. We stand by our opinions, but we don't expect everyone to agree with us. As objective as we try to be, our personal preferences can't help but be part of our experience. Like most restaurant critics, we feel that reviews should be seen as conversation starters, not as verdicts. Restaurants change. They get better and they get worse — and diners change, too. What was fabulous a few years ago may no longer be exciting.

Restaurant Prices

You might be surprised by how differently people perceive whether a restaurant is "Inexpensive," "Moderate" or "Expensive." After years of trying to educate people about *our* definitions, we have given up, and now just tell you how much entrées cost.

Every restaurant is rated from one to four dollar signs ($-$$$$).

$ The average entrée price is $10 or less

$$ The average entrée price is $10-$20

$$$ The average entrée price is $20-$35

$$$$ The average entrée price is $35 and up

Note that the $ only refers to the average cost of the *entrées* on the *regular* menu, not the overall cost of the meal, including appetizers, desserts, drinks, tax, and tip.

Special Features

Certain restaurants have special features that you may be looking for. These are

usually covered in the review, but also through the use of symbols:

The restaurant has a view of sunset during most of the year (remember, the sun moves through the sky as the seasons change, so the location of the sunset can vary).

The restaurant is either right on the water or there is an unobstructed view (for example, a beach walk or street) of the water.

The restaurant serves alcohol. The review usually indicates whether there is a full bar or just a beer and wine list.

The restaurant is near Kahului Airport (OGG).

The restaurant offers a children's menu and/or is loved by children. If this symbol does not appear, assume the restaurant is geared more for adults than children. This does not mean that your well-behaved child who is experienced at dining out is unwelcome — just check with the restaurant.

 Reservations are recommended or even required. During very popular travel times like Christmas week, Spring Break, and the summer months, nearly every restaurant will be very busy, so you might want to call for reservations, even if this symbol is not there.

 The restaurant has made some level of effort to include vegetarian options. There is only one all-vegetarian, full-service restaurant on Maui (**Fresh Mint**). All others with this listing have either a separate vegetarian menu or are considered vegetarian-friendly because they are willing to modify their meals or methods for vegetarians/vegans. If this is a concern for you, please notify the restaurant ahead of time so they can note your preferences for the kitchen.

 The restaurant usually offers a discount to diners who carry a Hawaii driver's license or other state-issued ID. Sometimes the discount is only offered at certain times or during certain months.

 The restaurant has a particularly romantic ambience and is good for a special occasion (for example a wedding dinner, honeymoon dinner, or anniversary).

 The restaurant has a consistently good Happy Hour: good drinks and food, and sometimes, depending on location, a good sunset view.

 The restaurant has live music on a regular basis.

 American Express accepted

 Discover accepted

 MasterCard accepted

 Visa accepted

CASH Cash only

A Note about Accuracy:

Travel information of any kind is subject to change at any time, especially information about restaurants on Maui. Restaurants open and close virtually overnight here, and we cannot guarantee that any reviewed in this book will still be open when you arrive, or that the hours, prices, and menu won't be very different. Just as an example, the night before this edition went to the book designer, we picked up some dinner at the only Chinese restaurant on Maui that we like. The owner informed us that they were closing at the end of 2011. Bummer! We pulled the review and had to find the many places in the book that we had mentioned East Ocean. All information is accurate as of publication — but for the latest updates you should register this book at www.TopMauiRestaurants.com/2012 and also pay attention to our email updates, **Aloha Friday**.

How We Review Restaurants

There are a great many food writers working these days — especially with the explosion of interest in this, the most primal of experiences. Many are very good writers, but not everyone approaches their work the way a journalist does. James' dad was a reporter, and he got the journalism bug early: the first time James hosted his own full-length radio show, he was only 16. He interviewed everyone from Supreme Court justices to pop culture icons like Dr. Ruth Westheimer to titans of industry like Ted Turner on a major talk radio station in Washington, DC. Molly wrote for the arts section at a Boston newspaper, and reviewed books for years … so it never occurred to either of us that we would approach restaurant reviewing in any way other than that recommended by the **Association of Food Journalists**:

Every restaurant is visited multiple times. Every restaurant has been visited at least twice, and in most cases, three, or more, times before we pen a review. We do this because every restaurant can have a stellar day, and every restaurant can have a terrible day. If a restaurant is inconsistent over time, it is hard for us to recommend it unreservedly, and we say so. We refresh our reviews on a regular basis, and certainly as close to publication time as possible.

We pay for every meal. If the restaurant offers a discount to locals or has a special running, we take the discount (we are ethical, but not dumb). At times we have been comped a dessert or an appetizer by our server. Very rarely is this because we have been recognized as critics; usually it is because we are good customers. To this day, some of our very favorite restaurants clearly have no idea that we write about them.

We dine under cover when possible. We used to be able to be completely "under cover," and most restaurants on Maui still have no idea who we are. But Maui is a very small island, and there is less than two degrees of separation between us and most restaurateurs. When everyone goes to the same movie theaters, shops at the same stores, and goes to the same beaches, it is easy to get to know others. And because we have so many other projects going in our businesses, some have put two and two together and do recognize us when we walk in the door (even after we use a different name for the reservation).

[NB: We've always suspected that there isn't much a restaurant can do to improve their performance, even if they do recognize us. But we were proven correct a couple of years ago when a friend of ours told a very expensive restaurant (*Merriman's Kapalua*) that we were coming that evening — and that we had previously had several disastrous experiences. Despite the warning, we still had an awful meal with excruciatingly slow service and food so salty we were still reeling the next day. You can't send out for good food, or train servers, if you just don't have it together. By the way, things may be looking up at *Merriman's* based on our last meal there. See the review for more details.]

Restaurant Reviews

808 Bistro *(American)*

808 Bistro is a funky restaurant in a funky spot, tucked back from South Kihei Road behind the decidedly rowdier ***Fred's Mexican Café***. Being in the rear of the complex works for them: they have a lovely slice view of the beach from their main open air dining room, with a beautiful patio/garden area in the back of the restaurant. They haven't renovated this space significantly since they opened (Greek Bistro used to be here), but it is quiet and comfortable. Prices are relatively low for the area, and it's also BYOB, which seems to be a draw for South Maui visitors suffering from Wailea Wallet Fatigue. The staff is unfailingly sweet (and cute), there's no corkage fee, and they supply wine buckets and ice for your cold beverages.

Charming funky turns to just plain *funky* funky when it comes to the food, which has gone downhill steadily since a rather promising opening in 2010. Terribly sloppy presentations, obviously commercial ingredients (and bottled sauces), a curious penchant for sugar (or too much vinegar, or both), and unappetizing recipes dominate the menu. The "pork and beans" is a plate souped with a "cassoulet" of oddly sweet cannellini beans, with a layer of overcooked spinach topped by a perfectly done but unfortunately glazed tenderloin (candy-sweet butterscotch). The sweet overwhelms the savory in this dish — nothing is subtle. The impression of having your dessert with your pork is disconcerting, at best.

The fish trio served three ways doesn't work in any of them. The pot pie is a ramekin filled with some short ribs and gigantic chunks of potato, briefly covered with a sheet of commercial puff pastry. With the exception of the acceptable flat iron steak and the average-but-tender braised short ribs (the same ones in the pot pie), dinner entrées fall flat. Vegetarians are out of luck.

The salads are nice, in general, but some of the most "popular" appetizers — the crab dip, the lox tart — are not. We do very much like the buffalo shrimp — we even bought some Frank's Hot Sauce to make our own at home — but we're not sure why you only get six medium-sized crustaceans when you're paying $11. And why does the macadamia nut banana foster come with pecans? And why, when we peek into the exhibition kitchen, is the microwave the most prominent appliance?

Breakfasts are pleasant with that beautiful beach view, if you stick with the egg dishes, but we do not recommend their "whale pie" or the tooth-achingly sweet banana bread French toast.

Address: 2511 S. Kihei Rd., Kihei, South Maui
Location: Across from Kamaole Beach Park II
Meals: Breakfast, Dinner
Hours: 7am-12pm (breakfast), 5pm-9pm (dinner)
Parking: Lot, Street
Phone: 808-879-8008
Website: www.808bistro.com

808 Deli *(American)*

This little deli tucked behind **Fred's Mexican Café** features creative and saucy sandwiches, paninis, hot dogs, salads, and breakfast sandwiches. Paninis are made to order (which you factor into the wait time) and we like them because they're not so cheesy that they sploosh all over your hand when you bite into the grilled sandwich. The $6 hot dogs are kosher and come with a wide array of toppings: avocado and mango salsa, kim chee, and sauerkraut. Sandwiches include deli meats, tuna salad and chicken salad. A good choice to take to the beach or on a long drive is the $10 boxed lunch, which includes sandwich, chips, cookie (homemade), and a drink. If you want to stay, there is a small bar area, or you can sit at one of **808 Bistro's** tables just a little farther back in the complex. They're closed for lunch, but offer you their lovely garden and beautiful slice-of-beach view.

Address: 2511 S. Kihei Rd., Kihei, South Maui
Location: Across from Kamaole Beach Park II
Meals: Breakfast, Lunch
Hours: Daily 7am–5pm
Parking: Lot, Street
Phone: 808-879-1111
Website: www.808deli.net

OVERALL:
3.2
out of 5 stars

$

A Saigon Café *(Vietnamese)*

A Saigon Café is one of our favorite restaurants, even though it features run-down decor, is difficult to find, and the waiters can't seem to stop telling cheesy jokes. We ignore the barely acceptable ambience and return our focus to the food, some of the freshest and most delicious on Maui: well-prepared Vietnamese classics, including a superlative pho.

There's a deep commitment to fresh food here. The owner, Jennifer Nguyen, stocks the kitchen with vegetables and herbs she's grown herself and makes a sincere effort to buy locally whenever possible. We've never seen a wilted lettuce leaf. The mint leaves that top many dishes are fresh-picked and snap crisply between the teeth. The fish is fresh and the shrimp are plump and pink.

Some of our favorite dishes include the crispy, spicy Dungeness crab, and the chicken and shrimp braised in a brown sauce in the traditional clay pot. If you like fish, ask the waiter what they have that day for whole-fish preparations. They can wok-fry or steam it — either style is delicious, so follow their guidance on which preparation to use on whichever fish they have that day. The wok-frying leaves a thin crust on the outside, which hides the tender chunks of flesh underneath and protects them from drying out. The black bean sauce is hearty and complexly spicy-sweet. The steamed version with ginger and garlic shuts our other senses down so that picking the fish off the bones becomes a meditation.

OVERALL:
3.6
out of 5 stars

$ $

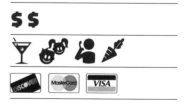

continued on next page

A Saigon Café *(continued)*

We *love* their "burritos." A stack of rice paper and a bowl of warm water are served first, followed, in short order, by a platter of raw shrimp, chicken, beef (or some combination), sliced cucumbers, pickled carrots, bean sprouts, fresh mint, and lettuce leaves. A fondue pot containing a light broth, pineapple slices, vegetables, and herbs bubbling over a carton of sterno appears next. The waiter will show you how to assemble your burrito, but essentially you drop your protein into the fondue to cook it while you dip your rice paper into the warm water to soften it. Then you pile vegetables, sprouts, mint, rice noodles, and hoisin sauce onto the sticky paper, and once your meat or fish is cooked to your liking, you place it on the bed of fresh food and carefully wrap the thin, stretchy rice paper around the whole thing. We like to place our burrito in a lettuce leaf to make it easy to bite. Delicious and fun, we leave it to the authorities to decide if the sterno presents a fire hazard.

There's finally a sign on the outside of this restaurant, but the inside could still use fresh paint, new tiles in the bathroom, new booths ... well, a big renovation. Some find the brusque, jokester waiters rude, but fans like us think of them as the "show" and laugh along with them. If your cell phone disappears during dinner, don't worry. It will reappear with the bill.

All jokes aside, the servers provide brisk, efficient service and are knowledgeable about the food they serve. The wine list is nothing special, but they have the usual Asian beers that complement the cuisine. We like their lemonade, which is sweet and made with both limes and lemons. We recommend skipping the Thai dishes and the desserts, (a five minute drive gets you to **Thailand Cuisine** for the first and **Ululani's Shave Ice** for the second).

Reviewing restaurants can be grueling work. After days of eating so-so meals that have lightened our wallets, added paunch to our waistlines, and flattened our taste buds, we make a trip to **A Saigon Café** to soothe our palates and remind us of how wonderful food can be.

Address: 1792 Main St., Wailuku, Central Maui

Location: This is "under" the highway overpass in Wailuku. As you drive into Wailuku on Kaahumanu Ave., look for the neon shooting stars and the pink building to the right of the highway overpass as you drive over it. Turn right on Central Avenue at the KAOI Radio Station intersection. Take your first right onto Nani St. Drive to the first stop sign. Turn right onto Kaniela St, and the restaurant is on the left.

Meals: Lunch, Dinner

Hours: M–Sa 10am–9:30pm and Su 10am–8:30pm

Parking: Lot, Street

Phone: 808-243-9560

Aina Gourmet Market *(deli)*

This classy deli and sundry shop is run by the same owners behind *I'o*, **Pacific'o**, the lu'au Feast at Lele, and the certified-organic farm O'o Farms. Both the gourmet deli items and the groceries reflect Chef James McDonald's fetish for all things local, organic, and dynamic.

Tucked in a corner of the stylish Honua Kai lobby, the deli is lovingly constructed from all recycled or up-cycled materials: salvaged granite countertops, Big Island eucalyptus flooring, and kiawe wood posts. A sustainable ethic reigns throughout the tiny deli: the servers wear hemp aprons, to-go packaging and cutlery is biodegradable, and all of the produce is harvested at the company's own O'o Farm.

For breakfast, we like the acai smoothie or any of the fresh baked pastries. But we usually stop here for lunch, on the way to or from the beach.

The fish wrap pairs the day's fresh catch with vine-ripened O'o tomatoes, roasted Maui onions, and remoulade sauce. The Local Beast sandwich comes on soft, whole-grain bread made locally at Home Maid Bakery and piled with hormone-free Maui Cattle Company roast beef. The parsley dill cream and horseradish is nice, but we ask for extra to make it a bit punchier. (We like a hint of that nostril-clearing bite.)

Sandwiches include a choice of chips, fruit, or salad. The gourmet salads are the best value; choose from beets with roasted garlic, orzo with smoked salmon and capers, fish ceviche, and potato salad tossed with strips of salami.

For dessert, we've been impressed by the handcrafted gelato and the fun cupcakes (we request these cupcakes when visiting friends from Lahaina ask "What can we bring with us?"). Deli servers are prompt and professional and willing to offer advice for island adventures.

You can score some great gifts for foodie friends here. Specialty groceries include tins of foie gras, microbrews, half bottles of bubbly, and local, pasture-raised eggs (a rare treat on Maui). O'o Farm recently began producing its own coffee, which you can buy here: 100% Arabica beans grown and roasted on the upper slopes of Haleakala. Four varieties include the chocolaty Mokka™ dark roast and a Red Catuai espresso roast. The in-store grinder is a thoughtful convenience.

The outdoor tables overlooking the koi pond are delightful, but you can also head across the lawn to Kahekili Beach — one of the island's most beautiful stretches of sand.

Address: 130 Kai Malina Pkwy., Ka'anapali, West Maui
Location: at Honua Kai Resort and Spa
Hours: Daily 7:00am-9:00pm
Parking: Valet, self-parking lot
Phone: 808-662-2832
Website: www.ainagourmet.com

Alive & Well *(Health Food Store)*

This small health food store has a good salad bar, sandwiches, sushi, vegan bakery items, and of course, groceries. It is good for vegetarians wandering Kahului or those looking for a break from rich food. The salad trio for $9.95 is a superb value if you mix the higher ticket items, such as quinoa and ahi. The power slaw is a perfect midday energy boost and daily soup specials include satisfying carrot ginger and Maui Cattle Company chili. Get excellent advice on vitamins and nutrition in the well-stocked supplement section from Dennis and Mona, the owners. They host a fascinating and informative weekly radio show called *Alive and Well!* on 1110AM.

Address: 340 Hana Hwy., Kahului, Central Maui
Location: on Hana Highway near BJ's Furniture
Meals: Breakfast, Lunch, Dinner
Hours: M-F 9am-7pm; Sa 9am-6pm; Su 10am-4pm
Parking: Lot Phone: 808-877-4950
Website: www.aliveandwellinmaui.com

Aloha Mixed Plate *(Local/Plate Lunch)*

Aloha Mixed Plate is a Maui institution. The turquoise-walled, tin-roofed restaurant lounges on the waterfront in Lahaina with one of the best views on the island. The gentle lapping of the water, the boats coming and going, and the sunset view make for an idyllic scene. The only problem with this scene? No alcohol this close to the water … you have to sit in the bar for the Happy Hour specials (from 2pm to 6pm beers are $1.75 and Mai Tais are $3).

The restaurant takes its name from the Hawaiian tradition of "plate lunch" or "mixed plate," which comes from the days when sugar plantations carpeted the islands and workers of several nationalities shared their food with each other on lunch breaks. Chinese workers brought noodle dishes like chow fun, Japanese brought their teriyaki and rice, and Filipinos brought adobo or slow-simmered pork. Koreans brought ribs, and the Hawaiians contributed their kalua pig. Plates were passed and each worker would take a portion from each dish, ending up with the "mixed plate" that perfectly reflects the melting pot that is Hawaii.

At *Aloha Mixed Plate*, you can get all of the above dishes in many different plate lunch combinations — mini and full portions — plus coconut prawns, Hawaiian classics like the salty lomi lomi salmon and the silky poi, kalua pig sandwiches, and teriyaki burgers, all at very reasonable prices. Rice and macaroni salad (two scoops rice, one scoop macaroni) always come on the plate to fill in the spaces. The noodles in the chow fun look fun and chow mein dishes are made in house and served with crunchy bean sprouts and snap peas in a Chinese take-out box. This is good food at great prices, but two signature dishes are a guilty addiction for many fans: the furikake garlic fries and the banana cheesecake lumpia, a multi-cultural confection in the spirit of the bygone plantation era. East coast cheesecake is slathered in caramel, wrapped in Filipino pastry, deep fried, and dusted in cinnamon.

Aloha Mixed Plate *(continued)*

The prices and fun, island-style atmosphere are key to this joint's attraction. There is nowhere else that serves fair-priced plate lunch *and* has an oceanfront location *and* offers tableside service *and* serves drinks (for $5.50, you might not mind that the mai tai features a lot of pineapple juice); you get a good value given the outstanding location. Servers tend to take your happiness for granted; they're gracious but not particularly attentive. We're usually looking out at the ocean anyway, and the restaurant's laid-back vibe is definitely Maui.

Address: 1285 Front St., Lahaina, West Maui
Location: Next to Old Lahaina Lu'au and across from Lahaina Cannery
    Mall
Meals: Lunch, Dinner
Hours: Daily 8am-10pm, Happy Hour 2-6pm
Parking: Parking lot.
Phone: 808-661-3322
Website: www.alohamixedplate.com

Amigo's *(Mexican)*

They say the family that cooks together stays together. We don't know how much "together time" the brothers who own these busy Mexican taquerias get, but we're glad they're cooking for us. The three locations — one in a backwater North Kihei strip mall, one in the back of the Wharf Center in busy Lahaina, and one in Kahului across from McDonald's — all serve up good quality Mexican dishes spiced with plenty of what we call Love.

Let's talk about Love, just for a moment. When we say a dish has a high Love quotient, what we really mean is that the person who prepared the dish was deliberate, thoughtful, and skillful.

We also mean the food tastes good.

We also mean ... oh, *darn it!*

We mean lots of things. Love in food is one of those ineffable, indefinable "you know it when you taste it" things, like the difference between good art and great art, or where erotica crosses a line and becomes pornography.

Anyway ... we feel — or taste — the Love in the food at ***Amigo's***. These guys have love for their food, their families, their culture, and for their customers. You can tell by the way you're greeted when you walk in. The smiles are warm, the advice on what to order is sound, and they bring the chips (freshly fried) quickly. You get your own salsa from the bar, which features a wide selection, all made in house. (They instituted a two-ramekin limit to the salsa, which we regularly break.) We like the chili verde, or green chili sauce served over pork. The sauce brings both full sweet flavors to the tongue and sneaking heat to the tonsils, just like it should. The pork

OVERALL:
3.6
out of 5 stars

continued on next page

Amigo's *(continued)*

is tender and flavorful. We also like the enchiladas, which feature fresh corn tortillas and generous fillings. You get a choice of red or green sauce for the top. We tend to get the red chili because we're often getting the green on another dish.

They have good burritos, flautas, chimichangas, and of course, tacos (flour or corn). We also like the chile relleno. A mild green pepper is stuffed with cheese, dipped in egg batter, and fried. The whole concoction is served with guacamole, pico de gallo, and ranchera sauce. The result is a crispy shell around a tender pepper that yields to the rather decadent cheese. The chicken mole is a commendable, if not outstanding version, of this traditional dish. The shrimp diabla (devil shrimp) is not for the faint of heart … but we adore the burst of flavor, and the way it clears our head.

The combination plates feature several house favorites and are a good value. They also come with the excellent spicy Spanish rice and delicious, perfectly seasoned beans, which taste like a family recipe (a good one). This is very good, fast Mexican food for takeout or dining in. If you choose to stay, they have bottled beer and generous margaritas to go with the daily specials. (We splurge and get the top shelf margarita, which runs you about $7 and is made with fresh juices.) The Kahului location is probably the least appetizing, as it's right off a gas station parking lot, but they've recently fortified the seating area's walls to create a more dignified atmosphere.

Address: 41 E. Lipoa St., Kihei, South Maui
Location: Just off South Kihei Road in the Lipoa Center.
Meals: Breakfast, Lunch, Dinner
Hours: Daily 9am-9pm
Parking: Lot
Phone: 808-879-9952
Website: www.amigosmaui.com

Address: 333 Dairy Rd., Kahului, Central Maui – Airport
Location: Across from McDonald's on Dairy Road
Meals: Breakfast, Lunch, Dinner
Hours: M-Sa 8am-9pm; Su 9am-9pm
Parking: Lot
Phone: 808-872-9525

Address: 658 Front St., Wharf Cinema Center, Lahaina, West Maui
Location: In the back of the Wharf Cinema Center across from the Banyan tree.
Meals: Lunch, Dinner
Hours: Daily 9am - 10pm
Parking: Lot, Street
Phone: 808-661-0210

Anthony's Coffee Co. *(Coffeehouse)*

Just about everyone stops into this Paia institution for a cup of joe at some point — including a cocker spaniel who waits patiently at the door for her owner to finish socializing. **We** come in for the decadent coffee ice cream-blended "Anthuccinos." Tasty breakfasts and pastries (muffins, donuts) make this a wise stop before you drive to Hana (they open waaaaaay early). The Benedicts come with veggies, turkey, ham, or kalua pork and reliably soft poached eggs. Locals swap their hash browns out for the proverbial two scoops rice, but you can opt for fresh fruit or tomato slices, if you like. They also do box lunches for your trip to Hana — call ahead and they'll have it ready for you when you arrive, or order their sandwiches, bagels, etc., to go. There are only a few small tables and a few counter stools and benches, so if you feel like a leisurely breakfast, head elsewhere.

If you like the brew, they sell their roast (the beans are roasted in house by the owner), as well as plenty of kitschy/silly souvenir type home décor items.

Address: 90 Hana Hwy., Paia, North Shore
Location: On Hana Highway across from **Flatbread Pizza Company**
Meals: Breakfast, Lunch, Snacks & Treats
Hours: Daily 5:30am-6pm
Parking: Street
Phone: 808-579-8340
Website: www.anthonyscoffee.com

OVERALL:
3.2
out of 5 stars

Antonio's *(Italian)*

Spicy, homemade Sicilian classics plus many daily specials are served at moderate prices in this teensy strip mall storefront. There's no gentle way of stating this: the walls are in dire need of a scrub. We'd be hesitant to eat here if we didn't have an unobstructed view of the kitchen, which in contrast looks well-kept. Red-checked tablecloths drape the handful of tables, verging on cheesy until you realize the entire cook staff is Asian and it just seems bizarre. (That's OK, though. One of the best Italian restaurants in Honolulu has an entirely Asian staff, too — there are simply more Asians than Italians in Hawaii. A love of good cooking can be inherited from any culture.)

Most everything is homemade. (We have our suspicions about the Thousand Island and Ranch dressings offered with the house salad, but the garlic bread's thick, fragrant mash is the real stuff.) The pink sauce — tomatoes, vodka, cream — is divine, better than we've had at pricier establishments. The stuffed pasta with gorgonzola, ricotta, and spinach touches our heart (and maybe puts a little extra strain on it, too). We also like the homemade sausages, tender and bursting with flavor. Daily specials usually feature a chicken, steak, and fresh fish. Many dishes are or can be made vegetarian-friendly.

OVERALL:
3.1
out of 5 stars

Antonio's *(continued)*

Lunches are mainly burgers, sandwiches, and basic pasta dishes. The wine list is limited but reasonably priced, and the tiramisu is lovely. Worth a stop if you're on the South Side looking for a moderately priced homemade meal. The menu is more creative than *Aroma D'Italia*, but that means there's a higher risk of inconsistency, too. The outstanding veal, for example, comes with a strange brown mushroom sauce. Swap that for marinara or pink sauce and you have a truly winning dish. When in doubt, let the waiter steer you. You may want to call ahead for reservations, as there aren't that many tables.

Address: 1215 S. Kihei Rd., Kihei, South Maui
Location: In the Long's Shopping Center
Meals: Lunch, Dinner
Hours: F-Su 11:30am-2pm; Daily 5pm-9pm
Parking: Lot
Phone: 808-875-8800

OVERALL:
3.7
out of 5 stars

Aroma D'Italia Ristorante *(Italian)*

Aroma D'Italia is a good choice for an affordable Italian meal. Located in the Foodland shopping center in Kihei, they have a corner location and a nice outside seating area that they've screened in and lit with fairy lights. Inside the restaurant is also a comfortable choice, although some find the lacey curtains, plump-Italian-chef salt and pepper shakers, travel posters, and the *Eh, Paisano!* -style music a little too much. We feel that this is a family-owned restaurant with homemade food, and if it is dressed a little like your Italian-American grandma, that's OK. Grandma makes good pasta. Actually, Chef Konrad Winder makes good pasta. He also makes decent marinara sauce, fine meatballs, delicious (but very cheesy) lasagna, passable sausages, and many other Sicilian classics. His daily dishes are particularly worth looking into.

The fresh fish is usually perfectly and tastefully prepared, and the lamb and beef specials are similarly tasty. We like the Italian sodas; perfectly flavored, bouncy on the tongue and creamy going down. Italian and American beers are also available, and there is a limited wine list. The homemade tiramisu is very nice. Service is consistent; many of the servers have been working here for a while, which is the sign of a good gig on Maui. This is a clean, affordable restaurant serving admirable, consistent family-style food, and our go-to restaurant when we're craving pasta in South Maui.

Address: 1881 S. Kihei Rd., Kihei, South Maui
Location: Kihei Town Center, Foodland's shopping center
Meals: Dinner
Hours: Daily 5pm-9pm
Parking: Lot
Phone: 808-879-0133
Website: www.aromaditaliamaui.com

Ba-Le Sandwiches *(Vietnamese)*

Nothing shoos away a threatening cold better than a flavorful bowl of *pho* — Vietnam's answer to mom's chicken soup. Whether it's piled with chicken, seafood, or slices of rare beef simmering in near-boiling broth, **Ba-Le's** pho is rich and unctuous, the noodles wide and slippery. The kitchen doesn't skimp on the fresh basil, bean sprouts, and jalapenos, all served on the side. Add a squirt of sambal (chili sauce) and good health is guaranteed. Whether we go for the *pho*, the noodle dishes, or one of their hearty sandwiches, our wallets stay about the same weight, and our bellies thank us.

OVERALL:
3.1
out of 5 stars

Ba-Le means "Paris" in Vietnamese, and believe it or not, this company makes great French bread — for Hawaii. (It's very hard to develop a good crust here, the clean air means less bacteria, which in turn means soft crusts.) You'll often see **Ba-Le** bread and cakes sold in local grocery stores on Oahu, even at picky, upscale **Whole Foods**.

These eateries feature a wide variety of hot and cold sandwiches made with their rolls and stuffed thick with ham, pate, or lemongrass chicken. Pickled daikon radish, slivered cucumbers, and carrots provide a crunchy, sour counterpoint. Most sandwiches cost under $7, which is a very good price on Maui. Meanwhile, the Vietnamese classics are also quite good. The noodle dishes feature well-seasoned grilled pork, lemongrass chicken, fried spring rolls, and many other fresh proteins that are prepared to order. For dessert, choose from a colorful selection of tapiocas — coconut or sweet potato. Skip the croissants, which tend to be limp. *C'est la vie.* While not fine dining, it is reliably good eats, and with several locations island-wide, they're easy to find.

Address: 1221 Honoapiilani Highway, Lahaina, West Maui
Location: Food court, Lahaina Cannery Mall
Meals: Breakfast, Lunch, Dinner
Hours: Daily 10am-9pm
Parking: Lot
Phone: 808-661-5566
Website: www.ba-le.com

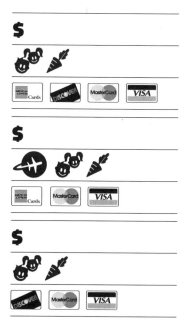

Address: 270 Dairy Rd., Kahului, Central Maui
Location: Food court, Maui Marketplace
Meals: Breakfast, Lunch, Dinner
Hours: M-Sa 9am-9pm; Su 9am-7pm
Parking: Lot
Phone: 808-877-2400

Address: 247 Pi'ikea Ave., Kihei, South Maui
Location: Pi'ilani Village Center, near Safeway
Meals: Lunch, Dinner
Hours: M-Sa 9am-9pm; Su 9am-8pm
Parking: Lot
Phone: 808-875-6400

continued on next page

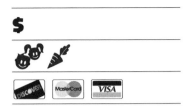

OVERALL:

2.5
out of 5 stars

OVERALL:

4.4
out of 5 stars

Ba-Le Sandwiches *(continued)*

Address: 1824 Oihana St., Wailuku, Central Maui
Location: Close to the overpass.
Meals: Lunch, Dinner
Hours: Daily 9am–9pm
Parking: Lot
Phone: 808-249-8833

Bangkok Cuisine *(Thai / Chinese)*

This is a small restaurant with crowded tables and a forgettable atmosphere. The food is inconsistent in preparation, generally bland, and even at its best not nearly as good as **Thailand Cuisine** or even **Dragon Dragon** a few blocks away. The "hands off" service borders on rude and it can be hard to get a server's attention — especially when they're on their laptop two booths over.

Address: 395 Dairy Rd., Kahului, Central Maui
Location: Near FedEx-Kinko's on Dairy Road
Meals: Lunch, Dinner
Hours: Daily 11am–9:30pm
Parking: Lot
Phone: 808-893-0026
Website: www.bangkokcuisinemaui.com

The Banyan Tree *(Pacific Rim)*

The Banyan Tree at the Ritz Carlton Resort in Kapalua is one of the finest restaurants on Maui, and would hold its own in any big city. Sequestered down by the resort's pool, we imagine the hotel's architect did not plan for this to be the resort's premiere dining spot. Luckily, the casual elegance of the open walls and glossy wood tables offers a pleasing counterpoint to the precisely-crafted, refined cuisine.

Chef Jojo Vasquez, who returned to the **Banyan Tree's** helm after a three-year whirlwind tour as sous chef to "Iron Chef" Morimoto, has the irrepressible enthusiasm of a child and the laser-like precision of a master. We're sooo glad he's back. His time with Morimoto-san clearly sharpened his personal quest for creative, boundary-pushing cuisine. If you aren't feeling particularly adventurous, this might not be the restaurant for you. We consider its departure from the norm an absolute treat from beginning to end.

Let's start with the bread. We usually don't review bread on Maui, since it nearly always ranges from just passable to disappointing (as we've said elsewhere, it's the clean air — no bacteria = no crust). However, the tradition at **The Banyan Tree** of serving the Egyptian spice mix *dukkah* with the sesame bread must be mentioned. The bread is soft and pleasant and a perfect transportation device for the *dukkah*. We often find ourselves finishing the entire loaf as we dip piece after piece into the dish of high quality olive oil, then into the crumbly mix of spices, nuts, and seeds. *Dukkah* means "coarsely ground" in Arabic, but we translate it as "heavenly."

Also heavenly is the Surfing Goat Dairy starter which pairs feta with roasted beets, red quinoa salad, and champagne vinegar. Or the hamachi crudo accompanied by dehydrated red peppers — delectably crisp wafers that melt against the fish. The seafood sausage appetizer, served with salmon roe, is decadent, and the pork belly steamed buns are less of a departure, but entirely satisfying.

Chef Vasquez's culinary fireworks include crisps, caviars, gels, foams, and dusts: the essence of an ingredient is isolated and presented in a novel way that often delights us, despite our knee-jerk aversion to molecular gastronomy in general. He particularly excels at tucking Persian and South East Asian influences into the menu here and there. The cumin crusted hapu (sea bass) served with harissa, a Tunisian chili sauce, is a welcome departure from the usual island-style seasonings, as is the steamed branzino (also a sea bass), which floats above the most delicate and delectable mushroom broth we've ever had. The drizzle of scallion oil and the crunchy leeks on top complement the tender fish perfectly; we had to pause, just for a moment, to appreciate the perfection of this dish. Chef Vasquez knows how to prepare and present fish.

We can't resist recommending the rib eye. The sous vide preparation — which involves submerging the vacuum-packed meat in gently boiling water — results in steak that is uniformly cooked and bright pink to its edges. Its moisture and tenderness are retained at their peak. While the rib eye may seem beyond the pale in terms of price, we have not once regretted ordering it.

While most fine restaurants on Maui can satisfy vegetarians, **Banyan Tree** *lavishes* them with a veritable cornucopia, including vegetarian entrées, sides, and a sampler of marinated shiitake mushrooms, turmeric-scented cauliflower, and a mushy but potent eggplant puree.

Desserts continue in the adventurous vein. A peanut butter parfait is served alongside a space-age vermillion globe that bursts with strawberry flavor against your palate. We especially like the house-made sorbets and ice creams: lavender, crème fraiche, and kinako (soybean flour — unusual, but tasty). The chocolate tasting dessert may seem too small — each of the three treats are the size of a Kit Kat bar — but it packs an outsize, intense chocolate experience. (Warning: ladies who enjoy chocolate, please be discreet ... it's not polite to moan loudly in public. Get it?)

The adage "you get what you pay for" certainly applies, as you'll see when you glance over the menu. This is one of the most expensive restaurants on the island, but it's one of the very few where we leave feeling we actually got our money's worth. There are some ways to cut back on the bill, and we recommend you take advantage of them. For example, each month the

continued on next page

The Banyan Tree *(continued)*

restaurant hosts a different winery for a chef's tasting menu, which is available throughout the month. At $130 per person for four courses paired with wines, it's not just an outstanding deal; it's also an opportunity to let the chef arrange an optimal succession of tastes. The featured wineries have included Cakebread and Stag's Leap. Another terrific savings occurs only on Wednesdays, when you can enjoy any bottle of wine for fifty percent off. And if you have a Hawaiian ID, you have no excuse — book your next special meal at *The Banyan Tree* for one of the best kama'aina deals on the island.

Service is usually good, and some servers are great. While the table settings are less formal than the prices would indicate (checkered napkins and table runners?), we don't care one whit once we taste the absolutely delicious food. Make your romantic evening complete with a post-meal stargazing session on the resort's quiet grounds.

Address: 1 Ritz-Carlton Drive, Kapalua, West Maui
Location: At the Ritz-Carlton Resort
Meals: Dinner
Hours: Tu-Sa 5:30pm-9:30pm
Parking: Valet, Lot
Phone: 808-669-6200
Website: www.ritzcarlton.com

OVERALL:
3.4
out of 5 stars

$ $

Beach Bums Bar & Grill *(American/barbecue)*

Picture a white, oval platter. On one side stretch out a glistening, mahogany brown half chicken. Watch as two long, thick beef spareribs (also deep red brown) climb in to spoon her from plump breast to tender thigh. Two bowls cuddle; creamed green beans piled with crispy onions; steaming baked beans.

When we taste the slow-smoked, top-notch Oklahoma-style barbecue at *Beach Bum's*, it's like watching Wilma Flintstone make food love to Fred. Delicious, guilty pleasure in a setting that — while the Harbor is under construction — might resemble the Stone Age. Smoking meat is a particular art form, one which takes both talent and patience. Beef ribs are rubbed out with a homemade spice mix before slow-cooking in the smoker. A half day later they emerge with long flanks charred and tender pink insides. They fall off their bone; they're done.

That so-seductive chicken is massaged with spices, wrapped in bacon, and set astraddle an open can of beer. She relaxes in the smoker's privacy while the liquid gold tenderizes her flesh and her cloak of bacon keeps the juices in.

There is no basting in the smokehouse tradition, so meats and sauces are judged as separate arts. Unfortunately, in our judgment neither of the two house barbecue sauces is a winner. The "spicy" is undistinguished except for a spiky mesquite flavor; the "mild" is sunk with too-sweet guava. (Combined, they make a decent sauce.)

Beach Bums Bar & Grill *(continued)*

All rubs, sauces, and sides are made in house, which we always admire in a tourist area. James, our Southern Boy, finds the comfort of home in the creamy green beans — but he adds a dash of salt. Molly's Boston roots want mustard added to the baked beans to dial down the sweet flavor — but she loves their tender texture. Fries are commercial shoestrings (but crispy), the mac-n-cheese average, the salads fresh but uninspired.

The open-air bar is often packed with rowdy local sports fans, but the service is still happy-touristy for the sunburned visitors dazzled by their Molokini snorkeling. We can put up with the toothy smiles ("**Hey**, how was your **day**? Where are **you** visiting from??) ...

...As long as the drinks still come fast and they check in regularly.

NB: Our ratings are for the barbecue, not the rest of the menu.

Address: 300 Ma'alaea Rd., Ma'alaea, Central Maui
Location: in the Ma'alaea Harbor Shops on the lower level, facing the
          harbor
Meals: Breakfast, Lunch, Dinner
Hours: Daily 8am–9pm
Parking: Lot
Phone: 808-243-2286

Betty's Beach Café *(American)*

This is a plum location overlooking the beach with a gorgeous ocean/sunset view. Unfortunately, the restaurant adage "the better the view, the worse the food" holds true here: commercial ingredients, sloppily prepared, and expensive considering the quality. The menu ranges widely and features sandwiches, seafood, and everything in between — including lobster for $13.95 on Wednesdays. Uninspired weekend brunches are buoyed by $2 glasses of champagne. The u-shaped bar is kitschy-cool to look at, but we wish they would live up to the location and serve a mai tai that isn't filled with coca cola and pineapple juice. They've made a nice renovation to the restaurant, and we like the super-over-the-top-fun Hawaiiana decor, but they are definitely relying on what the previous tenant also relied upon: a full view of the Feast at Lele lu'au show. The view alone brings in locals and tourists, but this doesn't seem quite fair to the lu'au, which is working just as hard to serve fabulous food as **Betty's** ... isn't.

OVERALL:
2.2
out of 5 stars

Address: 505 Front Street, Lahaina, West Maui
Location: At the back of 505 Front Street complex
Meals: Breakfast, Lunch, Dinner
Hours: Daily 8am–10pm; Bar until 12am
Parking: Lot, Street
Phone: 808-662-0300
Website: www.bettysbeachcafe.com

$ $ $

Big Wave Café *(Pacific Rim/American)*

At its best, **Big Wave** has been a moderately priced, no-frills place with generous portions of average food. In the last couple of years, the love has gone down and the portions, as well. There are now no substitutions (ever) on the specials, and if you want coffee with your $5 breakfast the bill will be $8. The breakfast fare is still satisfying, but the careworn attitude of the servers is not exactly a lovely way to start the day.

The early bird special is still available every day from 5-6:30pm, and they have lots of other price promotions in play, too. When the mood in the kitchen is good, the prime rib is an excellent deal, as is the coconut shrimp entrée. (We've noticed that moods tend to translate to the quality of the food.)

Address: 1215 S. Kihei Rd, Kihei, South Maui
Location: Long's Shopping Center
Meals: Breakfast, Lunch, Dinner
Hours: Daily 7:30am-9pm; bar open until 11pm
Parking: Lot
Phone: 808-891-8688
Website: www.bigwavecafe.com

Bistro Casanova *(Mediterranean/Italian)*

When a restaurant has heart and soul, you can always taste it in the food. But in the best restaurants, you can also experience it in the way the staff treats you, see it in the decor, and hear it in the "buzz" of the restaurant. Heart and soul is certainly evident at **Bistro Casanova**, Giovanni Capelli's newest venture. Sister restaurant to upcountry's institution, **Casanova**, **Bistro Casanova** reminds us that big-city style can blend with paradise.

The dark wood, hand-blown light fixtures, natural stone, and Mediterranean colors of **Bistro's** interior looks like a good restaurant *should* look. It's noisy, but the handful of tables outdoors allow for more intimate conversation. Shrouded by palms, the patio dining manages to evoke a casual elegance — even in dowdy Kahului.

Meanwhile, the menu — bistro specialties from France, Italy, and Spain — has settled into a routine for the kitchen. We haven't been able to get a good steak in Central Maui in ... well, in memory. But now we can, and do. The filets, rib eyes, and T-bones are grilled perfectly and served with your choice of several sauces, from a creamy green peppercorn brandy concoction to a Marsala wine and wild mushroom, to a béarnaise (and more). Served with a side salad dressed with excellent vinaigrette, the steaks also come with frites.

Chef David Gemberling is Belgian, and by tasting his *frites* we'd guess that he has been frying potatoes since childhood. Is there anything better than a serving of crispy-on-the-outside-tender-on-the-inside hand-cut potatoes? His are perfectly seasoned and Perfectly Addictive.

Bistro Casanova *(continued)*

The rest of the menu features more good bistro food, including an excellent duck confit. A leg of duck is roasted and carefully laid on top of a bed of tender, flavorful, slightly smoky lentils. Garnished with sautéed potato disks and truffle oil (which does what truffle oil does best: taste deliciously rich), this was eaten in its entirety.

The homemade pasta dishes are less consistently delicious. We've enjoyed the linguine al funghi — wild mushrooms in a creamy, garlicky pan sauce — and the calamari appetizer — lightly fried and served with a home-made tartar sauce. The paella is cooked to perfection (challenging in a dish combining everything from chicken to sausage to mussels and shrimp and clams and scallops), but too salty. So is the chicken cacciatore — though we like that it's organic. The smoked salmon over squid ink pasta is absolutely gorgeous, especially the studding of peas, leeks, and tobiko (salmon roe) … unfortunately, the flavor the servers rave about has escaped us on two occasions, possibly due to an excess of water in the pasta — we saw some separation in the sauce. The bolognese sauce, on the other hand, is flavorful and rich. The meatballs need less salt.

One of our all-time favorite desserts is Crêpes Suzette, and we've had a gorgeous, fresh-as-a-daisy version here. Unfortunately, its quality has slipped over the years: slightly stale crepes and nearly flavorless sauce. We're concerned: where has the sunshine gone?

At lunch sandwiches, savory crepes and panini round out the menu, as well as an extensive salad list. The Quawk salad with shredded duck, dried cranberries, and goat cheese over organic greens is ample enough to serve as a meal. We also like the caprese, which features Greek olives, feta cheese, and cucumber salad along with the obligatory slices of tomato, basil, and fresh mozzarella. Prosciutto is extra, but generously portioned, and if you're looking for something light before or after a movie, this is a good bet.

The tapas menu, served after 3pm, rotates with tempting specialties such as duck l'orange (can you tell we like their duck?), a juicy rib eye sandwich, and calamari in puttanesca sauce over polenta — all for under $10.

Reasonable prices for good to very good food is a compelling combination, but we resist recommending **Bistro Casanova** wholeheartedly because of chronic service problems. The wait at the door is often much longer than it should be — on one occasion the manager made us wait for nearly five minutes while he gave a sharp tongue lashing to an employee. The wait inevitably continues at the table, where the water, bread, and server are all slow to appear, and entire courses seem to arrive by parcel post. Service is friendly and knowledgeable, but this does not compensate for the inexcusable, interminable waits. We recommend the food, but please, don't arrive hungry.

If you're hosting a largish celebration of some sort — a birthday, rehearsal dinner, or reunion — the Bistro has an elegant private dining room. Dishes are served family-style on giant platters and, with a dedicated server or two you'll get all the attention you need.

continued on next page

Bistro Casanova *(continued)*

Bistro Casanova has set the goal of being an upscale-but-casual, unstuffy-but-professional neighborhood place welcoming to visitors as well as locals. When it opened in 2009, we predicted that it would thrive in the new location and perhaps become one of Maui's most successful restaurants. They're still a work in progress, and we're a little concerned that their love quotient has dipped slightly since they first opened … but overall, we're happy they're here.

NB: Check their website for promotions. As of publication, if you bring your boarding pass the day of your flight (before or after your flight) you get a complimentary crepe.

Address: 33 Lono Ave, Kahului, HI 96732
Location: At Kaahumanu Street and Lono Ave., turn onto Lono and make first left into parking lot
Meals: Lunch, Dinner
Hours: M 11am – 2:30pm; Tu – Sa 11am till closing
Phone: 808-873-3650
Website: www.BistroCasanova.com

Bistro Molokini *(American)*

The Grand Wailea is what we call the "Disneyland" resort. It's nearly cartoonish in its version of paradisiacal perfection: impossibly tall, skinny palms, golf-course-grass that is perfectly trimmed (but you never see them trimming it), and a water feature that loops throughout the grounds in roundabouts and waterfalls, with hidden grotto hot tubs and swim up bars. There's a bar in the pool restaurant, too, and ***Bistro Molokini*** bartenders make pretty good cocktails and "smoothies" that can feature both alcohol *and* ice cream.

The menu offers expensive, but decently made, items like ahi wraps, kalua pork nachos, big salads, and pizzas. There's also a small sushi selection, which is surprisingly good — and pricey. Service is efficient, if forcefully cheerful. This is a good place to spend your dining credit if you're taking advantage of one of Spa Grande's many package deals.

Address: 3850 Wailea Alanui Dr., Wailea, South Maui
Location: Grand Wailea Resort
Meals: Lunch, Dinner
Hours: Daily 11am-9pm
Parking: Valet
Phone: 808-875-1234
Website: www.grandwailea.com

Blue Moon *(American)*

Blue Moon is a local diner with lots of natural light from the plate glass windows, big tables crowded close together, and a big takeout/deli counter near the back. They feature plate lunch, seafood, steaks, burgers, and breakfast, but the food if average (with no exceptions we can find), and the coffee tastes burnt even when fresh. If you're in Kihei and looking for something relatively inexpensive and off the beach road, this is a decent option.

Address: 362 Huku Lii Pl., Kihei, South Maui
Location: Near the Tesoro station off the Pi'ilani Highway
Meals: Breakfast, Lunch, Dinner
Hours: M-Sa 7:30am-8pm; Su 7:30am-3pm
Parking: Lot
Phone: 808-874-8600

Brigit & Bernard's Garden Café *(German)*

This cozy little "biergarten" is lit with fairy lights and feels like a European oasis in the middle of the Kahului industrial zone. Its neighbors are fishmongers, body shops, an … ahem … "hostess bar" and window glass dealers. It is very popular with locals — including us — for good German dishes for both lunch and dinner.

The Wiener schnitzel and the Jaeger schnitzel are lovely, as is the bratwurst. (It's flown in, but delectable, especially the veal.) Many dishes come with a red cabbage as delicious as James's German grandma's, and the house bread — a hearty brown bread — is homemade and filled with love. (It's only available at dinner — it bakes during the day — and if Bernard doesn't have time to make it, they serve supermarket bread, instead. This disappoints, but we forgive.)

There's also an assortment of pastas, all of which we stay away from. There are always many daily specials, which tend to range from good to very good. If it's not on the menu, ask for the pork loin in their hearty port wine sauce. The rack of lamb is another good choice. Skip the desserts, but indulge in the excellent beer selection, including our favorite, Franziskaner Weissbeir.

Reservations are recommended because it's such a small place, but mandatory on Friday and Saturday nights in October, when they put out a huge Octoberfest buffet and party all weekend. If you're lucky, Bernard will come out of the kitchen and dance the funky chicken with his daughter while the oompah band plays.

Address: 335 Hoohana St., Kahului, Central Maui
Location: On the bend of the street, just off Alamaha.
Meals: Lunch, Dinner
Hours: Daily 11am-2:30pm & 5pm-9pm
Parking: Lot
Phone: 808-877-6000

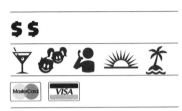

Bubba Gump Shrimp Co. *(American)*

At one time we would have shuddered to think we would recommend a chain restaurant that is **designed** to be a tourist trap ... but we can't help ourselves. If you like shrimp, don't mind paying prices that are nudged just a little higher than they should be, and if you won't hate yourself in the morning for contributing to their shameless commercialism (or being tempted to buy a t-shirt), **Bubba Gump's** is worth checking out.

First of all, it's on one of the best pieces of Front Street real estate: directly on the water with a front row view of the harbor, Lana'i, and sunset. We like to sit on the rail, and we wear clothes we don't care about too much — because we get sprayed nearly every time.

Every shrimp dish we can remember ever eating is on the menu, as well as OK steaks, pretty good fish dishes, and fried chicken that we like. But we usually order the shrimp sampler: a wired rack with arms holding paper cones filled with several different preparations ... this and the strawberry lemonade makes us as happy as *Forest Gump* when he runs without his leg braces. The overflowing bucket of peel-and-eat shrimp inspires one friend to spend lazy Sunday afternoons here with her sweetie.

If you haven't ever been to this theme restaurant paying homage to the 1994 classic Tom Hanks movie *Forrest Gump*, the incredible location and the friendly, efficient servers that keep the place running may be worth your stop. Everywhere you look there are details that tie into the movie; our favorite being the license plate-sized signs on each table. When you sit down, the green sign reads "Run, Forrest, Run!" When you're ready to order, or if you want to get your server's attention, flip to the red sign that reads "Stop, Forrest, Stop!" This system gets their attention so quickly that we sometimes muse it ought to be mandatory for all Maui restaurants.

The portions are the same whether you are there for lunch or dinner, and we like to eat mid-afternoon to avoid the crowds. We also like that our friends with kids can take their little ones here and totally relax, knowing theirs will not be the only table emitting spontaneous giggles and shrieks.

Address: 889 Front St., Lahaina, West Maui
Location: Right on the seawall on Front Street
Meals: Lunch, Dinner
Hours: Daily 10:30am–12am
Parking: Street
Phone: 808-661-3111
Website: www.bubbagump.com

Buzz's Wharf *(American/Pacific Rim)*

Buzz's is a Maui landmark, and it seems like nothing much has changed in the forty years they've been in business — from the bird of paradise napkin folds to the aloha print rattan chairs and stools. Located on the wharf in Ma'alaea, their great views — especially during whale season — are consis-

Buzz's Wharf *(continued)*

tent, and they're still using the same good ingredients, but the Love factor is slipping.

Or maybe it's just that the exquisite New Caledonia prawns they serve are no longer exclusive to their restaurant. We've had them at several other places that are just as good. But the "Sweet Prawns Tahitian" preparation at **Buzz's Wharf**, a baked dish using vermouth, dill, and parmesan cheese, has not been duplicated (that we've seen), and is still our favorite. The sweet (lobster-like), exceptionally tender shrimp are butterflied and perfectly set off by the slightly puckery sauce. Only five come on a plate, but if we ate more than that, we'd expire of a heart attack on the spot.

Fish dishes are generally OK, and only the lobster tail is truly expensive. If you're in Ma'alaea and have your heart set on fish, give **Buzz's** a try but keep your expectations in check.

Address: 159 Ma'alaea Boat Harbor Rd., Ma'alaea, Central Maui
Location: Ma'alaea Harbor Village, down on the water.
Meals: Lunch, Dinner, Pupus
Hours: Daily 11am–9pm
Parking: Lot
Phone: 808-244-5426
Website: www.buzzswharf.com

Café @ La Plage *(American)*

This little panini shop makes perfectly pleasant sandwiches for breakfast and lunch with fresh ingredients. We like that even though you order at the counter and they bring the food, they actually check back with you to see if you have everything you need. For essentially a takeout/internet place, that's a nice touch. Everything is made with care and attention, and the espresso drinks are *very* good. We skip the shave ice. This is a good place for breakfast before the beach, and an excellent choice for a beach lunch or a beach break.

Address: 2395 S. Kihei Rd., Kihei, South Maui
Location: In Dolphin Plaza across from Kamaole Beach Park I
Meals: Breakfast, Lunch, Snacks & Treats
Hours: M-Sa 6:30am - 5pm; Su 6:30am-3pm
Parking: Lot
Phone: 808-875-7668

Café Des Amis *(Mediterranean / Indian)*

This little bohemian Paia café has a handful of indoor tables in its tiny, sociable dining room and another smattering outdoors, where the fairy lit garden plays host to eclectic live music. The staff at **Café Des Amis** function as chef, barkeep, and server, so
continued on next page

Café Des Amis (continued)

depending on how hopping the joint is they can be sweet or slightly harassed. Service has never been quick, and you should avoid eating here if a leisurely pace drives you crazy or if your blood sugar is tanking.

Do come for the reasonably priced crepes, curries, and smoothies made from healthy, fresh ingredients. This menu is not extensive, but it's not meant to be. We like the quintessential breakfast crepe: ham, cheese, egg, and tomato. This makes a lovely light dinner as well. The lentil tomato crepe is basically an Indian dal wrapped up in a French crepe, and it's lovely. When we order the brie and apple crepe, we ask them to leave out the avocado, which turns the creamy texture of the brie into mushy ick in our mouths. All savory crepes come with huge dollop of sour cream and a small green salad (undistinguished, but fresh). For dessert, try the Maui cane sugar crepe with lime juice: crispy, tart, sweet. Or go Euro and dig into a pocket of melted Nutella.

Curries are good, and come in a few mild flavors. We ask them to take the heat up a notch or two, and the shrimp is our favorite. Each curry is served in a big bowl — nearly a serving bowl — with rice ladled next to the curry. If you like wraps and don't want so much rice, the curry wraps come with raita and mango chutney. The fruit smoothies are very fresh and creamy. The baristas know what they're doing and they've got superb Lavazza Italian espresso to work with. They list a handful of wines and beers, but we like their fantastic lilikoi margaritas.

This is a good place to stop when you're in the mood for something light but satisfying, and a great place to see Paia town neighbors hanging out with each other. The mismatched chairs (some of which are positively rickety) and the possibility of being showered upon (Paia gets some misty rain most afternoons) just reinforce the gentle non-conformist mystique of eating here. If you're sick of resort dining, *Café Des Amis* — with her fresh-from-windsurfing-servers — likely has the cure.

Address: 42 Baldwin Ave., Paia, North Shore
Location: Across from Mana Foods
Meals: Breakfast, Lunch, Dinner, Snacks & Treats
Hours: Daily 8:30am-8:30pm
Parking: Street
Phone: 808-579-6323

OVERALL:
3.6
out of 5 stars

Café Mambo and Picnics (Mediterranean)

After years of sampling *Café Mambo's* offerings, there are a few specific reasons we come to this funky, noisy, casual eatery.

1. The Crispy Duck Fajitas
2. The Happy Hour Burger and Beer Special
3. The Smoothies

We'll start with the crispy duck, which is rendered in its own fat and sau-

Café Mambo and Picnics *(continued)*

téed with a sweet sauce. The result is a luxurious concoction of caramel colored, tender shredded meat that is crispy and succulent, salty and sweet.

Whether you eat it on top of a bed of fresh greens (the salad), on a bun (the burger), or rolled in a flour tortilla with homemade salsa, guacamole, black beans and feta cheese (the fajita) is entirely up to you. All three preparations work for us, depending upon how hungry we are. The fajitas for two are large enough for four, while the single serving is large enough for two if you're getting other items. The salsa is somewhat flavorless, but the fresh greens that come with just about everything on the menu are dressed with tangy lilikoi (passion fruit).

We could end this review here, because the crispy duck is worth the trip to Paia. (We won't.)

Happy Hour, from 3pm to 6pm daily, is packed — you have to be willing to elbow your way to your seat past the boisterous wind- and kite-surfing crowd. The special price — at publication $3 on some of the most popular tropical cocktails and favorite beers — brings in lots of locals, as does the sensibly priced Burger and Beer special. Currently, for $9.95 you get a Maui Cattle Company burger with fries (or a green salad), and a beer. That is a very good deal for Maui, but we warn you now that if you like your burger less-than-well-done, please let them know that. Otherwise it's left on the grill too long and becomes a candidate for hockey practice. The tofu burger, which comes with a thick slice of cheddar, is also delicious.

If you're in the mood for something a little lighter, the hummus platter can be the perfect starter for a large group or an entire meal for one or two. The bright yellow hummus (from the cumin) is positively silky in texture, and when dipped with a warm pita triangle, mounds perfectly on the bread with a nice little tail hanging off. No mealy texture — our personal pet peeve — just creamy, earthy garbanzo flavors highlighted with warm, bright spicy tones. While you will see many other things on the menu, we recommend sticking to the appetizers, the fajitas, and the sandwiches. Although the paella is an honest effort, it is beyond this kitchen, and several of the other more expensive items are similarly too ambitious. Although we've focused on the duck, we must say that many vegetarian and vegan friends consider this the most vegan-friendly restaurant on the island, because many items can easily be slightly modified to remove the offending meat and dairy without losing flavor or style.

The smoothies are made with ice cream, so … well, isn't that enough? Breakfasts are good and include waffles, pancakes, omelets (a little over-done), hearty egg platters, and good burritos. Many of our readers recommend their boxed lunch for a road trip to Hana. The baristas work with Illy coffee, which is a good, moderately priced brand (if you're thinking everyone should be serving Kona coffee by default, check your wallet and see whether you really want to spend $6 on every cup you buy). There are free screenings of classic and cult classic films at **Café Mambo** on certain nights (call for a schedule). No food, but drinks and desserts are available.

PS: Did we mention the crispy duck?

continued on next page

Café Mambo and Picnics *(continued)*

Address: 30 Baldwin Ave., Paia, North Shore
Location: Across from Mana Foods
Meals: Lunch, Dinner
Hours: Daily 8am–9pm
Parking: Street
Phone: 808-579-8021
Website: www.cafemambomaui.com

OVERALL:

3.9

out of 5 stars

$ $

Café O'Lei *(Pacific Rim / American)*

Café O'Lei in Kihei is located on the second floor of Rainbow Mall, where several previous places opened and then closed in rapid succession. Despite the awkward location, ***Café O'Lei*** is packed even during tourist slumps. Chef Owners Dana and Michael Pastula have a magic formula that they apply to every restaurant: consistently good food is delivered at reasonable prices by hustling servers.

To start, we recommend the Manoa lettuce wraps. The chef combines chicken with water chestnuts, ginger, and hoisin sauce, and you spoon the mix into tender, fresh lettuce leaves and eat them like a burrito. We usually skip the flatbreads at ***Café O'Lei***, although they do have a good pizza oven (inherited from a former unlucky restaurant). The tower appetizer consists of three plates stacked with coconut shrimp, tempura fried ahi rolls and lightly battered calamari rings. Fried food fans, that one is for you.

We used to recommend the baked Maui onion soup. Then we went to Paris for six weeks, and were reminded of just how flavorful this soup can be when the onions are caramelized to their limits. Maui onions are exceptionally sweet, and while we appreciate that this kitchen uses plenty of thyme and brandy to keep the soup from becoming cloying and sugary, it's no substitution for the long-long-long caramelizing and more complex flavor of yellow onions. Still, good gruyere cheese tops the soup and then a puffed pastry crust forms a ballooning, crackly roof. The presentation is dramatic, and if you are looking for a little sip of bistro, this might be just the ticket.

We really like the braised shortrib. The cut isn't always the best, but the preparation makes up for it. The rib meat falls off the bone, cloaked in a deeply flavored ginger-shoyu glaze with sesame oil to smooth the flavors and siracha (red chili paste) to hit the top notes and singe the back of the throat with some heat. It comes draped over steamed rice, but we usually get the mashed potatoes instead. The chefs aren't afraid of butter, and neither are we.

Another dish we love here is the prime rib, which comes quivery and salty on the ridges. In fact, if we are craving meat and potatoes, this meal is on the short list for the reasonable price and excellent preparation.

Café O'Lei *(continued)*

Other good choices include a seared ahi in a spicy ginger butter sauce and light wasabi aioli, as well as jumbo shrimp laced with garlic butter sauce, basil pesto, and chopped macadamia nuts. Both of these entrées are under $20. Nightly specials usually feature a fresh fish, and are reliable in their preparation. If your table is craving sushi, it's pretty good. Desserts are focused on delivering more quantity than quality, so we usually skip them. The exception to this is when they have the banana lumpia concoction, which they do very well. The wine list is not particularly impressive, but they have a good beer selection and some pretty strong martinis.

If you can't visit for dinner, lunch is a very good value, and you'll be sitting in a packed restaurant amongst a gaggle of locals (realtors love this place). All sandwiches are under $10 and come with salads, and the fish dishes come with rice and salad. The tempura fish and chips lunch is a particular favorite. The fish is mahi mahi battered in a light, crispy tempura and deep fried to a golden glow. The quinoa salad with organic greens, goat cheese, and roasted peppers is an excellent choice at the healthier end of the spectrum. There's a Thai beef salad, too, but we save that dish for meals at ***Thailand Cuisine***. The blackened mahi mahi (Cajun-style) with papaya salsa is a standby; it shows up at dinner, too, but it's only $9 at lunch.

When the tourist season is roaring (generally during any public school holiday), lines can form, so we recommend reservations or calling ahead. The Kihei location is our fail-safe restaurant to take anyone who is not used to spending a lot on dinner out. The upscale-but-casual ambience, fair prices, generous portions, and abundance of tasty dishes makes this place a safe bet for people making this their "nice night out" or those who want a break from the resort prices. The Wailuku location has more limited hours and is only open on weekdays, but features a similar menu. The Dunes at Maui Lani location can handle special events, has a satisfying brunch menu, and is the home of the restaurant's catering service. A new location in Napili at the Napili Shores Resort brings this down-home restaurant to the West side.

Address: 2439 S. Kihei Rd., Kihei, South Maui
Location: Turn into the Rainbow Mall — which has a great many rainbow
          flags outside of it — and walk to the front of the building and
          climb the stairs.
Meals: Lunch, Dinner
Hours: Daily, 10:30am-9:30pm
Parking: Lot
Phone: 808-891-1368
Website: cafeoleimauidotcom.wordpress.com/kihei/

Address: 62 N. Market St., Wailuku, Central Maui
Location: Next to the Iao Theater
Meals: Lunch, Dinner
Hours: M-W 10:30am- 3pm; Th-Fr 10:30am-8pm
Parking: Street
Phone: 808-986-0044
Website: cafeoleimauidotcom.wordpress.com/wailuku/

continued on next page

Café O'Lei *(continued)*

Address 1333 Maui Lani Parkway, Kahului, Central Maui
Location: At the Dunes at Maui Lani golf course
Meals: Lunch, Dinner
Hours: Tu–Su 8:30am– 7:30pm; M 8:30am– 4pm
Parking: Lot
Phone: 808-877-0073
Website: www.dunesatmauilani.com

Address 5315 Lower Honoapiilani Hwy, Napili, West Maui
Location: At the Napili Shores Resort
Meals: Dinner
Hours: Tu–Sa 5pm–9pm
Parking: Lot
Phone: 808-877-0073
Website: cafeoleimauidotcom.wordpress.com/napili/

Cane and Taro *(Pacific Rim / Sushi)*

Cane and Taro is D.K. Kodama's newest restaurant in a renovated, prime Ka'anapali location. His success with **Sansei, Vino** (closed now) and his Oahu restaurants **The Counter** and **d.k. Steakhouse** suggests that this restaurant should be a slam-dunk, but in our experience it's not up to par with its siblings. Still, the location is hard to beat, and while the food isn't fantastic, it's at least as good as anything else you'll find in Ka'anapali (except for **Japengo** at the Hyatt, one of our new favorites).

When **Cane and Taro** first opened, it offered a greatest hits selection from all three of Kodama's other restaurants. Reading the menu felt like someone was throwing wild 95-mile-per-hour pitches at us — we kept thinking "How can they do great meatloaf *and* pull off the kampachi sashimi in ponzu sauce?" Ultimately the kitchen must've asked this same question, since the menu has since been drastically trimmed — probably for the best.

Tried and true favorites from Kodama's other venues have made the cut, including crispy crab wontons with wasabi aioli and sweet and sour sauce. The smallish selection of sushi includes the panko-crusted ahi roll with Waipoli greens and butter sauce and the "Dragonfly" — a spicy ahi roll draped with slices of ahi and avocado and finished with unagi glaze and a lovely chili aioli. These extravagant rolls can easily serve as an entire meal. Thankfully, the beloved Granny Smith apple tart with warm caramel sauce we love at other venues is also on the menu here.

Mom Kodama's plantation meatloaf is among the new favorites. Moist and drenched with an Asian-influenced gravy, it's meatloaf at its best. We like the crisp onion disc garnish, too — like a bonus onion ring. Speaking of crisp, the chicken wings have a wicked crunch to them (hear that? Molly's Boston background just slipped out) and come dressed in a beguiling spicy-sweet Korean-style chili sauce.

OVERALL:
3.2
out of 5 stars

$ $ $

Cane and Taro *(continued)*

Your best bet for dinner is to hit the early bird special. Order between 5:00pm and 5:30pm and get a substantial discount: 50 percent off Tuesday and Wednesday and 25 percent off the rest of the week. Not only do you get a deal, but you'll be treated to a spectacular sunset (almost guaranteed) immediately after. The open-air, shady dining room can feel under-renovated (the Rusty Harpoon was here for years), but the terraced design means most tables have a good view of the Pacific Ocean lapping up to Ka'anapali Beach's sugary sand. Watch your fingers as you adjust your chair — we've sat in several that are positively rickety.

Ironically, the most popular meal at *Cane and Taro* is new for Kodama: breakfast. He doesn't serve it anywhere else, but those ocean views must have convinced him to make a go of it. You can find standard breakfast fare, but also some only-in-Kodama-World items; the insanely decadent French-toast/fried-dough/fruit concoction comes to mind. First, Hawaiian sweet bread is stuffed with cream cheese and fresh fruit and crusted with macadamia nuts. Next, it's deep-fried and plated, then buried under a snowfall of whipped coconut cream. Berry compote tops off this breakfast treat. If you have a little girl (of any age), this will put a smile on her face. If you're feeling more butch, order the breakfast steak "medallions" paired with eggs and steamed rice.

The table service is not as good as it is at Kodama's other restaurants. But the bartenders are attentive, and drinks are delicious, especially the hibiscus margarita. The early Happy Hour (2-4pm) makes sense only in Ka'anapali, where most of the people taking advantage of the menu are definitely on vacation.

Address: 2435 Ka'anapali Pkwy, Ka'anapali, West Maui
Location: In Whaler's Village, right above *Hula Grill*
Meals: Breakfast, Lunch, Dinner
Hours: Daily 8am–10pm
Parking: Lot, validated parking
Phone: 808-662-0668

Capische? *(Italian)*

Capische? is one of a handful of Maui restaurants that could compete in the fiercely competitive markets of San Francisco, New York, Chicago, or D.C., and we deeply appreciate them for running their business as if every meal — and every diner — counts. It remains our favorite place on Maui for a romantic, no-holds barred (read: very expensive and very special) dinner.

The Hotel Wailea has a spectacular water feature that welcomes you with a koi pond at the entrance and then falls to flow underneath the hotel (Yes! Underneath!) into pools farther down the property. Unless you have already dined here and are somehow bored with the gemlike setting, we highly recommend making your reservation for just before sunset so that you can really appreciate the ambience and read your menu (the restaurant

OVERALL:
4.6
out of 5 stars

continued on next page

Capische? *(continued)*

is very dim after dark — so dark they think to bring a small flashlight with the bill).

Every table is outside, and most are on the rail overlooking the garden, the resort's villas, and finally, the lush volcano slope rolling down to the Pacific and the islands of Kaho'olawe, Molokini, and Lana'i. For a completely different feel, ask for a seat in the fragrant herb garden. And for the most exclusive experience, ask for reservations in their private dining room, **Il Teatro** (more about that in a minute).

The menu is creative and fresh Northern Italian with some French influences. While there are several standards that consistently please, it changes with the seasons and with the availability of local produce. Desperately fresh ingredients prepared perfectly are the key to the menu's outrageous success, which is why Chef Owner Brian Etheredge cultivates a vegetable garden at his home in addition to his herb garden at the restaurant, and brings in much of his produce from Hana Fresh in Hana and Michael McCoy, a farmer in Kula. Local fishermen know to stop by with that morning's catch. Beef and other meats are generally from high-end mainland purveyors (Snake River Farms is one), but that is not unusual at Maui's best restaurants. Local ranchers have not yet been able to provide a product good enough for truly fine dining. (And Maui needs a good butcher: some cuts we've had of local beef are rendered almost inedible by the … ermm … butchering.)

There is as much care and attention put into the appetizers at **Capische?** as into the entrées, and we often end up ordering more than one. (The kitchen is happy to split appetizers on two plates and bring them as separate courses.) We have several favorites worth mentioning to you. The Caesar salad: a head of Romaine lettuce is quartered and left undefended before the onslaught of shaved parmesan cheese and homemade croutons. This is drizzled with a garlicky, creamy sauce with a shot of balsamic vinegar to pucker it up.

Another favorite is the beef carpaccio braciola. Beef tartare is sliced thin, pounded thinner, and used to coat the bottom of a platter. An herb and greens salad is tossed thoroughly with tangy mustard vinaigrette and mounded with diced onions and fried capers (heavenly salty-crunchy capers) on top of the beef. Taken together the flavors dance a tango on your tongue — spicy and sultry, warm with that ineffable ingredient we call Love.

NB: The first time Molly ate this (in a rolled version, which you might request) she blushed and couldn't speak for several minutes. When she did, she said, "Either the chef is deeply in love with me, or he is deeply in love with this dish." It was like a scene from *Like Water for Chocolate*.

If the ahi bruschetta calls to you, answer. Perfectly seared ahi reclines on a slice of garlic toast while olives, capers, and a divine truffle aioli tumble onto the plate. It's hard to choose a favorite item, but if we had to, it might be the kabocha pumpkin gnocchi. Bathed in lavender brown butter, it's perfectly salty seared, and literally — we hate using such trite language, but it's the best way to say it — melts in your mouth. (We promise to not use that phrase again.)

Capische? *(continued)*

The caprese salad tastes so fresh we wonder if the basil and tomato were literally picked that hour, and the quail saltimbocca — wrapped in applewood bacon and laced with brown butter sauce — inspires one to bad table manners. We nearly always end up ordering at least one fish entrée at *Capische?* because here the exquisite Hawaiian species are deeply respected. We've never had a piece of fish anything other than perfectly cooked. To this day, the best fish of our life was an opakapaka (pink snapper) poached in olive oil barely floating in a pool of parsley pesto, topped with a salad of micro greens. The olive oil carefully sealed off the tender flesh and let it blossom into full flavor. The parsley pesto — a beautiful bright emerald — was fresh, light, and the perfect complement to the snapper. Chef Brian and Chris Kulis, his sous chef, know how to let the fish's natural flavors shine without mucking it up with too much other … *stuff.*

If you're in the mood for meat, the choices usually include Snake River Farms Wagyu (American Kobe) beef and Kurobuta the Kobe beef of pork. While not local, it is the best, and we never regret ordering it from this kitchen. We are not as big a fan of the pastas as some of our readers are, but that is more a function of how much else there is to enjoy, rather than a reflection of the pastas themselves. An exception: the ravioli, which comes in all colors as strikes the chefs' fancy. If it's black squid ink, orange pumpkin, or red roasted pepper, avail yourself. They're edible artwork. A perennial favorite is the signature cioppino of Kona lobster tail, shrimp, scallop, clams, fish, and king crab legs simmered in a savory, rich tomato saffron broth and ladled over *al dente* capellini pasta.

The servers are knowledgeable and many of them spend some time in the kitchen themselves, so do not be afraid to ask their opinion about the menu. Some will offer it whether solicited or not — we're not the only ones who have encountered service that suddenly veers away from relaxed and friendly to slightly panicked in its over-solicitousness — but regardless of individual mannerisms, they are well trained in the menu and can be relied upon for advice. They also hustle, and this is still one of the few places on Maui where if we ask for something, we get it nearly immediately. After dining here, we often have to remind ourselves to ratchet our service expectations down a notch or two at the next evening's restaurant.

The award-winning wine list should be shopped, and room in your evening's budget should definitely be reserved for one of their drop-dead delicious martinis (more on those below). We're afraid that we still do not love the desserts here, although we make exception for the sorbets made in house. You might not have room for anything more, anyway.

We spend at a minimum one special occasion every year at *Capische?* and often more than one. If you are celebrating, are ready to spend some money, and don't want to feel hurried (like you would be at *Mama's Fish House,* for example), this is our favorite choice.

For a truly exceptional experience, ask about *Il Teatro*, the private dining room off the herb garden, where the chef will cook a five course dinner for you personally at tableside. The opportunity to watch either of these

continued on next page

Capische? *(continued)*

Culinary Institute of America grads in action is spendy but worth it if you consider yourself a "foodie." You'll be treated to a professional cooking class — with some comedy — and an unforgettable meal. The room has two tables of ten, so depending upon how many other people are interested — or how big a party you have — it may or may not be available when you want to go. If you book a table at **Il Teatro**, you might consider hiring transportation to complete the fantasy evening.

If you are on a budget, the wonderful Happy Hour might be the way to go. The special menu includes $10 items that are not available at table, including a gorgeous antipasto board with salty-vinegary relishes made in house, and a lamb and mushroom ragu that is so satisfying you may not need a meal afterward. The ahi carpaccio is a revelation — the sashimi grade fish is sliced perilously thin, the local radishes also, and those fried capers stud the plate alongside sand-sized grains of sea salt. Delish. Drinks are half off for Happy Hour, which makes us very happy, because the bartenders are some of the best on the island. Mixology is an art, and some bartenders take a Jackson Pollack approach — throw a bunch of liquor together and see what sticks. It takes a great deal of restraint and creativity to combine alcohols and fruits and other flavorings in delicious ways, and we've been happy with each drink we've tried. The French Pear is a particular favorite: sparkling wine, vodka, and St. Germain, the liqueur made from handpicked elderflowers. Sweet, but not too, and luscious in its texture, it is perfectly clear and does not look nearly as frou-frou as it sounds. Another winner is the Watermelon mint martini: bright and clean and sparkly. If you're a fan of artisanal gins, The Hayman's Garden is a must-try: Hayman's Old Tom Gin, with lime sour, grapefruit juice, cherry liqueur, and rosemary — the fruit and vegetal notes are subtle, with a kick in the back of the throat that's energizing. These and the other $8 cocktails will put you well on the way to happy during the very civilized hours of 5-6:30pm. And if you feel so inspired, you can order from the full menu, even in the bar.

Capische? is not the most Hawaiian of restaurants, but it remains our favorite on Maui, and we're happy to see so many locals and visitors returning, and so many special events booking their parties here. (Note to brides: this is where we would want to celebrate our nuptials on Maui ... and there's a cupola on the grounds for the ceremony.) With seasonal kama'aina discounts and the new Happy Hour, no one has a reason to skip a visit.

Address: 555 Kaukahi St., Wailea, South Maui
Location: at the Hotel Wailea, this used to be called the Diamond Resort
Meals: Dinner
Hours: Nightly 5:30-9:30pm
Parking: Valet
Phone: 808-879-2224
Website: www.capische.com

Cary & Eddie's Hideaway Buffet *(Local/American)*

This restaurant fronting Kahului Harbor used to house an upscale chain steak house: **Chart House**. Now, it doesn't. While very popular with some locals for their buffet lunch and brunch loaded up with Hawaiian and local dishes, it's not popular with us. It's designed for — and perfect for — tourists who want to debark from the nearby cruise ship and then go right back on board without exploring too far.

Address: 500 N Puunene Ave., Kahului, Central Maui
Location: Right on the water, at the intersection of Puunene and Kaahumanu
Meals: Brunch, Lunch, Dinner
Hours: Tu-Sa 11am-9pm; Su 8am-9pm
Parking: Lot
Phone: 808-873-6555

Casanova *(Italian)*

At the intersection of Baldwin and Makawao avenues, **Casanova** is an upcountry institution and a gathering spot for the local community. It's really two restaurants: a daytime deli attached to a bistro with a dance floor, open for lunch and dinner. The kitchen sends out good food to both, the service is kindhearted and friendly, and the entertainment schedule is packed with everything from visiting DJs to saucy cabaret acts.

The deli offers simple omelets with fresh mozzarella and buttermilk biscuits for breakfast — not a bad option, but not the most imaginative either. For lunch, choose from a roster of tried and true sandwiches, of which the New York with meatballs, grilled onions and marinara sauce is a standout. The pizza is more of a platform for Italian vegetables than a typical pie, but it's hearty and delicious all the same. Baristas will learn your name and your drink of choice if you return for more.

For lunch at the adjoining bistro, the cioppino stuffed with chunks of seafood and shellfish is especially satisfying if the day has turned misty and cool — not infrequent in this neck of the woods. At dinnertime, the emphasis is not necessarily on giving you "the best night of your life," but we have had many good nights here — and three of our readers have reported spontaneous marriage proposals. **Casanova** carries an undercurrent of enthusiasm and happiness that is catchy. Perhaps it's because the building was originally a USO for American marines stationed nearby during World War II?

The menu is Italian and everything is made from scratch. The *carpaccio di bresaola* is thinly sliced beef rolled with fresh arugula, parmesan cheese, and a lemony olive oil dressing. There are some good flavors here, although we wish a little sharper pepper taste (capers?) were present. We like the *ravioli di magro al tartufo:* homemade raviolis stuffed with spinach and ricotta cheese in a moat of delicately flavored sage cream sauce. The steaks are good, and

continued on next page

Casanova *(continued)*

we like the fun presentation, where the mashed potatoes are shaped into a pineapple, with a little sprig of greens at the top to represent the crown. The aforementioned pizza makes a nice light meal or appetizer: the wood-burning oven turns out a pretty crust, and the simpler toppings are the best. (By the way, their bread is excellent because it's this pizza dough baked in their oven.) The bar is a typical nightclub's workhorse — standard stock in the well. But decent wines can be had by the glass, and there's Guinness on tap.

The tiramisu is slightly heavy in texture, but the flavors are strong and rich. The big bar area and the dance floor make the entertainment events and dancing nights popular. Make it a point to check out their schedule: there is something going on most nights of the week, and dining here before the show can earn you free admission.

Note to parents: your children can take to the dance floor — no one will mind.

Address: 1188 Makawao Ave., Makawao, Upcountry
Location: At Makawao Avenue and Baldwin Avenue intersection
Meals: Lunch, Dinner
Hours: M-Sa 11:30am-2pm; Daily 5:30-9:30pm; Pizza until 11pm on nights with entertainment
Parking: Lot
Phone: 808-572-0220
Website: www.casanovamaui.com

OVERALL:

3

out of 5 stars

Castaway Café *(American / Local)*

This quiet, beachfront bungalow café is relatively unchanged since the late 1970s. The reasonable prices and relaxed atmosphere have accrued local fans because you won't pay an arm and a leg in Ka'anapali for good pancakes at breakfast, sandwiches at lunch, or fish entrées at dinner. If you're hankering for macadamia nut pancakes drizzled in coconut syrup, consider this hassle-free spot over the crowded *Gazebo* down the road.

At night, the wine list offers some (very) surprising bargains.

Castaway Café consistently doles out decent (if somewhat unimaginative) dishes with a gorgeous view, and service that is hit or miss. If you're stuck in Ka'anapali and want a break from the resort prices (especially on wine), this could be right for you.

Address: 45 Kai Ala Dr., Ka'anapali, West Maui
Location: at the Maui Ka'anapali Villas and Resort
Meals: Breakfast, Lunch, Dinner
Hours: Daily 7:30am-9pm
Parking: Public Lot, then walk to the beach and you will see the restaurant on the beachfront at the Villas
Phone: 808-661-9091

Charley's Restaurant & Saloon *(American)*

New owners are re-shaping the menu at **Charley's**, but so far we haven't seen (or tasted) much to change our original opinion. This is a Maui institution, and its relaxed ambience (especially since a major renovation after a devastating fire), expansive menu, friendly service, and reasonable prices would be enough to take us most of the way to happy. The fact that Willie Nelson plays on a regular basis should take us over the top, but we just can't ignore the fact that whenever we stop in for anything other than breakfast, we want to delegate the meal-eating to someone else. We know plenty of locals who love **Charley's** and make it their favorite meeting place. Nostalgia dies hard, but die it must for us. Go for the live music and the drinks in the bar, and an appetizer or two while you listen. If you're hungry, a decent Maui Cattle Company burger will tide you over — but there is much better food (and drinks) on the corner at **Milagros** or down the street at **Flatbread**. Breakfasts are better, but we'd still prefer **Anthony's** or **Moana** or **Café Mambo.**

Address: 142 Hana Hwy., Paia, North Shore
Location: Right across from Indigo
Meals: Breakfast, Lunch, Dinner
Hours: Daily 7am-10pm
Parking: Street, Lot
Phone: 808-579-9453
Website: www.charleysmaui.com

Cheeseburger in Paradise / Cheeseburger Island Style *(American)*

If you're in the mood for an average-tasting, big, sloppy cheeseburger and a basket of fries in a restaurant built on ticky-tacky Hawaiiana silliness, a **Cheeseburger** restaurant might be your thing. While we find the nearly-trademarked "sassy" service (everything in this restaurant has a trademark — why not the service?) a little too real, some diners get a kick of out the impertinent teasing.

[We're not opposed to sassy waiters — read the review for **A Saigon Café**. We're also not unilaterally opposed to chain or theme restaurants — read the review for **Bubba Gump's**.]

The Lahaina location has stunning views of the harbor from their two floors of open-air dining rooms — as long as you sit on the rail. (If you're anywhere else, the packed-in-like-cattle seating might get old). Live music can be heard down the street and does much to draw in the customers for those hour-long waits. Kids *love* the noise and the water and the food, and if you've got them, you'll be happy they're happy. (But they might like the **Cool Cat Café** just as well, and that's a better burger. And they'll love **Teddy's!**) If you're there for breakfast, hanging over the water, enjoying the cool morning breeze can be kind of awesome — especially if you're craving a burger for brekkie. (They offer an "ali'i" cheeseburger topped with a fried egg and bacon.)

continued on next page

Cheeseburger in Paradise/Cheeseburger Island Style *(continued)*

The Wailea location at the upscale Shops at Wailea open-air mall is much more sedate, although the waits can still get long since this is the only moderately priced mall restaurant. Both locations have plenty of room for their cute t-shirts, tiki mugs, and cheeseburger-shaped earrings.

Cheeseburger Island Style
Address: 811 Front St., Lahaina, West Maui
Location: right on the sea wall, you can't miss it
Meals: Breakfast, Lunch, Dinner
Hours: Daily 8am–10pm
Parking: Street
Phone: 808-661-4855
Website: www.cheeseburgerland.com

Cheeseburger Island Style
Address: 3750 Wailea Alanui Dr., Wailea, South Maui
Location: The Shops at Wailea,
Meals: Breakfast, Lunch, Dinner
Hours: Daily 8am–10pm
Parking: Lot
Phone: 808-874-8990
Website: www.cheeseburgerland.com

China Boat / China Bowl & Asian Cuisine *(Chinese)*

China Boat and its sister restaurant, *China Bowl*, serve mainstream Chinese dishes. While the food is definitely "Americanized" Chinese, it is generally cooked competently. If you are from a city with top notch Chinese, you may want to go for Thai, Vietnamese, or Japanese restaurants while on Maui. If you really enjoy Americanized Chinese or have a nostalgic craving for it (we do, sometimes), the daily specials generally offer some good choices at *China Boat* and *China Bowl*.

China Boat
Address: 4474 Lower Honoapiilani Rd., Lahaina, West Maui
Location: In the Kahana Gateway Center
Meals: Lunch, Dinner
Hours: M-Sa 11am–2pm & Daily 5pm–10pm
Parking: Lot
Phone: 808-669-5089
Website: www.chinaboatkahana.com

China Bowl
Address: 2580 Keka'a Dr., Ka'anapali, West Maui
Location: In Fairway Shops
Meals: Lunch, Dinner
Hours: Daily 11am–9:30pm
Parking: Lot
Phone: 808-661-0660
Website: www.ChinaBowlMaui.com

Cilantro *(Mexican)*

Cilantro hits the spot when we're in the mood for fresh, inexpensive Mexican. Located kitty corner to Foodland in Lahaina, we love to buy some beer at the market and head here for a quick, satisfying meal rounded out by our own choice of adult beverage.

The gleaming exhibition kitchen is staffed by friendly chefs who work the tortilla presses, grills, and cutting boards in full sight while you place your order at the counter. The owner, though Persian, explored the heart of Mexico to find authentic recipes, which are best reflected in his house specialties and superb salsas.

Succulent roasted chicken provides the basis for some of our favorite dishes. The chicken is marinated in herbs and citrus before it is rotisserie-roasted. The constant spinning and the perfect balance of acidity leaves the flesh tender and pleasantly astringent. You can buy whole and half chickens to take home.

The Mother Clucker Flautas are particular favorites. Two flour tortillas are rolled up with secret spices and the delicious chicken, then flash-fried and smothered with *crema fresca* and mellow roasted jalapeno jelly. The tortillas end up crispy, while the chicken stays hot and melts into the creamy and almost-sweet jalapenos. Delicious.

Cilantro chefs know how to work a grill and how to treat fish's tricky protein with respect. The day's catch has good grill marks and is perfectly done. Our favorite so far is a flaky opakapaka on a bed of garlicky, spicy jicama slaw. (This slaw is so good we often take a to-go tub of it home.)

Taco plates include a trio of soft corn tortillas loaded up with that fantastic rotisserie chicken, al pastor, grilled steak, or roasted vegetables. The veggies aren't afterthoughts, either: grilled asparagus, zucchini, marinated mushrooms, and roasted green chilis and sweet onion rajas.

Salads are very good, fresh, and big. If you want a protein, you can add pork, chicken, steak, fish, or grilled shrimp. Try the margarita-reminiscent tequila-lime vinaigrette.

The only disappointment here is the burrito. Though giant, it's stuffed with too much fiesta rice and doesn't carry the same flavorful punch of the other dishes. Plus, it's wrapped in paper and served in a paper-lined basket, which we find unnecessarily cumbersome. If they lowered the rice to protein ratio — even if it meant a smaller burrito — and ditched the excessive packaging, we'd likely be enthusiastic fans of this too.

The chips are crisp and not too greasy, and the salsa bar features choices ranging from mild to crazy hot, each incorporating a different combination of the seven or eight different chilis stored above the register. You'll also find pickled vegetables and — of course — heaps of fresh cilantro. This is a very casual taqueria (paper plates and plastic utensils), clean, boisterous when busy, and brightly painted. The logos and marketing are so clever you could suspect it of being a chain, which it's not. Too bad. It knocks others

continued on next page

Cilantro *(continued)*

out of the water. For a cheap lunch or inexpensive dinner for two to ten, it's a dearly loved Maui institution and well worth your while.

Address: 170 Papalaua St., Lahaina, HI 96761
Location: Near Foodland
Meals: Lunch, Dinner
Hours: M–Sa 11am–9pm; Su 11am–8pm
Parking: Lot
Phone: 808-667-5444
Website: www.CilantroGrill.com

$

CASH

Cinnamon Roll Fair *(American)*

Just underneath Denny's in Kihei you'll find **Cinnamon Roll Fair,** a teensy storefront counter stocked with a few baked goods, including muffins and trays of sticky, gooey rolls with many, many spirals dripping cinnamon. They have a choice of toppings they'll put in little plastic takeaway cups, and many times we are jealous of vacationing people who are eating there, as if they are entitled to eat a cinnamon roll for lunch, simply because they are on vacation.

Address: 2463 S. Kihei Rd., Kihei, South Maui
Location: In the Kamaole Center
Meals: Breakfast, Snacks & Treats
Hours: M–F 6am–6pm; Sa–Su 6am–5pm
Parking: Lot
Phone: 808-879-5177

CJ's Deli & Diner *(American)*

CJ's is a down-home restaurant hoping to cater both to locals and visitors with comfort food at reasonable prices. Keeping in mind that everything in Ka'anapali is overpriced, they generally succeed.

We like the breakfasts best, especially for families who need a break from the resort prices. Pancakes and French toast and omelets are the best bets. Lunch and dinner entrées are problematic — maybe because the menu is so extensive for such a small eatery? **CJ's** serves everything from grilled salmon to mango glazed ribs to deli sandwiches and paninis. While we don't have a favorite, we do think the Hana Box Lunch is a good deal. For $12 you get a deli sandwich with the lettuce, tomato, and toppings wrapped separately so your bread stays dry. You also get chips, a drink, and a brownie. If you need a cooler, they'll loan one to you for a $5 deposit, which you can keep for the length of your stay. They'll even give you free refills on ice (good inducement to get you to come back for

CJ's Deli & Diner *(continued)*

another meal). We like the humor applied to the kids menu, which offers lizard toes and squid eyes soup (just kidding!) and promises no weird spices in the chicken dinner. If you're on the West Side, traveling with a family, and facing the dearth of inexpensive breakfast options, this this is a good stop.

Address: 2580 Keka'a Dr., Ka'anapali, West Maui
Location: In the Fairway Shops
Meals: Breakfast, Lunch, Dinner
Hours: Daily 7am–8pm
Parking: Lot
Phone: 808-667-0968
Website: www.cjsmaui.com

Coconut's Fish Café *(American)*

Eating at **Coconut's** feels like a mini-vacation. The casual, bright, order-at-the-counter fish shack atmosphere, the surfboard-shaped tables, the slim-cut staff t-shirts, and the plastic baskets filled with slow-cooked-fast-food is the perfect counterpoint to a sandy, salty day at the beach. Even when we're on a quick lunch break, our blood pressure stabilizes as soon as we sit down.

Coconut's is convinced that a fish counter can still serve healthy food; they lighten up on fat by substituting coconut milk for mayonnaise in the homemade condiments, and using an extremely light batter on fried items. Our personal philosophy is that all food is healthy if enjoyed in the proper spirit and in the right portions, and we do *not* believe in giving up flavor, for any reason. (We live to eat, we don't eat to live.)

In the case of **Coconut's** coleslaw, we're willing to concede that the substitution works; the coconut milk creams up into dense foam, and the cabbage and carrots hold their crunch better than in squashy mayonnaise versions.

We're also very pleased with the fish burger, which comes with that yummy slaw. The mahi mahi version is flaky and a little sweet, while the ono (our favorite) is firmer and more savory. They both arrive perfectly cooked with lovely grill marks, dressed sloppily (but sexily) in tomato, cheese, that decadent coleslaw, and tartar sauce. The fish can be rubbed with several flavors — blackened is a good choice — or grilled with butter. You can choose a sesame or whole wheat bun; or skip the bread altogether in favor of perfectly cooked, well-seasoned brown rice.

We're warming up to the fish and chips, which are decidedly different. To cut the fat and lighten the calorie count, the kitchen batters the fish in Italian bread crumbs. This results in a very light, very seasoned batter that effectively seals in the juices, but also makes the dish taste a little like the fish sticks we ate as kids. If you like your fish in a thick batter and enjoy that crisp sound when you bite it, you would do well to stick with the grilled fish burgers. The shrimp and calamari are fried in the same breadcrumb

OVERALL:
4.1
out of 5 stars

$

MasterCard VISA

continued on next page

Coconut's Fish Café *(continued)*

batter and the same advice applies.

The fish tacos are simply delicious. One order is $12 and nets you two plates, each with a layer of corn tortillas and a pile of perfectly grilled fish, mango salsa, tomatoes, cheese, and coleslaw. Almost impossible to eat with your hands due to the size, we dig in with a fork.

Another winner is the garlic steak sandwich. A generous 9 ounces of rib eye is grilled, sliced, and slipped between the folds of a garlic toasted bun. The meat is perfectly tender and perfectly done. The "special sauce" that comes on the side is a horseradishy-cream with a hint of garlic that just kills. This is a small place, and the owner is often on site. The last time we moaned out loud while eating this sandwich, he came over to tell us that it's inspired by the "steak" dinners his French mother cooked for his large family. She couldn't afford a great cut of meat ... but she *could* make this sauce, which they ate by the ladleful. He's serving a good cut of meat here, but *merci, maman*, for that sauce.

Seafood chowder is just silly to put on a menu on Maui. Who wants a cream-based hot soup? Everyone, including us. The New England style chowder is another recipe from *maman*, and **Coconut's** makes four batches a day to keep up with demand. Studded with perfectly tender ono, mahi mahi, and clams, it is creamy and perfectly seasoned. We can split a cup ($4) and be very satisfied.

Salads and burgers and pastas round out the menu, although we tend to return to our favorite, and we think about that garlic steak sandwich at random moments of reverie. There's also a very good children's menu.

Coconut's is one of the more thoughtful additions to the South Maui dining scene, and we cannot recommend it highly enough for a casual, moderately-priced meal prepared with careful recipes, high quality ingredients, and lots and lots of Love.

Address: 1279 S. Kihei Rd., Kihei, South Maui
Location: in the Azeka Mauka Marketplace
Meals: Lunch, Dinner
Hours: Daily, 11am-9pm
Parking: Lot
Phone: 808-875-9979
Website: www.CoconutsFishCafe.com

OVERALL:
3.7
out of 5 stars

Colleen's *(American / Pacific Rim)*

Colleen's is an upcountry favorite for comforting meals any time of day or night. Big portions and generally well-prepared classics are served in a clean, high-ceilinged, open, noisy joint.

The breakfast omelets are reasonable and tasty at $8.50, and the eggs Benedict come in several different styles — from ham, bacon, lox, veggie, crab, mahi mahi, and ono — all ono

Colleen's *(continued)*

(good). The tofu vegetable wrap is a favorite, as is the prosciutto tapas plate. Add a latte (very good) and you're all set for the day.

At lunch, you can't go wrong with a big salad topped with the mahi mahi or ono. The roasted eggplant sandwich with pesto, sun-dried tomato, carrots and melted muenster cheese is a winning combination of sweet, salty, and sumptuous ingredients. It's served on thick, toasted slices of whole wheat bread. A slice of pizza can be had immediately — the huge, doughy affairs weighed down with gourmet toppings are a meal unto themselves. Or if you're really hungry, get the beef burger (Maui Cattle Company beef, hormone free) and add fries and a pint of beer, all for $10.95.

At night the restaurant keeps the lights low and puts out votive candles and bluesy jazz. The wild mushroom ravioli is good, as is the creamy, comforting penne with vodka sauce and chicken. You might also try the seared ahi or the New York strip steak. The wine and beer list is short but decent. They make their own bread daily, and the espresso is excellent.

The waitresses (we've yet to see a waiter) tend to follow the owner's lead when it comes to service: socializing comes first, followed by efficiency. It's a place for North Shore denizens to see and be seen; if you're hip to the surfing scene, you might recognize world champions among those filling the booths.

This is a great alternative to Paia if you want to stray a little off the beaten path but still hang with the upcountry crowd. Right next door is Studio Maui, a yoga center and the site of many classes, workshops, and events to sustain your spiritual side.

Address: 810 Haiku Rd., Haiku, Upcountry
Location: Haiku Cannery
Meals: Breakfast, Lunch, Dinner
Hours: Daily 6am–9pm
Parking: Lot
Phone: 808-575-9211
Website: www.colleensinhaiku.com

Cool Cat Café *(American)*

The **Cool Cat Café** is a fifties-themed restaurant complete with checkerboard floor, jukebox, and pin ball machines on the top floor of the Wharf Cinema Center. There is typically a long wait to sit, but once you have a table, we find the service speedy. There is a lot of seating both inside (stuffy) and outside (breezy, if a little crowded in places). The menu has pretty good burgers, pretty good sandwiches, not so good fries or onion rings, and nice thick milkshakes. We like the Porky Pig, a kalua pig sandwich that looks undistinguished on its roll, but is surprisingly tasty (sweet and a little hint of sour), with good coleslaw on the side.

continued on next page

Cool Cat Café *(continued)*

A full view of Lahaina's historic banyan tree blocks most of the harbor and the ocean, but you definitely feel like you're getting a view of the action on Front Street. Live music and a full soda fountain and bar help to round out the relax-you're-on-vacation vibe.

They heavily promote themselves via other merchants (you'll be offered a coupon for a free root beer float at *Cool Cat* at least once as you walk down Front Street), but that doesn't mean they're not worth stopping in, if you're in the mood for a slightly overpriced, but comforting meal — or if you just want to people-watch from the lanai while sipping a $3 tropical cocktail. (The daily drink specials are downright cheap.)

If you can't get out to *Teddy's*, this is a good option for burgers in West Maui.

Address: 658 Front St., Lahaina, West Maui
Location: Upper floor of the Wharf Cinema Center
Meals: Lunch, Dinner
Hours: Daily 10:30am–10:30pm
Parking: Street, Lot
Phone: 808-667-0908
Website: www.coolcatcafe.com

OVERALL:
3.2
out of 5 stars

$

CASH

Costco *(American)*

We had to think long and hard about including *Costco's* food court, but the reality is that a reported 90% of Maui residents have a membership (it makes the cost of living here possible), and many, including us, eat in the food court for both the convenience and quality factor.

If you're a member, the only surprise will be how small the store is compared to others. Otherwise, you'll recognize the options and the prices. The pizza is heavy duty and one slice is like three everywhere else, and the hot dogs are Kosher franks, and still priced at $1.50, drink included.

Membership has its privileges, and at this location you'll be privileged to find a very good refrigerated foods section, much of which has locally sourced options, including local fish, when available. While we love locally-grown and raised food whenever possible, we admit to an addiction to the USDA Prime beef sold here. Their vegetables are surprisingly local (and very often organic), and the La Brea bread they sell in their bakery is the best "supermarket" bread on Maui.

You can also get lots of books on Maui, plenty of Hawaiian chocolate and macadamia nuts to bring home as gifts (all packaged for travel).

One of our top tips for visiting friends is to check out *Costco* as the first stop after picking up the rental car. (Or maybe the second stop, after a quick detour to Kanaha Beach Park, which is a gorgeous stretch of sand directly behind the rental agencies.) Pick up tasty treats, sunscreen at deep discounts,

Costco *(continued)*

and beautiful fresh leis at the best prices around. If you're disinclined to shop at big box stores, hit **Mana Foods** in Paia for much of the same — minus the Kosher franks.

Address: 540 Haleakala Highway, Kahului, Central Maui
Location: At the intersection of Dairy Road and Haleakala Highway
Meals: Lunch, Dinner, Snacks & Treats
Hours: M-F 11am - 8:30pm; Sa 9:30am - 6pm; Su 10am - 6pm
Parking: Lot
Phone: 808-877-5248
Website: www.costco.com

Cuatro Restaurant *(Latin/Asian Fusion)*

Cuatro, **Sansei's** sister restaurant in Kihei, is a nearly perfect square. This may seem trivial, but this *feng shui* fact seems significant to us. The sense of balance, harmony, and intimacy can also be found in the food, the wine list, and the service.

The food is a Latin-Asian-European fusion that makes liberal use of cilantro, truffle oil, balsamic vinegar, chilies, and butter (and many other things). In most dishes you can taste the four corners of the globe — and yet those far flung flavors don't fight with each other. The menu offers an easy approach for the spice-wary, with plenty of choices for those who are more adventurous.

A good example is the spicy tuna nachos appetizer. Six wonton, crisp and fresh, are laid on top of baby greens. A spicy tuna mixture that **Sansei** fans will recognize is scooped on top of each wonton. Next comes a layer of truffle aioli, then a cilantro pesto heated up with kochujang (a red chili pepper paste from Korea), then an avocado relish. Each serving ends up being either two perfect bites or one big mouthful of East-West Love.

The pupu steak is another good starter, and sized generously enough to be a small entrée. The steak is marinated until tender and then sautéed with earthy local mushrooms in a spicy teriyaki sauce. The sauce also features a little truffle oil, which melts the spice to the salty, and transitions the mushrooms to the meat. The end result is a cohesive taste experience that, in our opinion, is what good fusion is about: the sum must be equal to much more than the individual ingredients, and the different cuisines must marry each other, not threaten divorce.

The fresh fish of the day changes, of course, but can be prepared in one of four styles, each unique. You cannot go wrong with a fresh piece of mahi mahi sautéed with rock shrimp in a classic lemon caper butter sauce, but we like the more adventurous "house" preparation. Try a fish like ono or ahi blackened with Mexican spices, served over rice pilaf in a cumin-oregano beurre blanc with an avocado pico de gallo. Heat in the back of your throat, yes, but the rich beurre blanc and creamy avocado smooths it all out.

continued on next page

Cuatro Restaurant *(continued)*

Our favorite fish preparation, however, is the "Mauiterranean Grill." Garlic mashed potatoes are spread in a bed on the plate, with perfectly grilled vegetable slices on top — eggplant, onions, and whatever else is fresh. The fish is rubbed with what's almost a steak rub, grilled, and topped with tomato caper relish. The basil beurre blanc is not enough — it would be just spicy citrus and creamy nutty flavors. Where's the sweet to balance this out? It's in the balsamic syrup drizzled over the fish and the plate.

A very good meat entrée is the marinated pork. Pork is so easy to dry out, and so often rendered like sawdust, that we hesitate to order it. But this is so tender, juicy, and flavorful after its marinade and grilling session (Chef really knows how to *grill*) that we will order it again and again. Sweet green chilies in the *chili verde* sauce give way seamlessly to the sneaky heat in the back of the throat, and overall it's a satisfying dish. Another good choice is the roasted chicken breast. Stuffed with green chilies, ham, and a little pepper-jack cheese and then swathed in a southwestern butter sauce, it's perfectly tender and juicy. Is there anything better than a perfectly roasted chicken?

The one dish we do not care for is the shrimp scampi. The tomato sauce and the pasta are fine, but the shrimp are too often overcooked.

The wine list is very small, but carefully selected, and there are some bottled beers available. The keiki (children's) menu is simple: grilled fish, chicken, or steak, plus veggies and potatoes or rice. They can also get pasta with butter and cheese, or a cheese quesadilla.

Cuatro Restaurant operates like the best of city restaurants: proficient, energetic, confident, and hospitable — and it doesn't need a view to entertain you. Seating can be limited when they get busy, and they don't like to hurry tables — so calling for a reservation is recommended. There's also a Happy Hour special every day from 4-6pm with food discounts.

NB: Catering and private dining are also available. If you are planning a wedding or special event on Maui, put ***Cuatro*** on your list of places to check out for a delicious private dining event.

Address: 1881 S. Kihei Rd., Kihei, South Maui
Location: in the Kihei Town Center near Sansei
Meals: Dinner
Hours: Daily 4pm–10pm
Parking: Lot
Phone: 808-879-1110
Website: www.cuatromaui.com

OVERALL:
3.4
out of 5 stars

Da Kitchen *(Local / Plate Lunch)*

Engaging with a "Hawaiian mixed plate" could be called "eating until you're sore," and it's practically a sport in the Islands. A major distinguishing feature of good local food is that you get a great deal of it. Your paper plate or styrofoam to-go box should bend. Generally, it's served in casual, to-go joints.

Local food is not to be confused with Hawaiian food. Hawaiian foods are

Da Kitchen *(continued)*

traditional to these islands and include items like lau lau (butterfish, squid, or pork cooked in a ti leaf), lomi lomi (salt-cured salmon) and poi (taro root pounded into a nutritious paste).

Local food, on the other hand, is the best or favorite dishes from each of the cultures that make up the local population. Over the centuries, that has included Hawaiians, of course, but also Chinese, Japanese, Filipino, Koreans, and Portuguese. The favorite foods from each culture make their way into what we call Local Food. Just like visitors to New York should make a point to try the bagels, visitors to Hawaii should try Local Food. It is not fine dining, but skipping it is like skipping a lobster shack on the Maine Coast or a pig palace in Georgia.

We recommend *Da Kitchen* for your particular adventure. The restaurants are clean, the food is good, and the portions are Hawaiian-sized so you can split them and still have leftovers. Every order comes packaged for takeout, but if you want to sit and eat in the restaurant, there are plenty of chairs. You'll get your napkins and utensils with your order (the exception is the new Lahaina location, which is a sit-down restaurant with table service).

The combination plates are a good place to start. The kalua pork is good, as is the beef and chicken teriyaki. These dishes are often overly salty, but they are also meant to be eaten with the accompanying "two scoops rice" and one scoop of macaroni salad, which makes the seasoning more reasonable. Chicken katsu — breaded cutlets — is often too much bread and not enough chicken. We prefer the chow fun to the crispy noodles, and the ribs are pretty good when they are available. The tempura mahi is delicious and like everything else, big enough to split. The heftier fish basket with its abundance of fried fish, shrimp, and French fries could probably sink our battleship.

There is no special charm to either the ambience or the service, but if you're looking for a good meal at great prices and want to know "where da locals eat" *Da Kitchen* is da place.

Address: 425 Koloa St, Kahului, Central Maui
Location: Near K-Mart and the Airport
Meals: Lunch, Dinner
Hours: M-F 11am-8:30pm; Sa 11am-4pm
Parking: Lot
Phone: 808-871-7782
Website: www.da-kitchen.com

Address: 2439 S. Kihei Rd, Kihei, South Maui
Location: In the Rainbow Mall
Meals: Lunch, Dinner
Hours: Daily 9am-9pm
Parking: Lot
Phone 808-875-7782

continued on next page

Da Kitchen *(continued)*

Address: 658 Front St., Lahaina, West Maui
Location: Bottom level of the Wharf Cinema Center
Meals: Lunch, Dinner
Hours: Daily 11am–9pm
Parking: Lot (validated), Street
Phone: 808-661-4900

OVERALL:
4.2
out of 5 stars

$ $ $

David Paul's Island Grill *(Pacific Rim)*

One of the most memorable meals we've had at Chef David Paul Johnson's table started with a bean soup so hearty and creamy that we actually scraped the bottom of the bowl. The black beans, earthy-sweet and tender, were completely pulverized by a blending that lasted, according to the waitress, for at least fifteen minutes. The texture of the soup was a silky smooth cream. The *crème fraiche* dollop on top, when mixed in, gave a wonderful tangy counterbalance to the warm spices in the soup. Every once in a while, a dish is both perfectly balanced in flavor — earthy, sweet, spicy, pungent, salty — and also is utterly simple and straightforward. In other words: perfect. This soup is one of those dishes.

David Paul is known for bold flavors and fresh ingredients, and his menu changes with the seasons and the available produce, so the soup may not be on the menu when you visit. Every time we've been, it looks like a completely different menu, although there are always a few favorites from his previous menu at **David Paul's Lahaina Grill** (under different ownership and now named **Lahaina Grill).**

As mentioned, the menu is extensive, and if it seems too much to wade through the descriptions of each dish, you might try the tasting menu, which includes that evening's nine featured items as a four course menu. It usually includes the dishes Chef is most excited about that evening, with the most seasonal ingredients and the nicest combinations of flavors. The trick is that the whole table must order it, presumably for the kitchen's timing. It's an excellent way to sample a wide range of dishes without having to choose. Some substitutions can be made — for instance, we usually can convince them to include our favorite Triple Berry Pie on the dessert course. Although some find the portions too small, we find the meal more than enough food (how can you not be satisfied with four entrées?). At $75 per person at press time, this is a good value.

It is hard to comment on specific dishes without running the risk of disappointing you later if they're not there, but we have to write *something*, so here you go:

We love the cool, spicy watermelon gazpacho. When you sip from the lip of the martini glass, the first flavor to step forward is the intense watermelon, concentrated and sugary, which gently transforms itself to savory and then leaves a spicy backsplash that is intense but terribly satisfying.

David Paul's Island Grill *(continued)*

We also have enjoyed the butternut squash raviolis stuffed with mascarpone cheese and topped with a small piece of lobster. The decadent textures combined with the luxurious flavors ... we can't decide if this is a pasta, a main course, or a dessert (or all three).

Do not overlook the salads, which are just-picked fresh; we particularly love those involving diced roasted beets.

The pan-roasted seared snapper has been on the menu since day one — in fact, before the restaurant opened. Chef David Paul entered the recipe in the 2009 Maui Onion Festival cook-off and won top honors. It's easy to see (or taste) why. Hawaiian snappers, such as the delicate opakapaka, rank among the Islands' most delicious fish. Flaky, lightly perfumed of the sea, and with a more than adequate fat content, they offer an excellent platform for a sophisticated dish such as this one. The fish is roasted in olive oil, rendering it meltingly moist. It's laid on a soft pillow of rich and creamy polenta, surrounded by Maui onion jus. Magenta pickled onions crown the elegant presentation. With a biteful of fish, polenta, and jus we again experience that perfect mixture of earthy, sweet, spicy, pungent, and salty. A hint of truffle oil saturates the polenta, which is irresistible: baby food for the gods.

This brings us to a slight beef we have with the chef: an *over*-indulgence in truffle oil. There were at least six truffle-infused items on the menu at our last visit. This powerful, unctuous flavoring can elevate an ordinary dish to stardom (as in **Sansei's** truffle ramen, or the abovementioned polenta), but it can also pounce all over subtle flavors, trampling them with a single over-powering note. Truffle oil, while boosted by a sliver or two of actual truffle, is, for the most part, an artificial flavor. Our taste buds recognize this. When used sparingly, it's a fine exclamation point. In excess, either in a single dish or spread across a menu, it's too many exclamation points!!!!

Also, in the past, we've loved the chef's flamboyant use of garnishes. Perhaps it's the slow economy, perhaps a more sober mentality, but he seems to have restrained himself somewhat. Where are the crisp artichoke leaves, the parti-colored crucifers? The dishes taste just as decadent without the decoration, but we like it when chefs take extra steps to wow all of our senses.

Desserts are generally worthwhile, and Molly's favorite, Triple Berry Pie, is almost always available. Other than the food, there is a good wine list with dozens of wines by the glass. You can also visit their wine cellar to shop on your own and see the labels (all bottles are priced). This is a really fun way to pick your poison, and it makes good eye candy on the way to the elegantly appointed bathrooms.

The classy, contemporary restaurant is absolutely beautiful. The muted blues, greens, and mustards on the walls, the natural slate tiles on the lanai, the big mirrors, the exhibition kitchen, and the big square white plates remind us of upscale casual eateries in our old haunts. The view, however, is all Maui. If you sit on the open air lanai you will see one of the best wide-open views of Lahaina Harbor.

continued on next page

David Paul's Island Grill *(continued)*

Timing continues to be an issue with service at **David Paul's Island Grill**. While each server we've encountered is both knowledgeable and helpful, there is something seriously off about the pacing at this restaurant. It feels like every course comes four to five minutes (and sometimes longer) later than it should, and while water is poured immediately by the hostess, the first drinks and the bread come late. This could be caused by a slow kitchen, or a staff that hasn't yet set a successful rhythm, or both ... but in any case, it's a noticeable flaw and a consistent complaint from readers.

Come to think of it, we do have one other issue with **David Paul's Island Grill**. We think it should be located in Kihei, closer to our home.

Address: 900 Front St., Lahaina, West Maui
Location: Near Warren & Annabelle's and Hard Rock Café
Meals: Dinner
Hours: Su-Th 5pm – 10pm, F-Sa 5pm – Midnight
Parking: Validated for Lahaina Center parking
Phone: 808-662-3000
Website: www.davidpaulsislandgrill.com

OVERALL:

3.2
out of 5 stars

Dog & Duck *(Pub)*

This little dive of a pub is quietly (or not so quietly) making people happy with good music, good food, and good drinks poured by cute bartenders. The service is relaxed and friendly, and if you're looking for a simple lunch or cheap, this is a great place to check out if you like pub food.

You'll find standard fare like bangers and mash (sausages and mashed potatoes) and corned beef and cabbage, as well as steaks, burgers, and potpies. Specials can stretch to feature island flavors, even local fish over rice with well-made and tasty sauces. While most of the ingredients are commercial, they're prepared carefully and thoughtfully, and we enjoy our visits.

There is a small outdoor seating area on the wraparound porch, and while extra chairs and speakers may be inelegantly stashed in the corners of the pub, the atmosphere is pleasant and the locals friendly. There are televisions throughout the room and live music some nights (call for the schedule).

This is a good little Irish pub and a real gem if you're looking for a mellow time, good beer, and pretty good food.

Address: 1913 S. Kihei Rd., Kihei, South Maui
Location: Kalama Villages across from the Whale
Meals: Lunch, Dinner
Hours: Daily 11am-10pm, bar open until 2am
Parking: Lot
Phone: 808-875-9669

Dollie's Gourmet Pizza *(Pizza)*

This casual pizza joint in Kahana features a full bar, which makes it easy for locals and visitors to like. All told, the pizzas are fine, the service is fine, and the atmosphere is pleasant. Not a bad place to unwind without emptying your wallet in the process.

Address: 4310 Lower Honoapiilani Rd., Kahana, West Maui
Location: Kahana Manor Shops
Meals: Lunch, Dinner, Late-Night
Hours: Daily 11am–12 midnight
Parking: Lot
Phone: 808-669-0266
Website: www.dolliespizzakahana.com

Down to Earth *(Health Food Store)*

With the fast food chains packing Dairy Road, you might miss this healthy alternative, and that would be a shame. This small Hawaiian chain health food store has a good takeout/prepared food counter. It's also overwhelmingly vegan and all organic.

Prepared foods in the chill case include fresh spring rolls (tasty with peanut sauce — to which we add a squirt of siracha), "beautiful" wraps (basically a sandwich wrapped in a giant collard green), and simple but satisfying inari sushi (seasoned brown rice wrapped in a triangular pocket made of thin, wrinkly soybean curd). The self-serve salad bar features hot and cold items such as purple sweet potatoes, lasagna, chili, curries, millet cakes, mock tofu chicken, curried tofu (great, with apples, cashews, and raisins), and Greek salad. You pay by the pound, and can take out or eat in with the locals at the stools and tables available in the upper loft.

Address: 305 Dairy Rd, Kahului, Central Maui
Meals: Breakfast, Lunch, Dinner
Hours: M–Sa 7am–9pm; Su 8am–8pm
Parking: Lot
Phone: 808-877-2661
Website: www.downtoearth.org

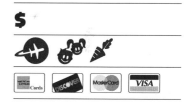

Dragon Dragon Chinese Restaurant *(Chinese)*

Maui lacks fantastic, lip-smacking Chinese restaurants. By all rights we should have plenty: Chinese immigrants helped build the island's infrastructure. But for some tragic reason, Oahu got the lion's share of dim sum while we were denied. That said, if you're craving Chinese, ***Dragon Dragon*** will do the trick.

continued on next page

Dragon Dragon Chinese Restaurant *(continued)*

Service is no-nonsense and the waiters are usually pretty good about steering you toward the best items of the day. (Just don't expect them to smile or be enthusiastic while answering your questions. These are a stoic bunch.) Any special made with fresh local Hawaiian fish is likely to be a standout. Sometimes they have a steamed whole fish with a tasty black bean sauce. Dim sum is particularly good here but served only at lunch time.

During the holidays this restaurant has fixed price specials for groups of six or more people, but make sure you call for reservations ahead of time. This is not a bad stop before catching a movie, but we prefer **Thailand Cuisine** or even the **Whole Foods** salad bar.

Address: 70 E. Kaahumanu Ave., Kahului, Central Maui
Location: Maui Mall
Meals: Lunch, Dinner
Hours: Daily 10:30am-2pm & 5pm-9pm
Parking: Lot
Phone: 808-893-1628

OVERALL:

3.1

out of 5 stars

Duke's *(Pacific Rim)*

The **Duke's** scene in Waikiki is well known; famed Hawaiian musicians drop in for jams and blissed-out patrons clink cocktails and cry "hana hou!" ("Encore!") all night long. On Maui, the off-the-beaten-path location of its sister restaurant, **Duke's Beach House,** precludes that kind of spontaneity, but presents an even more relaxing ambience. The entry serves as a mini-museum celebrating the life of Duke Kahanamoku — the legendary surfer, Olympic champion, and "Ambassador of Aloha." The patio's thatched umbrellas, tiki torches, and teak furnishings are embraced by tiered rock walls. On a small stage, wonderful Hawaiian musicians send the sweet twang of slack-key guitar and falsetto melodies adrift on the warm breeze.

If this were a museum, we'd love it. But it's a restaurant. And the menu fails to match the excellent ambience.

The "poke rolls" are an ill-conceived combination of a Japanese sushi roll and a Vietnamese spring roll, served hot … or at least warm. Raw ahi is wrapped with Maui onions in rice paper, and then seared. The result is a confusing, lukewarm mess.

The mango BBQ ribs might be tasty before they are burnt to a crisp (which they have been, twice). Our waiters, while both effusive and overly friendly, didn't notice that we didn't touch them on either occasion. Other dishes — even simple burgers — have been disappointments.

Cocktails are unimaginative (chip shots, beautifuls, and standard margaritas) and for dessert — surprise! The Hula Pie has found yet another home. The crème brulee trio — small pots of Kona coffee, Tahitian vanilla, and Hawaiian vintage chocolate — is unremarkable. And what do they mean by *vintage* chocolate?

Duke's *(continued)*

We like the organic fruit platter and steel cut oats served at breakfast. If there were live music during this meal, and we were in the mood for oats, we'd be here in a heartbeat.

Address: 130 Kai Malina Pkwy, Honokowai, West Maui
Location: at Honua Kai Resort
Meals: Breakfast, Lunch, Dinner
Hours: Daily, 7:30am-9:30pm
Parking: Lot
Phone: 808-662-2900
Website: www.dukesmaui.com

Duo *(American)*

Duo is so named because it is equally a steak and fish house ... but it also could be inadvertently advertising it's slightly split personality. Both the poolside breakfast buffet *and* a formal dinner venue at The Four Seasons, ***Duo*** bears a huge responsibility at the most exclusive resort on Maui. It must go from brightly-lit, comfy-cushioned, linger-and-read service in the morning to upscale, romantic, full service at night.

Let's start with breakfast. The open kitchen presents a big buffet with platters of pastries, fish, cereals, covered dishes mounded with sausages, scrambled eggs, and French toast, vats of miso soup and oatmeal. You can get fresh fruit and yogurt or made-to-order omelets. If it's a holiday, they are likely featuring a more expansive champagne brunch with a seafood bar, carving station, and piles of desserts. We like coming for breakfast on special occasions — not just because the food is good (which it is, and should be at these prices), but because the service is so wonderful. Every morning the kitchen makes a new smoothie "shooter," which is presented by the waiter during your meal. Whether it's carrots and orange juice or spinach, apple, mango, and lime, it's a well-balanced, thoughtful, healthy supplement. The servers are unfailingly pleasant and efficient, and this is one of the best places on Maui to feel true Aloha in the service. The bright-but-shady poolside location is cheerful, and you can see the ocean beyond the cabanas. It's just lovely.

At night, the lit-up pool's fountain, bubbling hot tubs, flaming tiki torches, and star-splashed sky serve as a backdrop for an elegant evening. A few modern décor elements and the gracious, restrained demeanor of the staff helps disguise the breakfast buffet's teak tables and waterproof seat cushions.

Duo's dinner menu used to be strictly a la carte: even the sauces had to be selected by the customer. We're very glad that their new menu dropped this conceit and now showcases nicely composed dishes that pair perfectly cooked proteins (fish, beef, elk, venison, duck) with some delightful sauce preparations and admittedly small side dishes.

OVERALL:
4.3
out of 5 stars

continued on next page

Duo *(continued)*

(Why small? We think they wanted to keep you ordering their rich and sizable sides: white cheddar-truffle mac and cheese, a stack of onion rings, unbelievably sweet and buttery corn from upcountry ... the skillet roasted vegetables are the only item on the side dishes menu that won't threaten a coronary by the time they bring the check.)

There are some good choices in the appetizer menu that could serve as a light meal: a nice pork pate served with grilled toast and a pungent fig mustard, a good crudo made from hamachi and radishes and studded with black sea salt, and the chop salad, which features spicy and bitter greens set off by creamy blue cheese, spicy-sweet pecans, teensy bits of pineapple and bacon, and a light papaya dressing.

The steaks at **Duo** are what you have in mind when you think "good steak dinner." Perfectly prepared and dressed in *just* the right sauces, we've never been disappointed when ordering from the "Land" side of the menu. The first time we had the dry-aged bone-in rib eye at **Duo** it earned a spot in our Hall of Fame as one of our all-time top meals. (We savor our favorite dishes again and again in memory.) On a whim, we ordered an unknown Lebanese wine, which had a medicinal flavor until paired with the tender and pink aged rib eye. Then, it was nothing short of magical: the wine tasted of passion and spurs, for some reason ... we imagined horses racing down an empty beach. Meanwhile, the meat tasted of smoke and honey. The combination was triumphant. We tried recreating it again, but while the steak remains exceptional, the mysterious wine is gone. We've also had the elk and the duck and venison preparations, and enjoyed each one. (Although none of them inspired equine fantasies.)

The fish entrées are all perfectly cooked, but perhaps less magical. The selection varies by season, of course, but usually includes a mahi mahi, snapper and ahi. A reliable preparation is the seared ahi with mushrooms swimming in a silky miso beurre blanc.

If you're really a seafood freak, you might check out the raw bar, available on certain nights (ask when you make reservations). It's on the left as you enter: a cart stacked with iced buckets of lobster, Markea prawns, crab, several kinds of poke, and oysters, which an attendant will shuck for you. This "endless catch" is available for $60. Most of it is cold-water, which means it was flown in from the East or West Coast, but some of the tastiest selections — the sweet Hawaiian slipper lobster and tender and crunchy octopus poke — were harvested from Island waters. We have a soft spot (read that: gluttonous appetite) for fresh oysters ... and really, *nothing* beats having someone shuck them for you. The green apple mignonette and kim chee aioli accentuate the brilliant briny flavors. Overall, the endless catch is a good value and James thinks it serves very nicely as appetizer, entrée, and sides.

The desserts are wildly innovative — from dense, chocolaty donuts in a cloud of Guinness ice cream to dehydrated chocolate mousse crisps. The menu changes often and most items on it are also available in tapas portions: miniature versions that you can mix and match. Some of these desserts have wowed us, others merely satisfied our sweet tooth.

Duo *(continued)*

The servers are exceptionally well-trained and attentive without being obtrusive (how *did* that steak knife get there without your noticing?) and they carry little pocket flashlights in case you forgot yours and need to read the menu (yes, the restaurant is *that* dark at night).

A sweet surprise accompanies your check: a giant spool of cotton candy. This carnival treat comes in sour apple, grape, or strawberry. It's fun and frivolous. And, of course, because it's the Four Seasons, you also get warm oshibori towels to wipe the sugar from your fingers.

Address: 3900 Wailea Alanui, Wailea, South Maui
Location: Four Seasons Resort
Meals: Breakfast, Lunch, Dinner
Hours: M-Sa 6am - 11:30am; Su 6am - 12pm, Daily 5:30pm - 9pm
Parking: Valet
Phone: 808-874-8000
Website: www.fourseasons.com

Eskimo Candy *(American)*

Eskimo Candy is a fish wholesaler with a lunch counter that serves fish plates, burgers, wraps, and ribs. The menu is pretty transparent about what you're eating. The Fish-n-Chips platter is advertised as "w/ frozen mahi" and "w/ frozen ono" ($6.95 each). The truth is that anyone selling you fish and chips on Maui is working with frozen fish — otherwise you'd be paying $16 for that plate — but few are willing to say so on their menu.

Of course, no other restaurant is hoping to sell you *fresh fish* to take home, either. We would buy more fresh fish and marinated fish from **Eskimo Candy's** retail operation if the prices were lower than they are at grocery stores. We do like their poke (ahi sashimi with spices), but we also like Foodland's.

The bottom line is **Eskimo Candy** provides good to average, inexpensive food in a clean, get-out-of-here-quick atmosphere. Outside tables don't have a great view (the street and parking lot), but the service is helpful and quick, and kids are very happy with the fish shack atmosphere and the menu.

Address: 2665 Wai Wai Pl, Kihei, South Maui
Location: Turn from South Kihei Road at Pizza Madness, Eskimo Candy is up the street on the right side.
Meals: Lunch, Dinner
Hours: M-F 10:30am-7pm
Parking: Lot
Phone: 808-879-5686
Website: www.eskimocandy.com

OVERALL:
3
out of 5 stars

$

Fat Boy Burger *(American)*

Fat Boy Burger is owned by the same crew who opened *Fat Daddy's*, but the love quotient is a notch lower. The menu is composed entirely of — you guessed it — burgers. There are lots of different special combinations — we count eight different sauces — and plenty of a la carte toppings, as well. While the toppings are fresh, the burgers themselves are average and greasy and overly salty. We're not sure whether the beef is commercial frozen patties or not — some servers have said Maui Cattle Company, fresh, hand-formed, while others say "it's frozen, I don't know where it comes from." The French fries are acceptable, but we like the tempura battered onion rings better. You place your order at the window, and pick it up when it's ready. The outdoor seating is comfortable, even though this patio (attached to Starbucks in the Kukui Mall) is pretty sunny during the day (most tables have umbrellas). Service is friendly, but the prices are a dollar or two more than they should be. If you are really craving a burger and want a quick, no-fuss meal, this is an OK option — but in a blind taste test, James named the "upscale" Angus burger at McDonald's a better sandwich. Believe it or not, it has a similar flavor, the toppings seem as fresh — and the price is right.

Address: 1819 S. Kihei Rd., Kihei, South Maui
Location: In Kukui Mall, next to Starbucks (on the same patio)
Meals: Lunch, Dinner
Hours: Daily 11am-9pm
Parking: Lot
Phone: 808-875-7777

Fat Daddy's Smokehouse *(American/Barbecue)*

Fat Daddy's makes good Texas barbecue by smoking meats in their own smoker behind the restaurant and serving them up with traditional sides like macaroni and cheese, baked beans, coleslaw, and cornbread. Everything is made from scratch. If you haven't had Texas barbecue, you should know that it's *supposed* to be bright pink inside and dark brown — charred — on the outside. The meat cures while soaking up the intense, wood smoke flavor. Once smoked, the meat is dressed with a sauce, which can be sweet or spicy, vinegary or tomato-ey, and this is served on the side or dashed over the top.

We like the brisket, the ribs, and the pulled pork. The sauce is too sweet on its own, but when paired with the meat, the woodsy char darkens the flavor and they balance each other out (use more sauce on the pork than you think you need). We like the watercress salad as a side because, while the bitter cress is used sparingly, it's nice with the sweet carrots, and the dressing is light and fresh. The cornbread we leave alone.

The plate combinations are a good value and big enough for most people to share. A full bar and several flat screen televisions make this an excellent place to hang out with your friends and watch the game. Kids also love this place for a filling, inexpensive casual family meal.

Fat Daddy's Smokehouse *(continued)*

Address: 1913 S. Kihei Rd., Kihei, South Maui
Location: Kalama Villages across from the Whale
Meals: Lunch, Dinner
Hours: W–M 11:30am–9pm
Parking: Lot
Phone: 808-879-8711
Website: www.fatdaddysmaui.com

Ferraro's Bar e Ristorante *(Italian)*

OVERALL:
4.2
out of 5 stars

Ferraro's is perched above stunning Wailea Beach, poolside at the Four Seasons, a resort that refuses to rest on its laurels. It'd be easy for the restaurant to skimp on quality and simply coast by on their absolutely perfect location — but it doesn't.

Clothed in white linen, tables are tucked under giant umbrella tents on several broad terraces, so just about everyone has a good view of the expansive green lawn rolling down to the ocean below. The large, columned bar built from warm stone provides sophisticated, no-reservations dining, while the surrounding tables can accommodate large parties.

Our favorite meal at *Ferraro's* is lunch, because the view is so pristine, the food so lovely, and the service so wonderful. It's fun to slide on big sunglasses, sip an expertly mixed cocktail and spy on the beautiful people lounging by the pool. Blueberry mojito? Yes, please. The wood-burning oven churns out good pizzas, the sandwiches are made with mostly local ingredients (get the lobster roll or lobster salad), and the salads are big and bold.

At dinner the atmosphere transforms (and the prices rise). Live classical music — gentle guitar, violin, or flute — wafts through the air just loud enough to enjoy without interrupting conversation. The sunset view defines the word *spectacular.*

Service is, to use James's word, "sterling." Friendly, knowledgeable, and relaxed, servers manage to guide, inform, and help you without being obtrusive. When they say "It's no problem," you actually feel that it isn't, for them.

The pasta dishes are lovely, and all can be split into half courses or appetizer sizes. We absolutely love the lobster linguini. It comes with a savory cream sauce and an incredibly generous serving of perfectly cooked lobster.

The bolognese has very clean flavors: not too spicy, not too sweet, not to salty. The veal, pork, and beef in the sauce are perfectly cooked and tender. For main entrées our current favorites are the sea bass with a slightly peppery watercress butter sauce, and the ciopella di mare, a lovely tomato-saffron-crab broth that is perfectly seasoned, with scallops, shrimp, lobster, calamari, and fish. James is tempted to tip the bowl to the back of his throat. When the kitchen is having a good night — which is most of the time — dinners are well worth the price.

continued on next page

Ferraro's Bar e Ristorante *(continued)*

Desserts are traditionally very good, and change regularly (as does the rest of the menu). If they have the cheesecake made with a super-light ricotta cheese and a disk of lemon gelato on top, we recommend it. The sugared pine nuts and rhubarb on the side make this dessert both refreshing and fairy-tale light.

Occasionally we are reminded that we are in a resort (not an independent) restaurant. Especially over the last year, a meals have ranked lower in the Love category. Some recipes didn't sing like they once did, and there were several ice-cold salads. In such a good restaurant, slip-ups and inconsistencies are more noticeable. The resort setting works to your advantage in other ways, however. If you fancy a wine or dessert served at *Duo* or the Lobby Lounge, you have only to ask and it will be retrieved post haste.

The little things, like the excellent house bread with olive tapenade threaded through it, two choices of sea salts, and the fact that coffee comes in a French press, up the ante for this restaurant making our favorites list. The wine list is good, filled with Italian bottles, but, as we mentioned, you can also order from the more extensive list at sister restaurant *Duo*. Parents with kids will rejoice to see the familiar, but sophisticated, children's menu, and be grateful that the more romantic tables are farther down the terraces, closer to the beach — far from their exuberant little dinner companions.

After filling our bellies with prosecco, pasta, seafood, and house-made ice cream, we saunter down to the beach path and listen for the eerie calls of native seabirds returning after their own adventures at sea.

Address: 3900 Wailea Alanui Dr., Wailea, South Maui
Location: Four Seasons Resort
Meals: Lunch, Dinner
Hours: Daily 11:30am - 9pm
Parking: Valet
Phone: 808-874-8000
Website: www.fourseasons.com/maui

OVERALL:
3.4
out of 5 stars

Five Palms Restaurant *(American/Pacific Rim)*

Five Palms is in one of the best waterfront locations on the island. Anchoring the north end of Keawakapu Beach, the view stretches out the Wailea coast, over the water to little crescent-shaped Molokini, and beyond to the majestic red mound of Kaho'olawe. Stunning.

Outdoor seating on the lanai is your best bet, and the best bet for food is breakfast. The garden Benedict — spinach and sun dried tomatoes — is a good choice. So is the banana foster pancakes (rum's in that pineapple sauce), and we also like their egg breakfasts. Lunches, which are served

Five Palms Restaurant *(continued)*

along with the breakfast menu from morning to Happy Hour in the afternoon, consist of large sandwiches with well-prepared steak fries. The burger is good (order it a little rarer than you normally would). So is the spinach salad with blue cheese and bacon.

A couple of times a year — Mother's Day and Easter — the restaurant puts on a really stupendous champagne brunch that we rarely miss.

We regularly meet friends for half-priced appetizers — sushi, ribs — and drink specials during Happy Hour, but we usually skip dinner, which doesn't measure up to other meals. Service is halfhearted, but the view makes up for most of it during daylight hours. After dark, however, there is nothing to look at but the plate.

One last thing about the view: during the winter months (peaking in January and February) Humpback whales come to calve just offshore here. Umm, like, right *in front of you*. Stupefying marine life shows are nearly guaranteed: the enormous animals leap out of the air, slap their tails, and blow off steam. Mama whales patiently teach their youngsters all the acrobatic tricks, demonstrating again and again exactly how to slap the water to achieve maximum effect. Grab a curbside seat for breakfast, order coffee or a mimosa, and keep your eyes trained on the horizon.

You may remember Canoes, *Five Palms'* sister restaurant in Lahaina. When they reopened as *Five Palms Lahaina* about a month before publication, they sported a new menu, more in line with what's on offer at the Wailea location.

Address: 2960 S. Kihei Rd., Kihei, South Maui
Location: at the Mana Kai
Meals: Breakfast, Brunch, Lunch, Dinner
Hours: Daily 8am–9pm
Parking: Lot
Phone: 808–879–2607
Website: www.fivepalmsrestaurant.com

Address: 1450 Front St., Lahaina, West Maui
Location: right on the corner where Front Street joins the highway.
Meals: Breakfast, Lunch, Dinner
Hours: Daily 8am–11pm
Parking: Lot (look carefully as you drive by, the intersection is very close).
Phone: 808–661–0937
Website: www.5palmslahaina.com

Flatbread Pizza Company *(Pizza)*

There are some restaurants that approach food as a life mission, and *Flatbread Pizza Company* counts itself one of those restaurants. *Sustainable, organic,* and *local* are more than watchwords here; they are a business decision for the company and a life choice for many of the staff members. The resulting food is delicious, and this is one of our favorite places on Maui.

Even deep dish pizza fans tend to ooh and ahh over the thin, irregularly shaped pizzas. The dough, made with local spring water, organic flour, cake yeast, and kosher salt, is densely flavored, chewy, and crispy in all the right places. The red sauce is made fresh in-house from organic tomatoes and several organic herbs. Toppings include a maple fennel sausage made from scratch, nitrite-free pepperoni, chicken, and plenty of veggies including sweet caramelized Maui onions. You can select your own toppings or choose from one of their thoughtful combinations. For locavores, a regularly updated sign listing which ingredients were sourced from Maui farms and ranches hangs to the left of the hostess station.

We especially like the sausage pizza with caramelized onions, sun dried tomatoes, mushrooms, mozzarella, parmesan cheese, garlic oil and herbs. It's a white pizza, but we occasionally get it with the red sauce added. Another perennial favorite is called the Pele Pesto, which features an luscious pesto of basil, macadamia nuts, and garlic. Goat cheese, fresh tomatoes, Kalamata olives, and herbs round out the pie. Best of all? The Pele Pesto with sausage added. Boo-yah!

Every day features two specials, one vegetarian and one meat. These tend to showcase the freshest and most unusual local ingredients the manager has found, but combinations can range from odd to unappealing. Sometimes they're winners, like a thin-sliced spicy potato pie. Other times, they're not: Caesar salad pie? Not for us. Unless a special really calls you, we recommend choosing from among the many regular combinations on the menu.

The large salads feature crisp, fresh greens, shaved carrots, chunky celery slices, and a smattering of dark arame seaweed. Their pineapple dressing, which we once thought too tart and sweet and not cohesive enough has been updated to a lovely, lingering, light vinaigrette. There is also vinegar and olive oil on the table and you can add optional dabs of Surfing Goat Dairy cheese.

Other than dessert — an overly sweet brownie sundae we skip — that's all that's on the menu: pizzas and salads. And that's all we need from *Flatbread*. Oh, except for a drink. There's a full bar, including the tasty *Maui Brewing Company* beers on tap. The signature drink on the mainland (this is a small chain from New England) is lemonade sweetened with maple syrup. In the colder climates of the northeast it can be served warm, but in Paia it is only served with ice. The iced version is still refreshing — especially since so few Maui restaurants make fresh lemonade at all — but not as tasty as we remember it. We suspect that with both lemons and maple syrup being very expensive on Maui, this drink gets a short shrift. The pomegranate ginger mojito is likewise a tad too subtle, but we like it anyway, with or without alcohol.

Flatbread Pizza Company *(continued)*

All Paia restaurants are noisy, and **Flatbread** is no exception. The big main dining room offers lots of seating options, from huge booths to smaller tables to tallboy chairs to couches and coffee tables to the bar itself. The brick oven is roaring inside, so we often sit out on the shaded lanai. Every Tuesday is packed as people turn out to support whichever local nonprofit gets 10% of that evening's sales. You might wait for as long as forty-five minutes on any given night, however, so consider calling ahead and putting your name on the list before you arrive.

Service can range from excellent and attentive to distracted and intentionally oblivious, and we suspect that training is sometimes left to previous employers. The person who delivers the pizza to the table is usually not the server, but the pizza maker, often wearing a heartfelt expression of humble pride as they describe the pie they made. There is no doubt that those who work the pizza oven — with their rippling windsurfer physiques, tattooed arms, and wild hair — are there to serve the Fire, the Bread, and maybe even the Divine in You. *(Namaste.)*

Address: 89 Hana Hwy., Paia, North Shore
Meals: Lunch, Dinner
Hours: Daily 11:30am–10pm
Parking: Street
Phone: 808-579-8989
Website: www.flatbreadcompany.com

Fred's Mexican Café *(Mexican)*

Fred's offers average Mexican fare to everyone from the families in the front dining room all the way back to the bar — where you can still get food, but the focus is definitely on the tequila.

When **Fred's** first opened, they tried: fresh food, stiff drinks, and truly reasonable prices. That was long ago. What used to be $2 Taco Tuesdays went to $2.95 — and the better ones are $3.95. We've had one too many too-fishy-tasting-fish-tacos, and the price of a margarita worth drinking has been pushed up to $illy. Service is still competent, and friendly, and the view is gorgeous. Still plenty popular, **Fred's** is fine if you ratchet your expectations to average and decide to splurge on a top shelf margarita (the house versions give us headaches).

Address: 2511 S. Kihei Rd., Kihei, South Maui
Location: Across from Kamaole Beach Park II
Meals: Breakfast, Lunch, Dinner
Hours: Daily 7:30am - 10pm
Parking: Lot, Street
Phone: 808-891-8600
Website: www.fredsmexicancafe.com

OVERALL:
2.6
out of 5 stars

$ $

continued on next page

OVERALL:
3.2
out of 5 stars

$ $

MasterCard VISA

Fresh Mint *(Vegan / Vietnamese)*

Fresh Mint is a crazy little restaurant in a crazy little building serving crazy delicious vegan food that satisfies even the most crazy carnivorous appetites. This establishment is not run so much like a restaurant as a home kitchen. So, let's set your expectations right up front.

Don't expect good service: it's just the owner and his wife serving and cooking, and they have trouble doing both at the same time. One of you might get your entrée ten minutes before the other one does — but that's OK, you'll want to share each one. Think of them as courses.

Don't expect a beautiful restaurant. The exterior (chartreuse) and interior (lavender) walls of this one-room eatery are a shade shy of psychedelic, the building dates back to sugar plantation days, and the bathroom is through the kitchen.

Do expect very fresh Vietnamese food made with care. The sauces are excellent and well made, and the soy meats are cooked so perfectly that the texture fools many a meat eater. Meatless ribs? Give them a try. The accompanying gravy is scrumptious. The pho, we feel, is less successful without the viscosity provided by the traditional beef broth. If you're a vegan, you should certainly stop in for a meal or two. If you're not, you might want to get a break from fish and steak.

Address: 115 Baldwin Ave., Paia, North Shore
Location: Past Mana Foods on the left side.
Meals: Dinner
Hours: Daily 5pm-9pm
Parking: Street
Phone: 808-579-9144

OVERALL:
3.2
out of 5 stars

$ $ $

DISCOVER MasterCard VISA

Gannon's *(American)*

Bev Gannon, Chef Owner of *Hali'imaile General Store* and *Joe's*, opened her latest venture in the old Seawatch location. We had always relied on Seawatch less for dinner (it was over-priced and average) and more for reasonably priced, good breakfasts and lunches. It's a million-dollar view from the 200 foot elevation, and we looooooooove watching whales breach in season from way up high while indulging in a great eggs Benedict: *Kihei Caffe* prices with Wailea views. Seawatch was additionally known for being a great spot for a catered party — to the chagrin of those dining at tables near the event lawn.

Surprisingly, all of this remains true under the new management, save for the killing blow: no breakfast on weekdays. Sure, breakfast is served after 10 am, but if you're not at work or frolicking in the water by then, we suggest shifting your priorities. Happily, the restaurant opens earlier on weekends (and even on weekdays during high tourist season), so our Benedict routine isn't completely dashed.

Gannon's *(continued)*

The Red Bar, with its sparkly bowling-ball-like countertop is sassy and fun — but marooned up on the golf course as it is it only attracts so much of a crowd. The bar has done its best to draw patrons by offering half off a decent selection of appetizers from 3pm-6pm — a good deal if you happen to be wrapping up your golf game or snorkeling trip.

Bev does comfort food well: smoky BBQ pork, salt-crusted rib eye, juicy, messy ribs with coleslaw, spicy blackened shrimp tacos and crab cake that doesn't scrimp on the crab. Go for lunch or Happy Hour and think of it as fancy picnic food, and you'll be satisfied. Sadly, dinners have disappointed, over and over. We've had terribly undercooked fish (which was not fixed by the waiter, but ignored), and watched as an entire table of companions pushed away their various dishes, barely touched. The steaks are a safe choice, but we're not sure how or why the magic gets lost at the dinner service.

Also, don't be surprised if you arrive to find a "closed for private function" sign taped to the door. (You can check the website to avoid this; the calendar is regularly updated.)

All of this said, we can and *do* recommend **Gannon's** for weddings and parties. Bev and her team are terrific caterers, and few locations on the island rival this one for sheer beauty and convenience. The process is made simple with online menus from which to choose.

Address: 100 Wailea Golf Club Dr., Wailea, South Maui
Location: On the Gold and Emerald Golf Course
Meals: Breakfast, Brunch, Lunch, Dinner
Hours: Weekdays 10 am-9:30pm, Weekends 8am-9:30pm
Parking: Valet, Lot
Phone: 808-875-8080
Website: www.gannonsrestaurant.com

Gazebo Restaurant *(American)*

The wait for a table at **Gazebo** is legendary. Unless you show up at least fifteen minutes before they open, you'll be waiting for up to an hour. We like to decide when we want to eat, and then arrive thirty minutes earlier. The free coffee bar on the deck of the pool (yes, you line up along a kidney-shaped pool) helps to keep the edge off the hunger.

Kids tend to love it here, and are treated well. If they have trouble waiting in line, send them to the giant checkerboard just beyond the pool. They can play a game with the coconuts painted red and black while you wait.

The tiny round restaurant has big picture windows all the way round (hence the name) and in whale season we like to sit facing Napili Bay, where the giant animals frolic in the early morning sun.

The food is average American breakfast and lunch fare, and we're afraid that

continued on next page

Gazebo Restaurant *(continued)*

the view often makes it taste better than it really does (views do that sometimes). We like the omelets better than the pancakes, which — despite their many raving fans — strike us as formulaic, even *with* the chopped macadamia nuts and the sliced bananas on top. If you like coconut syrup, you can buy some in any supermarket on the island, get a can of macadamia nuts, and pack them for home. Put them on your own pancakes with a dollop of Cool Whip for the same taste, without the too-steep price tag.

When on the West side for breakfast, we tend to migrate a little farther down the bay to **Sea House**, where the breakfasts are made with more care and better ingredients. We also like **Plantation House** for breakfast. **Mala** serves a great brunch on weekends.

Address: 5315 Lower Honoapiilani Rd., Napili, West Maui
Location: Outrigger Napili Shores
Meals: Breakfast, Lunch
Hours: Daily 7:30am-2pm
Parking: Lot
Phone: 808-669-5621
Website: www.outrigger.com

OVERALL:
4.6
out of 5 stars

Gerard's Restaurant *(French)*

Gerard's produces wonderful food. The restaurant is immaculately clean, down to the corners of the windows. They have *just* the right linens and polish the silver carefully. They serve the right food at the right time with the right wine, and the service is relaxed and attentive.

The food is high French, but Chef-owner Gerard Reversade uses Hawaiian ingredients deliberately and with great style, incorporating them seamlessly into dishes as if they always were part of the cuisine. There are also several bistro items on the menu. If you want a hearty and warming stew, try the meaty, savory, smooth *Boeuf Bourguignon*. If you want lots of flavors and textures, try the classic white bean *cassoulet*, stocked with tender, perfectly cooked chunks of meat and sausage. *Coq au Vin* rounds out the bistro menu with its slow-braised chicken — *fantastique!*

Few dishes warm you from the inside out as much as an authentic French onion soup — and this one is the best we've had in a restaurant. Caramelized onions abound in rich, house-made beef broth and blanketed by melted Gruyere and Parmesan — the browned edges of which are a sinful delight to crack off the rim of the bowl. This dish takes thirty minutes to bake, so you might want to phone in your order so the kitchen can have it ready for you when you arrive. Another good dish is the savory Souvaroff: delicate puff pastry sheets shelter quail and tender Hamakua mushrooms.

The eight-course *Degustation Menu* is a real treat. A *degustation* is a meal that is composed of a variety of flavors and textures, eaten with the intent of concentrating on the sensual and gustatory pleasures of the food. While the courses can change, the most recent menu does include many of our favorite dishes, so we'll look at it in detail.

The first course is the foie gras medallions, perfectly seared and placed upon a round of French toast, then drizzled with poha berry compote (sweet like honey with a little sour pucker). Next course is very rich wide, flat noodles with truffle butter sauce, accompanied by a duo of plump, sweet prawns sautéed lightly in hazelnut oil. Luscious.

Third course is a tiny bowl of a chilled cucumber soup. Swirled into the smooth, creamy, pale green soup is a white thread of Surfing Goat Dairy cheese. A little ball of tomato sorbet rests in the very middle, and when you stir this all together, you get a cool, sweet, tangy taste of summer with just a titch of spice from the sorbet.

For the next course, a simple spinach salad with two seared scallops arrives. Fifth course features a beautiful piece of snapper draped in a bright emulsion of orange and ginger. The fish is tender and slightly crisp from its bath in the oil in which it roasted; it rests on a perfectly seasoned and subtly flavored bed of braised fennel.

We should mention, here at *Intermezzo*, that each course is accompanied by a change of cutlery carried in silver trays, and the servers make sure that you know they're available with both explanations and anything else you may desire. The service is so quiet, professional, and genuine that it's a relief. We've never heard impossible questions like "How are the flavors?" or "Is everything tasting all right?" Instead we hear the classic "Is there anything else I can bring you?" which is more than enough inquiry.

The sorbet intermezzo is made in house, and served in a chilled martini glass with an ounce of champagne. It's like a fizzy, elegant fruit punch.

Our favorite course is the rack of lamb. Two lamb chops (the rack has been dismantled for you) are presented with the house *potatoes au gratin*, and a *flan* made from a green vegetable (watercress, spinach). The chops are generously sized, perfectly medium rare, crusted with a beautiful salt that keeps the New Zealand lamb succulent. The flan is subtle, but the fluffy potato gratin, with the wonderfully melty cheese, is decadent and comforting.

The final course is a dessert from their exceptional list. One of our favorites (you'll need several visits to try them all) is the classic *crème brulee*, which Gerard serves chilled and crusted with at least an eighth of an inch of raw Hawaiian sugar torched into a thick, hard caramel. Unlike many Maui versions of this dessert, we must actually stab at the dessert to break this crust and get to the custard, and the result is a mouthful of cool vanilla and slightly warm caramel. My, my, my.

Another favorite dessert is the *Mille-feuille*, or Napoleon. A spectacular puff pastry standing seven inches high, it features layers of "thousand leaved" puff pastry alternating with lemon curd and strawberries. Light, fluffy curd, crackly sounds as you break the pastry — and we complain there are so few good pastry chefs on Maui!!? To his great credit, Gerard is both lead cook and pastry chef.

continued on next page

Gerard's Restaurant *(continued)*

And the final favorite dessert: the Grand Marnier soufflé. Order it shortly after sitting down, as it takes time to prepare. Dizzyingly light and fluffy, sweet, aromatic and eggy in exactly the right proportion, this magical souf-flé-that-never-falls suggests that perfection is attainable after all.

After all that praise, we'll warn you against the Dusty Road, a simple combination of coffee and chocolate ice creams dusted in cocoa and macadamia nuts. It's nice … but when compared to the other sweet gems, it's a wasted opportunity.

The restaurant is located in the Plantation Inn, a gracious building well back from Front Street. There are no views to speak of, and there are three dining areas in the restaurant: inside in a very air conditioned and slightly stuffy parlor, outside on the lanai, or in a small, fairy-lit garden area. We like the porch best, where, even though the tables are very tight, we can see the dishes come out. Music plays to give quiet conversation some cover, but perhaps because of the close quarters, conversations erupt between tables, and we always meet nice people at *Gerard's*.

The wine list is lovely, the service is French, and if you want a special, quiet meal focused solely on the subtle pleasures of the palate, *Gerard's* is the place to be.

Address: 174 Lahainaluna Rd., Lahaina, West Maui
Location: at The Plantation Inn
Meals: Dinner
Hours: Nightly 6pm–8:30pm
Parking: Street
Phone: 808-661-8939
Website: www.gerardsmaui.com

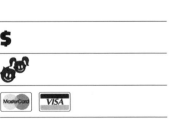

Giannotto's Pizzeria *(Pizza)*

Pocket-sized *Giannotto's* on Wailuku's Main Street serves New York style pizza with a really crispy, paper-thin crust that crunches under your teeth — and that salty cheese we haven't had since we left the Tri-State Area. Back home it would be average, and on Maui, it's nostalgic, but still average. The sandwiches, or subs, are similarly nostalgic — stuffed with fillings and a little greasy. Even so, the Philly cheese steak and chicken Parmesan editions are both pretty tasty, and for Maui, a steal at $6.95. The tiramisu is silky and rich.

Frank Sinatra and Bruce Springsteen albums line the walls beside faded high school sports teams pictures and baby photos. The owner's New Jersey roots are evident in his gravelly voice and business-like attitude, but he's been here long enough to have been softened by Aloha.

The few seats inside the pizza joint are supplemented by picnic tables out-

Giannotto's Pizzeria *(continued)*

side, and this is a good place to take the kids for a quick meal that no one will complain about on the way to the Iao Valley.

Address: 2050 Main St., Wailuku, Central Maui
Meals: Lunch, Dinner
Hours: M-Sa 11am-9pm; Su 11am-8pm
Parking: Street
Phone: 808-244-8282
Website: www.giannottospizza.com

Grandma's Coffeehouse *(Coffeehouse)*

On Sunday mornings, live music and livelier conversation erupt on the lanai (deck) at ***Grandma's Coffeehouse*** in tiny Keokea. Spindly coffee trees push through the decking and the view stretches from the summit of Haleakala all the way out to Kaho'olawe in the distance. (There's a reason Oprah lives up the street — it's drop dead gorgeous country.) As the story goes, Grandma Franco began roasting coffee in 1918. The family has kept at it and you can enjoy your Maui-grown cup of Joe chatting with long-time Maui residents who rarely get off the mountain. There's often a line out the door — ever since the Franco's expanded their breakfast menu — but it moves quickly.

Eggs and omelets come with commendably crisp breakfast potatoes and sweet corn bread. The crepes aren't as sophisticated as those at *La Provence* nearby, but they're still tasty. One of our friends swears by the oatmeal, piled high with fresh fruit and yogurt. You can also get acai bowls and smoothies. On weekends only, they offer a Benedict special. It is special — it comes on a cornbread waffle instead of an English muffin. Sadly, the waffle always tastes slightly burnt. Maybe they need to clean the griddle more often? We console ourselves with the pumpkin or zucchini bread in the bakery case — or if we're feeling naughty, a slice of rich tiramisu for breakfast.

One major flaw: no restroom. The nearest washroom is across the street at the park. On your way there, take a peek into the nostalgic general store and sweet Keokea Gallery.

Address: 153 Kula Hwy, Kula, Upcountry
Location: at Thompson Road
Meals: Breakfast, Lunch, Snacks & Treats
Hours: Daily 7am-5pm
Parking: Lot
Phone: 808-375-7853
Website: www.grandmascoffee.com

OVERALL:
3.8
out of 5 stars

$

OVERALL:

3.6

out of 5 stars

$ $ $

Hali'imaile General Store *(Pacific Rim)*

A cornerstone of the Hawaiian Regional Cuisine movement, for two decades this foodie oasis in the middle of the pineapple fields has been serving well-made, comforting, and delicious meals. The drive out to the restaurant, which inhabits a renovated plantation store, is idyllic just before sunset, when a golden mist overtakes the surrounding fields. We used to feel this restaurant was a must-try for visitors — but the golden glow has faded for us, as it has for some of our upcountry friends who used to be regular-like-clockwork patrons.

Perhaps it is that the menu hasn't changed in so long that it's gotten stale … and the few newer items we've tasted haven't been inspired. Celebrity chef Bev Gannon certainly works hard — she's a terrific caterer — but something's off, both here and at **Gannon's**. As a New York City newspaper travel writer said when we shared a meal here, "now I see why you two have to revisit even the most reliable of restaurants — places go downhill when they rest on their laurels."

We still recommend a visit if you want well-executed meals with good service — just stick to the reliable dishes. For example, our long-time favorite appetizer, the Sashimi Napoleon, still makes us curl our toes with happiness. Layers of sashimi, smoked salmon, caviar, and won tons stack up on a bed of crisp salad greens laced with tobiko caviar and wasabi vinaigrette. The whole contraption looks delicate, but it's tougher than you would think to destroy it with a chopstick or a steak knife and render it into bites. Your server is happy to do the honors and demonstrate how to chop it for you. The smoky, spicy, sweet flavors with the crisp, crunchy, silky smooth textures define pleasure. The "crab" pizza is famous, but it's never been our favorite, and that hasn't changed.

The seasonal fish dishes are generally reliable, including the macadamia nut preparation with the killer mango lilikoi butter sauce. We also like the peppery-but-sweet Thai chili sauce on the seared ahi dish.

Chef Gannon always does ribs well, and we still like the baby back ribs with spicy, tangy, sweet barbecue sauce. The mashed potatoes that come with many dishes are noteworthy for their creamy texture and buttery flavor. If you are looking for something a tad lighter, the simply prepared roast chicken dish usually features astringent asparagus extravagantly wrapped with prosciutto. (It's only a *tad* lighter.)

The desserts are as rich as the main courses, including a too-sweet pineapple upside down cake and one of James's all-time favorite desserts: a chocolate pastry shell filled with caramel and chocolate and macadamia nuts, topped with whipped cream.

Special mention must be made of the drinks, because the bartenders here love their work and make killer cocktails (though they can be slow to deliver). Our favorite is their mai tai, which is served in a hollowed out pineapple. The pineapple juice comes from the walls of the fruit, so we recommend waiting for your first sip until after the concoction marinates for at least two minutes. It's worth the wait for one of the freshest, most delicious versions on the island.

Hali'imaile General Store *(continued)*

The restaurant's setting is kitchen-kitsch: bold colors, big ceramics, lots of framed photos of Chef Gannon and her celebrity clients. The front room of the restaurant is loud. The quieter back room is better for larger groups, and the walls double as a rotating gallery exhibit of some of Maui's best artists. Each new collection is based on a single theme and it's fun to guess what it is while studying the diverse paintings.

One of the first female celebrity chefs and one of the twelve founders of Hawaiian Regional Cuisine, Bev Gannon does carefully hire her servers. They genuinely love food and really get to know her menu and recipes, so the service is both attentive and a celebration of your meal.

Occasionally, the restaurant offers a substantial discount if you bring in a canned good to donate to the Maui Food Bank. It's also always a good idea to call or check the website for special deals. If you dine here you can present your receipt to either **Gannon's** or **Joe's Bar & Grill** for a discount within a certain time frame.

Address: 900 Hali'imaile Rd., Makawao, Upcountry
Location: Turn from Baldwin Ave. or Haleakala Highway
Meals: Lunch, Dinner
Hours: M–F 11am–2:30pm; Nightly 5:30pm–9:30pm
Parking: Lot
Phone: 808-572-2666
Website: www.BevGannonRestaurants.com

Hawaiian Moons Natural Foods *(Organic/Vegan)*

This medium-sized health food store is the place to shop in South Maui for a small, but careful, selection of groceries, produce, vitamins, and beauty items. Prices are high compared to other health food stores on the island, but those other stores are very far away from Kamaole Beach Park I. We think of this as a convenience store that sells health food.

The prepared foods bar is very good and well-shopped, so it turns over frequently. The hot entrées can be tasty but tend to be on the bland side (the mock chicken is pretty good and the baked yams are scrumptious). The fresh fruit smoothies are especially recommended. Check their website for coupons offering discounts on the deli.

Address: 2411 S. Kihei Rd., Kihei, South Maui
Location: Across from Kamaole Beach Park I
Meals: Breakfast, Lunch, Dinner
Hours: M–F 8am–9pm; Sa–Su 9am–9pm
Parking: Lot
Phone: 808-875-4356
Website: www.hawaiianmoons.com

OVERALL: **3** out of 5 stars

OVERALL:
3.6
out of 5 stars

$

Honolua Store *(American/Local/Plate Lunch)*

Kapalua's gorgeous coast invites some of the wealthiest of the wealthy to live and play there, and the restaurants — some of the best on the island — are as expensive as the view. That's why budget-friendly *Honolua Store* is such an unexpected treasure. Steak and eggs for only $8.75? Whoa! Stop the car.

Built out in a recent expansion, this general store and deli carries not only the typical resort sundries, but many specialty items: locally grown produce, wine, cheese, and … crème brulee served in half a pineapple! (This fantasy dessert was an all-time favorite at the bygone Chez Paul restaurant in Olowalu; somebody wisely revived the recipe.) Beyond the dessert case and espresso bar you'll find a small deli and grill serving an eclectic collection of local plate lunch favorites and more gourmet salads and sandwiches. Breakfast is a steal, with steak and Benedicts well under ten dollars. For lunch or dinner you can get sandwiches (the pulled pork is tasty), burgers, pizza, (eh … just okay) and local and plate lunch dishes. (Who can argue against a side of chili for a buck fifty? Obviously not the resort staff, many of whom eat here at lunch.)

If you're looking for a break from the resort prices and formality, grab a seat at the picnic bench outside and talk story with the locals while tossing back simple but satisfying fare. And just in case you forgot you were in well-heeled, eco-savvy Kapalua, you can rest assured that the café's pretty to-go packaging is fully biodegradable.

Address: 900 Office Rd., Kapalua, West Maui
Location: In the Kapalua Resort
Meals: Breakfast, Lunch, Dinner
Hours: Daily 6am–8pm
Parking: Lot
Phone: 808-665-9105
Website: www.kapalua.com

OVERALL:
4.2
out of 5 stars

$ $ $

Honu Seafood & Pizza *(Seafood / Pacific Rim)*

It's hard to imagine an improvement on *Mala Ocean Tavern's* view, but its new sister restaurant next door, *Honu Seafood & Pizza*, is somehow closer to the water, closer to the turtles nibbling seaweed at the shoreline, and, to our mind, that much nearer to heaven.

When we heard Mark Ellman was opening a new restaurant in Lahaina we were thrilled. Then we heard it was supposed to remind us of an East Coast fish shack. Hmmm … Really? With so many wonderful fish to choose from here in Hawaii, why import from the Atlantic? And who needs more fried food in their diet?

Our doubts are dished: *Honu* isn't the closest thing you'll find on Maui to an East Coast fish shack (*Paia Fish Market* may be closer in spirit), but it's so, so much more.

Honu Seafood & Pizza *(continued)*

Like an oyster, its exterior is rough at the edges. But inside is a an elegant bar and sunlit, airy dining room with an unobstructed view of the surf that nearly tumbles up to the oceanfront tables. This ranks amongst Maui's best waterfront settings, and they have maximized the outdoor seating with plenty of tables on the rail.

Appetizers and sides feature heaping portions are heaping and novel preparations. Vegetarians can happily dine on the left half of the menu, and you can easily be full and happy just ordering two or three and a drink. (The beer list spans continents.)

Honu has a fish shack's requisite assortment of rolls: decadent fried clam, oyster, crab, and lobster. It's got fish and chips and filets done three ways. But it's also got a bevy of unexpected items: chickpeas (deep-fried and salty, brought with your water), sprouted lentils, authentic Naples pizza, and fried pig's ears.

The pig's ear appetizer is a heaping pile of slender, slightly chewy, mostly crunchy bits fried up light and airy (think tempura). Lavender is a nice touch, but gets lost in the fried intensity. The Korean aioli that comes alongside is more sweet than spicy. If you've never had pig's ears, this is a very good version to sample.

The Ipswitch clam appetizer is addictive, and the clams are flown in from the Northeast, if not specifically from Ipswitch, Massachusetts. The briny meat positively sparkles in the slightly sandy texture of the batter. These also come in a roll.

We were skeptical of the steamed mussel appetizer, which too often disappoints. We ended up fighting our friends — and the busboy — for the last of the dish. The portion is generous, and it comes with enough toast points to sop up the broth. You need them — or a spoon, which we resorted to — because this broth is eat-it-up yummy. Tomato-based and fragrant with lots of garlic, herbs and olives, we had to promise our friends we would come back (and back again) to have another bowl. In fact, this and a beer is the simple-but-delicious celebratory meal we're planning for when this edition of the guide is finished.

The fish and chips basket is the best we've had in a long time. The fish (ono in ours) has paper-thin lemon slices threaded around it before it is tempura-battered and fried. The sour-bright lemon flavor permeates the fish and the tender rind lends a textural switch-up that's beautiful. The portions are huge — you can easily split a basket — and you also get a mix of sweet potato and russet fries: hand-cut, well-seasoned.

At $25, we expect a lobster roll to overflow, and it does. The preparation is exactly what one expects in a New England fish shack: large chunks of Maine lobster bathed in warm butter spilling out of a homemade roll grilled golden. All breads are homemade, and all sandwiches come with both an incredible house tartar sauce and the aforementioned aioli. In case you're from farther down the Eastern Seaboard, there's also a small tin of Old Bay on the table.

continued on next page

Honu Seafood & Pizza *(continued)*

NB: If you want lobster, we recommend the roll over the cocktail appetizer, which features more claw meat and is priced the same. But ask for the excellent cocktail sauce, on the roll's side.

A word about sauce. Everything from the oyster's mignonette to the lobster roll's tartar sauce is praiseworthy at **Honu**. (When was the last time you praised tartar sauce?) The cocktail sauce in particular should be bottled; rockets of fresh horseradish erupt most pleasantly in your mouth. We only wish there was a little more of this heat in the Korean spicy aioli.

Persian spices are in short supply here on Maui, but they're laced throughout **Honu's** menu, including the lamb riblets. Tasty, healthy Middle Eastern staples such as quinoa, lentils and hummus accompany main dishes. The most delectable braised kale salad — a real winner and something we would order over and over — comes with pomegranate and Medjool dates.

Phew. That's just the regular menu — most rolls, appetizers, salads, and pizzas are available all day long. But there are also "Daily Specials" — soups, appetizers, and entrees — that appear on the right side of the menu. There are also some excellent specials.

Presented on a bed of red and white quinoa, the lehi (silver mouthed snapper) was perfectly sautéed: moist throughout, it's flavor accentuated by preserved lemon. The hedonistic veal osso bucco sprawled on its bed of creamy marscapone grits and braised kale tossed with pomegranate and lemon vinaigrette.

Another sumptuous dish — surprise — fried chicken. The tender-but-crispy buttermilk-fried chicken served boneless (!!) and piled on perfectly salty-sweet grits with a delicious mango sauce and seared asparagus was so delicious it inspired a fork fight. Our friend who had the good taste to order it ended up guarding his plate with his elbows. The filet Oscar — rib eye topped with Dungeness crab and a rich béarnaise sauce — was perfectly prepared. The Molokai sweet potatoes — which are a lovely purple color, but quite stiff on their own — were delectable. The secret? Enough butter and seasoning and just plain old puree-ing to render them creamy and silky and bring out their earthy goodness. Even the simple sautéed veggies that come with many entrées are Perfectly Done.

We have conflicted feelings about the spicy Dungeness crab entrée. It's exquisitely flavored, gorgeous and perfectly addictive, but also the very messiest thing we've ever eaten in public: we half-jokingly requested newspaper to spread on the table, and a floor-length bib. The first hint of trouble was a look of tremendous concentration on James's face, the second was a cessation of conversation as he cracked shells and clawed the crab meat out. Whatever lay beneath the crab — quinoa we think — was largely ignored, because his hands were so slippery he couldn't hold a fork. As the flesh under his fingernails began to burn from the spices, he started working faster and faster, hoping to be able to finish before he succumbed to the need for a good long hand washing ... or a shower. The two moistened towels delivered with the plate were appreciated, but not nearly enough. A most delicious, but seriously rude, dish; we recommend ordering it, especially if you don't mind looking like a four-year-old who got into the finger paints.

Honu Seafood & Pizza *(continued)*

Some items weren't as satisfying: the grilled octopus is perilously close to rubbery when cooked just a little too long, which it was, twice — is the grill cook not as persnickety as the fry cook? The clam chowder seemed like a no-brainer, but it fell flat — too much butter, not enough savor, overcooked fish. The crab macaroni and cheese was promising, but the huge bowl rendered the bottom layers mushy while the top layers of panko crunched up under the broiler. The Molokai prawns with lemongrass sauce were similarly promising — those prawns are rich and hearty — but fell flat in the execution: not the full flavor we know they can deliver, and overcooked. The Italian sausage pizza was fine, but we'd focus on other items.

Happy Hour is a good time to come, for a discount off the entire menu, plus drink specials. And if you have a state ID, ask about their kama'aina deals.

Honu is a relatively new restaurant, and it hasn't hit its full stride in terms of service. The spirit is willing, but the large menu and the emphasis on daily specials seems to flummox a few servers, some of whom we worried were about to fling themselves onto the rocks just outside the window. The kitchen sends out dishes at reasonable times, considering everything is made to order — and yet, we've had the wrong ones delivered to us, and then the right ones delivered, but a couple of minutes apart. Waiting for your companion to be served when there's a bowl of steaming mussels (did we tell you about the mussels??) tempting you is to be in a terrible, terrible position.

We trust that Chef Ellman — who is spending plenty of time here, as are his wife and daughters — will get this kind of thing sorted out as time goes on. Even the best food can't always save a meal from off-putting service.

You never know whether new restaurants will keep their happy enthusiasm going, and we're a little worried that *Honu's* shine will wear off. For now? It's close to perfect.

Address: 1295 Front St., Lahaina, West Maui
Location: right next to Mala, behind the Lahaina Cannery Mall
Meals: Lunch, Dinner
Hours: Daily, 11am-10pm
Parking: street, lot
Phone: 808-667-9390
Website: www.honumaui.com

OVERALL:
3.4
out of 5 stars

Hula Grill *(Pacific Rim)*

Hula Grill is a nearly irresistible restaurant if you're walking by Whaler's Village. It's so friendly looking, with its sandy Barefoot Bar and upscale dining room menu. The late afternoon music (don't sit too close or you won't be able to hear anyone but the vocalist) and the sunset views draw us and many others like a magnet.

The appetizers and sandwiches in the Barefoot Bar are average to good, if somewhat overpriced (Ka'anapali again). The real pull here is the sand, the pretty good drinks, and the view of the beach walk (bikinis, muscular chests, salty hair) and the sunset.

Dinner inside is not nearly as compelling; the food becomes less interesting and more expensive. However, as one of just a handful of dinner restaurants in the resort, you may end up here at least once, and some good choices include the steaks and the fish specials. Kids like their menu, too. We appreciate that the ingredients are locally sourced, and those searching for gluten-, nut-, or dairy-free options will discover plenty of choices.

Like its sister restaurant ***Leilani's*** next door, ***Hula Grill*** belongs to the T S Restaurant empire, with the added benefit of having celebrated Chef Peter Merriman as a partner. While we prefer ***Hula Grill*** to ***Leilani's*** (better food, atmosphere, and service), neither establishment elicits our excitement.

Address: 2435 Ka'anapali Parkway, Ka'anapali, West Maui
Location: Whaler's Village
Meals: Dinner, Pupus, Happy Hour
Hours: Daily 5pm–9:30pm, Barefoot Bar 11am–11pm
Parking: Lot (validated)
Phone: 808-667-6636
Website: www.hulagrillkaanapali.com

OVERALL:
4
out of 5 stars

Humuhumunukunukuapua'a *(Pacific Rim)*

The signature restaurant at The Grand Wailea floats in a lagoon stocked with umilu, brilliant turquoise fish whose fins gracefully cut the surface as they circle meditatively. The open air restaurant has a thatched roof, tiki torches, and a large central bar with a wraparound fish tank — home to at least one brightly painted humu (the restaurant's namesake, which translates to "fish with a nose like a pig"). The sunset view is unbelievable and the setting positively theatrical. The temptation must be mighty to allow the ambience to do most of the work, but that's usually not what we find.

Chef Isaac Bancaco is a local boy who spent several years in trendy kitchens in Boston and L.A. before returning to his roots. Evidence of his commitment to uber-fresh Maui-grown produce is everywhere on his seasonal menu (which changes quarterly) and his prix fixe farmer's menus (which change monthly). Two menu items never change, however: the lemongrass ahi traps and the catch-your-own-lobster. Since the restaurant opened nearly two decades ago, the "traps" have entrapped many a hungry diner, including ourselves. Morsels of glistening red ahi are stabbed with lemongrass stalks, wrapped in nori and fried. The result is a crunchy, soft, fragrant, salty, mouthful of goodness — albeit a pricey one at $16 for four bites. The catch-your-own lobster is self-explanatory — only at **Humu**, you get to reel your bristling Hawaiian spiny lobster up from the saltwater lagoon. (Before invoking your inner Hemingway and reaching for the biggest bad boy, you might want to keep the price tag in mind: $52-58 per pound; minimum 2 lbs.)

As we mentioned, the menu shifts seasonally, and most often, the new offerings are good ideas executed well. When we went last, the hamachi carpaccio was a colorful treat, seasoned with black Hawaiian salt, fiery chili, and yuzu (an intensely fragrant Japanese citrus), and topped with tiny snowballs of celery ginger granite. The scallops (available as an appetizer or entrée) came stacked: each huge, nicely seared scallop sat atop a fantastic coconut rice croquette and a layer of braised greens, crowned by a fresh mandarin slice. It's a pretty presentation, but we wished for a punchier counterpoint to the sweetness — perhaps a tad more of the electric green basil oil that decorated the plate?

The Kobe short ribs were first seared in mustard then braised for five hours in dashi. Ours were fatty but, we confess, heavenly. We spooned all of the meat's lingering juices up with the heart of palm potatoes and nearly licked the plate clean.

At another visit, this time during a five-course prix fixe affair — (these are offered regularly, check the website) two courses featured crab and mahi mahi "two ways." The first way, as a crudo, was well-executed, but unexciting and unsurprising. The second way was a tempura with a curiously bland curry sauce that did not like being paired with that crab: the two fought so ferociously most of us left it in our bowls, barely touched. (The mahi mahi, on the other hand, loved this preparation.) Later there was a *perfectly* done lamb course with a wine reduction so excellent we reached for our spoons, followed by the aforementioned short ribs. These big dinners are challenging, there is no doubt. The chef's challenge is to create a soup-to-nuts meal that, hopefully, surprises and delights with each turn out of the kitchen. The food is well-prepared, and the price is right — we just wish each course was consistently delicious, because otherwise the evening can turn into a challenge for the diners.

Service historically has been slow — both in the kitchen and on the floor — and it still drags. Because of this, we prefer the tables edging the bar to those in the dark, cavernous dining room. They're serviced by the cocktail waitresses who hustle a little more — plus there's that gajillion-gallon fish tank to gaze at in the interim. We vacillate on the bar's ostentatious drinks: sometimes we're genuinely in the mood for an outrageous Disneyland tropical libation served in a whole coconut or decorative tiki mug. But at

continued on next page

Humuhumunukunukuapua'a *(continued)*

these prices ($14–$36 per beverage), not often.

While some of the menu items are exorbitantly priced, the majority are average for Wailea. Check the restaurant's website for specials — as we went to press, they were offering 50 percent off lobster entrées before 6:30pm.

Address: 3850 Wailea Alanui Dr., Wailea, South Maui
Location: Grand Wailea Resort
Meals: Dinner
Hours: Nightly 5:30pm–9:00pm
Parking: Lot, Valet
Phone: 808-875-1234
Website: www.grandwailea.com

OVERALL:
3.8
out of 5 stars

$

CASH

Ichiban Okazuya *(Japanese)*

Well off the beaten path, this one-room kitchen belongs to a bygone era. The word "okazuya" is Japanese for "side dish shop" and refers to the days when bachelors left for work on the sugar plantations with rice in tow and in need of tasty sides to spice it up. They picked from piles of delicious, pre-prepared meats and vegetables — fast food — at an okazuya.

Few of these nostalgic to-go shops remain on Maui, and this one's definitely the best — even though it has terrible parking and nowhere to sit. When we're hankering for chicken katsu, we head to Wailuku and join the line out the door at ***Ichiban***. Chicken katsu — for the uninitiated — is chicken meat that's been breaded in panko (ultra-light, flakey bread crumbs) and deep-fried until dark golden. Pieces are then sliced into two-inch chunks and served with katsu sauce — a sort of glorified ketchup. Admittedly, fried chicken is hard not to love, but this version, crispy on the outside and bursting with moist flavor inside, is lip-smacking good.

Don't be shy when you push past the screened wooden doors to get to ***Ichiban's*** counter: the staff is friendly and will crack jokes at their own expense. Point to what you want. Everything is sold by the piece, so you can get as many or as few of the shrimp tempura as call you. (Hooray!) Pans are piled high with tempura of every sort (we also love the sweet potato and asparagus), firm noodles, nishime (a savory vegetable stew), and broccoli steamed to its emerald peak of color. The fried, fluffy tofu balls are sweet and creamy — almost like dessert — and sell out early. If you want the best selection, get here before noon. And if you don't know what something is, ask.

It's easy to miss the list of fish on the right hand wall, but it's worth checking out. The cooks will speedily pan-fry your choice of ahi, teriyaki salmon, or misoyaki butterfish. We regularly order the salmon and pair it with warm hijiki salad. The teriyaki is mild (rather than syrupy-salty, like at some places) and the fish is perfect. The dark flecks of hijiki seaweed are warm, having been sautéed lightly in sesame oil with shitake mushrooms and carrot.

Ichiban Okazuya *(continued)*

Everything at **Ichiban** is made that morning or while you wait. Nothing has ever been stale, greasy, or over-salted here, which is more than we can say for most plate lunch places. Top your plate off with spicy kim chee, then head to a nearby park or beach to dig in. We recommend heading to Kanaha Beach by the airport, or up to Iao Valley; any further and your tempura will get soggy.

Address: 2133 Kaohu St., Wailuku, Central Maui
Location: Turn from High Street onto Kaohu.
Meals: Lunch, Dinner
Hours: Daily 10am-2pm (lunch) 4pm-8pm (dinner)
Parking: very little street parking
Phone: 808-244-7276

I'o *(American/Pacific Rim)*

 I'o's Chef Owner James McDonald is so dedicated to fresh, local ingredients he started his own organic farm in Kula. After nearly a decade in operation, O'o Farms supplies the vast majority of produce and herbs to his restaurants **I'o** and **Pacific'o**. Feast at Lele, his lu'au, also benefits from this farm's largesse.

Chef James's drive to wow the diner is evident in the evolution of his food, and this makes him one of our very favorite chefs on the island. While **Pacific'o** stays true to his fusion roots serving the exciting, bold flavors that put him on the beach in Lahaina in the first place, **I'o**, just next door, now takes a simpler approach. Chef James's commitment to food is fundamental: extraordinary ingredients — he buys fish from fishermen who land just offshore to show him the day's catch — prepared as simply as possible.

The clean flavors and sheer sensuality of his signature dishes often gets us at a gut level (pardon the pun) ... but it also engages us intellectually and emotionally. Try the crab cake that spills its solid lumps from a light panko crust with a luxurious miso aioli on the side. Don't miss the fresh and delectable green papaya coleslaw that beds the cake. One of our favorite salads is the perfectly roasted beets, drizzled with a rich pesto and kissed by creamy, salty feta cheese.

Now ... for the entrées. It pains us to say this, but the newest additions to the menu take simplicity too far. We know Chef James has his heart in the right place and he has mad skills to back his passion up. But recently, he seems to have taken a detour by deconstructing his dishes, perhaps too severely. Proteins, vegetables, and starches are served individually. First you choose from the hot or cold greens, then from a "risotto bar," and finally add a fish or meat. We so trust his palate and his guidance on this menu that we end up lost. On several visits in the last year, we felt we ordered badly (and received little guidance from the waiter). As each dish arrived — a perfectly cooked opah filet lonely and unadorned in a pool of sauce (a rich but un-

OVERALL:
3.6
out of 5 stars

continued on next page

I'o *(continued)*

distinguished goat cheese fondue), a carrot risotto — we realized that we needed those greens that we had neglected to order (nothing had called to us). The O'o Farm medley — a bowl of roasted sweet potatoes, squash, and shallots — promised to remedy the imbalance. But what may have been a lovely meal on one plate, where the ingredients could work together, was a disappointment when served separately. None of the dishes had enough star power to stand on their own. The love seems to be slipping in the kitchen, too — that risotto was not nearly as brilliant as we've had in the past. Not as bright, too crunchy. The vegetables were slightly charred.

Luckily, many of Chef McDonald's top entrées are still on the menu, intact: the "Crabby Catch," a light but hedonistic combination of oven-roasted fish and crab salad, and the "Lamb Pa," a trio of perfectly grilled chops doused in Madras curry sauce. Another favorite, the succulent "Three Little Pigs," garlicky, braised pork cheek medallions, are available a la carte.

The wine list is highly rated, and each item on the menu lists a wine suggestion. The large number of wines by the glass is a sign that the owners (Chef James has two business partners) care about your experience — they are willing to break open a bottle for just one serving. The martinis are **excellent**.

We love the beachfront location — spectacular at sunset — and the modern lines and colors on the interior. Despite the romantic garden seating, we choose to sit on the rail inside because Feast at Lele, Chef James's beautiful lu'au experience, is right next door. While we enjoy hearing the music, it can be a little loud if you're outside.

The waiters generally know food, and know the menu, but they (or the kitchen?) can be very slow, and at times we've had a dish arrive cooler than it should be because of it. Plan for a leisurely paced meal, and keep the bread on the table.

While this latest menu isn't our favorite, we're 100% confident that Chef James will wow us again in the near future.

Address: 505 Front St., Lahaina, West Maui
Meals: Dinner
Hours: Nightly 5:30–10pm
Parking: Lot, Street
Phone: 808-661-8422
Website: www.iomaui.com

OVERALL:

3

out of 5 stars

Isana Restaurant *(Korean / Sushi)*

Isana is a good Korean restaurant featuring yakiniku style barbecue, which you cook yourself on the tabletop. A sushi bar is set off to the side, and their late night half-price specials pack in the locals. Service is generally friendly, but can be brusque, dismissive, and disarmingly honest (we've been told bluntly not to order something because it's not a good dish). The ex-

Isana Restaurant *(continued)*

pansive space holds many large barbecue tables, and there's karaoke late at night. Quite a trip.

We recommend the sushi, especially the spicy scallop dynamite, which lightly dresses tender, well-seared scallops with the spicy Japanese mayonnaise (we also like the shrimp version). The uni is usually very good, also. The rolls are fresh but somewhat unimaginative — the soft shell crab roll, for instance, comes with (surprise!) crab ... and not much else.

For Korean barbecue we especially recommend the kalbi meat marinated in soy and the spicy pork loin. The banchan, or side dishes, that accompany the barbecue include a creamy, very egg-y potato salad, pickled daikon, steamed broccoli, and fiery kim chee, among others. A minimum of two dishes is required for the barbecue, which pushes the bill up significantly if there are just two of you. Portions are generous, so if you split between four people, it's a much better deal. Prices will seem high to those who know the cuisine, but it's the only tabletop Korean on Maui.

Address: 515 S. Kihei Rd., Kihei, South Maui
Location: Across from Sugar Beach
Meals: Lunch, Dinner
Hours: Daily 11am-10pm; Sushi bar is open until 12am
Parking: Lot
Phone: 808-874-5700
Website: www.isanarestaurant.net

Izakaya Matsu *(Japanese)*

In Japan (and even on Oahu, which caters to more Japanese visitors) izakayas are everywhere. Like Spanish tapas bars, izakayas are essentially taverns that serve small plates of food to keep drinkers happy and sated. On Maui, we have only one: *Izakaya Matsu*, the humble Japanese eatery in a South Maui strip mall.

Portions are small, but that's expected at an izakaya. (Remember to think of these as tapas, not entrées.) Come for the cooked dishes rather than the sushi, which is adequate, but better elsewhere. The service is friendly and welcoming, but also rather flustered: if you are not (or they *think* you are not) familiar with the food, they may steer you toward the $26 sushi combination platter and away from some of the other more interesting choices.

The okonomiyaki is a dense, savory Japanese pancake made of cabbage, ginger, seaweed, and bonito flakes, and thoroughly doused in tonkatsu sauce. The use of the word pancake may be misleading if you haven't had this dish before — there is a strong seafood flavor.

The onigiri (rice balls) have been overcooked on occasion, but on others perfectly delicious. Rice is packed with salty ume plums or salmon and then

continued on next page

wrapped up in a piece of seaweed (nori) like a little Japanese taco. The ginger pork dish features thin slices of pork grilled perfectly and sauced with a tasty ginger sauce. The hama kama is one of our favorite dishes: the cheek (kama) of a hamachi (hama) is cooked until super tender. You pick the flesh off the bones with chopsticks: creamy and juicy. Many dishes come with a small green salad, which has, truly, one of the lightest and most addictive ginger miso dressings we've had.

The takoyaki (usually octopus, but sometimes squid) is mixed with a fluffy dough and fried — but the winner is the tempura, which, when bit, makes an audible crackling sound. Fresh grated daikon and ginger on the side — delish. The beef tongue with salt — which they push in hand-written notes on several walls — is a success when sliced thin enough to offset the inherently rubbery texture, less so when thicker. Is the salt placed alongside *really* rock salt? We suspect MSG …

We've had undistinguished potato croquettes (we want a zesty sauce), but perfectly crisp gyoza — and this is probably the only place on the island where you can get Orion beer, which is from Okinawa. There are also good sake choices. Call ahead if you want to try their fun shabu-shabu. (Shabu-shabu is like a Japanese fondue — you dip thinly sliced meats and veggies into boiling broth.)

We can usually get out of here with full bellies for under $30 per person — including a beer or two — and that alone makes us happy.

Address: 1280 S. Kihei Rd., Kihei, South Maui
Location: in the Azeka I Marketplace
Meals: Dinner
Hours: Tuesday–Sunday 5:30-9pm
Parking: Lot
Phone: 808-874-0990

Japengo *(Japanese / Pacific Rim)*

Just about everything about the Hyatt's new restaurant *Japengo*, which reportedly means "Land of Mystery," is magical. The resort spent a bundle of time and energy renovating the former Cascades, a lovely but underappreciated spot for sushi. You will spend a bundle of money dining at its replacement, *Japengo*, but if you're a sushi purist, it will be worth it.

Each corner in this chain restaurant (Café Japengo came first, in the Hyatt La Jolla) feels like your own cubbyhole — whether you're beneath the manicured hau trees in the entry, at the sushi bar, in the dark paneled dining room, or overlooking the resort's fantasy pool. Every time we've dined here, we felt so snug and intimate we've forgotten we were smack dab in the center of a huge resort.

Lanterns shaped like mushrooms and sea urchins hang over the bar, which sends out chilled sake and inventive cocktails, including a sake-fresh-lime-cucumber-ginger-ale concoction that had us smiling from the first to last sip. The "Moon Bar" also offers Golden Star sparkling jasmine tea. It's bizarrely expensive — $25 a bottle — so we're bummed we crave it.

Let's start with the sushi, which is exemplary — and better be for its steep price. (This is not an inexpensive restaurant: it didn't occur to us that we would be charged for a bowl of edamame, let alone **$8**.) The moriawase platter is pure heaven. Depending on your inclination — or whatever is freshest — you'll receive creamy slivers of uni (sea urchin), poached baby abalone grown on the Big Island, ruby red maguro (tuna), and translucent hirame (Big Island flounder) arranged like petals around an upright lemon.

Farther down the list, a whole seared madai (Japanese pink snapper) rests on a bed of fresh seaweed, shiso leaves, and daikon ribbons. His (or her) tail is turned up and the belly meat is sliced *just so* — slightly morbid, perhaps, but irresistible.

Sashimi comes with our all-time favorite condiment, fresh wasabi root, served with a do-it-yourself sharkskin grater and tiny broom for sweeping the shavings onto your plate. Pale green and pungent, the fresh root grows on the Big Island and packs less of a punch than its powdered form. This rare luxury is free with the $60 platter and $8 a la carte.

The ample sushi rolls (eight pieces) are stuffed with rice, far too big for one bite, and large enough to be a meal on their own. The over-the-top presentations of some of the more complicated rolls are pure eye candy — if Willy Wonka made sushi, this is what it would look like. We've had the mahmay (pastel green soy paper wrapped around rice, ruby red ahi, avocado, and crab, drizzled in an orange Thai chili sauce), the blackened ahi (a California roll draped with blackened ahi and avocado slices, with a cascade of ponzu-marinated onions, garlic, and spicy dynamite sauce), and the tootsie (soft shell crab, snow crab, cucumber, shiitake mushrooms, avocado with a lobster-teriyaki sauce). If we closed our eyes, we wouldn't be able to differentiate amongst these monstrous creations. There are just too many flavors — it all comes out to spice-sour-sweet-mush. (Disclaimer: we are not fans of over-the-top rolls in general.) Our advice is to choose the simpler rolls, the hand rolls, and the nigiri, which includes novelties like kaibashira scallop, and sweet Markea prawn served raw with a fried head. (Oh, heaven.)

Toro — that most delectable belly cut of the blue fin tuna — is listed "as available." We've sworn off blue fin, ourselves, because it's being hunted to extinction — availability is not likely to last.

Sushi can be the entirety of your meal here, and you may be tempted to skip the main menu, but we recommend taking another look. The chef says many of the recipes are family heirlooms, and some taste like it. The steamed Manila clams swim in a broth of miso, ginger, lemongrass, Thai basil, and sake that warms the belly. The emperor's ponzu sauce, made with several types of sea vegetables, steeps for four months before it is ready. It accompanies the duck potstickers — which are delicious but still not addictive. Mahi is served atop a tower of forbidden rice, plump and moist in

continued on next page

Japengo *(continued)*

a lemongrass beurre blanc.

The grilled ahi perches in a similar fashion — a large slab over a mountain of garlic fried rice and Hamakua mushrooms, laced with a rather anemic wasabi butter. But why not slice the ahi before serving? That way we — or they — could have seen right away that the fish was more medium than the promised rare.

We've had the filet twice — once perfectly cooked, once a tad overdone. It's a smallish serving partnered with prawns (again, fried with the head on). Oddly enough, the side dish is most memorable: potatoes whipped with kim chee and edamame. Please, if you're ever invited to Thanksgiving at our house, bring this.

If you've been in the mood for duck, try the "Chinese-style" dish. Half a duck is served, nicely roasted, on a platter with a pile of perfectly sautéed vegetables (asparagus, onions, green beans, peas) and tiny, salty, delectable bacon lardons. The puddle of plum sauce is sweet and studded with sesame seeds — too bad it soaks the bao buns. Oh, well, a little soggy or not, our recommendation is to slice the duck thin (ask for a steak knife) and pile it, the veggies, and the sauce into a bun. Enjoy.

Vegetarians are out of luck. Unless they ask for something special from the kitchen, the only things sans meat are cucumber and natto (fermented soybean) rolls.

The desserts don't dazzle, despite fun offerings such as mochi ice cream and profiteroles dusted in macadamia nut brittle and sea salt.

Service is unpredictable. The waitstaff are pleasant and proud of their menu, but we wonder — is the kitchen so very far away? How else can they excuse their frequent, extended absences?

We're pleased to be able to recommend *Japengo*, just as we once did the previous restaurant in this location. This is pricey-but-good food in the otherwise rather barren Ka'anapali restaurant scene.

Address: 200 Nohea Kai Dr., Ka'anapali, West Maui
Location: at the Hyatt Regency Ka'anapali
Meals: Dinner
Hours: Daily 5:00pm-11pm (bar) 5:30pm-10pm (dining)
Parking: Valet, some self-parking
Phone: 808-667-4796
Website: www.hyattregencymaui.com

Jawz Tacos *(Mexican)*

Jawz started out as a taco stand just outside of Makena's Big Beach, and that's still our favorite place to get their food. If you go to their sit-down restaurant in North Kihei, you'll find a slightly more refined grill on their fish and a huge salsa bar with salsas ranging from sweet to heat, diced onions, pickled carrots, sour cream, wasabi Asian sauce, and many other yummy toppings. The burritos and tacos themselves are sold to you barely dressed, so take advantage of the bar.

We like the fish (they also have steak, pork, chicken, and shrimp), but don't think this is the place to get inexpensive ahi, because when you shred and grill ahi it just tastes like canned tuna. Get the ono or the mahi mahi instead. The tacos come with cilantro-pesto rice, which is a little odd, but does add interesting texture. Fresh-squeezed lemonade is rare on Maui, because lemons can be extremely expensive here. While *Jawz* has a huge vat of fresh lemonade, it's anemic (we suspect a cost control issue). They also make a pretty good margarita and sell Mexican beers. The Happy Hour specials (Monday — Saturday from 3 to 6pm and all day Sunday) make an inexpensive meal even cheaper, while the large tables and surfing movies on the televisions make this is a pleasant place for a quick lunch or dinner.

There are now two trucks in Makena, one parked before the big red pu'u (volcanic cinder cone) and one parked across the first entrance to Makena State Beach Park. Only one has the giant shark fin on top, but both serve the same tacos, plus smoothies and shave ice.

Address: 1279 S. Kihei Rd., Kihei, South Maui
Location: Azeka Mauka Marketplace
Meals: Lunch, Dinner
Hours: Daily 11am-9pm
Parking: Lot
Phone: 808-874-8226
Website: www.jawzfishtacos.com

Address: Makena Alanui Rd., Makena, South Maui
Location: By entrance to Makena State Beach Park
Meals: Lunch
Hours: Daily 10am-4:30pm
Parking: Street
Phone: 808-874-8226

Joe's Bar & Grill *(American)*

Chef Bev Gannon has reversed the typical Wailea equation (great views, but less than great food) to give us home-style comfort food in a setting that — while quirky — still provides a lovely vista. *Joe's* is perched on stilts over the tennis courts at the Wailea Tennis Center. There's a clear view over the courts, golf course and ocean, and you can see great sunsets there. The restaurant

continued on next page

$ $

itself is open air and features a deep bar made of copper, wide planked floors, and large tables that are somehow still intimate. We love coming with a few good friends to commune over the big plates of steak, fish, pork loin, and meatloaf.

The meatloaf is thickly sliced from a large loaf made with moisture-retaining veggies and tender beef. The sweet-sour-spicy barbecue sauce is key to this dish's success: savory, comforting flavors. Served with steak fries or mashed potatoes, this is the manliest meal on Maui.

We also like the diver scallops, which come in plump little islands of perfectly seared flesh on silver-dollar-sized discs of tender yellow potatoes. Beautiful deep green beans accompany the shellfish, and the whole dish is sauced with a light-but-rich shallot butter. Also try the ribs, which we love at **Hali'imaile General Store** as well, and the prime rib with the stunningly simple au jus.

Appetizers and salads are simple and aboveboard and generally very good. As purists, we feel the 'ahi carpaccio is weighed down by too much sauce: truffle oil, a mass of capers, shaved Parmesan and lemon dill aioli end up taking away from the fish. But the shrimp cocktail is excellent. The secret to this dish is not just super-fresh shrimp, but the spicy cocktail sauce. Bev's version is freshly spiced with horseradish, but also lemony highlights, and a hint of sweet. We also like the simple wedge salad with homemade blue cheese dressing.

The desserts are generously proportioned and straightforward, just like the rest of the meal. One exception: the "Not Your Usual Crème Brulee." This de-constructed dessert is a mash-up of blueberries, strawberries, and custard. Since our favorite part of crème brulee is cracking the caramelized shell, the magic is lost for us.

One of this restaurant's quirks is that the parking lot is set up the steep hill from the restaurant, making for something of a climb after your meal (it's downhill on the way in). To address this, there's always someone in a golf cart ready to shuttle you back and forth. It's good service, which is matched throughout the meal by the rest of the staff.

For stargazers, **Joe's** is a frequent haunt of local celebrities. Bev's husband Joe was in the entertainment business for years (evidenced by the concert light cans hung over the tables and the photographs of rich and famous guests lining the entry). His friends often drop by for a quiet bite to eat. Mauians don't raise much of a fuss over celebrities, which we see regularly, and that keeps them coming back.

Prices are moderate for Maui and certainly for Wailea, the view is good (although we have to note the thwacking tennis balls can interfere for some people), and the service is just as good as the food.

Address: 131 Wailea Ike Place, Wailea, South Maui
Location: Wailea Tennis Center
Meals: Dinner
Hours: Daily 5:30-9:30pm
Parking: Lot
Phone: 808-875-7767
Website: www.bevgannonrestaurants.com

Joy's Place *(Vegetarian/American)*

Joy's serves high quality sandwiches, salads, and soups to go. The ingredients are invariably fresh and local and whether your thing is nut burgers or free range turkey (roasted in-house), you'll find excellent choices.

Sandwiches are generally filled to bursting, and they use sprouted breads or locally-made herb breads. Among our favorite lunches is a turkey sandwich transformed into a wrap, employing a large collard green as the encasement. No matter where you fall on the vegan to carnivore spectrum, we also recommend trying the falafel with the homemade tahini caper sauce.

Smoothies are available, as are pasta salads and soups made fresh from whatever is best in season. The prices aren't rock bottom, but there's a lot of love and very good ingredients, and you definitely get the quality you pay for. Plus, Joy and her fellow chefs are unfailingly sweet (if somewhat distracted) and their good juju goes straight into the food.

Joy recently launched a line of raw and live foods called, appropriately, Joy's Live. A variety of dense, nutrient-packed morsels can be had from the refrigerator next to the register. While the $5 price tag on the raw cacao truffles might give you pause, we encourage you to try them. Even a sliver of the mint truffle is supremely satisfying, though we rarely resist popping an entire one into our mouths. If you can't get to Kihei, **Whole Foods** also carries the Joy's Live line.

If you're considering Subway for a beach lunch, dash that from your mind and head to **Joy's** as a healthier alternative.

Address: 1993 S. Kihei Rd., Kihei, South Maui
Location: Island Surf Building
Meals: Lunch
Hours: M-Sa 8am-3pm
Parking: Street
Phone: 808-879-9258

Julia's Best Banana Bread *(Banana Bread)*

If you or your traveling partner has nerves of steel, you should drive around the West Maui Mountains from Kapalua to Wailuku. The views are unbeatable, the land wild and rugged, and the trade winds blowing in from the west make the air on this side crystal clear. When you hit Kahakuloa (Kah hah koo LOH ah), the teensy fishing village, look for the green road-side stand. If it's before 2pm, Julia may still have some bread for you. Made with local bananas, it's succulent, moist, and sweet. Is it the best in the world, as the signs proclaim? Not necessarily ... but it's delicious in its context, and if you're driving out this way, you should get a loaf or two. The coconut candy is also very good.

If you don't want to drive out to Kahakuloa, you can order the bread from

continued on next page

Julia's Best Banana Bread *(continued)*

her website (*so* this century) or you can try **Julia's** bread at **Flatbread** in Paia. They heat it in their fiery, wood-burning furnace and top it with chocolate sauce and macadamia nut ice cream as a dessert. It's not as yummy when it's not as hard-won, perhaps ... but at least **you** don't have to make the drive.

Address: Honoapiilani Highway, Kahakuloa, West Maui
Location: past Kapalua where the highway gets very narrow
Meals: Snacks & Treats
Hours: Daily, 9am - 5:30pm or when sold out
Parking: Lot
Website: www.juliasbananabread.com

OVERALL:
3.1
out of 5 stars

$ $ $

Kai Wailea *(Sushi)*

Kai Wailea's sister restaurant, **Kaiwa** in Waikiki, is well-known for unique, creative sushi and Japanese dishes served in an elegant, comfortable restaurant with excellent, traditional service. The service is not always up to par, but the food usually is here in the Shops at Wailea.

They've narrowed the menu down a bit since they first opened, which was a good choice. The more extravagant sushi platters are still here, but not as many of them — we don't risk the heart attack that threatened the first time we saw the prices.

The food is good to great, with fresh sushi, including some creative combinations, and some really excellent cooked dishes. They now offer a $60 tasting menu in the evening, which is a good way to go. The five course meal features a hearty miso soup, which comes studded with local vegetables, a tasting of the day's freshest sashimi, a tempura (a little soggy) and robata–yaki (teriyaki chicken and beef) course, and a choice of three entrées: a generous and delicious sushi platter, a super-tender rib eye loaded up with grilled veggies, or a lobster tail on our last visit. The sushi platter has enough for two to split with ease, but you won't want to skip that steak, either. Dessert is also included, but we're too full for it. (This is fine, because desserts are not their strength.)

Lunches feature several meal combinations, including a $16 version that includes that incredible rib eye, a sushi roll (your choice), salad, and miso soup. The beer and sake list are very good, and service is good, too — until they get busy.

This is still an expensive restaurant, especially if you focus just on the sushi ... but the value they offer has climbed considerably since their opening, especially if you take advantage of their fixed price meal.

Address: 3750 Wailea Alanui Dr., Wailea, South Maui
Location: The Shops at Wailea
Meals: Dinner
Hours: Nightly 5pm-10pm; Late Night Happy-Hour F-Sa 9:30pm-12:30am
Parking: Lot
Phone: 808-875-1955
Website: www.kaiwailea.com

Kihei Caffe *(American)*

Locals and tourists flock to **Kihei Caffe** for breakfast. The counter is manned by the owner, who oozes true Aloha spirit, and the service is fast (with a little less Aloha).

Order inside — you have to navigate a maze-like, roped-off line to get to the register — and then go find a seat. If you sit before you order, you actually mess with a system that works really well. (You also risk being scolded by a server.)

This island version of a greasy spoon has a view of Kalama Park and a slice of the ocean beyond, and serves no-frills breakfast and lunch dishes. We're not huge fans of the average breakfast fare, but we come anyway because we can get in and out quickly, and the coffee is good. At the counter, you'll be confronted with a tray of oven-hot sticky buns and cinnamon rolls slathered with creamy frosting. We appreciate that these and the muffins are baked in-house, rather than procured from **Costco**, as is the case with so many breakfast places. Fans praise the cinnamon roll French toast, a special that isn't on the menu and only offered sometimes. We have to take their word for it, since we've never been there when it was available. The egg plates come with pretty good (if dense) biscuits, and the bacon is thick and tasty. The stack of three pancakes is fluffy and filling. The veggie scramble, a bowl-shaped medley of spinach mushrooms, bell peppers and more is a decent and substantial breakfast for vegetarians. (Vegans can request it sans eggs and cheese.) We recommend elsewhere for lunch.

The outdoor seating invariably puts us at the mercy of obnoxious sparrows, but that's true at any of the outdoor restaurants on the island. What we don't see anywhere else are the wild chickens that calmly forage under tables for dropped bits. The servers clear plates quickly to discourage the wildlife from feeding and to remind us that we shouldn't linger when other diners need tables.

Address: 1945 S. Kihei Rd., Kihei, South Maui
Location: Kalama Village across from the Whale
Meals: Breakfast, Lunch
Hours: Daily 5am–2pm
Parking: Lot, Street
Phone: 808-879-2230

Kimo's *(Pacific Rim/American)*

This waterfront restaurant is run by a very successful family of businesses, T S Restaurants, which chooses gorgeous beachfront locations, decorates them with lava rocks, tiki torches, and lots of wood, and serves up big portions of average-to-good steaks, chicken, fish dishes, and their famous Hula Pie — a huge slice of macadamia nut ice cream cake slathered in fudge and whip cream. Sister restaurants on Maui include **Leilani's on the Beach** and **Hula Grill** in Ka'anapali and **Duke's** in Honokowai.

continued on next page

Kimo's *(continued)*

In general, we find the food undistinguished. Service is fine, if a little forced, drinks are strong, and the location, location, location never, ever disappoints. The sunset view from **Kimo's** can make even the most average of fairly priced food seem much more than average, and we think that accounts for much of this restaurant's popularity.

Address: 845 Front St., Lahaina, West Maui
Meals: Lunch, Dinner
Hours: Daily 11am-10:30pm; Bar is open till 1:30am
Parking: Street
Phone: 808-661-4811
Website: www.tsrestaurants.com

Ko *(Pacific Rim / Local)*

This well-intentioned restaurant at the Fairmont Kea Lani in Wailea has a brave mission: to elevate bygone sugarcane plantation-era food from peasant to high cuisine. (Ko is Hawaiian for sugar.) The resort's culinary department asked employees to share their family's cherished, handed-down recipes and the resulting menu is a tribute to Hawaii's cultural melting pot.

The idea hasn't always translated well into reality. We've been disappointed in the past on several occasions; while we appreciated the resort's initiative to serve local cuisine made with fresh, local ingredients, we ultimately gave **Ko** a pretty rough review.

Since then, we've had one thing new to the menu that we love: the paniolo (cowboy) rib-eye steak. Rubbed in red Molokai salt and raw Maui sugar, this prime cut of meat is served with pohole fern shoots. Pohole ferns are a local delicacy that grows wild in damp forests. When blanched, they're tender, crunchy, and leave a funny numbness on your tongue.

Even so, the restaurant is undergoing a massive renovation as we go to press, so we are refraining from giving a full review. (Because, well, because we can't.) When it re-opens, we'll give it another chance, particularly because we always love **Ko's** contributions to local food festivals. The small plates they serve at, say, The Taste of Wailea, part of the Maui Film Festival each June, have made us wonder if the golf course location inspires more cooking magic than the resort kitchen.

Hopefully, when the restaurant re-opens (possibly by February 2012) the food will rise to the occasion of its new surroundings, which promise to be quite beautiful.

Address: 4100 Wailea Alanui Dr., Wailea, South Maui
Location: Fairmont at Kea Lani
Meals: Dinner
Parking: Lot, Valet
Phone: 808-875-4100
Website: www.fairmont.com

Kobe *(Japanese Steakhouse)*

Teppanyaki is just plain fun, dontcha think? (James does — he begs Molly to visit **Kobe** at least once a quarter.) Japanese chefs juggle knives and throw fire while they prep, sear, and serve your meal tableside ... it is Food Theater (and everyone gets a front row seat at the U-shaped tables).

Kobe is one of the only teppanyaki places on Maui, and we're glad they're here, because it's pretty darn good food, and a pretty darn good show. (Just don't sit upstairs, where the ventilation is less than adequate.)

Visitors flock here, but so do more than a few locals, who appreciate the large quantities of food and the good fried rice (made in front of you, of course). We particularly like the scallops, which we've always had perfectly cooked. The steak is a good cut, especially when we upgrade to the filet.

The seasonal opakapaka (Hawaiian pink snapper) is tender and takes well to the super-hot grill. Keep in mind that they're not using the very best oils or brandies, and set your expectations accordingly. We skip dessert and head to **Ululani's Shave Ice** or **Ono Gelato** for after dinner treats.

Reservations for the teppanyaki are recommended, but you can also get sushi at Oku's sushi bar — a restaurant within the restaurant. Bonus: it's open until almost midnight, so bar-hoppers can sate their night owl cravings with straightforward, fairly decent sushi.

If you've got kids — or, ahem, a guy who's a kid at heart — we recommend **Kobe**.

Address: 136 Dickenson St., Lahaina, West Maui
Meals: Dinner, Late-Night
Hours: Daily 5:30pm-10pm; Sushi Bar until 11:30pm
Parking: Lot, Street
Phone: 808-667-5555
Website: www.kobemaui.com

OVERALL:
3.4
out of 5 stars

$ $ $

Koiso Sushi Bar *(Sushi)*

The secret is out about **Koiso.** After several years of singing Sushi Master Hiro-san's praises we find we can't get in if we just show up. We have to call and make reservations. That's OK with us — he's worth the extra planning, and we can't begrudge sushi lovers such an excellent experience, or Hiro-san the business.

Hiro-san's domain is in the back of Dolphin Plaza in Kihei, and frankly, it's tiny and doesn't look very inviting from the outside. The two glass walls are plastered with posters, a crowded bulletin board features hundreds of snapshots of his loved ones, and the back wall is littered with various hand lettered signs detailing the day's fish. There are maybe a dozen seats at his L-shaped sushi bar and one table for four. He doesn't like to seat regulars at

OVERALL:
4
out of 5 stars

$ $

continued on next page

Koiso Sushi Bar *(continued)*

the table, perhaps because he knows that watching him work is part of what makes this place magical.

Yes, we said magical. If you've seen a Harry Potter movie, you'll recognize the phenomena we encounter at *Koiso*. Despite the fact it's like he opened his restaurant in his living room, once we sit and look over the fresh fish, something shifts. Just as the brick wall in the train station disappears when a wizard runs into it, when we sit and ask Hiro-san to feed us, the brick wall of everyday life — all the problems, worries, and stress — drops away and reveals a magical place where time seems to stand still and even the most independent-minded diners can't help but smile at each other and strike up a conversation.

It's the impeccably fresh fish, of course. Some is local, and some is from Japan — the fishermen call him in the wee hours to let him know what they've got. If he likes the sound of it, they put it on a plane and it arrives on Maui in time for him to pick it up at the airport, tote it back to Kihei and prepare it for that evening. With fish this delicious, you cannot help but revel — and since everyone else is reveling, you have instant friends on either side.

The magic isn't all in the fish — some of it comes from Hiro-San himself. Watch him as he prepares your meal, and you will see him moving his entire body as he works. All movements come from his abdomen, not his shoulders. He is anchored to the floor, but light on his feet. Every movement is precise, and every movement counts. His long knife flashes as he slices and flips and scoops — we can't always follow the blade as it blurs with speed. Watching Hiro-san is an education in what it means to be a Sushi Master (which he is). Dedicating yourself to making sushi is an act of love, and we've seen his face dissolve into concentration, relaxation, and peace.

We like to sit down and ask Hiro-san to feed us. He picks the best of what he has and prepares a lovely plate. This is not the place for fancy rolls; this is straight up classic sushi. If the Molokai shrimp is fresh, we order a pair of those plump shellfish, and he bakes the heads until they're crisp and crunchy between our teeth. The baby abalone grown on the Big Island is tender, served sliced in its own shell with a shiso leaf and kalamansi lime. The miso soup is hearty from the earthy mushrooms that fill the bowl, yet still light and clear in the broth. Sake and beer are both available and the waitress keeps the water glasses filled and the drinks coming.

This is not a restaurant for big parties or sushi newbies — if you need beginner chopsticks you're probably better off at *Sansei* — but if you have respect and admiration for sushi and want to spend an hour with a Master, call *Koiso* and see if they'll take your reservation. Keep in mind that this is a tiny place, and deeply personal. Hiro-san likes to populate it with people who really appreciate his food. If you suspect you are getting the cold shoulder, and you really want to visit, we suggest showing up a little later in the evening — maybe around 8pm — and quietly stepping just inside the door. Wait for him to acknowledge you and then bow a little and hold up your fingers with the number of people who would like to eat. If he likes the look of you — if you look respectful and knowledgeable he'll either

Koiso Sushi Bar *(continued)*

remove one of the "reserved" signs from in front of an empty chair or tell you about how long the wait will be.

And no matter how long that wait is, once you get your sake, listen to a few minutes of the music (usually a female vocalist singing "The Girl from Ipanema"), and start watching Hiro-san work, your own brick wall will fall, and you will join us and all of Hiro-san's other fans in joyful communion.

Address: 2395 S. Kihei Rd., Kihei, South Maui
Location: Dolphin Plaza across from Kamaole Beach Park I
Meals: Dinner
Hours: M-Sa 6pm-10:30pm
Parking: Lot
Phone: 808-875-8258

Kula Lodge Restaurant *(American)*

Kula Lodge sits high up on Haleakala and features tumbling (as in hold on to something or you'll fall over at the beauty) views of Maui's central valley, the West Maui Mountains, and both sides of the hourglass shaped island. "Sweeping" does not do this scene justice.

The inn's fireplace and dated, wood-paneled interior make for cozy meals. The food is average at best, and costs more than it warrants, but the view helps take the edge off, as does the fact that if you're this high up on the mountain, you likely are hungry and limited in your dining options. We recommend it for breakfast over other meals, though the gourmet pizzas — baked in the outdoor brick oven — are a good choice for lunch or dinner. We also recommend that you leave time to take a walk around the beautiful grounds to digest both your meal and the incredible, nowhere-else-on-Maui scenery. If you want to take the view home with you, stop into the Curtis Wilson Cost Gallery in the lodge's lobby for a startlingly real portrait of the eye-popping landscape. There's also a sweet general store next door, where you can stock on up on snacks and handcrafted gifts.

Address: 15200 Haleakala Hwy, Kula, Upcountry
Meals: Breakfast, Lunch, Dinner
Hours: Daily 7am-9pm
Parking: Lot
Phone: 808-878-1535
Website: www.kulalodge.com

L&L Hawaiian Barbecue *(Local / Plate Lunch)*

L&L is a Hawaii-based chain that serves plate lunch up as fast food: they scoop two scoops of rice and a mountain of macaroni salad onto a plate, and then you tell them what meats you want. We like the barbecue chicken and the beef short ribs

continued on next page

$

MasterCard VISA

L&L Hawaiian Barbecue *(continued)*

with spicy and sweet sauce. The katsu chicken can be dry. The prices have gone up (the $5 combo platter is now $10), but you can still score a deal with a "mini" plate by sacrificing one serving of rice. **L&L** has expanded outside of the islands, but if you don't have one in your hometown, you might want to check it out for decent, inexpensive local food.

Note: Fast food on Maui doesn't mean the lines move fast. As the bumper sticker says, *Slow down, this ain't the mainland.*

Address: 270 Dairy Rd., Kahului, Central Maui
Location: Maui Marketplace
Meals: Lunch, Dinner
Hours: Daily 9:30am–9pm
Parking: Lot
Phone: 808-873-0323
Website: www.hawaiianbarbecue.com

Address: 1221 Honoapiilani Rd., Lahaina, West Maui
Location: Lahaina Cannery
Meals: Lunch, Dinner
Hours: M–Sa 9am–9pm; Su 9am–7pm
Parking: Lot
Phone: 808-661-9888

Address: 247 Pi'ikea Ave., Kihei, South Maui
Location: Pi'ilani Village Center
Meals: Breakfast, Lunch, Dinner
Hours: Daily 4:30am–9pm
Parking: Lot
Phone: 808-875-8898

Address: 790 Eha St., Wailuku, Central Maui
Location: Wailuku Town Center
Meals: Breakfast, Lunch, Dinner
Hours: M–F 9am–9pm; Sa–Su 8am–9pm
Parking: Lot
Phone: 808-242-1380

OVERALL:
3.2
out of 5 stars

La Provence *(French)*

La Provence has excellent pastries in a breathtakingly beautiful location. Get there early (before 9am) to beat the cyclists and morning dog walkers who race there for almond and chocolate croissants, palmiers, and plump fruit tarts. The mango-blueberry scones are positively scrumptious — and huge. The plain croissants are — sincerely — the best we've had outside of Paris: simultaneously buttery and flaky. Perhaps because of the bakery's high elevation it's able to accomplish what no other Hawaii bakery can. The French owner lives up to the stereotype: a fussy, grouchy perfectionist. Full breakfasts are served *al fresca*, only on the weekends. It's worth a Sunday

La Provence *(continued)*

drive to get the flawless eggs Benedict or a crepe stuffed with salmon, pesto and béchamel sauce. The egg and crepe dishes come with tender, whole potatoes, crisp on the outside and soft inside. To top it off, you also get a lovely Kula greens salad with a tart lilikoi dressing, made from fruits off the vine that tangles round the bakery's perimeter.

The coffee is excellent; the espresso less so. It's a family run establishment, and if the employees are having a bad day, so are you. We prefer to approach their occasional surliness as part of the entertainment; it's like a ticket to France at a fraction of the cost. Besides, the views ease any agitation you might work up while waiting ... for ... your ... check ... Oh, forget it! Just go to the counter and pay there!

CASH

La Provence has a wood-burning pizza oven and serves dinner according to the chef's whim, but we can't recommend it. Their unpredictable hours and slow service turns from charming to grating the darker and colder it gets outside.

Address: 3158 Lower Kula Rd., Kula, Upcountry
Meals: Breakfast, Lunch
Hours: W-Su 7am-2pm
Parking: Lot
Phone: 808-878-1313
Website: www.laprovencekula.com

Lahaina Coolers *(American)*

Lahaina Coolers is a pleasant, open-air restaurant with an active bar, big menu, and plenty of sports on the television. Service is quick and friendly.

Breakfasts are very good with big portions and speedy delivery (don't you hate waiting for breakfast?). Try the French toast, perfectly doused with cinnamon. If you're an eggs-in-the-morning type, we like the Surfer, an egg burrito with Portuguese sausages, peppers, onions, and salsa on the side, as well as rice and well-seasoned beans.

Lunch is good, with sandwiches, burgers, and pretty good pizzas. We like the pork tacos, which feature a smoky pulled pig that's roasted in-house. The ingredients are fresh and the recipes creative. We usually recommend moving on for dinner, or sticking to a drink and an appetizer.

OVERALL:
3.2
out of 5 stars

Address: 180 Dickenson St., Lahaina, West Maui
Meals: Breakfast, Lunch, Dinner, Late-Night
Hours: Daily 8am-12am; bar until 1am
Parking: Street
Phone: 808-661-7082
Website: www.lahainacoolers.com

OVERALL:

4.2

out of 5 stars

$ $ $ $

Lahaina Grill *(Pacific Rim)*

Lahaina Grill is a workhorse of a restaurant that consistently creates very good to great meals with some of the best service on the island. From the hostess to the bartender to the servers to the sommelier who works the floor, each employee possesses poise, tact, and knowledge of their product. Whew! What a relief on island where truly exceptional service is in short supply.

David Paul Johnson first opened this restaurant in 1990 (he sold the restaurant nearly a decade ago, and they dropped his name in late 2007), and Chef/Owner Jurg Munch — is there a better name for a Chef? — continued many of his signature flavor combinations. This is a restaurant where every dish is designed to make you say "Wow!" from its presentation to its flavor profile to its exuberant use of high-end ingredients.

The European/Asian fusion cuisine crosses all sorts of boundaries, like the kalua duck quesadilla (sweet) bursting with roasted Maui onions and spiked with poblano peppers (heat). We like the plate of three separate seafood appetizers called the Cake Walk, because it lets you sample several standouts. The crab cake combines Kona lobster, scallops, crabs and panko with an exceptional spicy mustard sauce. The sweet Louisiana rock shrimp cake has a binding problem (sometimes) but the seared ahi cake — just a darling slice of fish over a disc of sticky rice — is perfect. The accompanying wasabi sauce is light, simple, and clean-flavored; an excellent example of how swinging for a homerun often results in one.

The Kona coffee lamb is a perennial favorite: a majestic, perfectly Frenched rack of lamb daintily laced with an excellent cabernet demi-glace rendered even more dark and spicy by Kona coffee.

If you've not had ahi yet, the sesame crusted seared version here is extraordinarily popular. We understand why — the flavors are excellent and the dish a powerful example of Hawaiian Fusion — but we still have to argue with the overuse of Maui onions in the crust, which are too overpoweringly sweet when combined with the bed of vanilla bean rice. We love, however, the apple-cider-and-soy-butter vinaigrette used here, because it sharpens the flavors and balances out the sweet a little. Another popular dish is the mahi mahi, which comes with a delicious beurre blanc sauce; we ask for a lighter hand with the gorgonzola to keep the delicate fish flavor coming through.

The menu's true star is the seared ahi and Hudson Valley foie gras. This decadent appetizer is guaranteed to be your most memorable dish: ample portions of rare, ruby-red ahi and creamy goose liver, both seared to perfection. The accompanying fig compote and duck demi-glace provide a sweet and salty counterpoint to the exquisite richness.

If you're a vegetarian, you're in luck, as several items are designed to give you a full, satisfying meal. We like the entrée featuring a tall "stack" of goat cheese, fresh tomatoes, grilled eggplant, marinated Portobello mushrooms, and roasted red bell peppers, all finished with a sweet Maui onion sauce.

Plenty of well-prepared sides are also vegetarian and sourced from local farms. While the creamed Kula spinach is perhaps too heavy with cheese

Lahaina Grill *(continued)*

for our taste (mascarpone, ricotta, and reggiano take it out of the veggie category and into dessert) the curried cauliflower is delightful.

Lahaina Grill's lovely dessert menu is really worth saving room for. Try the Road to Hana, Maui: a concoction that secrets away chocolate cake, chocolate mousse, and a delicious macadamia nut caramel under a coating of chocolate ganache. An S-curved crisp — representing the S curves on the famous road — balances on top.

The excellent wine list (heavy on California) and the genuine and efficient service make for a lovely dinner for two or ten. Make sure to ask advice from the restaurant's sommelier, a super-friendly fellow with an intuitive knack for picking the right bottle for the job. There may be too much bustle for a truly intimate meal, but sometimes a little noise screens out other diners and lets you focus on yourselves ... and the food.

There is no view, but the giant paintings from local artist (and fan) Jan Kasprzycki illustrate the dining experience perfectly. This has often been voted the best restaurant on Maui, and we understand why. While the menu hasn't changed much over two decades, it's always a pleasure to dine here, and this is one of our favorite restaurants. Sometimes, if we haven't made reservations (recommended), we just sit at the bar, where the full menu is available.

Note: if you celebrate a special occasion here, this is one of the few Maui restaurants who follow up with you later with birthday and anniversary cards that include price promotions.

Address: 127 Lahainaluna Rd., Lahaina, West Maui
Location: Just off Front St. near Cheeseburger in Paradise.
Meals: Dinner
Hours: Daily 6pm-10pm
Parking: Street
Phone: 808-667-5117
Website: www.lahainagrill.com

Lahaina Pizza Company *(American)*

This deep dish pie place used to be part of a mainland chain — BJ's — before it went independent and changed its name. The owners haven't changed, but something in the kitchen did: what used to be pretty good pizza is now simply average. The pizzas are too often doughy (a risk with this style) and lack the crispy edges that used to charm us. Toppings are still generous, but lack flavor and punch. The sauce is still red, but has lost its tomato flavor. The fabulous sunset view of Lahaina Harbor from their second floor location is still inspiring, however, and we still love the live music every night. Funny enough, we like the Buffalo wings well enough to make a point of stopping in once in a while: the huge platter piled with brilliantly orange thighs, wings, and drumsticks comes with fire on the

continued on next page

OVERALL:
3
out of 5 stars

Lahaina Pizza Company *(continued)*

chicken and cool blue cheese dressing on the side. Pair those with a beer and you are good to go. Service is proficient once you get a seat, but lines can form on busy nights. If you're going berserk trying to find parking, there's a free (shhhhh) public lot directly behind this section of Front Street, on Luakini Street.

Address: 730 Front St., Lahaina, West Maui
Location: Across from the sea wall, near the intersection with Dickinson.
Meals: Lunch, Dinner
Hours: Daily 11am-10pm
Parking: Street

Leilani's on the Beach *(Pacific Rim)*

Leilani's is a T S Restaurant (like sister restaurants *Hula Grill, Kimo's* and *Duke's*) with — of course — one of the best locations on the beach walk in Ka'anapali. Lava rock walls and wood beams soar through the two story restaurant, and the food is exactly what you might expect from a place with such a great view: only as good as it needs to be. T S Restaurants tend to deliver on views and service but not so much on creative dishes. This works for us when we're looking at breakfast places or burgers for lunch, but not so much for fresh fish at dinner. If you stick with the beachside grill (downstairs), the prices go down and the value proposition goes up. Ka'anapali is designed for tourists, and it has more than its fair share of expensive restaurants serving average food to people who did not rent a car. This is certainly one of those restaurants.

Address: 2435 Ka'anapali Pkwy., Lahaina, West Maui
Location: Whaler's Village
Meals: Lunch, Dinner
Hours: Daily 11am-11pm
Parking: Lot
Phone: 808-661-4495
Website: www.leilanis.com

Leoda's Kitchen and Pie Shop
(Hawaii Regional Cuisine, Bakery)

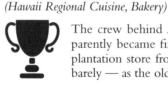 The crew behind *Aloha Mixed Plate,* and *Star Noodle* apparently became fixated on pies ... so they renovated an old plantation store from the ground up. (You'll recognize it — barely — as the old Chez Paul location.)

The adorable new (open less than a month at publication time) eatery offers a wide range of items served in pie tins. The menu is a naughty gourmet goodie bag: an abundance of pork (the roast pork hoagie even comes with "ham drippings"), fried stuff, haute (hot) dogs, pickles, organic garnishes, and, of course, pies.

Leoda's Kitchen and Pie Shop *(continued)*

We came full from a meal at **Honu** on our first visit — which was the second day they opened. We stopped in just to sample the dessert pies. We raved in public about what we found, and so did others — at our last visit right before publication they were sold out of pies at 4pm in the afternoon. The secret to a great pie is tender, flaky crust, which they have mastered ... but just listen to the fillings: apple crumb with a layer of caramel, perfectly tender apples, and an excellent streusel, three berry pie with the perfect bright squeeze of lemon, snappy banana cream, and a macadamia nut chocolate praline that has us begging for mercy. The cream and chocolate pies are both topped with a thick whip cream that tastes slightly of marshmallow ... or vanilla ... or angel wings. We get lightheaded after our second bite. Meanwhile, the fragrant yuzu tart is tangy and sweet — a lemon bar dressed up for the prom. Don't fret that these pies are only 5 inches wide, because each serves four handily. Eat more and you might knock yourself out cold. (But they also refrigerate well — so if you are tempted, get one for later.)

After this first visit we were so ratcheted up we tried every one of the hand-held and pot pies. Darn it! The crust is still tender and flaky, and we like the concept: folding ingredients into a pie crust, and then hand crimping the crust to make a pocket pie. Too bad the fillings on the savory pies are universally bland. The carnitas pie isn't spicy enough, the Kula corn is sweet, but little else, and the mushroom pie is very ... mushroom-y. The berry and apple handhelds are similarly disappointing — what happened to the perfectly balanced and more flavorful sweet versions we ate just a few days earlier? Even the otherwise wonderful crust on these handhelds is hampered by their bath in the deep fryer — it kills some of the flavor, and makes the pies heavier than necessary. Tragic! The pot pies don't fare much better; we *adore* the cheddar and herb crusts, but the steak and chicken fillings, respectively, are blah.

The kitchen is still working things out — this is very early in their career and we normally would not even include a review. The reason we do is because the crew behind this restaurant are talented and usually find a good balance between quality, price, and experience — so we want you to hear about it. We think they'll be around for a while.

We're happy to say that **Leoda's** sandwiches and hot dogs are good. And — Hallelujah! They bake their own bread! You can buy a loaf to take with you — for only $6. The ahi sandwich is perfectly rare, and comes with a lovely pesto (although there is not enough of it — and it's not evenly distributed enough to make every bite delicious). The burger is fine, and the hand-cut fries are yumsters.

Another favorite is the ... fried salad??!! Brussels sprout leaves are fried until slightly crunchy. The addition of celery leaves and a few sprigs of mint has us smacking our foreheads, wondering why we've never thought to add these extras to salads at home. The burnt orange vinaigrette is candy-sweet, but mixed liberally over the bitter Brussels, it's perfect.

The charming décor blends a good ol' American pie theme with lovely local accents: Haleakala Dairy milk bottles serve as vases for fresh flowers, and

continued on next page

Leoda's Kitchen and Pie Shop *(continued)*

old photos of former Olowalu residents grace the walls. We just wish they could do something about the dull roar that seems to emanate from the walls — the exhibition kitchen can be heard everywhere, and the "buzz" in the room is several decibels louder than comfortable. At least you don't worry about your conversation being overheard (or, at times, heard at all).

Leoda's opened with both barrels roaring, and they are certainly charging forward and being welcomed by locals and visitors alike, even with prices just slightly higher than comfortable (it seems like everything should cost $1-$2 less). Service is definitely still working the kinks out, but we predict they'll continue to refine and improve, and find a comfortable formula that works — just as they have at their other properties.

We give them a trophy because we couldn't stay away from those dessert pies if we tried.

Address: 820 Olowalu Village Road, Lahaina
Location: Halfway to Lahaina on Honoapiilani Highway
Meals: Lunch, Dinner
Hours: Daily 10am–8:00pm
Parking: Lot
Phone: 808-662-3600
Website: www.leodas.com

OVERALL:
3.3
out of 5 stars

Longhi's *(Italian)*

Longhi's is a Maui institution that's a good choice for big group meals. Most dishes are served family style and many tables and booths are big enough for eight (or more). The restaurants are "clinky" — which is our word for the pleasant sound a restaurant makes when it's busy and people are eating a lot.

The menu is Italian, and everything is made in-house. Pastas are not listed on the regular menu because they want you to order exactly what *you* like. They can do just about any shape and any traditional sauce competently, but nothing blows our socks off. The steaks are good and sometimes excellent, but keep in mind that the a la carte menu means that when you ask for a steak you'll get a steak — no sides unless you order them. We recommend the asparagus or French fries.

The shrimp dishes are well made, including the signature Shrimp Longhi, a platter of shrimp perched on garlic toast points and ladled with a buttery white wine sauce. We recommend getting fish at another restaurant.

Salads are fresh, although the dressings aren't exciting. The exception is the endive salad, which is a real treat. Slightly bitter, long leaves of Belgian endive are laid out like little canoes, then filled with gorgonzola cheese crumbles and candied macadamia nuts. Delicious, fresh-tasting honey vinaigrette brightened with mint and spiked with scallions tops the dish.

Oddly, one of the things we like best at *Longhi's* is the doughy, cheesy pizza

Longhi's *(continued)*

bread served gratis with your water. One is topped with mellow tomato sauces, the other with sweet roasted jalapenos. We ask for this comfort food even when we come for breakfast.

Breakfasts are elegant, with actual fresh-squeezed orange juice (a rarity on Maui) and excellent coffee made with French press. This is not the cheapest breakfast menu on Maui, but they make their baked goods in house, and we like it. Benedicts come on huge slices of toasted Italian bread. Lunchtime offers a menu with many of the dinner items with smaller portions (and a lower price tag), plus a very good burger.

Service is inconsistent. We've had terrific, attentive waiters, and bumbling, oblivious ones. The Wailea location is large, open-air, and has a quieter atmosphere than the Lahaina location, where the noise — and sometimes the exhaust fumes — from Front Street can be overwhelming. Upstairs, on the checkerboard dance floor, you can whittle your pasta away dancing to live rock and jazz and DJs from Thursday through Saturday evening.

Address: 3750 Wailea Alanui Dr., Wailea, South Maui
Location: Shops of Wailea
Meals: Breakfast, Lunch, Dinner
Hours: Daily 8am–10pm
Parking: Lot
Phone: 808-891-8883
Website: www.longhis.com

Address: 888 Front St., Lahaina, West Maui
Meals: Breakfast, Lunch, Dinner
Hours: Daily 7:30am–10pm
Parking: Valet, Street
Phone: 808-667-2288

Lulu's *(American)*

Lulu's is a scene, and that's the main reason to go. The food is beside the point when the servers are this cute, there's an eating contest, or a good local band playing. Drinks are fine, but you may have to wait a while to get yours (we notice that James is more forgiving than Molly when the waitress smiles her apologies). Burgers are fine (they serve one with peanut butter that is really surprising, in a good way). Other typical sports bar items like nachos and spicy chicken wings are fine, too.

The dive bar vibe is undercut during the daytime and early evening hours when lots of families with kids come. At night, salsa fans invade the dance floor, swinging one another around like practiced acrobats in spiked heels.

On a second floor in Kalama Village with a beautiful view, the open-air restaurant draws a lot of tourists looking for a break from the heat, but also

continued on next page

Lulu's *(continued)*

locals looking for Happy Hour and hanging out, too. The farther back into the restaurant you go, the darker the ambience.

Address: 1941 S. Kihei Rd., Kihei, South Maui
Location: Second Floor, Kalama Village
Meals: Lunch, Dinner, Late-Night
Hours: Daily 11am-10pm; Bar until 1am
Parking: Lot
Phone: 808-879-9944
Website: www.lulusmaui.com

OVERALL:
2.6
out of 5 stars

Lulu's Lahaina Surf Club *(American)*

Lulu's Lahaina has ample seating at the bar, where you can watch jaw-dropping surf footage or your favorite sports team on big screen TVs. The menu goes beyond basic bar food, but we recommend sticking to appetizers and cocktails. Fancy margaritas are rimmed with Li Hing Mui powder and the mai tai comes to the table in a Maui Gold pineapple. The large dining room is decorated with authentic surf memorabilia, deep booths, busy pool tables, and a stage for live music, and plenty of room to dance. NB: This restaurant is not owned by the same owners as the Kihei ***Lulu's***.

Address: 1221 Honoapiilani Hwy, Lahaina, West Maui
Location: Lahaina Cannery Mall
Meals: Breakfast, Lunch, Dinner, Late-Night
Hours: M-F 11am-2am; Sa-Su 7am-2am
Parking: Lot
Phone: 808-661-0808
Website: www.luluslahaina.com

CLOSED FOR RENOVATIONS
No ratings available while restaurant is renovated.
Check MauiRestaurantsBlog.com for Updates.

Ma'alaea Waterfront Restaurant *(Pacific Rim)*

The ***Waterfront*** is a Maui institution that was once one of our favorite places but has been disappointing us terribly for the last few years. In mid-2011 this fish restaurant on the lower level of an out of the way condominium in Ma'alaea closed its doors for "renovations." We were skeptical that they would re-open, especially when the September date got pushed back to October, and then to "indefinitely." However, it looks like they may have found a new place: a decidedly better spot in the space where Ma'alaea Grill once operated. That restaurant has beautiful views and is well-situated at the back of the Maui Ocean Center complex. Better parking, easier to find — hopefully this move will be inspiring (if it happens), and they'll get their mojo back in their new digs. Check their website or their Facebook page, which they regularly update, to see if they're open.

www.facebook.com/WaterfrontMaui
www.waterfrontrestaurant.net
Phone: 808-244-9028

Mai Tai Lounge *(Pacific Rim)*

When we think of the **Mai Tai Lounge** we feel all soft and fuzzy.

We think it's because we usually go at around 4pm, when the view from the open-air lanai is all hazy with golden afternoon light and the little boats in the harbor line up, and the water sprays the side of the building, and we start with a mai tai, which is served in a wide, low bowl with a long straw and, when we drink it, we smile at each other and then we take another big sip and the people we are with start being really funny, like really, really funny, and then we drink some more, and have a nacho or something and then Molly realizes she's all done with her drink and maybe she has to pee and she goes to the bathroom, but sheesh these chairs are really tall and she realizes that they make very, very strong mai tais that taste very good, which is what she thinks about while she is in the bathroom, which is very clean, she notices, and when she gets back to the table hey, James ordered another mai tai for her, which she probably shouldn't have, but at this point she knows she'll have to wait much later than planned to drive home anyway, so why not have another yummy mai tai, and oh, we were planning on ordering food, too, but then maybe we don't need to order food because we just had a lot of pineapple juice and guava juice and lime juice and some nachos and isn't that enough to get us through, and maybe we should go somewhere really *great* for dinner, because after all we deserve it, a really excellent meal is so wonderful and so now it's sunset and we've been here over two hours and James wants to go and the server was sooooooooo nice so he leaves a big tip and then we take a long walk to sober up a little, and now it's like whatever, 8pm and we're still in a really good mood, but we're hungry and can't drive all the way back to the South side when we're *so* hungry and maybe still don't trust ourselves to drive so we decide to go to **David Paul's Island Grill** and we spend way more on dinner than we meant to that night but that's OK because the food is soooooo good, and when we get out, the plumeria trees are all dropping their flowers and, even though we usually don't like Lahaina because the whole town feels like a tourist trap, tonight it just seems so **magical**.

Address: 839 Front St., Lahaina, West Maui
Meals: Lunch, Dinner, Happy Hour
Hours: Daily 11am-10pm
Parking: Street
Phone: 808-661-5288
Website: www.maitailounge.com

Main Street Bistro *(Pacific Rim)*

Main Street Bistro is a lunch and light dinner restaurant in Wailuku, and we recommend that you stop in on your way to or from Iao Valley. Chef Owner Tom Selman is well known on Maui for making straightforward dishes — crab cakes, roast beef sandwiches, potato macaroni salad, fried chicken — with a precise hand and careful flavors.

continued on next page

Main Street Bistro *(continued)*

We hear a jangle in the restaurant from the happy clinking of knives and forks and the lively chatter of locals who live and work on Main Street in Wailuku. The rather haphazard decor — big Hawaiian prints, cane chairs, local art, and the exhibition "kitchen" (read: grill) is definitely designed — or not — for those who come for the food, not the ambience. It's clean and the tall ceilings let in a lot of natural light, so we forgive that we have to take a key attached to a large wooden spoon into the office building next door to find a bathroom.

Try the roasted beet salad. The beets are tender and sweet, the onion a little pickled from the light, refreshing pear vinaigrette, and the candied cashews add crunch. We also like the straightforward grilled steak salad, with slices of beef laid on peppery arugula and topped with bleu cheese. The fried chicken is called "southern" but we find the batter not quite as crispy as that implies. It is, however, tender, juicy, and despite the rather flat breading, better than any of the katsu we've had on the island. If you're offered mashed potatoes with your meal, they're prepared in our favorite style: skin still on, handmade, chunky, well-seasoned, tender not mushy. The crab cakes come on a toasted bun or on a salad, and they are well made and have a tangy, delicious remoulade. We love the onion rings, which are razor thin and tangle on the plate.

Service is efficient, kind, and neighborly, and you can see Chef Tom working away every day of the week. The restaurant is closed after 7pm and on weekends, but sometimes stays open a little late for First Fridays, the town-wide art celebration on the first Friday of each month.

Address: 2051 Main St., Wailuku, Central Maui
Meals: Lunch, Dinner
Hours: M-F 11am-7pm
Parking: Street
Phone: 808-244-6816
Website: www.msbmaui.com

OVERALL:
4
out of 5 stars

Makawao Steak House *(Steakhouse)*

Sometimes it's fun to knowingly walk into a time warp, and when that's what we want, we eat at ***Makawao Steak House***, which feels exactly like an upscale-rural steak house, circa 1975. The cozy lounge features a big wood-burning fireplace that is necessary in the winter months. You can order the full menu here, and the service is just as good as it is in the restaurant proper (which is to say unpretentious, relatively efficient, and usually friendly). The several dining rooms slowly fill up with rough-riding, sunburnt paniolo (Hawaiian cowboys), who've cleaned up for a night on the town. A tidy, charming room in back is reserved for high tea — a favorite for birthdays and bridal showers.

There are no surprises on the menu: big steaks, jumbo prawns, and a sprawling, quivery prime rib. The sides are limited but acceptable, and the salad bar is an almost frightening relic from the era we're revisiting: Iceberg let-

Makawao Steak House *(continued)*

tuce, shaved carrots, sliced cucumbers, commercial croutons, ramekins of sunflower seeds and raisins, commercial dressings you ladle over your plate … everything you could have wanted before you found out about heirloom tomatoes. Your server will likely recommend the calamari appetizer, an odd combo of fried, breaded calamari steak and caper butter sauce. We feel funny about this dish — the same way we feel about marshmallow cream. It's tasty but not quite right in its core; we feel guilty after eating it.

The wine list is not creative, but it has a decent selection. Don't expect guidance from the restaurant about what to eat or drink. As one waitress said to a friend of ours playing big city foodie, "your options are laid out on the menu and are self-explanatory." Desserts are basically mountains of whip cream, chocolate, and ice cream.

So why eat here? One reason: the prime rib. Pink through and through, it's tender enough to sever with the edge of your fork, and served in two sizes: huge and gargantuan. While tucking away half of your portion, your mind will helplessly stray to the delicious sandwich you'll make tomorrow for lunch with the other half. The accompanying horseradish cream could be spicier and the *jus* less salty, but in all truth the meat is as good as we've had at a Four Seasons buffet — for far less coin. It comes with rice, which we swap out for creamy garlic mashed potatoes.

After gorging ourselves on this (and skipping dessert) we step out into the cool, crisp air on Makawao's main drag and look up at the spangly night stars. If you remember what the night skies looked like in 1975, you probably remember stars like these.

Address: 3612 Baldwin Ave., Makawao, Upcountry
Meals: Dinner
Hours: Nightly 5:30pm-9pm
Parking: Street
Phone: 808-572-8711

Makawao Sushi & Deli *(Sushi/American)*

Tucked into the back of a little storefront on Baldwin Avenue in Makawao is a tiny little sushi bar — maybe six seats and two tables — where a competent chef makes plate after plate of reasonably good, fresh sushi. We skip the miso (salty) and order a few rolls when we're upcountry and want fish. We don't arrive hungry, though, because while the chef is good, he's not quick. (We've caught him sitting down with his customers — while we were waiting for our sushi!) If you're in the mood for sandwiches, the deli at the front of the store features the usual choices and makes them generous in size. The milkshakes are very good, creamy and thick and made with Roselani ice cream (local, good), which you can also get in cones. The coffee and espresso is very good, and the pastries are worth tucking into,

continued on next page

OVERALL:
2.8
out of 5 stars

$ $

especially the brownies.

Address: 3647 Baldwin Ave., Makawao, Upcountry
Meals: Breakfast, Lunch, Dinner, Snacks & Treats
Hours: M–Sa 8:30am–8:30pm; Sushi Bar opens at 12pm
Parking: Street
Phone: 808-573-9044

Mala Ocean Tavern and Mala Wailea *(Pacific Rim)*

Mala Ocean Tavern is one of our favorite restaurants because it serves fantastic food in a lively, casual restaurant smack dab on the water. We don't come here when we want an intimate, romantic meal — the tables are so close you're likely to find out a lot about your neighbors — but when we want to celebrate with friends, or just have a beer at sunset, this is our pick.

The fabulous Maui Chef Mark Ellman — other restaurants include ***Penne Pasta***, the original ***Maui Tacos***, the fabled (and long-closed) Avalon and the new ***Honu*** next door — has crafted a menu packed with a long list of small tapas-sized dishes and plenty of hearty entrées. His skill with flavors and his insistence on local, organic, and healthy ingredients makes his food both opinionated (he insists on telling you that the dark, flavorful bread is made with flax seed) and dastardly delicious.

The pale green edamame dip that comes with your water says a lot about the meal to come — nothing is going to be done exactly as expected, but everything will be done with care and attention, and all surprises will be good ones (like the spicy salsa served at the same time, which stirs up the edamame's mild flavors).

The crunchy, panko-crusted calamari is one of our favorite items on the menu (and on the island). The fish is lightly battered and just barely fried, so it stays delicate and tender. The accompanying aioli and the mojo verde (pesto made from cilantro and tomatillos) are addictive. We ration it. We also like the ahi "tartare" — chopped fish, capers, lemon, red onion on slices of crispy lavosh bread.

The burger is made with Kobe beef, applewood bacon, caramelized onions, and blue cheese, and, when cooked medium, is perfect. We love the baby back ribs mainly for the voluptuous sauce. The seared sashimi with a shiitake mushroom ginger sauce is earthy and spicy, and the Yukon gold potatoes on the side are mellow and buttery. The adult mac and cheese is a dish to which we'd normally turn up our noses, but here, we have to admit: it's divine. We can hardly wait for the molten layer of mozzarella, pecorino and Maytag blue cheese to cool enough to eat. Delectably crisp on the edges, the cheesy crust gives way to juicy Ali'i mushrooms and macaroni aswim in rich sauce.

When in season, get the opakapaka, or pink snapper, in whatever prepara-

Mala Ocean Tavern and Mala Wailea *(continued)*

tion is on the menu. When they have it, the wok-fried moi is incredibly tender, and the ginger black bean sauce is as good as **Spago's**.

The vegetable sides here are outstanding, and represent one of the island's best bangs for the buck. Heaping portions of spicy sugar snap peas doused in fiery sambal and ginger sauce, Brussels sprouts charred in butter till caramelized, and gem-like purple sweet potatoes can be had for a fraction of an entrée price — but could easily serve as dinner when combined.

Lunches are less expensive and excellent, and their weekend brunch menu is wonderful (French toast fans, this one's for you). While the atmosphere is totally different, we recommend heading here over **Sea House**, and certainly **Gazebo**, if you're in the mood for a good brunch on Saturday or Sunday.

If you're here at Happy Hour, they have good drink specials and many of the small plates are available. We've sat on the lanai many times to watch the water and the turtles — sometimes dozens of them — feed on the rocks just below the restaurant at low tide. The wine list is selective, and there is a good selection of beers on tap. Service is generally very good, although there are some quirky personalities at both locations.

We rate **Mala Ocean Tavern** a 4 for ambience, but **Mala Wailea** doesn't warrant the same top rating. It has the sort of clunky hotel restaurant atmosphere that just can't be helped when you're in a Marriott. The big chairs and long tables and rather disjointed spaces — from lounge to lanai to dining room — make for a very different feeling than the Lahaina location. The view is nice, overlooking the Marriott's pool and the beach walk below, with Molokini beyond, but the farther inside the restaurant you are, the less relevant it is, and the more aware you are of the self-conscious decor. There is substantially more room here, however, and if you're with a big party you can expect to be situated in a nice, relatively private alcove of your own. The menu is the same in Wailea as in Lahaina, and the kitchen is finally executing at a level comparable with the mother location. We have come to love the Happy Hour in Wailea almost as much, even without the turtles. Both locations feature absolutely top-notch bartenders who can deliver if you ask them to make you something special.

Address: 1307 Front St., Lahaina, West Maui
Location: Across from Lahaina Cannery Mall
Meals: Breakfast, Brunch, Lunch, Dinner
Hours: M-F 11am-9:30pm; Sa 9am-9:30pm; Su 9am-9pm
Parking: Lot, Street
Phone: 808-667-9394
Website: www.malaoceantavern.com

Address: 3700 Wailea Alanui Dr., Wailea, South Maui
Location: Wailea Beach Marriott Resort
Meals: Breakfast, Dinner
Hours: Daily 6:30am-11am; 5:30pm-9:30pm; bar 5pm-10pm
Parking: Valet, Lot
Phone: 808-879-1922

OVERALL:
4.2
out of 5 stars

OVERALL:
4
out of 5 stars

OVERALL:
4
out of 5 stars

Mama's Fish House *(Pacific Rim)*

Readers consistently ask us these three questions:

Should I drive the Road to Hana?

Should I get up for sunrise at Haleakala?

*Should I go to **Mama's Fish House**?*

Our answer is the same for all three questions: It depends.

The decision to go to Hana, Haleakala, or **Mama's Fish House** is deeply personal and requires careful examination of your true desires, expectations, and motivations. We leave the first two questions to another section of this book, and will address **Mama's** here. While we can't offer advice to you directly, we can tell you the parameters by which we would make the decision.

Mama's is a landmark, an institution, and a well-run, profitable business that brings joy and happiness to tens of thousands of diners every year. If this were Florida, it would be Disney World or Epcot.

When we first made this comparison, we heard from the restaurant that they resented it. They pointed out the careful choices in decor, the one-of-a-kind items that had been brought back to Maui from journeys to the South Pacific. They felt we were saying they are just a tourist trap. Well, we're not saying that — at *all!* To start, we don't think *Disney* is a tourist trap. Disney offers its guests the best in entertainment — the best singers, dancers, rides, parades, high quality souvenirs, the most beautiful landscaping. They control every aspect of your experience with the intention of making sure that you feel *happy*. Are they popular? Absolutely. Does it cost an arm and a leg to go there? Yup. Does this mean it's not worth it? No — you either love the world they have created for you, or you don't. There is no middle ground.

Mama's also offers a highly controlled experience. The owners toured the South Pacific in a sailboat many moons ago, and they've recreated the experience for you here, both in the Tahitian-inspired cuisine and the sea-spray-kissed atmosphere. **Mama's** also offers the *best*. The fish is unequivocally fresh. The tropical fruit, the vegetables, the seaweed, the ferns, the roasted macadamia nuts and everything else are of the highest quality (and the menu lists where each ingredient comes from, including the name of the fisherman, his boat, and how he reeled his catch in). The preparations are painstakingly developed and carefully made, and delicious across the board.

The show starts when you hand your keys to the valet (there is no self-parking). Walking down to the restaurant and the grounds, we still marvel at how perfectly Hawaiian this place is. The restaurant sits on what is called Mama's Beach, which offers one of the most breathtakingly beautiful views available. After you check in at the hostess/souvenir/gift kiosk and walk through the narrow walkway to get inside, the restaurant, the gracious ceilings and wide open walls and fresh breezes create a perfect setting for a terrific meal. In this parallel reality, you go "on vacation" for the length of your meal — even if, like us, you already live on Maui.

Mama's Fish House *(continued)*

From the start the service is like clockwork. Servers bring menus, drinks, dishes and then clear them away with a regularity that can seem precisely timed. We suspect that it is. This is a restaurant — one of the few on the island — that can fill every table several times in one afternoon or evening — and they do not particularly want you to dawdle over dinner.

The strength in this food is not gourmet flourishes, but fresh food cooked simply and garnished perfectly. The menu is focused, but perfect. The fresh fish of the day is listed, along with the best preparation to complement it. The pork and steak dishes are similarly developed with perfection in mind. One of our favorite preparations is a simple butter lemon sauce with macadamia nuts, because it is Just Done Right. The beef Polynesian, served in a grilled papaya, is a medley of medium rare morsels spiced with chili and lime. The ceviche? Out of this world — and we love the giant fried sweet potato chips that accompany it. This fresh-and-simple-and-perfect ethic stretches even to the drink menu. The mai tai is strong and sweet. Our favorite nonalcoholic drink *on the island* is the coconut mint concoction that blows our senses with its straightforward freshness. In general, there's a lot of coconut on this menu, and tropical fruits figure heavily into the savory dishes.

The desserts warrant your attention. The insanely beautiful Tahitian black pearl is a glossy globe of ganache ensconced in a pastry shell and surrounded by sunrays of lilikoi sauce. In the center of the "pearl" hides a soft lilikoi cream. The sleek Kuau pie is an addictive slice of silky chocolate atop caramel cookie crust. The house-made ice creams are fabulous — especially the banana and coconut — and are delivered to your table with a song if it happens to be your birthday.

If you want to take advantage of the superlative view, lunch time may be a good time for you to book a table (or walk in). The menu is reduced in size but not in quality, and the prices are slightly (but not much) lower. Another strategy we suggest is to make this the meal you eat right before you get on a plane to leave Maui, especially before a red eye flight to the mainland. It may seem odd, but it makes sense: you can be sure you will enjoy your meal, that it won't last overly long due to slow service, and you're only fifteen minutes away from the airport.

Sometimes, we simply head to *Mama's* to indulge in resplendent drinks and dessert. We sit at the bar and act like we live this luxuriously all the time. (Whenever we've tried this, though, we've always caved and ordered an appetizer or two.)

The bottom line for us is that we like *Mama's* exactly for what it does: provide a one-of-a-kind experience. You get an excellent, fresh meal with incredible views and very well-trained service. We do not expect or want it to change any more than we'd want Disney to stop doing what Disney does. You can have a wonderful meal elsewhere on the island — that's true. But only *Mama's* gives you *Mama's*.

That is our long-winded answer to *"Should I go to **Mama's Fish House?**"*

continued on next page

We hope it is helpful.

Address: 799 Poho Pl., Paia, North Shore
Meals: Lunch, Dinner
Hours: Daily 11am–10pm
Parking: Valet
Phone: 808-579-8488
Website: www.mamasfishhouse.com

$

CASH

Mama's Ribs & Rotisserie

Mama's Ribs is a family-run joint that sells ribs, pulled pork, pot roast, and rotisserie chickens for takeout (there are a few tables, but the strip mall location is pretty barren for a meal). Ribs are slightly dry and not juicy enough for us in the Napili location, but better in Kihei. We like the tangy-sweet-sour barbecue sauce. The pulled pork is similarly prepared, but the rotisserie chicken is tender and juicy. You can get a whole chicken for $15.99 and a half chicken for $9.99. If you don't want to go to a supermarket for your chicken, this is a notch above it in quality, a couple of notches above in price. For sides, you can do the slaw or the macaroni salad or the cornbread and be pretty happy.

Address: 5095 Napilihau St., Napili, West Maui
Location: in Napili Plaza
Meals: Lunch, Dinner
Hours: Daily 11am–8pm
Parking: Lot
Phone: 808-665-6262
Website: www.mamasribsmaui.com

Address: 1819 South Kihei Rd., Kihei South Maui
Location: in Kukui Mall
Meals: Lunch, Dinner
Hours: Monday–Saturday 11am–8pm
Parking: Lot
Phone: 808-875-7755

Mana Foods *(Organic/Vegan)*

This is the best independent health food store on the island, and an excellent place to stock up on essentials (and indulgences) before heading out to Hana. The barely reconstructed warehouse space hosts nearly everything you could want to buy for healthy grocery items, amazing produce sourced locally, and an array of natural cosmetics and remedies. We forgive the crowded aisles, sudden ramps in the flooring, and mismatched tiles because the prices are often lower than elsewhere, and we can find things here we can't anywhere else. We approach the scarcity of parking and the strange cast of characters lolling about at the door as a sort of Zen thermometer. If we

Mana Foods *(continued)*

are relaxed, we find the circus charming and fun. If we happen to be extra hungry or in a hurry, we find our annoyance quotient tips in the other direction. The cure? An immediate dose of chocolate.

Fortuitously, the entrance to **Mana** is lined in every conceivable gourmet chocolate bar, including those laced with chili pepper, goji berries, and bacon. The chocolate selection is reason enough to visit this grocery wonderland.

The prepared food section includes an ample salad bar with wild greens, quinoa, green papaya salad, stuffed grape leaves, decent sushi, sandwiches and wraps. The attendants will scoop hijiki salad, curried chicken, and lovely eggplant parmesan into to-go containers for you. They can also make smoothies, sandwiches, or burritos, and slice free-range and organic meats and cheeses to order. Of special note are the phenomenal vegan desserts. The silken tofu chocolate mousse with walnuts is dreamy, as is the tapioca with layers of fresh fruit. We also highly recommend the dark Ukrainian sourdough bread they make in-house.

The produce aisle offers every variety of fruit grown in the Islands, including many you may not have heard of. Luckily, a produce guru stands by, waiting to slice you a sample. (Sadly, the best service is had in this aisle — otherwise it's rather disinterested, even in the vitamin room.) Ask lots of questions and learn how to select the ripest, most mind-blowing mango or cherimoya. Dried fruits and nuts are available in the bulk room; try the whole dried bananas or sliced, dehydrated mango.

Paia is home to many surfers who come from all over the globe for the big waves, so **Mana** stocks plenty of gourmet and European treats (European butter, Greek yogurt, Nutella). Although it's small, it manages to carry as comprehensive an inventory as the best health food stores on the mainland. Did we mention the huge chocolate bar selection as you walk in? Our only complaint is actually a request. The closest place to sit and eat is several blocks away. May we suggest the owners consider opening the rooftop for *al fresca* dining?

Address: 49 Baldwin Ave., Paia, North Shore
Meals: Breakfast, Lunch, Dinner
Hours: Daily 8:30am–8:30pm
Parking: Lot, Street
Phone: 808-579-8078
Website: www.manafoodsmaui.com

Marco's Grill & Deli *(Italian)*

Marco's is a popular restaurant with a great central location: right on the corner of Dairy Road and Hana Highway. If you are just getting on or off a plane, this is a good place to get a meal that will, as one of our best friends, a foodie from New York City who grew up in New Jersey put it, "weigh you

continued on next page

OVERALL:
3.3
out of 5 stars

Marco's Grill & Deli *(continued)*

down, but in a good way." The owner, Marco, grew up in Philadelphia and owned a deli/diner in New Jersey, and you can tell. The tiled floors, art deco booths, and snappy service will be familiar to anyone who's ever stopped off the Turnpike looking for a bite to eat.

The sausages are ground on premises, and the pasta is made in house. All the sauces are from scratch. We like the rigatoni in the creamy, perfectly seasoned vodka sauce, which comes in half and full sizes. The ravioli stuffed with ricotta and prosciutto has been described as "pockets of love." The chicken Parmigiana sandwich is hearty and crisp. The portions are generous. While in the past we've felt that the menu was slightly over-priced, Marco hasn't raised his prices in years and now a meal here nearly feels like a bargain.

There are no surprises on the breakfast menu, but the food is good and the price is right and you can get it any time (just like in Jersey). Kids love the chocolate chip pancakes.

We often visit **Marco's** with modest expectations and are satisfied with the good value it offers. We recommend it if you need a filling, familiar meal in central Maui.

Address: 444 Hana Hwy., Kahului, Central Maui
Location: On the corner of Hana Highway and Dairy Road
Meals: Breakfast, Lunch, Dinner
Hours: Daily 7:30am-10pm
Parking: Lot
Phone: 808-877-4446

Market Fresh Bistro *(Pacific Rim)*

Market Fresh Bistro's mission is in its name: only the freshest local ingredients. Chef Owner Justin Pardo's goal is to cook food grown or raised within 100 miles of his small kitchen, and he's well on his way. Local farmers and growers knock at his back door, supplying him with all sorts of excellent ingredients, and his menu changes regularly with what's available.

Although it is true that ingredients are precious, at **Market Fresh**, they are treated as *too* precious. They need to be roughed up a little more — spiced, charred, blended, pureed, oiled ... whatever. We want to see (and more importantly, taste) those ruby red beets *reborn* on the plate, after a little alchemy in the kitchen.

We recommend **Market Fresh** for breakfast or lunch, when the (still spendy) prices are more in line with the level of cooking magic on offer. As you might guess, Chef's strengths are perfectly cooked proteins: fish rendered firm and flaky; beef seared well with rich, melting meat inside; pork that is tender and moist, not dried out or tough. We've enjoyed several nice sides: potato gratins stacked high on the plate, the thin slices of potato soaking up excellent cheese until starch and dairy melt together; wild rice with wheatberries and diced carrots (precise, brilliantly orange quarter-

Market Fresh Bistro *(continued)*

inch cubes). The tiramisu is light in texture and perfectly clean in the flavors (although we'd like those flavors a little stronger). Breakfasts feature strong egg dishes. There is no corkage fee if you bring your own libations (no liquor license — but ***Rodeo General Store*** is just across the street).

Service is also, often, too precious. The host and hostess (co-owners, along with the chef) linger at the counter and watch customers eat. They're cordial enough, as long as you appear to be enjoying your meal. Then, they're happy to talk about the farms they support. If they see or hear or smell even a whiff of disgruntlement, however, don't expect any sympathy: they believe in their product and they expect you to do so, as well. If you don't ... well ... the door is right over there. Can't you see it? Why haven't you left yet?

The one-to-two person kitchen can be slow, but even so weekend brunches are extremely popular with the upcountry crowd, some of whom are passionate true believers in the mission of this restaurant. We love the casual location — in the courtyard behind ***Makawao Steak House***. You can sit inside at the small tables with the lace curtains blowing in the fresh breeze, or outside under the shady trees.

Address: 3620 Baldwin Ave., Makawao, Upcountry
Location: in the courtyard behind Makawao Steak House
Meals: Breakfast, Brunch, Lunch, Dinner
Hours: M–W 8am–4pm; Th–Sa 8am–3pm & 5:30pm–9pm; Su 9am–3pm
Parking: Street
Phone: 808-572-4877

Matteo's Pizzeria *(Italian/Pizza)*

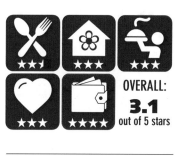

OVERALL:
3.1
out of 5 stars

We used to go to ***Matteo's*** when we were in the mood for moderately priced (for Wailea) pasta and sandwiches and wanted to eat outside with a view. We're sad to say the value has dropped here, and the love has left much of the food (although they're still the smiley-est of kitchens). Overlooking the golf course and perched just above The Shops at Wailea, it is still an uber-popular place for families looking for a break from resort prices. Uber-popular is another way of saying: expect a line out the door during regular meal times.

So many tables and plastic chairs have been squeezed into the dining area that now the only view now is of the party you're sitting next to — or nearly on top of. While we appreciated the self-service aspect (you order at the entrance, take a number, and a server delivers your food to the table) as a cost-saving measure that benefits both the owner and the customer, we aren't as fond of other measures: garlic bread made from hoagie rolls, for example.

The owner is from Italy via the Four Seasons resort down the street and

continued on next page

Matteo's Pizzeria *(continued)*

he can cook a mean lamb ragu when he's in the mood. Too often, he's not.

Classics that used to be hearty and tasty — the eggplant and chicken parmesan for example — are have become sloppy in their preparation and overly salted. Too often, they're overcooked. If you believe in cheese, you're in luck, because most everything comes with it.

Salads remain a good choice — they're fresh and the simple oil and the vinegar dressing is nice. The vine-ripened Maui tomatoes served with the Caprese are lovely accentuated by a balsamic glaze and basil oil. The basil tomato sauce is still simple and made with a light hand. We also like the pink vodka sauce, which is rich without being cloying.

If we're getting pizza, we ask them to lighten up on the cheese, and we choose the "thick" crust. The thin crust, while it has its fans, doesn't hold a candle to **Flatbread's**.

The pizza is still decent and the prices are still fair, given the restaurant's well-heeled address. We just wish popularity hadn't gone to this restaurant's head.

Address: 100 Wailea Ike Dr., Wailea, South Maui
Meals: Lunch, Dinner
Hours: M-F 11:30am-9pm; Sa-Su 5pm-9pm
Parking: Lot
Phone: 808-874-1234
Website: www.matteospizzeria.com

OVERALL:

3.6

out of 5 stars

$

Maui Bake Shop & Deli *(Bakery, deli)*

In a 100-year-old building with a massive brick oven, pastry chef Jose Krall turns out decent breads, delectable pastries, satisfying breakfasts and savory sandwiches. Closed for several years before its recent renovation, expansion and reopening, **Maui Bake Shop** is even better than before.

Now, in addition to faultless croissants and Italian espresso, you can enjoy a Monte Cristo (!!) or a crab Benedict for breakfast, along with excellent coffee. James's heart nearly stopped the first time we found a complimentary, fresh *Wall Street Journal* on our Saturday morning breakfast table. If you're heading out for a morning hike in Iao Valley, this is the place to come for breakfast beforehand. Or stop for a hearty French dip or pastrami sandwich for lunch afterwards. Or do both. The menu is large enough to explore over a couple of visits.

We can't say enough about the pastries, which are European (don't look for a big pie or cake — tarts and tortes are the norm). Beautiful and yummy: we love the macaroons, and the checkerboard cookies, and the strawberry shortcake ... and ... and ... and during the holiday season, there are yule logs, marzipan animals, and breads shaped like crabs!

Maui Bake Shop & Deli *(continued)*

The lines can get long, and the same person taking your order is likely to bring it to your table, so things can slow down — but, still, it is definitely worth a stop.

Address: 2092 West Vineyard St., Wailuku, Central Maui
Location: At the corner of North Church Street
Meals: Breakfast, Lunch, Dinner
Hours: M–Sat 6am–2pm
Parking: Street, Lot
Phone: 808-242-0064

Maui Brewing Company Brew Pub *(American)*

 Beer lovers should absolutely visit **Maui Brewing Company Brew Pub**, the island's only microbrewery. The sustainably-minded company crafts excellent, national award-winning brews, and we especially recommend the pale, clean-flavored Bikini Blonde and the dark chocolatey CoCoNut Porter.

Ordering a flight of beer lets you sample several at once — including the short-run beers that are only available here. We like getting a flight when we sit at the bar, because they line up the little glasses — maybe two ounces each — on the three inch wide strip of eternally-regenerating ice that circles the bar and keeps the drinks cool.

The food menu is standard pub fare, decently made. We like their slider, a small Maui Cattle Company burger that is well made and perfect with a beer. The fish and chips platter is good: a beer batter, of course, and we appreciate the well-executed traditional taste and light, fluffy, crunchy crust. The same holds true for the beer battered onion rings. If you haven't had enough beer by the time dessert comes around, the CoCoNut Porter float — a scoop of ice cream with the porter poured over it — is an ingenious response to the root beer float. (For those who don't imbibe, they also make actual root beer. While too sweet for our taste, we love that it's made with cane sugar, honey and vanilla bean, all grown on Maui.) We also like the Baby Cake, a chocolate cake made with CoCoNut Porter.

[A note about CoCoNut Porter: it lends itself to both drinking and baking due to its complex, deep, dark flavors of chocolate, malt, and sometimes we taste honey. Made with toasted coconut and winner of several national and international awards, it's really something special.]

The brew pub looks like a brew pub should: concrete floors, long tables, high-ceilings and lamps made from — what else? — tiny kegs. It is buzzy-sounding from the people and the televisions over the big u-shaped bar, and you shouldn't come if you're looking for a romantic meal. You should come for the beer and to get away from the palm trees, wine lists, and pretentions so easily found elsewhere. Service is best if you sit at the bar.

continued on next page

Maui Brewing Company Brew Pub *(continued)*

If you love the beer, you can get it at many grocery stores around the island. Don't bother looking for bottles, as this ecologically-friendly company chooses to can their brew so that it travels better, recycles easier, and keeps the beer fresher. Also consider stopping in to their tasting room at their brewery down the road in Lahaina. If you like what you taste, share the Aloha by asking local stores back home to carry their brews.

Address: 4405 Honoapiilani Hwy, Kahana, West Maui
Location: Kahana Gateway
Meals: Lunch, Dinner, Late-Night
Hours: Daily 11am–12am
Parking: Lot
Phone: 808-669-3474
Website: www.mauibrewingco.com

Maui Coffee Roasters *(Coffeehouse)*

We like *Maui Coffee Roasters* because, in addition to serving their own roast (which you can buy, of course), they make excellent, fresh sandwiches and salads. They aren't fancy, but they're simple and straightforward and made with care. You have to wait a while for your food, but you get your coffee right away (they put it out in a coffee bar). For breakfast, there's an insane bagel sandwich with egg, cheddar cheese and jalapeno that will stoke your fire — if you can handle it. The casual, arty coffeehouse atmosphere attracts everyone from students to business people and lends itself to working on the laptop, chatting with companions or quietly reading a paper. This is our favorite place to hang out in Kahului when we're not running errands. From 2-6pm they host "Happy Cappy Hour," during which their commendably crafted cappuccinos are only $1.

Address: 444 Hana Hwy., Kahului, Central Maui
Meals: Breakfast, Lunch, Snacks & Treats
Hours: M–F 7am–6pm; Sa 8am–5pm; Su 8am–2:30pm
Parking: Lot
Phone: 808-877-2877
Website: www.mauicoffeeroasters.com

Maui Culinary Academy Food Court and "Class Act"

The University of Hawaii - Maui College runs the *Maui Culinary Academy*, a respectable cooking school. The students — who in just a little while will be on the line at some of the island's best restaurants — have to practice, practice, and practice. One of the ways they do this is by making all of the food court offerings, which makes it one of the best lunch places

Maui Culinary Academy Food Court and "Class Act" *(continued)*

in central Maui.

The dining room is a noisy cafeteria with big round tables, so if you're thinking of sitting by yourself, think again. You'll find sandwiches, sushi, a great salad bar, hot entrées, and pastries, all at student prices (average $3-7 per person). The food court is open every weekday during the college term, and it's kind of fun to see how eager the students in their chef whites are to make sure you're happy with your meal. Be sure to take a spin by the pastry room windows at the far end of the cafeteria, where you can gawk at the student's creative attempts at wedding cakes.

If you're looking for a more upscale lunch, on Wednesdays and Fridays the students serve a four course meal in *Class Act*, their snazzy restaurant upstairs, which actually has a darn nice view of Kahului Harbor. Seating is limited, so be sure to call for reservations. If you forget, you can snag a seat at the bar. To be clear, this is a class, not a restaurant — it's only open when class is actually in session. Every week it's a different cuisine, based on what skills the students are honing. At only $30, participating as a guinea pig diner is a great deal. Call for menus, dates, and reservations. The academy also produces its own line of culinary products: flavored sugars and salts, salt rubs, jellies, and a terrific cookbook filled with recipes representing the island's full range of ethnic flavors.

Address: 310 W. Kaahumanu Ave., Pa'ina Building,
Maui Culinary Academy, Kahului, Central Maui
Meals: Lunch
Hours: (Food Court) M-F 11am-12:30pm when school is in session;
(A Class Act) when class is in session
Parking: Lot
Phone: 808-984-3280
Website: www.mauiculinary-campusdining.com

Maui Tacos *(Mexican)*

Maui Tacos was the brainchild of Mark Ellman, the superior Maui chef (***Mala, Penne Pasta***, and ***Honu***). It has since become a national chain, but the Maui locations — of which there are several — are still making every dish to order and using good, fresh ingredients. Has the love left, now that Mark Ellman is no longer in charge? Yes, but not completely.

The "surf" burritos, tacos, and plate lunch dishes come with beans and rice. As many Californians point out, this is not true Mexican, but it's still good, inexpensive, fast food. There are numerous vegetarian options and the huevos rancheros breakfast is pretty tasty. The salsa bar features homemade salsas in a range of spices and flavors. There are also pickled carrots and sweet Maui onions. If you're looking for a quick bite while shopping or after the beach, this is a popular choice.

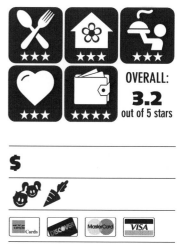

continued on next page

Maui Tacos (continued)

Address: 840 Wainee St., Lahaina Square, Lahaina, West Maui
Meals: Lunch, Dinner
Hours: Daily 10am–8pm
Parking: Street
Phone: 808-661-8883
Website: www.mauitacos.com

Address: 275 Kaahumanu Ave., Kahului, Central Maui
Location: Queen Kaahumanu Center
Meals: Breakfast, Lunch, Dinner
Hours: Daily 9am–9pm
Parking: Lot
Phone: 808-871-7726

Address: 247 Pi'ikea Ave., Kihei, South Maui
Location: Pi'ilani Village Shopping Center
Meals: Breakfast, Lunch, Dinner
Hours: Daily 9am–8pm
Parking: Lot
Phone: 808-875-9340

Address: 5095 Napilihau St., Napili, West Maui
Location: Napili Plaza
Meals: Breakfast, Lunch, Dinner
Hours: Daily 9am–8pm
Parking: Lot
Phone: 808-665-0222

Address: 2411 S. Kihei Rd., Kihei, South Maui
Location: Kamaole Beach Center
Meals: Breakfast, Lunch, Dinner
Hours: Daily 9am–8pm
Parking: Lot
Phone: 808-879-5005

OVERALL:

3

out of 5 stars

Maui Thai *(Thai)*

Maui Thai is in the way back of the Rainbow Mall and serves OK Thai food at decent prices. We like their wide chow fun noodles with chicken or shrimp, their red pineapple curry, and their peanut-y panang curry. The atmosphere is forgettable, but the service is good. This is an acceptable choice — but no replacement for — driving to Kukui Mall to check out ***Thailand Cuisine***. (You know, it's not *that* far.)

Address: 2439 S. Kihei Rd., Kihei, South Maui
Location: Rainbow Mall
Meals: Lunch, Dinner

Maui Thai *(continued)*

Hours: M–F 11am–2:30pm; Nightly 5pm till closing
Parking: Lot
Phone: 808-874-5605
Website: www.mauithai.com

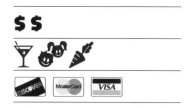

Merriman's Kapalua *(Pacific Rim)*

By all rights **Merriman's Kapalua** should be one of the best restaurants on the island. Chef Owner Peter Merriman is a founder of Hawaiian Regional Cuisine and famous for his eponymous restaurant on the Big Island of Hawaii. He's also played a big part in encouraging local farmers to raise delicious and organic produce. Unfortunately, all of the passion and quality we associate with him have not been coming through in the food or the service at this very expensive restaurant. The restaurant's record was 0 for 8, until our most recent visit, right before publication. Now they are 1 for 9.

Chef Merriman has been doing something right at his flagship Waimea restaurant, which is as popular as it was twenty years ago, so perhaps sending his top chef over to the Kapalua location is an attempt to correct some of the problems that have plagued this restaurant (desperately salty food, poor execution of otherwise decent-seeming recipes, startlingly bad service).

Rather than go over our many notes on failed dishes and dismal evenings, we'll give you the highlights of this one last visit, in hopes that it augurs a shift in the restaurant's potential to live up to its stunning, jewel-like setting.

This *is* one of the prettiest places on Maui. Located on Kapalua Bay, its dark wood, open walls, gentle breezes, shimmery tiled ceiling make an enchanting place to dine. There's an enormous lanai below the restaurant, complete with a copper fire pit, and sitting out there under the deep dark spangly night sky is enchanting. On the night in question, we didn't sit out here, but we had occasion to skirt its edges, more than once, due to an odd automobile situation.

We have mixed feelings about mandatory valet parking, and this evening demonstrated one reason why. As we pulled in, the lot had plenty of room, partly because there were so many cars parked on the circular drive, tilted, half on the curb. Not interested in putting our car in what looked like a precarious position, we asked if we could park ourselves, and the valet directed us to the public beach next door. Fine. Well, it *would* have been fine, if he'd also indicated how to *find* the restaurant from the lot in the dark. The lot is fenced and without lighting: we were at a loss. Ultimately, we hiked up a steep grass slope to enter **Merriman's** from the back. Not an auspicious start to our evening.

We perked up when led to a table against the rail, where a handful of other diners also clustered. (The bar area, on the other hand, fairly bustled.) Our waiter appeared promptly and rattled off the specials, answering our questions with knowledge and friendly competence. We ordered cocktails and a few items. *continued on next page*

Merriman's Kapalua *(continued)*

We started with the pupu taster, which is a large square platter with four small plates, each containing one of the evening's featured appetizers. It arrived within minutes — almost suspiciously fast — and before our cocktails. The offerings were fine, with a few exceptions. The best was the miniature tomato salad: a vibrant tomato topped with a smear of avocado cream and morsels of Keahole lobster. The tempura-fried goat cheese was a pleasant ball of warm, creamy chevre (local, from Surfing Goat Dairy) with a thin crisp crust, too-sparsely garnished with slivered onions in mint vinaigrette and strawberry. The Kalua pig and sweet onion quesadilla was standard fare, enlivened just slightly by the house-made kim chee and a liquefied mango chili dipping sauce. The ahi sashimi was disappointing — a tad mealy, as if it had been sitting for a while — and the accompanying pohole fern and tomato salad was limp and duller in color than we expect. Pohole ferns are crunchy and bright green when fresh and degrade to a duller color and gummy texture when they've sat for too long. These weren't yet old, but they certainly weren't fresh, and looked and tasted as if they'd been made too early in the day to serve now.

The lobster bisque was beautiful: cinnabar liquid studded with creamy white chunks. It tasted delicious, too — but calling it lobster bisque is a cruel joke. There was no lobster ... at least not in the flesh. The sumptuous, tomato-based broth must have been cooked with lobster shells, as it had a rich, unmistakably lobster-y aroma ... but those creamy white chunks were not lobster meat. They were hearts of palm. Their stiff crunch felt like a trick. We flagged down our waiter to ask "Where's the lobster?"

No luck. Our server was clearly feeling stretched too thin, and was simply not available. It was then that we realized we had never received our cocktails. Was this an issue at the bar, or had the order never been placed? We never found out (or got a drink). As the next course arrived, practically on the heels of our "lobster" bisque, we gave up on solving the mysteries of soup and spirits.

Our half portion of the opakapaka special arrived, which was lovely, moist and flaky, beneath its thick, crunchy crust of sesame seeds. A nice hint of heat emerged with each bite, and we delighted in the light but chewy morsels of eggplant spaetzle that surrounded the filet. Properly cooked fish, we noted; a nice change from the raw-in-the-middle or rubbery-like-a-tire preparations we've had here previously.

Lamb is served in a different fashion each night, and tonight's edition featured both meat from the leg (grilled) and shoulder (stewed). The lamb was cooked perfectly. The leg meat had a prime char and a nice honeyed taste — evidence of a quality spice rub. The shoulder was tender and bursting with flavor, and the complex, thick sauce was punctuated by star anise. The seasonings were perfect — not even a pinch too much salt — and the smooth-whipped garlic mashed potatoes and gently braised kale were both just lovely. Hurrah!

Desserts have traditionally been very good here, and we were pleased to find that this is still true. The chocolate purse dessert is the deepest, darkest, most decadent we've ever had and beats out ***Roy's*** chocolate soufflé for

Merriman's Kapalua *(continued)*

flavor, texture, and certainly for creativity. A cinched pocket of baked phyllo dough gives way to dark, mousse-like Waialua chocolate. The ribbons of Earl-Grey-scented caramel decorating the plate are a perfect enhancement to the chocolate and phyllo, along with a vanilla ice cream speckled with bits of bean.

Overall, the evening was a marginal success. Dishes were decent, although we can't say anything was over-the-top outstanding (and some of those appetizers did not feel prepared to order, and the hearts-of-palm-for-lobster trick still galled). The portions were exactly enough to sate our hunger. Service was spotty, but not so much that it ruined our experience. We weren't angry or defeated, as we have been at the end of previous meals. We really *want* to like this restaurant, and we really don't want to see it sink into the [tourist] trap: relying on the romantic location to feed its guests. With this new menu, the kitchen has taken steps in the right direction. Perhaps things are turning around.

We were in for one final shock, however. When the bill arrived, we were stunned by the $40 charge for the half order of opakapaka. Since the average price of full-size entrées listed on the menu was $37, we could hardly have expected a half portion to exceed that. Upon inquiry, we learned that the full portion of opakapaka cost $47. Had we known, we certainly would have opted to pay seven dollars more for double the amount of fish. We felt tricked — again. At least they didn't charge us for the drinks we'd never had.

On our way out, we scrambled back down the hillside, along with another couple struggling even more than we were. A few strong lanterns are needed before someone takes a tumble. Back in our car — safely parked on level ground — we agreed that we cannot recommend this restaurant with confidence, yet, but that we can raise their ratings, slightly, conservatively. Perhaps **Merriman's Kapalua** is addressing some of its problems — most of which are pretty basic. We certainly hope so, because this location — and your taste buds — are worth a great restaurant.

Address: 1 Bay Drive, Kapalua, West Maui
Location: in the Bay Club
Meals: Dinner
Hours: Daily 5:00pm - 9:00pm; Bar Menu, Su- Sa 3:00pm - 8:30pm;
Happy Hour, M- F 3:00pm - 4:30pm
Parking: Valet
Phone: 808-669-6400
Website: www.merrimanshawaii.com

Milagros Food Co. *(Mexican)*

Milagros is our go-to place when we want an island-style Tex-Mex meal made with fresh ingredients accompanied by a killer margarita. The only problem is getting a table at this super-popular, super-visible corner restaurant in Paia. Note to

continued on next page

OVERALL:
3.4
out of 5 stars

OVERALL:
3.2
out of 5 stars

CASH

Milagros Food Co. *(continued)*

Texans: we know that this is not real Tex-Mex. There is no real Tex-Mex on the island. Want to move here and open a restaurant? That would be great!

What this *is*, is well-prepared, generously portioned food. We love the blackened ahi taquitos, which are spicy and tender inside their super-crispy tortilla shells. The fish sandwich comes with an excellent cut of sashimi-grade ahi, and you can get it blackened. The burgers are generous and satisfying.

The salad plates are more like platters, and the baby spinach salad with seared ahi on top is the perfect light lunch, with leftovers. The enchiladas are excellent, especially the spicy shrimp and seafood versions. The ahi tacos are strangely delicious. We say strange because who would've ever thought that adding avocado and sweet chili sauce to a fish taco would be such a slam-dunk? We love the big chunks of fish, but sometimes suspect that they aren't always the freshest. And we resent that the prices spike in the evening for the same dish. But that hasn't dissuaded us yet. Breakfasts are average but beautiful in the morning air.

The outdoor seating is hot in the sun (depending upon the angle, the awning doesn't shade the whole lanai), but perfectly cool at night and in the morning. The people-watching on that active corner is hard to beat. The inside seating is cramped and unpleasant. The drinks are strong, and we already mentioned the margaritas, but we will again, because these (any of these) are the best on Maui. They stock an impressive array of top shelf tequilas, including anejo, reposado, and plata varieties.

By the way, Happy Hour drink specials can be had from 11am-6pm.

Address: 3 Baldwin Ave., Paia, North Shore
Location: Corner of Baldwin and Hana Highway
Meals: Breakfast, Lunch, Dinner
Hours: Daily 8am-10pm
Parking: Street
Phone: 808-579-8755
Website: www.milagrosfoodcompany.com

Mixed Plate *(Mexican / Local / Plate Lunch)*

Mixed Plate in the Pukalani shopping center has a split personality: half plate lunch place and half taqueria. The Mexican owner makes wonderful tamales (a little heavy on the masa, but generally full of flavor) and her chipotle pork or chicken mole and are not to be missed. Unfortunately, you're more than likely to miss both exquisite dishes, because since the restaurant relocated to this spot, the chef shifted the menu towards her local plate lunch clientele and away from slowly simmered Mexican heaven. You can still get a few South of the Border specialties: tacos, enchiladas (and mole if you call ahead) — but the buffet is now dedicated to fried chicken and chili poppers. If you're exploring upcountry and need a snack — the $2 tamales are a delicious option. Make sure to get some super-sonic hot sauce on the side.

Mixed Plate *(continued)*

Address: 55 Pukalani St., Pukalani, Upcountry
Location: In the Pukalani Terrace Center
Meals: Breakfast, Lunch
Hours: M–Sa 6am–3:30pm
Parking: Lot
Phone: 808-572-8258

Moana Bakery & Café

Moana Bakery & Café is adjacent to the *Mana Foods* parking lot, and it's worth heading over for a meal or at least an espresso and pastry to go.

We'll start with the pastries, which are excellent. The apple strudel is filled with more apples than anything else, and the crust flakes off under the slightest pressure from your fingers. That is a satisfying event on an island with so few pastry shops. You can also get a cherry strudel — fresh made — and a coconut empanada, which is a kind of turnover filled with a luscious coconut filling.

Breakfast is wonderful here, and it's our favorite place to stop on the way down from sunrise at Haleakala Crater or the way out on the Road to Hana. The burritos are hearty and filling and the eggs Benedict — including several vegetarian versions — are well-made. We like the guava mimosas and the spicy bloody Mary's.

The barista and bartenders know what they're doing — when you can get their attention. Prices are a little spendy, but at least the quality of the food and the portions match them.

All ingredients are as fresh and local as possible, and at dinner, the lively kitchen sends out many fresh fish dishes, an excellent rack of lamb, and many vegetarian dishes: spicy Thai noodles, pesto pasta, etc. There's eclectic live entertainment (call for the schedule, or you might get stuck with an amateur open mic night when you were hoping for sultry jazz) and local art on the walls. The restaurant rambles from the big front windows to a rather dark exhibition kitchen, and if you have a big party you won't feel too crowded. Service is Paia style — which means very cute, but equally (if not more so) slow.

OVERALL:
3.2
out of 5 stars

$ $

Address: 71 Baldwin Ave., Paia, North Shore
Meals: Breakfast, Lunch, Dinner, Snacks & Treats
Hours: Daily 8am–9pm; Su–M 4pm – till closing
Parking: Lot, Street
Phone: 808-579-9999
Website: www.moanacafe.com

OVERALL:

3.2

out of 5 stars

MonkeyPod Kitchen by Merriman
(Hawaii Regional Cuisine)

Hip marketing is a science in this new Wailea restaurant. The décor is stylish, bright, and fun, with surfboards hanging from the rafters and Japanese fishing floats rising in a motionless tide behind the bar. The clever logo may be too clever: two readers have earnestly asked if we have eaten at "MonkeyPoo" ... because the "d" is so close in size to the "o." The logo decorates a raft of merchandise waiting just inside the door, next to the typically cheerful host/ess. The staff here tends to believe in the product. We want to believe in it too — it's just so darn cute — we just wish the execution were more consistent.

Their ambitions are high. They broadly announce a commitment to local and sustainable produce, meats, and fish on the menu, website, and in their tableside talk. The menu reads well, filled with tempting items in nearly every category: pizza, burgers, inventive appetizers and salads. Their beer list is incredible.

The actual food too often disappoints. We've had OK calamari, and it's not hard to put a smile on the face when truffle oil and parmesan cheese is sprinkled on fries. The first time we had a roasted butternut squash pizza with caramelized onions, rosemary, and pine nuts, we yummed and oohed and ahhed. Every other time we've had it we've been struck by mealy squash and bland flavors. How does this happen? Lack of love. (In general the pizzas are undistinguished, except for, perhaps, their excess of cheese.)

The slider trio, a much-recommended appetizer, consists of three bland burgers dressed differently from each other and made from different types of patties (we've had crab, kalua pig, beef, and on another occasion, taro). We are bored with all three equally.

The pumpkin ravioli is normally quite decadent: roasted squash (a favorite ingredient here — but it could always stand a little more roasting) with chevre, spinach, and sage brown butter. Unfortunately, it's been served to us tasting like rancid butter — leaving us to wonder if anyone consistently inspects or tastes the food before it leaves the kitchen.

The fish tacos are three corn tortillas with small portions of fish, Tex-mex roasted tomato salsa, a sprinkling of cilantro and a squirt of lightweight avocado crème. Flavor?

We've had the dry mein noodles on four different occasions. The first and third times, we loved them. The Iwamoto Natto saimin noodles (made in Paia by long-time noodle makers) were firm and yellow with just the right chewiness. Tamarind added a nice accent to the dressing. The green beans were a pert and lively green; they popped in the mouth. The Tamashiro tofu (from another local purveyor) was soft and pillowy; a nice contrast to the other textures. Unfortunately, our other encounters with this dish have left us disappointed. No pop, no contrast. The noodles are consistently good — but the love quotient is too inconsistent to recommend the preparations.

The fresh gnocchi is lovely on its own, but is buried under so many sautéed mushrooms, chard, tomato sauce, and chevre that it soups up — before you can finish, the gnocchi is soggy.

MonkeyPod Kitchen by Merriman *(continued)*

Speaking of soggy, the only time the pie crust has a texture — other than "cardboard" — is when the filling separates and soaks it. This is sad — not only because we love pie (see ***Leoda's Kitchen and Pie Shop***) but because the servers are so excited about "only having cream pies" for dessert. Why is this a good thing? We've had banana, chocolate, vanilla, and strawberry, and they all suffer from a strange lack of flavor. Cream pie doesn't have much texture ... so eating bland versions is akin to swallowing a light and airy spoonful of spackle.

The servers are generally tone-deaf to whatever's happening at the table, and seem oblivious when dishes are sent back nearly untouched. We've asked two where they have worked before, and both have said they were "in finance" in New York before moving here and getting this gig ... so perhaps they just don't realize that when food is good, it's eaten.

Despite the inconsistency, this restaurant attracts a surprising number of people in its prime location at the head of Wailea. Our suggestion is to go here for drinks at Happy Hour. Good money was spent on a space-age cooling system designed to keep brews at the perfect temperature, and the selection is serious — almost Bostonian. The cocktail recipes are original, including a much-lauded Mai Tai topped with lilikoi foam.

The restaurant seems to realize this is their strongest offering: the bar offers two Happy Hours complete with drink specials, from 3pm to 5:30pm and again from 9pm to closing.

PS: If you are wondering if the "Merriman" in the name is Chef Peter Merriman, it is.

Address: 10 Gateway Plaza, Kihei, South Maui
Location: In the Wailea Gateway Plaza, where the Pi'ilani Hwy meets Wailea Ike Drive
Meals: Lunch, Dinner
Hours: Daily 11:30am-11pm
Parking: parking lot
Phone: 808-891-2322
Website: www.monkeypodkitchen.com

Monsoon India *(Indian)*

Most attempts at Indian cuisine on Maui are futile stabs in the dark or unwitting happy accidents. That's why we're so blissed out, man, that the nicest server on the island, Hari, and his Chef Bindeshor rescued the rather odd location at Menehune Shores in North Kihei and kept it Indian with ***Monsoon India***.

The symphony of flavor in Indian *masalas* (spice blends) makes our eyes water and our taste buds intone "Namaste." Sweet and pungent cardamom, nutty and citrusy coriander, earthy and warm cumin ... you must surrender

OVERALL:
3.8
out of 5 stars

$ $

continued on next page

your taste buds completely to get just how special they are. The explosive feeling in the mouth — on the tongue, under the tongue, in all corners of the cheeks, at the back of the throat, even into the sinuses — can take some getting used to. But once you submit to the spices, you crave them.

Monsoon India's masalas are timid for our taste — is it the condo location? — which is why we were grateful when on our first trip Hari gently suggested we order everything "hot" ... we suggest you do the same if you're hoping to clear your sinuses. (Every curry can be prepared to your preferred spice level: mild, medium, or hot.)

The menu is simple, well-organized, and explains Indian so well that even the most cautious diners can feel confident. Our personal favorites include the masala curry — sprightly tomatoes and velvety cream blended with herbs and spices — which is delicious with either their tandoor oven-roasted chicken or the pillowy shrimp. The chicken korma is creamy and soothing. We also like the saag, finely chopped spinach with cream and spices, with tender lamb. The samosas (dumplings with meat or veggie fillings) are perfectly crispy on the outside and moist inside. The mango chutney is just spicy enough to offset the fruit's sweetness; we could eat it with a spoon.

We would like to spend three paragraphs on the naan (but we won't). On an island where most bread is fair to middling, eating this fluffy-crispy Indian flatbread is heaven. We like the garlic and the cheese versions, but we get a basket of plain to go with our meals so they don't interfere with the spices in the dishes. Every visit finds the rice pudding creamier and more nurturing with its hint of cardamom. The mango lassi — a traditional yogurt drink — is tangy, mellow, and sweet.

Despite the urgency in a name like ***Monsoon India***, the kitchen tends to be slow (don't come with low blood sugar and order samosas immediately). The servers are sweet, sometimes overwhelmed, but usually open your BYOB wine or beer without being prompted (bring your own, as there is no liquor license at this time). The live music (jazz and Hawaiian standards) on Saturdays and every other Tuesday night adds elegance and calm to the sometimes rushed feeling of the service. The open-air restaurant is so breezy our napkins blow away, which is too bad because the view of the West Maui Mountains makes us drool. Their budget (or building permit) must not allow for good lighting at night ... but ... STOP. The bottom line is this: the food and the smile on Hari's face render our complaints nitpicky.

This is lovely food served by lovely people in full sight of one of the loveliest views on the island. Visit on Sundays for a brunch buffet — and locals, heads up: they now deliver tiffin lunch packs (minimum of ten) and pick up the empties later.

Address: 760 S. Kihei Rd., Kihei, South Maui
Location: Menehune Shores condos in North Kihei
Meals: Lunch, Dinner
Hours: Daily 11:30am- 2:30pm, Dinner 5pm- 9pm Su Lunch Buffet 11:30am-3pm
Parking: Lot
Phone: 808-875 6666
Website: www.monsoonindiamaui.com

Moose McGillycuddy's *(American)*

The American classics at **Moose's** (burgers, sandwiches, steaks, fish) are supplemented with Americanized ethnic foods (fajitas and pastas). The purpose of this restaurant is to feed you large portions of average food while plying you with average drinks and two-for-one coupons for breakfast (look in the tourist magazines) — but also to give you a killer view and fresh breezes in your hair. The Happy Hour specials, late night dining, and good breakfasts are definitely bonuses. Service, unfortunately, is inconsistent, but the second story locations make for expansive and pleasant views that take the sting out of waiting for your drink.

Moose's is worth visiting if you're in the mood for a bar scene and a drink special. We also like the breakfasts at both locations because the focus is on good food and big quantities (which is important at breakfast). This is where we take our less adventurous relatives when they come to visit, they love it.

Address: 2511 S. Kihei Rd., Kihei, South Maui
Location: Above Fred's Mexican Café
Meals: Breakfast, Lunch, Dinner, Late-Night
Hours: Daily 7:30am–1am
Parking: Lot, Street
Phone: 808-891-8600
Website: www.mooserestaurantgroup.com

Address: 844 Front St., Lahaina, West Maui
Meals: Breakfast, Lunch, Dinner, Happy Hour, Late-Night
Hours: Daily 7:30am–1:30am
Parking: Street
Phone: 808-667-7758

Mulligans on the Blue *(American)*

Mulligans on the Blue has a beautiful view. It's halfway up the rolling green golf course, and the sunset is sweeping and nurtures the soul. There's a lot of live music and plenty of famous musicians hang out here (and one or two have thought of buying it for themselves). The menu lists typical pub fare like shepherd's pie (no), and burgers (yes), but the food is beside the point. Drinking a pint of tapped Guinness counts as a meal, right?

"Right," say our Irish friends back home, unless they insist on drinking Murphy's instead. At **Mulligans**, both are on tap (because we're in Hawaii, not Boston, so we don't have to choose sides in the stout controversy).

Service is not good, especially during concerts when the music is loud and the waitresses are overwhelmed by the number of diners and drinkers. We recommend if you order a few appetizers to go with your beer, you order everything up front and plan on going back to the bar to get your refills from the source.

continued on next page

Mulligans on the Blue *(continued)*

There are as many games on as there are televisions (we counted eight at last visit), and the bar opens at 8am on the weekends so sports fans can have their oatmeal while they watch their favorite team.

Address: 100 Kaukahi St., Wailea, South Maui
Location: on the Wailea Blue Course
Meals: Breakfast, Lunch, Dinner, Late-Night
Hours: M-F 10am-1am; Sa-Su 8am-1am
Parking: Lot
Phone: 808-874-1131
Website: www.mulligansontheblue.com

Nick's Fishmarket *(Pacific Rim)*

One time we sat down at **Nick's** and watched three servers collide over one water glass as they rushed to be the first to fill it. We wouldn't mention it if it weren't such a perfect illustration of our general experience of **Nick's** over the years: the overeager service and romantic, delightful ambience will never, ever make up for the unforgivably expensive, mostly bland food.

The food sounds promising — especially the signature dishes, like the tempura ahi rolls and the wasabi-beurre blanc laced fish of the day. But the ahi in the ahi roll is gray around the edges and has lost most of that pleasant red-pink of fresh sushi, and three hours later we're still finding gummy bits of tempura in our teeth. (Did they make the roll, flash-fry it, refrigerate it, and then serve it hours later? We don't know, but we can't imagine how else crispy tempura gets so mushy.) The scallops are only seared on one side (why?) and the sauce is their standard beurre blanc, which usually begins to separate by the time it gets to the table.

The menu reads like a shopping list at a gourmet store — each dish features at least one item (if not two or three) designed to trigger your "wow — that's expensive!" reflex. We're not against upscale or luxurious ingredients, of course ... far from it. But too often, the combinations just don't work. Too many flavors competing for our attention — and too little satisfaction. Each plate is designed to appeal to the eye with elaborate flourishes and a rainbow of colors, but ultimately these are beautiful but empty promises.

Dessert is often better — get the flaming strawberries, as trite as it may sound, or the bananas Foster — and we really like their Kona coffee. We appreciate the excellent wine list, but this, like everything else, is overpriced.

The servers are exceptionally friendly, although so hurried we've seen chairs knocked into and drinks slopping over the lips of glasses as they stop short. They have also picked up the excruciatingly bad habit of asking "how does everything taste" during dinner. Or worse, lately: "Everything is great, right?" How can you say "no," to someone who just filled your water glass after each sip you took? They're just doing their job.

The setting could not be in a more perfect location. The koi pond at the

Nick's Fishmarket *(continued)*

Fairmont Kea Lani is our favorite place in any Maui resort, and passing by it to get to the restaurant is a pleasure. The interior of the restaurant is like a dream of upscale luxury, and the sunset views of the pools, grounds, and sea are fairytale romantic. They're just not enough.

For this reason, our sole recommendation is to come here just before sunset, during Happy Hour. From 5:00-6:30pm, specialty cocktails (mangotini, a good ginger martini) are **$6** and local brews are **$4**. Kick back a few oyster shooters (in a tomato gazpacho with a daub of cucumber sorbet), toast the gorgeous view, and head elsewhere for dinner.

Address: 4100 Wailea Alanui Dr., Wailea, South Maui
Location: Fairmont Kea Lani
Meals: Dinner
Hours: Daily 5:30pm-9:30pm
Parking: Valet, Lot
Phone: 808-879-7224
Website: www.nicksfishmarketmaui.com

Nikki's Pizza *(Pizza)*

Nikki's Pizza is one of the few places in Ka'anapali with good food priced proportionally. Pizzas are made to order (you can also get slices), there are enormous sandwiches and heroes, and pretty good shave ice (a little icy, but the best option if you're not driving down to Lahaina to try **Ululani's**).

Nikki's has carried us through several forgot-it's-lunchtime blood sugar crises. We like the Greek salad, which is fresh and crisp, and we like the calzones and the wraps.

The food court location is less than glamorous, but it is air conditioned. You can also sit outside, or, of course, get your food to go and eat it at your condo or on the beach.

Address: 2435 Ka'anapali Pkwy, Ka'anapali, West Maui
Location: Whaler's Village
Meals: Lunch, Dinner, Snacks & Treats
Hours: Daily 10:30am-9pm
Parking: Lot
Phone: 808-667-0333

OVERALL:
3.4
out of 5 stars

North Shore Café

This cute, quirky little café occupies an old plantation house. You sit on the lanai (the front porch), which might've been the living room at one time. The friendly, but not particularly genteel, service might have you feeling like family by the time you leave.

continued on next page

OVERALL:
3.6
out of 5 stars

North Shore Café *(continued)*

The prices are a nod to the locale: $5.75 for Haiku's telephone prefix and $8.08 for Hawaii's area code. The portions are extra-large, so it's no wonder the lanai fills up early with locals. It's a great value for satisfying breakfast fare with plenty of options — from steak and eggs to the quintessential loco moco (hamburger patty topped with gravy and a fried egg, over a huge mound of white rice).

We love that they have an omelet called "Kanak Attack," (in reference to kanaka maoli, or native Hawaiians) though we can't imagine finishing the three-egg marvel stuffed with ham, Portuguese sausage, bacon, Vienna sausages, onions, and cheese. Instead, we opt for the "Onolicious Latkes:" two hash browns with a bit of crab mixed in, topped with roasted vegetables, two poached eggs, and béarnaise sauce. Every variation of the standard eggs-toast-meat-potato breakfast is available, and organic eggs can be had for a few bucks extra.

Our excitement at trying the taro pancakes fizzled upon learning they're made from the grocery store mix, but they're only $1 apiece, if you want to try them. We prefer the macadamia nut short stack drizzled in pure maple syrup.

North Shore Café is a lovely window into life on Maui's windward side. Come here on your way to Hana, or just on a day exploring this less touristy, rainforested corner of paradise. Rub elbows with windsurfers and pig hunters alike. If you're caught by a brief but drenching Haiku shower upon leaving, look for the rainbow and count your blessings.

Address: 824 Kokomo Rd., Haiku
Location: Across from Haiku Cannery
Meals: Breakfast
Hours: Daily 7–2pm
Parking: small parking lot.
Phone: 808-575-2770
Website: www.northshorecafe.net

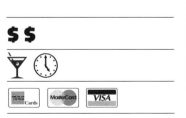

Ocean's Beach Bar & Grill *(American)*

Ocean's is a big sports bar in South Kihei that serves average food at average prices and opens up their big windows to let in plenty of light and air. It's as pleasant a sports bar as you'll find on Maui, with friendly (if inconsistent) service and good Happy Hour specials. Stop in if you want a brew and some company.

(But beware: they have Jagermeister *on tap* here.)

Address: 1819 S. Kihei Rd., Kihei, South Maui
Location: Kukui Mall
Meals: Lunch, Dinner
Hours: Daily 11am-2am (Kitchen closes at 10pm)
Parking: Lot
Phone: 808-891-2414

Ono Gelato *(Gelato/Ice Cream)*

Gelato, or Italian ice cream, is a most virtuous choice for a frozen treat. We will now prove this to you:

Most ice creams have air mixed into the final product to make it "lighter" and therefore "lower in calories" — but the reality is you're buying and eating air. Super-premium brands have less air, which accounts for their richer, denser texture and flavor (and higher price tag).

Gelato follows this logical process and leaves as much air *out* of the cream as possible. However, there is much less fat in gelato than in ice cream, and that's because — despite the dense, creamy texture — gelato is made with more milk (and less cream) and therefore has less fat!

A dense product creates dense flavors. Because the flavors are so strong, it's a very satisfying dessert, and we find we can barely finish anything larger than a small cup (automatic portion control).

There, that's our proof. *You're welcome.*

If you get the fruit flavored sorbets at **Ono Gelato**, one of our top dessert places, you'll be doing even more good for your body. Made with filtered water and local, organic, sustainable fruit, the flavors are intense and hard to find anywhere else. Try the tangerine in season (Molly loves it with vanilla or sour cream to make a creamsicle flavor), or the lilikoi (passion fruit), both of which are only made from local, organic fruit. The Kula strawberry is similarly luscious and usually available year round. We've seen dragonfruit, mango, lemon, lime, and raspberry, along with countless other tropical flavors. We never miss the dairy.

The dairy flavors use organic milk as a base, and with the exception of a few traditional Italian flavors that are imported from Italy (hazelnut, etc.) these are made from local ingredients. Try the sultry vanilla, the sour cream (tastes like cheesecake!), and pistachio (James's favorite). The Quark is another delicious choice. It's made with Surfing Goat Dairy cheese blended with lilikoi, for a lilikoi cheesecake flavor. We love the dulce de leche and the mint. If you want to combine flavors, they can pack two or three into even the smallest cups or cones, but of course they also have big waffle cones to fill up (if you can handle them). They are generous with samples.

The Kihei store tends to make more adventurous and less traditional flavor combinations — including some with brownies, cakes, and other baked goods made fresh in house. The owner of this store has also opened up a sister store, **Maui Gelato**, in Dolphin Plaza across from Kamaole Beach Park I. We like these stores in particular for their mini-sized waffle cones, cake popsicles, and "spirited" gelati flavors (try the limoncello, made with the local liqueur Mauicello).

All of the shops are bright, clean, and well stocked with plenty of pre-packed pints, gelato cakes (what a way to celebrate a birthday) and non-gelato items. In addition to the loose leaf teas, handmade local jelly beans, coffee, and t-shirts, the Lahaina location also serves stuffed croissants and cupcakes with patio seating out back that hangs over the ocean. We rarely pass up an opportunity to visit **Ono Gelato**.

continued on next page

Ono Gelato *(continued)*

Address: 115D Hana Hwy, Paia, North Shore
Meals: Snacks & Treats
Hours: Daily 11am - 10pm
Parking: Street
Phone: 808-579-9201
Website: www.onogelatocompany.com

Address: 815 Front St., Lahaina, West Maui
Meals: Snacks & Treats
Hours: Daily 11am - 10pm
Parking: Street
Phone: 808-495-0203

Address: 1280 S. Kihei Rd., Kihei, South Maui
Meals: Snacks & Treats
Hours: Daily 11am - 10pm
Parking: Lot
Phone: 808-495-0287

OVERALL:
4
out of 5 stars

Pacific'o *(Pacific Rim)*

Sitting on the rail at **Pacific'o** at Happy Hour makes us very, very ... happy.

There's a beautiful view of the beach and the harbor, and the sunset views are fantastic. If we're lucky we get to see a fresh-caught tuna carried from the beach landing where the fishermen sell their day's catch up through the restaurant and past our table. Add this "just caught" freshness to the rest of the menu, the vast majority of which is made with food grown on Chef Owner James McDonald's O'o Farm in Kula, and our foodie souls relax.

Thankfully, the recipes do justice to the quality of the ingredients. This is Pacific Rim at its best: local ingredients meet European and Asian flavors to fuse into plate after plate of food love (when the chefs are on their game, which is usually).

The appetizers and small dishes really shine. For example, we love the diver scallops roll. Scallops are seared golden brown, slathered with arugula pesto, and then rolled up with coconut rice, sliced, and bathed in a sauce made with citrusy yuzu and limes: perfect acidity to counter the sweetness.

Of all the tomato salads on the island, the tomato "stack" at **Pacific'o** is our favorite. Ripe tomato slices alternate with slabs of tangy, house-made buttermilk cheese and fresh basil leaves. They rise a few inches with artichoke hearts slipping in between a couple of layers. A carefully balanced vinaigrette made with roasted red peppers and curry is what really brings the flavors together — perfectly seasoning the sweet and tangy in the cheese and tomatoes.

Visitors go gaga over macadamia-nut-crusted fish, and **Pacific'o** dishes up

Pacific'o *(continued)*

our favorite version of it: a Thai peanut sauce, creamed up with coconut, is the perfect background to the tropical fruit salsa. Mahi mahi is good, but you can trust the server to steer you toward another fish if something special has come in. The Bling Bling dinner is a lovely Pacific Rim version of surf and turf: petite filet mignon paired with a poached lobster with a ginger butter sauce. The tempura asparagus that's served with this is crispy and light.

The Hapa/Hapa tempura appetizer is our favorite. The chef takes the two best fish of the day's catch, cuts them for sashimi (two big blocks of fish — hapa means half), wraps them in seaweed, flash fries them in tempura batter, and plates them side by side with a ying-yang of sauces. The white miso sauce is very good, but the brilliant lime basil sauce has us stealthily licking our fingers.

Chef McDonald's food is exuberant, fresh, and delicious, and if you haven't had Pacific Rim yet, this is a great place to try it. While we love the food at dinner, the ambience can suffer if you like quiet with your meal. Between the nearby *Feast at Lele* lu'au and the nightclub upstairs, timing your meal for romance can get tricksy. We do not come when we want quiet — we come when we want this food. If you want a more sedate experience, we highly recommend *Pacific'o* for either Happy Hour or lunch, when the menu is less complicated and also less expensive. We take a table on the rail to get a higher view and stay out of the sun (but then again, we live here).

Overall the service — while some individual servers are very good — can be lacking. We've seen hostesses flustered by walk-ins when the restaurant is empty and servers who size up guests who ask a lot of questions about the menu, as if dining is a foodie competition. (To be fair, we know plenty of foodies who like to catch a server in a mistake — if you're reading this, you know who you are. Stop it, relax, and enjoy your meal.)

It shouldn't be hard to relax at the far end of Lahaina, where the traffic is slower and the salt breeze wafts through the boutiques at 505 Front Street. *Pacific'o* (and *I'o*) benefit from some of the easiest, hassle-free parking: street parking, a free public lot, and an underground garage.

Pacific'o is a bright restaurant with good energy, both in and out of the kitchen. We come here when we want to digest some of that brightness ourselves. Special events here are usually over-the-top, because the party-patio atmosphere can't be had anywhere else, and Chef McDonald seems to really like hosting and cooking for a party. If they are hosting a film on the beach, having a special dinner, or doing any sort of a ticketed event, we recommend checking it out.

Address: 505 Front St., Lahaina, West Maui
Meals: Lunch, Dinner
Hours: Daily 11:30 am-9:30pm
Parking: Lot, Street
Phone: 808-667-4341
Website: www.PacificoMaui.com

$

Paia Fish Market *(American)*

This is a good place for a relatively quick fish burger. It doesn't look like it'll be quick when you see the line for the order counter or the packed communal tables, but somehow by the time you finish placing your order — or at least once your number is called and you get your food — seats will open up for you.

The menu is on the blackboard, and consists of seafood dishes and fish burgers, nearly magical for their sheer heft: it's impossible to purchase a filet that fat for the same price at a grocery store. Ignore the other offerings; they're mostly dismal.

You can get any fish you like for your burger, but we heartily recommend the opah, or the ono, which is a tender, white fish named for what it is — ono means "delicious." Opakapaka, or pink snapper, is another top choice, when available. A piece of grilled fish — perfectly cooked — is placed on a bun with homemade slaw (good), shredded cheese (commercial), and a tomato slice. No matter how many times we have this burger, we enjoy it well enough to stop talking for a few minutes so we can concentrate. You can get a single portion of shoestring fries with your burger, but we order the larger basket to share. They're nicely seasoned with spices and salt.

Address: 100 Hana Hwy., Paia, North Shore
Location: Corner of Baldwin and Hana Highway
Meals: Lunch, Dinner
Hours: Daily 11am-9:30pm
Parking: Street
Phone: 808-579-8030
Website: www.paiafishmarket.com

$ $

Penne Pasta *(Italian)*

Penne Pasta is a good choice for no-frills, no-surprises, well-priced Italian food. Well-known Maui chef Mark Ellman (***Mala*** and the brand new ***Honu***) opened this small, amiable eatery and then passed it on to his sous chef, who continues to cook the same authentic Italian — and some Italian-American — dishes for $18 or less. (In Lahaina? Yes. In Lahaina.)

The pastas are cooked al dente, and the sauces are homemade and taste that way (good). If you're from the East Coast and have a fondness for baked penne, the version here is cheesy and has good flavors (not completely bland like so many are). We like the bolognese sauce with its tender meat, and the slightly spicy meatballs. The house salad is very good and comes with an excellent piece of homemade crostini. Even better is the ample Nicoise salad, with roast potatoes, garlicky seared ahi, olives, and a lovely red onion Dijon vinaigrette. Pizzas are thin crusted and good. The oven-roasted squash is sweet and flavored with plenty of butter, sage, and almonds.

Penne Pasta *(continued)*

The daily specials are worth ordering. The regulars include a succulent roast chicken, a spicy and hearty sausage with pasta, and a tender and meaty lamb osso bucco (the new owner inherited the recipe, originally from Mark Ellman's grandmother.) Each special comes with a small salad.

You order at the counter and take a number back to your table (inside or outside), so your server can find you when your food is ready. Beer and wine are available and we always find something simple to go with the meal. The clean, well-lit restaurant features blond tables with aluminum legs and lightweight chairs (some folding), and you'll see that most of the cost of the meal goes into the ingredients, not the dishes or the ambience. In a town where everything is overpriced, this is a relief.

Address: 180 Dickenson St., Lahaina, West Maui
Meals: Lunch, Dinner
Hours: M-F 11am-9:30pm; Sa-Su 5pm-9:30pm
Parking: Lot, Street
Phone: 808-661-6633
Website: www.pennepastacafe.com

Pineapple Grill *(Pacific Rim)*

We like **Pineapple Grill** for its creative Pacific Rim cuisine and for the way Chef Ryan Luckey works so hard for every bite. We have no doubt he is spending most nights in his kitchen: he often greets guests from the hot line with a smile. Chef Ryan was born on Maui — one of the few great island chefs who can make that claim — and his love for his home is in the food. The overall ethic is fine dining in a casual atmosphere, and he focuses on using locally raised vegetables, fresh and sustainable fish, and island-bred beef.

We like to order a mai tai, because — although pricey, as everything else is on the menu — they're so darn good. We also like to come a little early and sit at the big square bar to drink it, because looking at that ceiling — painted to look like you're underwater — is just very cool.

Must-orders include steamed Manila clams that come plumped up in a black bean butter broth enriched with truffle oil and studded with shiitake mushrooms. The fragrance as we lean over the bowl is overwhelmingly rich, and we save rolls for sopping up every delicious, savory drop. We also like the crispy duck spring rolls, sweet and tangy inside with a sour-sweet relish on the side. And partly because it's just so unusual for Maui, we love the cheese plate (sometimes we save it for dessert), which comes with several cow, sheep, and goat selections, including the delicious local Surfing Goat Dairy chevre.

We don't often order salmon, because it is a cold water fish and not local to Maui. However, it is tangy-sweet here, seared in a miso preparation

continued on next page

OVERALL:
4
out of 5 stars

Pineapple Grill *(continued)*

and served with cold soba noodles, vegetables, and a citrus-y ponzu sauce. Another favorite is the ahi encrusted with pistachio and wasabi. These flavors — familiar to those who know Pacific Rim fusion — are outstanding together. The sweet, nutty, pale green pistachios love to dance with the sinus-scorching wasabi, and the ahi's firm, dramatically pink flesh stands up to them in both texture and flavor. The filet is served atop a marvelous mound of deep burgundy "forbidden rice." You can get this dish as either an appetizer or an entrée.

The Asian braised short ribs are another winner: simmered for hours in aromatic juices, the meat falls off the bone. The pineapple relish is a tad sweet with also sweet kalbi demi-glace, but we find ourselves greedily devouring it all anyway.

Our very favorite entrée is the rack of lamb with a veal cabernet reduction. The strong, sweet and dark flavor of the glaze strengthened by a hint of molasses is the perfect complement to the delicate but robust lamb. It comes with a beautiful serving of mashed purple sweet potatoes from Molokai. It is so easy to get these potatoes wrong — they are not particularly flavorful — but Chef Ryan knows to beat them until they are almost like candy.

The pineapple upside down cake is made with the sweetest pineapples on the planet: Maui Gold. The rum caramel sauce is dessert on its own, and the perfect topping for the macadamia nut ice cream they serve a la mode. This is a rich and sweet dessert, so make sure you have room before you order (it's hard not to finish once you start).

The wine list is excellent, and they carefully pair wines to food (the restaurant is heavily involved in the Kapalua Wine and Food Festival each year). There are also plenty of wines by the glass, and you can be assured these are kept at an appropriate temperature. (In so many island restaurants, the reds are too warm from languishing on shelves and the whites are too cold from sitting in the fridge.) The after-dinner drinks are worth looking at, too, especially the martini made with a shot of espresso.

There can be a tension in the service that is palpable: we wish the staff were a little bit less intense when we're spending plenty of money, and a little more attentive when we're not.

With every course worth your dollars, and the wine and drink list, too, this can turn out to be an expensive meal, and we don't recommend coming when you're on a budget. Many are fooled by the casual atmosphere of the bar area when they enter. It can look like this restaurant-on-a-golf-course is more affordable than it really is. The large tables and comfortable rattan chairs definitely look like an afternoon with the boys after a few rounds is in order, perhaps not a four star meal. At the tables up front the view of Molokai and the ocean is rather eclipsed by the brightly lit tennis courts. We prefer to sit to the left, where we can look across the golf course to the mist-shrouded West Maui Mountains. Larger parties are in luck here, because there are several large round tables that can sit up to ten, making a group get-together more pleasant.

We recommend ***Pineapple Grill*** for a thoroughly satisfying meal from start

Pineapple Grill *(continued)*

to finish, whether you are a twosome or a twentysome.

Address: 200 Kapalua Dr., Kapalua, HI 96761
Meals: Lunch, Dinner
Hours: Daily 11am–9pm
Parking: Lot
Phone: 808-669-9600
Website: www.pineapplekapalua.com

Pita Paradise *(Mediterranean)*

OVERALL:

4

out of 5 stars

$

Pita Paradise has served wonderful Mediterranean food at very reasonable prices for more than a decade. The little restaurant tucked in the back of Kalama Village is one of our favorite places for a quick and delicious lunch. When we learned that the owners were opening a second location in diamond-plated Wailea, we were thrilled: Now we can dig into tasty gyros and fish kebabs at Kihei's affordable prices with Wailea style. (Truth is, the prices in Wailea are a tad higher, but still below those at neighboring restaurants.) The new restaurant has a lovely *al fresca* dining area, with a huge fountain that absorbs any traffic noise from the highway nearby, and service is gracious.

The gyros are excellent and feature flavorful free-range New Zealand lamb that is grilled perfectly. The pitas are fresh and warm and the ziziki sauce is tangy and cool with cucumber flavors, while the shredded lettuce and the tomato slices bulk up the sandwich and lighten the heavier lamb.

Johnny, one half of the couple who owns both restaurants, is a fisherman and catches the daily special himself, so order with confidence that whatever it is — aku, ebi, or mahi mahi — it will be ultra-fresh. You can order it as a pita, salad, or kebab. We enjoy pasta dishes elsewhere.

The hummus is good, and our vegetarian friends love the veggie wraps and pitas. The rice pilaf, which comes alongside the pita sandwiches, can be a little too salty (and is cooked with chicken broth — so vegetarians, beware).

Local brews and decent wines are available. We are not huge fans of the baklava ice cream cake, but others are. We like that it drips with honey — isn't baklava basically a device with which you inject honey into your veins? — but it needs more pistachio and half as much ice cream. Check their website for coupons; right now there's one for free ziziki bread.

Address: 1913 S. Kihei Rd., Kihei, South Maui
Location: Kalama Village
Meals: Lunch, Dinner
Hours: Daily 11am–9:30pm
Parking: Lot
Phone: 808-875-7679

continued on next page

Pita Paradise *(continued)*

Address: 10 Wailea Gateway Place, Kihei, South Maui
Location: Wailea Gateway Center, where Pi'ilani Highway bends and turns
        into Wailea Ike Drive
Meals: Lunch, Dinner
Hours: Daily 11am-9:30pm
Parking: Lot
Phone: (808) 879-7177
Website: www.pitaparadisehawaii.com

Pizza Madness *(Pizza)*

OVERALL:

3.4

out of 5 stars

$

Pizza Madness is filled with huge bronzed wall and ceiling sculptures of undersea creatures — turtles, squid, a huge shark — devouring slices of pizza. They made us laugh the first time we saw them, and they still delight our inner children.

The exceptionally dark wooden paneling on the walls, the huge slabs of tables anchored to the walls, the long benches, the televisions, and the plate glass windows that let in plenty of light, make this a great place for large groups to eat. The bar and the many smaller tables for two and four make it acceptable for couples looking for a quick meal. While the art is perhaps the source of the "madness" in the name, the pizza is all East Coast middle-of-the-road 'za.

If a junior high school student imagined the perfect pie, this would be close. The crust isn't thick, or thin, there's plenty of cheese (we ask them to lighten up), and the choice of toppings is exactly what you expect: sausage, meatballs, pepperoni, and plenty of veggies. (You can also get pineapple and jalapenos.) The sauce is made in-house and not spicy enough, but they're not trying to make great pizza, they're trying to make American pizza. It's good, and we like the homemade sausage and the fact that we can get an individual size for less than $7.

Sandwiches are reasonably priced, and the homemade meatballs with green peppers on a grinder are a very good representation of this classic comfort food. Pasta is best eaten elsewhere.

The salads are little more than iceberg lettuce with tomato wedges and cheese, but we're not here for salad. On the other hand, the full bar sells pitchers of beer (unheard of on Maui) and pitchers of soda, too (another first). The servers are speedy and very friendly.

Pizza Madness serves that comforting middle ground that few other restaurants here do: decent food at decent prices with good service and a fun, clean, good atmosphere.

Address: 1455 S. Kihei Rd., Kihei, South Maui
Location: Near Maui Dive Shop
Meals: Lunch, Dinner
Hours: Daily 11am-10pm
Parking: Lot
Phone: 808-270-9888
Website: www.pizzamadnessmaui.com

The Plantation House Restaurant *(Pacific Rim)*

The view from **Plantation House** is unlike any other on the island. The restaurant sits high above sea level in the middle of the Kapalua golf course, which rolls down to the ocean with sky-high, ramrod-straight ironwood trees marching down the volcano beside it. You can see Molokai's dramatic shape rising out of the Pacific, and often dramatic shafts of light piercing dramatically dark clouds, and even a dramatic rainbow or two. It's very ... **dramatic**, and best seen from a table close to the front of the restaurant, preferably at a window. (Ladies, bring a wrap, it can be chilly in the breeze.)

We wish the food matched the superlative views ... but it doesn't always. We stay away from most of the "from the land" entrées and focus on the fish, which are where the chef excels. Your waiter will inform you what the fishermen reeled in and you select from five preparations. Our favorite is the Mediterranean. A filet is coated with a crust of sweet Maui onions and spicy, hearty mustard, served over more Maui onions that have been roasted until the sugar is completely caramelized, and a light and fluffy couscous. To cut this joyful sweetness, a fried caper sauce is ladled over the top. The spicy, peppery sauce pulls out the flavors of the fish — which otherwise would be smothered in this crust — and the fried capers give a satisfying crisp texture.

We also like the pistachio-crusted preparation with spinach, but we feel the **Roy's** or **Pineapple Grill's** version is better. The wine list is very good, and the drinks are well-prepared if a tad unimaginative (don't forget, this is the golf course's restaurant).

We like the breakfasts, which are reasonably priced given the million dollar views. Good options include the eggs Benedict, the spinach and cheese omelet, and the sweet French toast. Service can be all over the place and has ranged from barely there to totally engaged and friendly. A large seating area in the middle of the restaurant is elevated by a few steps, making **Plantation House** good for group meals (wedding rehearsal dinners, family celebrations) where the large menu can please many at once.

Address: 2000 Plantation Club Dr., Lahaina, West Maui
Meals: Breakfast, Lunch, Dinner
Hours: Daily 8am-9pm
Parking: Lot
Phone: 808-669-6299
Website: www.ThePlantationHouse.com

Polli's Mexican Restaurant *(Mexican)*

Sometimes the iconic sign "Come on in and eat or we'll both starve!" is a sign a restaurant has a good sense of humor — other times, that it truly wants you to eat there for charity's sake. We aren't sure which applies to **Polli's**. We haven't seen much of a sense of humor on display here, but it seems busy enough that they don't need to beg.

continued on next page

Polli's Mexican Restaurant *(continued)*

The fare is sloppy, cheesy, average Mexican food at generally reasonable prices, and more so when you take advantage of the daily specials. Served with a mix of flour and corn tortilla chips, the salsa is very good, the guacamole, as well — but why do you have to pay for your chip basket? We are surprised at how much we like the tender pork with chili verde. The burritos are generous and the cheese sauce is not too overpowering. The bar at this tiny, cowboy-country sit-down restaurant is packed with locals who watch the surf flicks on the TV. The margarita is nothing to write home about, but if you must have one and can't drive down to **Milagros**, **Polli's** will just have to do.

Address: 1202 Makawao Ave., Makawao, Upcountry
Meals: Lunch, Dinner
Hours: Daily 11am-10pm
Parking: Street, Lot
Phone: 808-572-7808

Pulehu, an Italian Grill

Elegant and moderately priced, **Pulehu** is an attractive option for resort guests and locals alike. Several tables overlook a serene koi pond; they're tables worth asking for. The remainder fan out around a glass-enclosed demonstration kitchen.

While waiting for your breadsticks, try the signature strawberry limoncello martini. The fancy designer cocktails don't exactly match the Italian menu, but they're fun: many feature crushed macadamia nut-rimmed glasses and Kula lavender syrup. The dinner menu also features some very nice dishes. The wood stone pizzas are true flatbreads — cracker-thin, crisp crusts amply slathered in classic toppings. The flavorful cappannone features a dousing of tomato sauce, smoky chunks of apple wood bacon, melted blue cheese, walnuts, and a handful of fresh arugula. Yum.

We also like the risotto-crusted fish (monchong on our last visit) — a novel preparation of an old favorite. A modest layer of crisp risotto blankets the filet, keeping it moist and flaky. Served atop roasted vegetables in a thin pool of pesto butter, this is simple and delicious.

Other dishes are good without being spectacular: the sausage, spinach and mushroom lasagna is a thick and cheesy slab, the chianti-braised short ribs do not offend in any way, and the butternut squash ravioli with sage brown butter are good representations of this rich dish. The calamari has been rubbery and the crab dip with roasted garlic looks and just *is* unappetizing. We've had a nice dish of strawberry guava sorbetto, however, and the gelato is also nice.

Service vacillates between overly-friendly to inattentive, and the host/ess stand is not always manned, for some unknown reason.

The early bird special is nice: if you arrive by 6pm, you can indulge in a

Pulehu, an Italian Grill *(continued)*

three-course prix fixe menu for under forty dollars. The restaurant also offers half-off kama'aina discounts on Thursday evenings after 8pm, for those with a local ID.

Pulehu is only "An Italian Grill" for part of the week. On Tuesday and Wednesday nights, it transforms for special events — some private, some open to the public. Creative wine dinners include blind tastings and themed menus. Recently the sous chef shared specialties from her home country in a Thai dinner, and to celebrate the restaurant's first anniversary, they threw an indulgent Chocolate and Truffle Decadenza.

With the lovely location and good food, this is a good restaurant to consider if you are planning a reception or party.

Address: 6 Kai Ala Dr.,   Lahaina
Location: In the Westin Ka'anapali Ocean Resort
Meals: Dinner
Hours: Daily 5:30-9:30pm Thursday through Monday
Parking: valet and self-parking lot
Phone: 808-662-2655
Website: www.pulehurestaurant.com

Rodeo General Store *(deli)*

This general store and deli has lots of good choices for prepared meals: breakfast burritos, veggie curries, chicken enchiladas, and lamb with couscous and raita. This is not standard to-go fare: the chefs are also caterers, and they've developed their recipes carefully after years of experience here and in restaurants across Maui.

The chill cases are stocked with everything from decent sushi to raw cashew spreads. Vegetarians and vegans will be very happy here. Fresh soups include carrot ginger, Italian lentil, coconut broccoli, and a chili so hearty our fork stands straight up.

Rodeo General has connections to *Alive and Well*, the natural foods store in Kahului, so some menu items are the same. For instance, both places offer a terrific "salad trio" deal. You have more options at *Rodeo*: a power slaw with kale (energizing), beets and greens (nourishing), seaweed salad (slimy), tortellini (somewhat stale), and quinoa (yes, please). You can throw in a meat entrée for no extra cost, too. The steak poke — chopped morsels of Maui Cattle Company beef seared medium rare and tossed with onion, chili peppers, garlic, and tomato — is delicious, as are the Thai turkey burgers with sweet chili sauce. The chicken salad, on the other hand, could do with half as much mayonnaise.

Sandwiches are made to order, and the flank steak on house-baked focaccia with roasted red bell pepper, cheese, and horseradish sauce, ranks among Maui's better sandwiches.

continued on next page

Rodeo General Store *(continued)*

There is delicious chocolate cake in the chill case, along with vegan tapioca in two flavors: lilikoi and mocha. Also check out the intensely flavored gelato made from local fruit.

As a grocery, **Rodeo** meets the needs of Upcountry gourmets who can't get down to **Mana Foods**. The produce selection is slim, but mostly local. The microbrews and imported wines are well-picked. One thing you can get here you can't get anywhere else: giant bags of fresh, restaurant-style made-on-Maui tortilla chips. If you're planning a fiesta, these are essential.

A second location, which just opened in Kihei, is more of a resort sundry shop, due to its more touristy location. It doesn't have a full-scale deli, but you can get all of the chill-case items and a few pre-made sandwiches. Perhaps they'll scale up as more of us locals discover they're here (their permanent sign just went up last night as we pen this). Kihei is, after all, home to the biggest population of permanent residents on the island.

Address: 3661 Baldwin Ave., Makawao, Upcountry
Location: just below the intersection of Baldwin and Makawao avenues
Meals: Breakfast, Lunch, Dinner
Hours: 6am–10pm
Parking: street
Phone: 808-572-1868

Address: 1847 S. Kihei Rd., Kihei, South Maui
Location: Sandwiched between Kukui Mall and KFC.
Meals: Breakfast, Lunch, Dinner
Hours: 6am–11pm
Parking: lot, or public lot just across the street
Phone: 808-633-4990

Roy's Bar & Grill *(Pacific Rim)*

Roy's — owned by Roy Yamaguchi, one of the founders of Hawaiian Regional Cuisine (HRC) and a James Beard Foundation Award Winner — is now an international chain, and they've got their system down. The service is attentive, the food consistently well-made, and the menu — which changes on a regular basis — is created by chefs who know his vision and can execute against it. Joey Macadangdang, the executive chef here on Maui, has a fan base of his own.

Yamaguchi was one of many HRC chefs to open a restaurant in a strip mall, away from the all-important beachfront real estate. He maintained that his food was so fantastic it didn't need a mesmerizing view. We agree. (Though we have yet to tire of gazing at the sunset.) Yamaguchi's Kahana location is particularly un-glamorous — parked next to McDonald's in the less-trafficked end of West Maui. In January 2012, the restaurant will relocate to a ritzier and far more popular intersection: the entrance to Ka'anapali. While

OVERALL:
4.3
out of 5 stars

$ $ $

Roy's Bar & Grill *(continued)*

the transition hasn't occurred at publication, but we're certain the seasoned staff at **Roy's** will handle it well. We still feel confident recommending our favorite dishes from the award-winning menu.

First, we order dessert. Made to order, the melting hot chocolate soufflé takes a while to attain its molten perfection in the oven, so ordering it first means they can time it to be ready when dinner is cleared. You might as well order one for each of you. We've never been able to share the soufflé — even with each other. The slightly crunchy skin gives way to a sinfully rich center, while the raspberry coulis and the simple vanilla ice cream sets off the dark chocolate perfectly. Many restaurants offer lava cakes, but this demolishes the competition. We've been known to phone in an order for this soufflé and arrive as it's pulled from the oven, in time for drinks and dessert.

Once that is taken care of, we order our meal. We often order a selection of appetizers rather than focusing on the entrées, because there are so many good choices. We especially like the Szechuan flavored baby back ribs and the potstickers, but an excellent thing to do is order their "boat" of the best appetizers of the day. It serves two easily for a light meal, especially when you add a spicy tuna roll, hot melting chocolate soufflé, and one of their strong rum cocktails — our favorite, so far, being a lovely lilikoi colada made on the spot by a friendly and creative bartender (standard disclaimer: lilikoi may not be in season when you go).

Our favorite entrées on **Roy's** "Classics" menu — dishes which are usually available — include the misoyaki butterfish, which is sweet, falling-apart tender, and rich, and the roasted macadamia nut mahi mahi lavished with buttery lobster sauce. We also looooooove the pistachio and wasabi crust on the ahi, finely chopped and beautifully seared to the pink fish, and the avocado mousse served on the side is surprising (still, after all these years) and perfectly creamy. The tenderloin is perfect. The shrimp and butternut squash risotto — usually available in the fall — is plush, perfectly made, and comforting.

If you aren't a chocoholic, we also love the banana crisp for dessert, which has an excellent pudding texture that contrasts nicely with the gingery, nutty topping.

The wine list is excellent and the servers are helpful at picking something that will go with these intense flavors, but we often choose to drink a lighter, Asian beer with our meal so that it doesn't compete with the food.

Our friends with children love **Roy's** for nice dinners out because the children's menu is coursed so they don't get bored, and the first course arrives *immediately*. There are crayons for the picture books, too.

A meal at **Roy's** still feels like a celebration to us, even if we're just stopping in for a light meal. It's not particularly quiet and romantic, but we love that we can come by ourselves or with friends — or with friends with kids — and enjoy our meal. There's a joyful, playful energy to this restaurant that pours out of the kitchen and saturates the mood (and the food), and we've never felt let down as we walk back to our car.

continued on next page

Roy's Bar & Grill *(continued)*

Address: 4405 Honoapiilani Hwy., Kahana, West Maui
Location: Kahana Gateway Center
After January 2012
Address: 2290 Ka'anapali Pkwy, Ka'anapali, West Maui
Location: Ka'anapali Golf Course, right at the main entrance to Ka'anapali
Meals: Dinner
Hours: Nightly 5:30-10pm
Parking: Lot
Phone: 808-669-6999
Website: www.RoysRestaurant.com

$ $

Ruby's *(American)*

This be-bop diner at Queen Kaahumanu Mall is the go-to place for kids of all ages. The big burgers wrapped in paper so they don't spill, the thick milkshakes, the reasonably good fries and onion rings, and the clean, red-boothed restaurant bring in crowds from open to close. If it's your birthday, don't tell them unless you're ready for a crew to come out and sing to you their own special song. (You will also get a free sundae, no matter what your age is.)

Other items on the menu include pretty good dinners like fresh-roasted (in-house) turkey dinner and fish and chips. The sauces and salsas and gravies are made in house, too. Salads are commercial, but crisp, and the appetizers are large and can serve as entrées.

The servers are efficient and attentive, and we often leave happy to have dined in a well-run restaurant. On weekends there is often someone wandering the tables, creating balloon animals to order. Ask for a monkey climbing a palm tree, the surfer, or the mermaid. ***Ruby's*** is a good, inexpensive choice for a quick meal at any time of day. Check with the info desk at the mall for coupons offering 25% off your entire meal.

Address: 275 W. Kaahumanu Ave., Kahului, Central Maui
Location: Queen Kaahumanu Center
Meals: Breakfast, Lunch, Dinner
Hours: M-Th 7:30am-9pm; F-Su 7:30am-10pm
Parking: Lot
Phone: 808-248-7829
Website: www.rubys.com

Ruth's Chris Steak House *(American)*

We do not normally review chain restaurants, but we make an exception for ***Ruth's Chris***, because 1.) The service is excellent and 2.) A good steak dinner is a wonderful way to celebrate any occasion.

Ruth's Chris does steak great honor and features lovely locations in Wailea

Ruth's Chris Steak House *(continued)*

(dark-paneled, intimate), and Lahaina (same paneling, same half-round booths, with a lovely view of the ocean thrown in).

Beef is one of our favorite ways to get protein, iron, B vitamins, and zinc into our diet. We're not sure that we *need* the sizzling butter sauce that dances around the steaks — which are served on exceedingly hot plates dotted with parsley — but we don't *mind* it. Seared at 1800°F, the filet is tender enough to cut with a butter knife, and the rib eye is our favorite cut. The sustainable foodies in us wish the beef were local, but we admit, grudgingly, that local beef is not yet as beautifully textured or consistently high quality as the beef from the Midwest.

Ruth's Chris does use local ingredients in their side dishes — and the flavor results are excellent. The salads are crisp and colorful Kula greens and other vegetables grown on Haleakala (not in California). The well-balanced dressings are homemade. The steakhouse salad — iceberg, micro greens, carrots, tomatoes — is generous and delicious with the traditional blue cheese dressing. The Caesar is garlicky and has an excellent anchovy flavor without the chunks of fish that can distress some diners.

Sides are typical of steakhouse menus and plenty big enough to split. We can't help but love the simplest: potatoes whipped with butter until pillowy and seasoned with a sure hand, and spinach so perfectly integrated with cream that it becomes almost spinach *butter*.

The wine list is very good, and we like that they have several half bottles and glasses available.

The service, however, sets ***Ruth's Chris*** apart. Servers show up on time, check back often without interrupting, and clear and clean without being intrusive. They know the menu, can offer good advice, and exude genuine hospitality. They also handle that crucial skill, upselling, with poise. This is so universally true in our experience that we once asked a server in Wailea what the restaurant's secret is.

"We all 'hui it up,'" he said, "and work as a team."

"Everyone, back and front of the house, understands that the success of the restaurant rides on our shoulders, and that everyone must be fully committed, trained well, and working hard all the time."

We commented that this level of service isn't always found on Maui.

"Well, we all have mortgages and families," he replied, "and we know that diners are the ones who pay us. So we stay focused on you and make sure you're happy, even if you're not at 'our' table."

"If someone gets off track, we all make sure that they get back on, in a hurry."

Might we humbly suggest that this attitude be adopted by other Maui restaurants?

continued on next page

Ruth's Chris Steak House (continued)

Address: 3750 Wailea Alanui Dr., Wailea, South Maui
Location: in the Shops at Wailea
Meals: Dinner
Hours: Nightly 5pm–10pm
Parking: Lot
Phone: 808-874-8880
Website: www.ruthschris.com

Address: 900 Front St., Lahaina, West Maui
Location: at the very end of the seawall, near the Hard Rock Cafe
Meals: Dinner
Hours: Nightly 5pm–10pm
Parking: Lot (validated), Street
Phone: 808-661-8815

OVERALL:
3.8
out of 5 stars

$

CASH

Sam Sato's *(Local / Plate Lunch)*

Some say that expectations are pre-meditated resentments, and we think this is especially true when it comes to restaurants. We recommend you reign in your expectations before sliding into a booth at **Sam Sato's**. We also recommend being in the mood for noodles. This humble little diner will never get a Michelin star, but it has been ladling out hot ramen since 1933, when it opened in Camp 3, a sugar plantation village in Sprecklesville. The noodle house's loyal customers have followed it faithfully through three migrations before it finally settled in Wailuku's drab but functional Industrial Park.

On an island where entrées regularly exceed $30, it's easy to understand the popularity of a clean, home-style joint where pennies still count as relevant currency. The restaurant's claim to fame — the dry noodles and the manju — cost $6.50 and 70 cents, respectively.

There's a line out the door for both breakfast and lunch. Customers write their names on a list outside and wait (usually) patiently for a booth inside the jam-packed room. The windows are framed by palaka (Hawaiian cowboy plaid) curtains, and five original paintings of earlier incarnations provide the decor. Once seated, you won't wait long to eat: service is friendly, brisk, and efficient.

Order the dry noodles, in particular the "super dry" version, which adds bok choy and carrot to a large bowl of firm, yellow noodles, pink-edged fish cake, roast pork slices, slivered egg, and crunchy bean sprouts. A small, salty cup of broth comes on the side, as does a squirt of hot Asian mustard. We were once instructed by a "regular" to mix a little shoyu into our mustard and pour *that* over the noodles. Good advice, because otherwise the broth is fairly standard chicken stock. (Do-it-yourself-noodles don't charm everyone, but it's tradition — and at these prices, we're happy to participate.)

The noodles are made by a family operation in Paia and have a lovely integrity: flavorful, with good texture that doesn't turn to mush when subjected to steamy broth. In fact, the noodles don't even get mushy overnight — something you discover when you take half of your bowl home. (You can also buy packages of these noodles at Ah Fook's, the Asian market in the strip mall on the corner of Kaahumanu and Lono in Kahului.)

We come for the noodles, not for the plate lunches or burgers, which are not nearly as charming or tasty. But we do save our cash to buy a paper bag of manju and turnovers on the way out. Manju is a Japanese confection, kind of like a little pie — a pastry wrapped around a sweet filling. The manju sold here are baked (elsewhere they're fried) and come in two flavors: adzuki and lima bean. Both are delicious. All of the turnovers are worthy, but our favorite flavor is the creamy, bright orange pumpkin, available in season.

Address: 1750 Wili Pa Loop, Wailuku, Central Maui
Location: In Wailuku Industrial Park
Meals: Breakfast, Lunch
Hours: Daily 7am–2pm
Parking: Lot, Street
Phone: 808–244–7124

Sansei Seafood Restaurant & Sushi Bar
(Sushi/Pacific Rim)

Once when we visited **Sansei** someone at the next table asked us what the name of the restaurant meant. We didn't know, but as a group speculated it could mean "circus" because of **Sansei's** slightly rowdy, cheerful, bustling approach to Pacific Rim and sushi.

[We looked it up later, and *sansei* actually means "The U.S.-born grandchild of Japanese immigrants to America." Ahhhh. We take a moment now to honor Chef Owner D.K. Kodama's Japanese grandparents who immigrated to America and gifted us his hurly burly, exuberant approach to Japanese cuisine.]

The menu at **Sansei** is several pages long and features chicken, beef, fresh fish, and even a few pasta dishes, but most diners go for the outrageous and flamboyant sushi.

It's visually stunning. For example, the caterpillar rolls slinks across the plate with brilliant green avocado-slice scales. Under the avocado are layers of ahi and salmon, which are wrapped around seaweed, around rice, around eel. Ah, it's an eel roll!

Most of the rolls are like this, with garnishes and tricks and treats hidden in the layers. When we want simple, we order sashimi, especially a couple of the more elegant presentations, like the Kenny G, which is delicate slips of kampachi layered with ponzu sauce.

continued on next page

Sansei Seafood Restaurant & Sushi Bar *(continued)*

The miso butterfish and the rock shrimp dynamite are must-orders. The butterfish — so named for the rich and velvety texture and taste — is cooked and beautifully glazed with a salty-savory-sweet brown sauce. The rock shrimp dynamite is a dish piled with teensy popcorn shrimp flash-fried in panko batter and bathed in spicy mayonnaise.

If you have sushi newbies in your party, *Sansei* is an excellent place to bring them to try out a few pieces. It's fresh, it's delicious, and the servers have plenty of beginner chopsticks to hand out. Best of all, if they really don't want sushi, the wide-ranging menu won't make them feel left out (and the chicken teriyaki is better than we've had anywhere else). The crab ramen is a superb, surprising blend of Dungeness crab meat, cilantro, Thai basil, and jalapeno in a truffle-infused broth. It's light and soulful all at once. The seafood ravioli (shrimp, lobster and crab) appetizer is on the smallish side (we eat them too quickly to count) but it comes slathered in a super-rich Madeira cream sauce and slivered shiitake mushrooms.

For the most part, this is not a sushi purist's place. Don't come here for dazzlingly adept sashimi platters, or even for more obscure types of nigiri, such as uni (sea urchin). But *Sansei* does have a few tricks up its sleeve for true aficionados. If you don't mind eating off a fish carcass, ask the waiter if the sushi chefs have a "hama kama" left. The phrase refers to the cheek (kama) of the hamachi (hama). This tender, fatty, delectable part of the fish is virtually useless in sushi preparation, but absolutely delicious baked and served with a dipping sauce and salad. Since they butcher at least one hamachi per day, they usually have cheeks available. You will sometimes see it on the daily special list, but if you don't, you can ask if they have it. Be aware that you will be served a big fish jaw — including bones and fins — but this is the perfect dish to work over with chopsticks.

Service is generally efficient, and dishes come out as soon as they are ready, so we never sit hungry for long. The wine and beer list are very good, and the restaurants are large and rather noisy. (This is not the place to come for a quiet, intimate meal.)

Even when tables are available in the busy restaurant, we like to sit at the sushi bar or the cocktail bar, so we can watch the show. Watching a sushi chef work is just plain fun. At *Sansei*, it is also fun to watch the bartenders, because they throw glasses and spin drinks and they'll invent a cocktail for you on the spot. (The full menu is available at both the sushi and cocktail bar.)

Both locations feature sushi price promotions. Their most popular is the Sunday and Monday early bird: 50% off food (with a few exceptions). This discount applies to all comers in the Kihei location, but only to locals with a Hawaii State ID in Kapalua. If you decide to go for this super-good deal, call to find out when the promotion starts, and then plan on showing up at least thirty minutes before the restaurant opens, because the lines form early (bring a beach chair and a book).

The late-night half-off-sushi specials are particularly fun if you like Karaoke — get in early to put your name in. Call the restaurant for details on price promotions because they can change with the seasons and the night of the week.

Sansei Seafood Restaurant & Sushi Bar *(continued)*

Address: 1881 S. Kihei Rd., Kihei, South Maui
Location: Kihei Town Center near Foodland
Meals: Dinner, Late-Night
Hours: Nightly 5:30pm-10pm; Th-Sa 10pm-1am
Parking: Lot
Phone: 808-879-0004
Website: www.sanseihawaii.com

Address: 600 Office Rd., Kapalua, HI 96761
Location: At the Kapalua Resort
Meals: Dinner, Late-Night
Hours: Nightly 5:30pm-10:30pm; Th-F 10pm-1am
Parking: Lot
Phone: 808-669-6286

Sarento's on the Beach *(Italian)*

As mentioned in the Introduction, ***Sarento's*** inspired us to write this book in the first place. The Italian menu is focused on providing important-sounding and expensive ingredients in flamboyant preparations that don't always work as well as they should (especially at these prices).

There are some items that are well-prepared, including a decent cioppino with lobster, scallops, crabs, and fish that satisfies our cravings *di mare*. We've had good steaks with competent sauces, too.

That's where the hope dies. Some of the least successful items we've had are marked as "recommended" on the menu. For example, the Chopped Salad "Gabriella" is a bleary, mucky mess of feta, shrimp, onions, avocado, artichokes, tomatoes, and skinny strips of romaine lettuce. The overall visual impression is not appetizing, and the flavors and textures terrorize each other, and our palate. On a recent visit we could not eat more than two bites — and the busboy cleared it without comment. Another "recommended" dish, the grilled ahi, comes as a giant slab of gray fish (cooked way more than the promised medium rare) piled on dense goat cheese gnocchi, which are little more than balls of goat cheese. The puttanesca sauce that tops the whole sad affair is one-noted (garlic), except for the sour vinegar — perhaps from the overuse of bottled caper water? The veal marsala is not described on the menu, but if it had been, we might have skipped it just because it comes with spaetzle. First: why not noodles? It was chewy to the point of rubber, and the sauce was so flush with mushrooms that it lost all hint of wine. These, too, were cleared without comment.

The restaurant is very proud of its service, or "hospitality." According to Webster's, *hospitality* is defined as the "friendly reception and treatment of guests or strangers." We're afraid that ***Sarento's*** staff exhibits less hospitality — which is genuine, unforced, and relaxed — and more of what Miss Manners calls "fits of hospitality." A fit of hospitality is entertaining people who do not want to be entertained; or entertaining when you can't genuinely put your heart in it. The feeling that we're entering a place where we will

continued on next page

Sarento's on the Beach *(continued)*

be entertained with at-your-elbow-service, whether we like it or not (and we don't) — is a serious problem at **Sarento's.** Why must we constantly be interrupted? Isn't a romantic location like this a place where people go to pretend they are the only two people in the world?

[We know some people who love the doting service, who think it's wonderful that they take a sip of water and someone immediately tops off the glass, who love the clasped hands and practiced smiles. We're just saying that for this kind of money you can have a glorious Italian meal at **Capische?** or **Ferraro's.** You may not be hovered over, but you will assuredly enjoy your food more.]

The new breakfast menu seems promising — the Benedicts in particular. Unfortunately, the dishes are terribly complicated (and priced that way). There is no simple egg dish — omelets are available, but not just eggs, and toast, for example. The hash browns are russet, sweet, and Molokai sweet potatoes, and so dry that they crumple off the fork. The different potatoes clearly need different cooking times — bits are raw while others overcooked. The standard Benedict is adequate, but the other versions are, like the dinner dishes, just too much. Why can't even breakfast be simple, here? We find ourselves enjoying the pancake — it tastes like a mix — only because it is what it promises to be, with no odd or unappetizing sides. This is one of the prettiest breakfast views on Maui — the restaurant sits right on Keawakapu beach in Wailea — but **Five Palms** is right across the sand and offers a much better meal.

A word about the prices: they are sky-high, particularly given the quality of food. At our last dinner visit we refused all drinks and ordered only recommended dishes. When the waiter set the bill in front of us, he opened it and, as he fiddled with the ticket (it wasn't quite *perfectly* straight), he noted the total.

"Wow, you got out of here with a *bargain*!" he exclaimed. Our shock must have been evident — although he may not have realized we were as shocked at his calling anything we'd just had a "bargain" as we were that he would make a comment like this.

Realizing he'd made a mistake, he tried to fix it with a joke (well, we *think* it was a joke): "Well, I mean, most people spend a lot more than *that* here. Usually when I bring the bill, they go through each dish, saying 'I didn't like that, take it off.'"

"They're in sticker shock," Molly suggested, "they try to negotiate the bill down?"

"Yeah," he shrugged, and zipped away, before we could determine whether what he'd just said was a joke, or actually happens.

Address: 2980 S. Kihei Rd., Kihei, South Maui
Location: Next to the Mana Kai
Meals: Breakfast, Dinner
Hours: 7am-11am (breakfast), 5:30pm-10pm (dinner); bar until 12am
Parking: Valet
Phone: 808-875-7555
Website: www.tristarrestaurants.com

Sea House Restaurant *(American/Pacific Rim)*

If the thought of the breakfast line at **Gazebo** drives you crazy (it does us), take comfort in knowing that we think your best bet for breakfast in Napili is actually their neighbor, **Sea House**.

Sea House is the main restaurant at the Napili Kai, a resort that oozes the relaxed Aloha spirit Maui is famous for. The service is friendly and efficient, and the breakfast fare is wonderful. We like the hearty panini, the giant baked egg frittatas, and the friendly egg scrambles. But one of our very favorite breakfast items is the Dutch Baby pancake.

Of course, **Sea House** calls it a Crater Pancake. Essentially a giant custard, it comes topped with lemon juice and powdered sugar, and it's perfect. Creamy textured. Crisp on the outside. Bright-flavored and sweet without being cloying: Delicious! The Haleakala Pancake is the same confection, but topped with cinnamon, sugar, apples, and pineapples. Too sweet, in our opinion, but some disagree.

We don't recommend lunches and dinners here, but we do drive from South Maui to have breakfast meetings here ... and if that doesn't sound like a big deal, ask a local what would taste good enough for *them* to drive one hour before eating breakfast.

The location — immediately on the water — offers beautiful views and fresh air and the same whales (in season) that you can see from the more popular (why?) **Gazebo**.

Note: our ratings are for breakfast only.

Address: 5900 Lower Honoapiilani Rd, Napili, West Maui
Location: Napili Kai Beach Resort
Meals: Breakfast, Lunch, Dinner
Hours: Daily 7am-9pm; Bar until 10pm
Parking: Lot
Phone: 808-669-1500
Website: www.napilikai.com

Shaka Pizza *(Pizza)*

Shaka is an East Coast-style pizzeria, and it wins lots of local awards ... but keep in mind that pizza is not indigenous to Maui. The crust is okay, but the tomato sauce is lacking the complexity we want in really good pizza, where the sauce is the star of the show. You'll do better with the white pizza — cheese, olive oil, garlic, and gourmet toppings like clam and spinach. We also like the pesto pizza.

The menu also features sandwiches, but we find everything a tad overpriced for what we're eating. The open air restaurant seats a lot of people and the pies are large, so this can be a good place to have a casual meal.

continued on next page

Shaka Pizza *(continued)*

Address: 1770 S. Kihei Rd., Kihei, South Maui
Location: Across from Kukui Mall
Meals: Lunch, Dinner
Hours: Su-Th 10:30am–9pm; F-Sa 10:30am–10pm
Parking: Lot
Phone: 808-874-0331
Website: www.shakapizza.com

Son'z at Swan Court *(Pacific Rim)*

There's a restaurant proverb that (like all proverbs) is almost always true: the better the view, the worse the food. The proverb holds at **Son'z**, the fine restaurant at the Hyatt. A sweeping staircase brings you down to one of the most romantic places on Maui: a waterfall-fed pond dotted with elegant white swans. Protected from the beach-walk-gawkers, this is a beautiful spot for an intimate evening. If we could eat the view, we would, happily, and it would be delicious.

Unfortunately, we can't. We must rely on what's coming out of the kitchen. The menu is similar to that of sister restaurants **Sarento's on the Beach** and **Nick's Fishmarket**, including the strained descriptions, overly friendly handwriting font, and extremely high dollar amounts next to each item. The overly complicated recipes result in plates that always look very colorful (all of the primary and many of the secondary colors are represented), but never blow us away with taste (strange, how so many ingredients result in so little flavor).

Our overwrought imaginations come up with all sorts of scenarios to explain why the service, which is *very* attentive, strikes us as panicked. Is there someone in the kitchen holding a gun to their heads? Do they all have nails sticking up through the soles of their shoes? We have a bias against service that is obtrusive. Don't refill our glass of water between each sip, and don't ask us more than once how we like the "flavors." (Especially when we don't.) And if you can't make an honest recommendation, find a way to guide us besides repeating what's listed on the menu.

If you are staying in Ka'anapali and want to eat a romantic dinner without driving into Lahaina or out to Kapalua, we recommend heading upstairs to **Japengo** or to the pool for '**Umalu**.

Address: 200 Nohea Kai Dr., Ka'anapali, West Maui
Location: at The Maui Hyatt hotel near the swan pond
Meals: Dinner
Hours: Su-Th 5pm–10pm; Fr-Sa 5pm–10:30pm; Bar until 12am
Parking: Valet
Phone: 808-667-4506
www.hyattregencymaui.com

South Shore Tiki Lounge *(American)*

We can't help but like ***Tiki Lounge***, the open-air, thatch-roofed bar in Kalama Village. The food (sandwiches, hot dogs, nachos) is average, but the drinks are generally good, and it's got a fun, relaxed vibe that just works, and has for a while.

Live music, surfing videos projected on a giant screen … it's a nice little joint for a drink and an appetizer. For some reason it's been hyped as a good place for vegetarians, and while we do appreciate that they offer veggie burgers and faux hot dogs, we can't get behind the crumbled veggie patties used in the chili and curry plate. We'd also be considerably happier if the coleslaw wasn't served in styrofoam cups — just like it is at ***KFC***. We do like that they use "smart fry" oil for their French fries. Snacking on bar food is so much better without the guilt factor.

Address: 1913 S. Kihei Rd., Kihei, South Maui
Location: Kalama Village across from the whale
Meals: Lunch, Dinner, Late-Night
Hours: Daily 11am–2am
Parking: Lot
Phone: 808-874-6444
Website: www.southshoretikilounge.com

OVERALL:
3.2
out of 5 stars

$ $

Spago *(Pacific Rim)*

A reader once sent us a thank you note — handwritten — specifically to thank us for including ***Spago*** in the book. "I eat at the original [Spago] all the time," he wrote, "and when I read your review of the Maui location, I was suspicious. How could a resort version possibly capture the energy and passion I love? And why would I want to visit a chain restaurant in Maui? I was so wrong — and you were so right: it's its own restaurant, but still belongs to Wolfgang Puck."

We're happy to hear this of course, particularly because we have never felt let down by this restaurant, either. Walking into ***Spago*** at the Four Seasons Resort Maui feels like an event. The dark paneled, glitzy bar is accented by fresh pincushion proteas. Giant orange and pink sea anemones reach out from huge, splashy prints in the lounge. It's one of few places on Maui where your heels can't be too high or your décolletage too glittery — a little extra glamour and bling fits right in. You might expect the food to falter in such a showy environment; instead, each dish is attended to with fastidious care.

Our single favorite item served in any Maui restaurant is the spicy ahi tuna poke in sesame miso cones. To make these little handfuls of love, fresh ahi is chopped and mixed (pureed?) thoroughly with chili aioli, the full-flavored Tosa soy sauce, plenty of green onions, pickled ginger, and the crunchy, brilliant orange tobiko (flying fish roe). Meanwhile, black and white sesame

OVERALL:
4.6
out of 5 stars

$ $ $ $

continued on next page

seeds are combined with a little flour, butter, corn syrup and miso paste, rolled into circles, baked, and carefully formed into little cones (one person does the cones, all night long). The ahi mix is carefully spooned into the cones, garnished, and slid into wooden carriers. The small portion is three, and the large is five. They are incredibly expensive — several dollars apiece — but we don't regret ordering them. And if we need to, we order an extra one or two to round out the number and avoid petty fights.

(We're spending a lot of time on this appetizer because it is emblematic of what you will find at *Spago*: layers of flavors carefully thought through and then enthusiastically assembled by people who know what works and how to execute night after night.)

When you bite into a cone, it does not crumble (the corn syrup, we think, lets it bend rather than snap), and you get at least two or three full bites out of each one. The spicy poke (which means "chopped fish") dissolves on your tongue, sending spicy heat to the back of your throat and filling your entire mouth with flavor. While the fish brings the spice, the cone brings a crunchy/chewy texture and sweet, mellow, cool flavor. It's like candy sushi. We were once treated to a veggie version, where diced hearts of palm replaced the ahi. Amazingly, it was just as good. So you see, we think you should order this appetizer.

Another delight is the Thai coconut soup with lobster. Kaffir lime, galangal, and chili mingle with bright vegetables cooked to their peak. The broth is impossibly light and flavorful, making us wonder if there is a Thai fairy godmother waving a wand in the kitchen.

Entrees we particularly like include the wok-fried moi (when it's available; you might want to call ahead and ask). The fish, which at one time was only eaten by Hawaiian royalty, is small, exquisitely tender, white, and flaky. The preparation preserves all the moistness and keeps out the oil. Served over jasmine rice, shiitake mushrooms and hearts of palm, garnished with kaffir lime and Thai basil, it's a great example of Thai flavors fusing with Hawaiian fish. The server will debone the fish for you tableside. There is nothing more special, in our opinion, than a properly prepared moi at *Spago*.

Neither of these dishes are budget items, but *Spago* is not a place to visit when you feel strapped for cash. However, we will point out that even the most inexpensive item on the entrée list, the pan-fried chicken, is ridiculously tasty. The chicken is delicate, moist, tender, and laid over a healthy helping of delicious, creamy mashed potatoes laced with local goat cheese and oyster mushrooms from upcountry Maui. Molly's been known to crave this dish, even with all of the other excellent choices available.

Other entrées include grilled Chinois lamb chops (perfectly done every time we've had them), and diver scallops sautéed until tender and an interesting contrast to the spicy eggplant puree underneath. If you are a meat eater, we also like the simply prepared prime rib and the Japanese rib eye.

If you are a vegetarian, ask what the kitchen can do for you, because they can whip up a series of gorgeous courses just for you, based on your preferences and what is best that day. There is an unabashed love for ingredients

Spago *(continued)*

here, and we think the true test of a chef's creativity is how well he knows his vegetable garden. One course that stands out for us was a remarkable homage to the local tomato: a simple yet stunning shot glass of tomato water, a rich and foamy tomato "cappuccino," and a delicate caprese salad sprinkled with teensy micro basil leaves.

Desserts are good — though the molten lava cake simply isn't **Roy's** chocolate soufflé. Instead try the lilikoi meringue pie: a tart passion fruit custard topped with snowy meringue. Fruity, fragrant, and not overly sweet.

The wine list is extensive and the guidance from servers and the sommelier is both professional and friendly. Service is exceptional, but be prepared for a leisurely pace to your evening. You will likely be at table for at least two hours, and you will not be rushed out the door. During that time, however, service will be attentive and well-paced. Don't be afraid to ask for exactly what you want here, or, alternately to place your fate in the hands of the very capable chef.

The beautiful, uber-chic restaurant has wonderful open-air sunset views, but can be a little breezy in the evenings, so if you get chilled and have a table on the rail, bring something to cover up. (And if you forget, the bend-over-backwards-to-please-staff will fetch you something.) Despite its romantic appeal, this restaurant can easily accommodate large groups and children who think restaurants are a treat. A three course keiki (children's) menu will please most small fine diners with its cheese pizza appetizer, chicken fingers, steak, fish, pasta, and ice cream sandwich dessert.

Spago attends to every little detail, and does so with friendly, unpretentious, knowledgeable competence. It's one of our favorite special occasion restaurants on Maui, and we recommend dining here.

Address: 3900 Wailea Alanui Dr., Wailea, South Maui
Location: Four Seasons Resort
Meals: Dinner
Hours: Nightly 6pm-9pm, bar open until 11pm
Parking: Valet
Phone: 808-874-8000
Website: www.fourseasons.com

Star Noodle *(Asian/Noodles)*

Even though it's hidden up at the top of Lahaina's industrial park, this tiny dining room is often packed for lunch and dinner. The hip, metropolitan ambience and the fresh, reasonably-priced cuisine attract plenty of locals, including us.

The kitchen staff took a research trip to New York City before crafting their menu, and they aspire to the greatness of legendary noodle houses like Momofuku and Wagamama. To some extent, they succeed.

We like to order several appetizers as a full meal, because they are both rea-

continued on next page

OVERALL:

4.2
out of 5 stars

$ $

Star Noodle *(continued)*

sonably priced and generously portioned. We nearly always get the steamed pork belly buns, because they are just lovely, and nearly irresistible at $9. Served in a bamboo basket, the thick slabs of pork have a crunchy crust of seared fat — exactly the indulgence one looks for in a pork bun. The buns are soft and sweet, stuffed with Japanese cucumber and green onions.

Another under-$10 treat is the pan-roasted Brussels sprouts, with their perfectly charred outer leaves. Served with bacon and lick-the-plate kim chee puree, the appetizer portion is generous, though you and your companion might still fight over the last tender quarters.

The Vietnamese crepe is another standout, and big enough to serve as a satisfying, inexpensive ($10) meal. The crunchy folded crepe — which is more egg-y than pancake-y, to set your expectations if you've never had this classic dish — gives way to a medley of shrimp, pork, and bean sprouts. Add crisp butter lettuce, slivers of carrots and cilantro sprigs for even more flavor and texture.

The pohole fern salad is bright and crisp, perfectly dressed and mixed with onions, seaweed (kombu) and shrimp (ebi).

Most of the noodles are made in-house, as you would expect in a place that puts "noodle" in its name. They also make the several types of dashi (soup stock). Sadly, we're not huge fans of the noodle bowls.

The Star Ramen *should* be the menu's star, and its extra umami flavor certainly has its fans. The dashi's smokiness comes honestly — it's extracted from the pig bones that were smoke-roasted for long hours in the traditional imu from at Old Lahaina Luau. The result is a viscous and deeply flavorful stock, but that's part of the problem: it's too dense, it's too rich. When the traditional egg is dropped in the bowl, it just gets more intense.

While the Hapa Ramen is a lovely thought: two broths ying-yanged in the same bowl that you mix yourself after admiring the presentation ... it is similarly too heavy. Halve the richness and we'd be better able to evaluate the broths for their inherent flavor.

Some of the noodles dishes are downright confusing: the Look Funn noodles are tight little rolls arranged in a row besides a spattering of shrimp and scallops in black bean sauce. Neither element is powerful enough to survive the separation. The Lahaina Fried Soup isn't soup at all — it's a pile of thick noodles covered with crumbled pork on the dry-ish side.

The simpler noodle dishes fare better, particularly the garlic noodles. These feature both fresh and fried garlic and just enough (garlic) oil and soup stock to bring everything alive. We don't even mind the candy-like bits that stick in our teeth.

Where this restaurant really excels is in the daily specials, so pay attention when the server goes over them. We particularly loved a delectable scallop dish topped with fried Brussels sprout leaves and served with kim chee mashed potatoes. The dusting of furikake (sushi seasoning) finished off this plate perfectly.

Star Noodle *(continued)*

We're never wowed by a malasada that isn't scorch-your-mouth hot, but we admit the fried dough balls so named on the dessert menu are fun, and their accompanying dipping sauces are nice, too. We like the unique house-made sorbets and ice creams even better. Frosty spoonfuls of sumptuous sour cream or perfumed lychee are a lovely final note to a meal here.

Service is knowledgeable and efficient. There's a full bar at the back of the room, and plenty of sakes and sake cocktails — even better — to try. We particularly like the Nigori cosmo and the berry sparkler (sparkling sake, lychee liqueur, and lemon). Prices are generally fair, making it easy to add a drink to an already reasonable bill.

On an island with plenty of sunset views and palm tree flourishes, it's a relief to relax in this comfortable restaurant filled with modern lines, blond wood, river stones and slate tiles. The floor to ceiling windows bring in plenty of natural light and also offer a panoramic view of the faraway ocean (once you look past the parking lot and the industrial park). Several smaller tables line the window, but strangers don't mind sliding in beside one another at the expansive twenty-seat communal table that dominates the center of the room. Charismatic screen prints by graffiti master Shepard Fairey complete the nod to the urban concept at work here.

What's not-so-urban — and not-so-Maui-an, either — is the Absolutely Fabulous Bathrooms. Thank you, to whoever designed these chic oases — the pocket doors, barn-door latches, river stone walls and beautiful sinks are unexpected, and appreciated.

Address: 286 Kupuohi St., Lahaina, West Maui
Location: Turn from the highway onto Keawe St. and head up the hill away from Lahaina Cannery Mall. Turn right on Kupouhi (there's no other option) and follow it up to the very top of the park. The restaurant is on your right.
Meals: Lunch, Dinner
Hours: Daily, 10:30am–10pm
Parking: Lot
Phone: 808-667-5400
Website: www.starnoodle.com

Stella Blues Café *(American)*

Stella Blues serves American comfort food in a fading Grateful Dead-inspired restaurant. The large, noisy rooms, outdoor seating, pool tables, and commodious concrete bar keep its fans coming back, and back, and back.

Sadly, the heart seems to have gone out of this formerly fabulous, friendly restaurant. We used to look forward to coconut shrimp that were perfectly prepared (crunchy and sweet outside, tender inside). We loved their baby back ribs with a fruity barbecue sauce. The roasted chicken with mashed potatoes, creamed corn, and wilted spinach was one of our favorite meals. We even liked their tofu stir fries and curries.

continued on next page

Stella Blues Café *(continued)*

Sometimes the magic is still there, but a lassitude has crept into the kitchen that makes the food inconsistent. One visit will be wonderful, the next awful. The service is still efficient and unobtrusive and friendly, but there's something off for us and the high prices (which have crept up over the years) are now off-putting compared to what's on the plate, no matter how big the portions remain. Breakfast is a little perkier, but not much.

Address: 1279 S. Kihei Rd., Kihei, South Maui
Location: Azeka Mauka Marketplace
Meals: Breakfast, Brunch, Lunch, Dinner
Hours: Daily 7:30am–10pm
Parking: Lot
Phone: 808-874-3779
Website: www.stellablues.com

$
🐾
CASH

Sunrise Café *(American)*

We would call this hole-in-the-wall family-run business quaint if they served excellent — or even just good — food. Instead, we call it something unprintable because of the bad coffee, disinterested, lazy, almost hostile service (we've waited thirty minutes to get that bad coffee), and mediocre, commercial ingredients prepared with very little love or attention to taste. While we like the idea of eggs Benedict served with lox on a bagel, it's not as good as it sounds. The pancakes are stiff, and everything takes thirty minutes longer than it should. The pineapple juice is thirst-quenching, though we suspect "fresh squeezed" might be an "exaggeration." The prices are low, especially for Front Street, but we think they survive — and have lines out the door — only because they're one of the only places to get breakfast in Lahaina town. Go to *Moose's* or *Lahaina Coolers* instead.

Address: 693 Front St., Lahaina, West Maui
Location: Next to the library, tucked down the block from the activities booth
Meals: Breakfast, Lunch
Hours: Daily 6:30am–5pm
Parking: Street
Phone: 808-661-8558

Sushi Paradise *(Sushi)*

If there isn't room at *Koiso* and our sushi craving will not go away, we head to *Sushi Paradise* for fresh, no-frills sushi. The owner is as picky about his fish as Hiro-san is, and puts out a great plate.

This small, Spartan restaurant next to Long's in Kihei is often a victim of its own popularity. It can't accommodate crowds and the waitress/hostess will turn guests away when the seats are full. With several tables in addition to the sushi bar, the wait can get looooong because the owner

Sushi Paradise *(continued)*

is the only sushi chef, and, unless you're sitting at the bar where the action is, the quiet room can be very ... quiet. On the other hand, if a big group of fans comes in, it can get rowdy quickly.

Our advice: order edamame and sunomono (seafood salad with substantial slivers of seafood and sea vegetables) to snack on while you wait. When they do arrive, the sashimi platters and nigiri are more than capably prepared — generous slices of fresh fish often hang over the sides of the rice, completely obscuring their platform. While the prices are similar to other sushi places around Maui, we don't get that same magic feeling we get from Hiro-san ... but if it's sushi you must have, this is a good option in South Maui.

Address: 1215 S. Kihei Rd., Kihei, South Maui
Location: in the Long's Shopping Center
Meals: Dinner
Hours: Tu-Su 6pm-10pm
Parking: Lot
Phone: 808-879-3751

T. Komoda Store and Bakery *(Bakery)*

This ninety-year-old general store and bakery may look like it's been boarded up or condemned, but ***Komoda's*** isn't closed permanently ... just sold out for the day. If the weathered storefront is open, there's probably a line. Get here early (before 10 a.m.) for delicious malasadas, the Portuguese donut rolled in sugar. Malasadas tend to be oilier than regular donuts and are served in paper bags to absorb the extra greasiness. They're best when piping hot, straight out of the wok or fry pan. If your arrival coincides with the baker's and fresh, hot malasadas are on hand, get a half dozen plain and eat them on the spot. Otherwise, try those filled with sweet guava (some say too sweet) or red adzuki bean paste (yum). You can also get macadamia-nut-covered stick donuts (glazed donuts with a stick stuck in them, so your fingers don't get too sticky), decent cream puffs (the pastry shells are exquisite, the custard-y cream just okay), and fluffy butter rolls.

Komoda's donuts and cream puffs have won an enthusiastic following as much for their flavor as for the nostalgia of their environment. This is a glance backward in time to how Maui used to be, before its population exploded and big box stores overwhelmed small mom and pops like this one. It's humble and dusty in the corners, but sweet and quirky. We've peeked into the kitchen and been reassured to see everything is squeaky clean and made by hand — the same way it's been done for decades.

If you're a donut fan, this is worth the trip up to Makawao and the pastries generally still taste good the following morning. If you order ahead, they won't run out of whatever you're interested in. Note: closed on Wednesdays, which somehow is when we get motivated to visit.

continued on next page

Address: 3674 Baldwin Ave., Makawao, Upcountry
Location: Just down from the corner of Makawao and Baldwin, the building looks closed up
Meals: Breakfast, Lunch, Snacks & Treats
Hours: M–Tu and Th–F 7am–5pm; Sa 7am–2pm
Parking: Street
Phone: 808-572-7261

OVERALL:

3.1

out of 5 stars

Taqueria Cruz *(Mexican)*

Taqueria Cruz makes decent Mexican food by hand and to order. (We know it's made to order, because it takes an intolerably long time for it to come out of the kitchen.) Their blackened fish taco makes the most flavorful choice; most other items are blander than they should be. The seating is outside, in the strip mall's courtyard, and local musicians like to set up and play for tips in the evenings (we don't always like what we hear, though, and the amplifier is often turned up to 11).

We recommend ***Taqueria Cruz*** for those with a low spice tolerance who like the flavor profile of Mexican food. The ingredients are fresh and the prices moderate.

Address: 2395 S. Kihei Rd., Kihei
Location: in Dolphin Plaza across from Kamaole Beach Park I
Meals: Lunch, Dinner
Hours: M–Sa 11am–8pm
Parking: Lot
Phone: 808-875-2910

OVERALL:

3.6

out of 5 stars

CASH

Tasaka Guri Guri *(Guri Guri)*

Guri-Guri is a local frozen treat that is something like ice cream, something like sherbet, but not really either one. The story is that it was made for Japanese plantation workers and sold as "goodie-goodie" (which they pronounced guri-guri).

This third-generation family store is a Hawaiian institution and people visiting from other islands make a point to stop in and get a tiny Dixie cup filled with little scoops of this treat. There are two flavors — strawberry and pineapple — and you can combine them if you like. Two scoops (the size of a melon ball) cost you $1.

Made with (as far as we can taste; the exact recipe is a closely guarded secret) strawberry guava or pineapple juice, 7 UP, sweetened condensed milk, and one other "mystery ingredient," you won't be surprised to hear that the flavor is more sweet than fruity, but very refreshing. A recipe you can make at home in your ice cream maker (or without) is on our blog, just search for "guri-guri" at www.MauiRestaurantsBlog.com/guri-guri. Kids of all ages back home will love you for it.

Tasaka Guri Guri *(continued)*

Address: 70 E. Kaahumanu Ave., Kahului, Central Maui
Location: in the Maui Mall
Meals: Snacks & Treats
Hours: M-Th & Sa 9am-6pm; F 9am-8pm; Su 10am-4pm
Parking: Lot
Phone: 808-871-4513

Tasty Crust *(Local/Plate Lunch)*

You probably have a version of **Tasty Crust** in your own hometown. Picture the diner that's been open since the fifties (or earlier), hasn't updated (or cleaned) since the seventies, serves cheap food and lots of it, and brings in business mainly because old habits die hard and food eaten in childhood automatically attains a nostalgic pleasure. The popularity with visitors is limited to, as far as we can tell, people who don't read this book, but it has its fans from other islands, too. While this is a "landmark" and an "institution," we wouldn't choose to eat here unless it was our job — and the staff and owners probably don't care either way. Sticky tables, surly (at best) service, and stiff pancakes ... it compares about the same to our greasy spoons back home, but without our personal nostalgic ties.

Address: 1770 Mill St., Wailuku, Central Maui
Meals: Breakfast, Lunch, Dinner
Hours: Tu-F 6am-10pm; Sa-Su 6am-11pm; M 6am-3pm
Parking: Lot, Street
Phone: 808-244-0845

Teddy's Bigger Burgers *(American)*

Teddy's Bigger Burgers is a burger joint that started in Honolulu, but now has locations in places as far away as Washington state and Tokyo. We are really, really glad they finally came to Maui. Their burgers are delicious: hand-formed from ground chuck that has never been frozen. They are cooked to order, so this is not very-fast food, but it is well worth the wait. The toppings are fresh and the buns are fresh, and the special sauce — they call it Super Sauce — is a nice combination of tang and sweet. We also like that they come in three sizes: 5 ounce, 7 ounce, and 9 ounce. The 5 ounce is plenty for us, especially when we're getting their specialty burgers. The Cajun burger is nice and spicy, and the pepperjack cheese adds a creamy kick. The volcano burger, with jalapenos, pepperjack cheese, and their super spicy BBQ sauce, is also delicious.

If you prefer, they also have a flavorful fish sandwich and can make chicken breast, veggie and turkey versions of their burgers. They treat these sandwiches are carefully as they do the burgers, making sure they are tender and

continued on next page

perfectly cooked. The fries and onion rings are good — not spectacular — but the shakes are so thick we can't draw them up through a straw. Try the creamsicle and pineapple flavors, but the chocolate and strawberry are delicious, too.

Combination meals are a good value: under $10 for a 5 ounce burger, fries, and soda. If you want to substitute a specialty burger or shake, that's possible.

The service is friendly and efficient, but patient, which you will appreciate once you get up to the front of the (usually) long line. The restaurant is spotlessly clean, and the walls — a yellow that is usually only seen in kindergartens — are painted with fun murals of surfing burger slingers. Every fifteen minutes or so a server roams the restaurant offering packets of wet naps. We appreciate this, much as we appreciate this delicious representation of classic, all-American fare.

Address: 335 Keawe St., Lahaina, West Maui
Location: In the Lahaina Gateway Shopping Center, in the back near Foodland
Meals: Lunch, Dinner
Hours: Su-Th 10am-9pm. Fr-Sa 10am-10pm
Parking: Lot
Phone: 808-661-9111
Website: www.teddysbiggerburgers.com

Thai Chef *(Thai)*

Thai Chef is a little hole-in-the-wall dive without a liquor license or its own restroom, but it serves some of the strongest Thai food on the island, and offers an exceptional dining value.

Tables are crammed together and chair legs practically overlap each other, but patrons — many of whom have brought their own beer — don't care at all once the friendly and enthusiastic servers bring the food. It's super-fresh, well-prepared, and authentic. The menu covers everything you expect it to, including lots of vegetarian options.

We adore the pad Thai. This popular noodle dish is often the first one tasted by those new to the spicy, flavorful cuisine — which means it is often dumbed down: a bland pile of noodles with peanut bits dumped on top. ***Thai Chef*** treats it with great respect, making sure that the noodles are the perfect dense, scrumptious texture, the egg is tender, the protein (our favorite is pork) well-cooked, and the sauce ... oh, this sauce. You might think "peanuts" when you think of this dish, and you would be correct, of course. But it's not just peanuts. It's also tamarind, and fish sauce, and rice wine vinegar, and scallions, garlic, cabbage, lime, red chili peppers ... only the best things in life. Here you taste all of these in a perfect blend — sweet, spicy, sour, salty. The chopped peanut garnish isn't just grit: it has a salty sweetness all to itself. We usually order Thai food "Hot" (and sometimes

OVERALL:
3.6
out of 5 stars

$ $

Thai Chef *(continued)*

"Thai Hot"), but here we order this dish Medium. They are not afraid of insulting Western palates, and their Medium would be Hot at *Thailand Cuisine*, for example.

Another must-try is their snapper (opakapaka, or Hawaiian pink snapper, in season) with ginger sauce. The fish filet is steamed, skin left intact, until it is Perfectly Done. If you've never had this snapper, it's a real treat — tender, moist, and delicate. In this sauce, it's *sublime*. Fresh ginger, onions and carrots are slivered — toothpick-sized — and sautéed with spices and fish sauce to render a pungent, slightly sweet, fiery gravy. This one, we order Hot. Every time we eat this dish, we have the same thought: this same preparation could easily fetch three times the price if served at an upscale restaurant. It's $13.95.

Other good choices include the larb: minced chicken, beef or pork (we like pork, again), grilled and combined with onions, bean sprouts, mint and cilantro with fish sauces and other spices. Lovely. The cabbage leaves are not decoration — eat them along with the meat to cool down the dish and add crunch and texture. We also like the curries, and the Evil Prince tofu. Vegetarians will l-o-v-e the clean flavors and super-fresh food, as well as the many vegetarian options.

We are not such huge fans of many of the appetizers. The crab and pork toast never works for us, and the spring rolls are greasy. But the fish cakes are nice, and the cucumber vinaigrette that comes with is light and flavorful. We also like the green papaya salad.

Despite the occasional long wait for a table and the cramped seating, there's a lot of love coming out of that tiny kitchen, and we're happy there's such good Thai in Lahaina. We also love that it's BYOB.

Address: 878 Front St., Lahaina, West Maui
Location: In the Old Lahaina Centre near KFC
Meals: Lunch, Dinner
Hours: M-F 11am–2pm (lunch), M-Sa 5pm–9pm (dinner), closed Sunday
Parking: Lot (drive past the restaurant for spots that aren't reserved)
Phone: 808-667-2814
Website: www.thaichefrestaurantmaui.com

Thailand Cuisine *(Thai)*

Thailand Cuisine is one of our favorite island eateries and one of our main "comfort" restaurants. If we've had an exhausting day or feel a little cold coming on — or even if we just want a meal before or after a movie — we walk in, sit in the first booth they point to, and surrender to the quiet, capable service.

If you already like Thai food, you'll recognize the quality dishes. The usual suspects — pad Thai, soups, curries — are freshly made and well spiced.

OVERALL:
4.4
out of 5 stars

continued on next page

Thailand Cuisine *(continued)*

Although we personally like our Thai "hot" (spicy) or "Thai hot" (volcanic), even the milder versions are flavorful. We love the *Tom Ka Gai*; spicy coconut soup studded with big, fresh mushrooms, slices of ginger, basil leaves, and your choice of chicken and/or shrimp. The *Tom Yum* soup is another comforting brew, this one spicy and sour from the kaffir lime.

The green papaya salad is crisp and puckery, studded with finely chopped peanuts. It wakes up our palate for whatever main course we're ordering. The *Yum Nuer*, or Beef Salad, piles marinated beef on top of a delicious medley of vegetables. We often order this dish if we're in the mood for a light entrée.

The Crispy Chicken is a generous mound of deep fried chicken that comes with a complex, spicy red dipping sauce. We also like the Evil Prince curry with tofu, a blend of lemongrass, basil, chilies, and coconut milk. The Pad Pet is one of our favorites — a savory brown sauce with your choice of protein. You might've guessed by now that we're fans of duck done well and this humble kitchen turns out a delightful duck in red curry.

Dishes are served family style, and you can get sticky or brown rice on the side. Served in a slender woven basket, the sticky, glutinous rice is like candy — sweet, chewy, and addictive. The ingredients are fresh and local, with many coming from the owner's garden. Beer and wine choices are limited, but they always have the light Thai beer *Singha* on hand, which is, of course, perfect. Before we can order dessert, the mild-mannered servers often deliver a free dish of coconut milk tapioca pudding to the table. We also like the sweet mango (when they are in season) over sticky rice.

Their combination dinners (for two, for three, for four) include some of the best items on the menu, and we recommend them for their value. Just about every dish can be made vegetarian, which our herbivore friends appreciate — doubly so since their half of the menu is titled "Vegetarian Lovers."

Both locations are consistent and offer both dine in and take out. The dining rooms are wood paneled and have plenty of statuary and traditional décor, but also comfortable booths and real napkins. The Thai music videos blaring on the TV make us giggle, but the pretty blue matching china — from the teapot to the soup bowls — evoke that sweet, cared for feeling we've had at grandma's or a beloved aunt's. The moderate prices, excellent service, and delicious food make these little Thai joints a must-try.

Address: 70 E. Kaahumanu Ave., Kahului, Central Maui
Location: in the Maui Mall
Meals: Lunch, Dinner
Hours: Daily 10:30am-3:30pm; Su-Th 5-9:30pm; F-Sa 5-10:30pm
Parking: Lot
Phone: 808-873-0225
Website: www.thailandcuisinemaui.com

Address: 1819 S. Kihei Rd., Kihei, South Maui
Location: in the Kukui Mall
Meals: Lunch, Dinner
Hours: M-Sa 11am-2:30pm; Nightly 5-10pm
Parking: Lot
Phone: 808-875-0839

$ $

Three's Bar & Grill *(Southwestern, Pacific Fusion, Sushi)*

Three's Bar & Grill is owned by three ambitious chef-owners, each of whom has his own perspective on food (Pacific Rim, Hawaiian, and Southwestern). When it first opened in 2010, we were exhausted just trying to read the almost terrifyingly sprawling menu. Each cuisine was so thoroughly represented that trying to figure out what to order was next to impossible, and the kitchen struggled to send out consistently delicious dishes. We feared these young chefs — who also have a catering business together — were more focused on protecting their own dishes than figuring out what their customers wanted to eat. The menu — and most of the dishes — needed some serious editing.

Our fears were unfounded. Over the months the menu became tighter and more focused, while the font increased and the number of pages shrank. They've pared out the less successful dishes — these cuisines don't always blend well — and developed an interesting offering. Their original slogan, "Wailea food at Kihei prices" has not exactly been lived up to — they have a way to go before their product is "Wailea" great — but the prices are indeed reasonable. (Entrees are usually under $16.) These owner chefs clearly care about their business, their customers, and their food, and we see ample evidence that they will only continue to improve as time goes on.

We like anything that pairs the kalua pork and sweet CoCoNut Porter barbecue sauce: they come as a sandwich (with Asian slaw) and in a quesadilla (with spiced mango chutney). Sweet, smoky, messy … we are glad these dishes have survived every menu iteration. We also like their build-it-yourself burger. The coconut-crusted fish sandwich (whatever's available that day) is also nice, and comes with a tasty pineapple Asian slaw. The specialty fries are worth the upgrade — we like the sweet potato and the roasted garlic.

The papaya salsa on the fresh fish preparation is the perfect sweet counterpart to the blackened crust, and the "deluxe" Hawaiian loco moco is the best representation of this staple we've had. This dish is not for the faint of heart (and we have to share it). Eight ounces of burger, two eggs (your choice of style, we like over easy), and onion rings come over sushi rice. The wild mushroom gravy is flavorful and earthy, and the bacon just pushes this to the limit. It's also available for breakfast, and we've seen more than one single guy polish it off before heading to work. (Or surf.)

The ribs come flavored by a nice rub and slathered with a sweet-heat barbecue sauce (guava and chipotle), plus wasabi mashed potatoes and that Asian slaw. We skip the flatbreads, which have been soggy too often.

Salads are fresh, and the lilikoi vinaigrette is tart, but not *too*. The sushi is good, if you're in the mood, and the wasabi cocktail sauce that comes with the raw oysters is very nice. We like that you can order one oyster at a time, rather than committing to a whole plate. This flexibility is carried into the dessert end of the menu, too, where there are several tiny little desserts offered for only $3. The price is right, but they're not skimpy on the presenta-

continued on next page

tion or ingredients: just miniaturized. One of their teensy sundaes carefully topped with whipped cream and hot fudge, and a cup of their excellent coffee make a satisfying end to a meal. The prices are low enough that we don't mind spending a little more on these "extras."

That coffee — an excellent blend from Maui Oma, the local roaster — is part of what brings us back in for breakfast. We like the egg breakfasts best, because they are most consistent. The French toast is candy-sweet (caramelized on the edges) and we just don't find the guava jelly and lilikoi cream cheese fillings appealing. The pancakes have ranged from fantastically delicious to passable to inedible on three separate occasions. The Benedicts are solid, and the lobster Benedict, if you can stomach it for breakfast, is almost too-silly luxury ... but for $15.95, not a bad deal.

Service is good and seems efficient, although we have to say we have rarely been able to experience it without a chef-owner stopping by at least once to see how we are being treated. We're not sure if they treat all of their customers this way or if it's because they know who we are. (James judged a cooking competition that Chef Cody Christopher won, right around the time this place opened.) It's certain that one of the reasons this restaurant continues to improve is because the chef owners are invested in its success — and at least one of them is always on-site.

The restaurant is located in the old Bada Bing! location, and they wisely gutted the wreck and made the interior welcoming and level-floored and well-lit. There's a large lounge area to the left, separate from the rest of the restaurant, with a big bar, comfortable couches, and lots of live music. If you're wondering where the night life is on Maui, it's here — their permit allows dancing and serving alcohol until a crazy-late 2am.

To the right as you enter is the small dining room — which feels more like a hall, and probably was at some point — and an outdoor lanai that is breezy (sometimes too breezy) during lunch, but shady and pretty during breakfast, and cool at dinner. Unfortunately, the large tree that shades it also drops all over the lanai. This and the wind blowing in dirt and sand make it almost impossible to feel clean. Every time we visit, we notice the dirt on the lanai and around the front entrance of the still rather ramshackle building. Someone should be sweeping up at least once a day, and probably twice, and a power wash once in a while wouldn't hurt. For this reason, sitting inside, for us, is nicer, even if it is a bit stuffy and loud when the music is pumping in the lounge.

The very reasonable prices, generally good food, and excellent cocktails (try the margarita) make this a good choice for families and anyone else looking for a decent meal that won't burn a hole in your pocket.

Address: 1945 S. Kihei Rd., Kihei, South Maui
Location: In Kalama Village, near Serendipity.
Meals: Breakfast and Lunch Wed-Sun, Dinner
Hours: Daily Mon-Tues 3pm-10pm, Wed-Sun 8:30am-10pm
Parking: Lot
Phone: 808-879-3133
Website: www.Threesbarandgrill.com

Tommy Bahama's Tropical Café *(American)*

Despite our reluctance to eat in a clothing shop chain, we always have a great time at **Tommy Bahama's**, and it's one of our favorite Happy Hour places in South Maui. **Tommy's** menu is filled with hyperbole (every item reads like the most extravagant, to-die-for dish you could ever hope to eat) and Wailea's characteristically high dollar signs. But the food that's presented is consistently fresh, well-prepared, and delicious. The staff is uniformly gracious from the hostess to the busboy.

We love the appetizers, especially their ahi poke, a simple, fresh, delicious representation of the Hawaiian-style sashimi. The ahi tuna is uniformly chopped small, mixed with creamy mayonnaise and plenty of spices, then layered with guacamole to smooth out the flavors. Served over crispy flatbread and tortilla chips, it is one of our favorite ways to celebrate.

The scallop sliders are a lighter takes on the beef slider — replace the red meat with the tender seared scallop and you get a fresh burst of sweet fish that perfectly sets off the spicy slaw on top. The simple, macadamia-nut-encrusted goat cheese served with mango salsa is also a favorite. Texture and flavor are well-balanced in all of their appetizers. We also like the buttery crab bisque, the crab cakes, and the coconut shrimp, which are usually well prepared and not overcooked.

The cheeseburger has a good sear and sweet and melty honey roasted onions. The pork sandwich with the blackberry brandy sauce continues to be one of our favorite items; savory and sweet and generously sized. The chopped salad with chicken is chunked up with apples, nuts, bacon, and corn, and completely satisfying as a light main entrée. Ribs fall off the bone (and we always take some home).

The steaks are good cuts and prepared well. They often have good specials, and sometimes excellent deals on three course fixed price menus (the portions are often smaller, but we still leave plenty full).

Desserts are excellent at **Tommy's**, and we often come here late just for a little something sweet. We were skeptical when a reader (who is now a friend) told us that the butterscotch pudding was "the best dessert on Maui," but we were converted upon the first taste. Made from scratch and spiked with plenty of whiskey, the creamy, beautifully browned pudding comes in a giant (**giant**) goblet coated on the inside with a chocolate ganache and topped with homemade whipped cream. While we like the brownie and the key lime pie, this pudding is what we talk about later. (And you will, too.) Ask for the smaller size unless you are splitting it with your companion.

There's live music at night, and the open-air restaurant features wide, comfortable booths and large tables. It's even prettier with its recent renovation, which left the central bar intact: big, square, and comfortable for hanging out at Happy Hour or any other time.

OVERALL:

4

out of 5 stars

continued on next page

Tommy Bahama's Tropical Café *(continued)*

Address: 3750 Wailea Alanui Dr., Wailea, South Maui
Location: at the Shops at Wailea
Meals: Lunch, Dinner
Hours: Daily 11am-10pm
Parking: Lot
Phone: 808-875-9983
Website: www.TommyBahama.com

Tropica *(Pacific Rim / American)*

Tropica, the beachfront dinner restaurant at The Westin in Ka'anapali, features giant thatched umbrellas, a central koi pond, and a beautiful "wall of water" fountain at the back of the somewhat cavernous, open-air restaurant. If the Hawaiiana theme, slightly too loud (but good) live music, and vacationers passing close to your table don't bother you, we recommend *Tropica's* menu for fresh, local ingredients prepared with care. The prices are high, yes, but Ka'anapali is overpriced in general, and this is one of the better options in the resort area.

The wide-ranging menu features many very good appetizers, thin crust pizzas, several salads, and well-composed fish dishes, steaks, and meats. Wine suggestions are listed with every item. We like to share several appetizers (portions are smaller than they should be) and add a salad or pizza to make a full meal. We enjoy the New Caledonia Prawns — the sweet, tender shrimp meat is respected and not overcooked, and the uni butter that surrounds each large prawn adds a briny flavor with a decadent texture. The roasted lamb loin with light and creamy polenta is perfectly satisfying. We also appreciate the organic chicken: braised in lavender (though we couldn't taste it) and finished with a sweet shoyu sauce and a medley of Asian vegetables. Many of the entrées incorporate novel sauces or spices, which we approve of, but in general we find their application too timid (something that can happen at resorts, where chefs have to cater to customers who might only be eating at their restaurant because they're staying at the hotel).

If you must stay in Ka'anapali for dinner, this is among your best options; otherwise head to *Japengo*.

Address: 2365 Ka'anapali Pkwy., Ka'anapali, West Maui
Location: Westin Ka'anapali
Meals: Dinner
Hours: W-Su 4:30pm-9:30pm
Parking: Valet
 Phone: 808-667-2525
Website: www.westinmaui.com

OVERALL:
3.4
out of 5 stars

Ululani's Hawaiian Shave Ice *(Shave Ice)*

This is the only place on Maui we recommend you go to for shave ice. And you're in luck, because it's one of the best in Hawaii. With three locations — and a new one opening in Kihei in early 2012 — you really don't have an excuse. If you're visiting, make your first stop early in your stay, because you will want to come back at least twice before you leave. If you live on Maui, why aren't you there right now?

Shave ice (not "shaved ice"), will remind you of a snow cone, but keep in mind that its legacy is east, not west — it came to Hawaii from Japan. The texture is flakier and lighter than an Italian ice or snow cone on the mainland. That said we still find most of the shops on Maui serve crinkly ice studded with chunks. Because they're often using inferior syrups, the dominant taste is "sweet," no matter what flavor you choose. Not exactly good eats.

Not so at *Ululani's*. The texture of the ice — delicate flakes that nearly float down off the blade — is exactly like the fluffy, large-crystal snow that falls when winter sets in earnestly in colder climates. The ice melts instantly when it hits your tongue, sweeping the flavors you've chosen throughout your mouth. The pure water combined with the delicious homemade syrups make for a refreshing "sip" in every "bite."

The syrups are made by hand and tested until the recipe is just right, and they are beautiful. When we watch the Guava poured on the ice, for instance, we can see the fruit puree. The syrups taste like what they are, because they are made from what they are. For example, lilikoi (passion fruit) is made from lilikoi. Coconut is made from coconut. Maui cane sugar is the sweetener (no corn syrup), and that makes a huge difference in the *flavor* of the sweetness.

After watching them make shave ice, we have realized that making good shave ice is a lot like making good espresso. Every step of the process represents an opportunity to refine technique. The amount of pressure exerted on the ice, the speed of the blade as it shaves off the paper-thin slices, the way the ice is mounted in the cup, the subtle hand pressure used to form the perfectly round ball of ice, the careful pouring of syrups so they don't mix, but meet exactly ... it's just like watching an experienced, talented barista.

In addition to just ice and syrup, try a base of ice cream to give a different texture as you drill through layers of ice to the creamy layer below. Toppings include a drizzle of evaporated milk, which hits a nice smooth note right off the top. There are at least 30 flavors to choose from, but you can have many in combination on a single ice. The strongest seller — and with good reason — is a combination of coconut and dulce de leche that is decadent and unforgettable.

Co-owners Ululani and her husband, David, share a lovely story about growing up loving shave ice on Oahu, moving to the mainland, and missing it terribly. They opened their first place in Seattle with some retirement

OVERALL:

4.6
out of 5 stars

$

CASH

continued on next page

Ululani's Hawaiian Shave Ice *(continued)*

funds, and in 2008 moved back to Hawaii to open up their first Lahaina shop.

We're so glad they brought their icy Aloha home to all of us. If you are looking for a taste of pure Hawaii that also is a delicious food on its own, *Ululani's* is a must stop. If you are at the airport in the afternoon, you can make this your last (or first) taste of Maui.

Address: 819 Front Street, Lahaina, West Maui
Location: In the Old Poi Factory — near and on the same side of the street as Cheeseburger in Paradise.
Hours: Daily 11am-10pm
Parking: Street
Phone: 360-606-2745

Address: 790 Front Street, Lahaina, West Maui
Location: On the other side of the street from Cheeseburger in Paradise!
Hours: Daily 11am-9pm
Parking: Street
Phone: 360-606-2745

Address: 333 Dairy Road, Kahului, Central Maui
Location: in the same shopping plaza as Amigo's, right across from Mc-Donald's
Hours: Daily, 11am-6pm
Parking: Lot
Phone: 360-606-2745

NEW SOUTH MAUI LOCATION OPENING SOMETIME IN 2012:

Address: S. Kihei Rd., Kihei, South Maui
Location: The official location has not been announced as of publication, but the likely location is where the Suda store once was, next to ABC Store in North Kihei. From Wailea/South Kihei take the beach road (N. Kihei Road) north and look for it on your right-hand side. Check their website for an update.
Hours: Daily, 11am-6pm
Parking: Lot
Phone: 360-606-2745
Website: www.ululanisshaveice.com

OVERALL:

3.4

out of 5 stars

'Umalu *(Pacific Rim/American)*

The poolside restaurant at the Hyatt is above average hotel cuisine at average (read: exorbitant) Ka'anapali hotel prices. The wide-ranging menu, however, is likely to have something for even the pickiest of eaters, and we think vegetarians will be particularly happy with the varied and tasty preparations.

Appetizers are sized big enough to share or use as an entrée. We especially like the Snake River Farm Kobe sliders. The American Kobe beef is used

'Umalu (continued)

to create a tray of three burgers topped with rich gorgonzola, caramelized sweet Maui onions, and a delicious aioli. With a poi (taro) bun, this is a really decadent, tender, sweet burger. Another good choice is the large platter of ahi nachos. Taro chips and sweet potato chips line the bottom, topped with a very good, balanced ahi poke, goat cheese, and guacamole made from edamame beans. The soft textures of the guacamole and the cheese meet the firmer fish, and contrast with the crisp chips. We like the unusual chips for the nachos.

Sandwiches and pizzas are available, as well as several really generous dinner-sized salads. The ingredients are fresh and local, and there is some care put into the recipes and the execution. We actually find ourselves fantasizing, on occasion, about the Korean beef bulgogi sandwich. Slices of tender and sweetly spicy marinated rib eye steak are piled onto a toasted ciabatta roll along with salty ribbons of miso-dressed cabbage slaw. Sour, salty, sweet, earthy and pungent? Check. Served with a small dish of suitably fiery kim chee, it's a resort version of Korean street food, and we give it a messy thumbs up.

Service is fine, but harried when busy. The pools at the Hyatt are spectacular. If we wanted to have lunch in Ka'anapali, we would likely choose *'Umalu* for its choice of indoor or outdoor seating, pretty views, and relatively good value for the resort area.

Address: 200 Nohea Kai Dr., Ka'anapali, West Maui
Location: Hyatt Regency, right on the beach walk
Meals: Lunch, Dinner
Hours: Daily 11am - 9:30pm
Parking: Valet
Phone: 808-661-1234

Vietnamese Cuisine *(Vietnamese)*

This sister restaurant to Wailuku's **A Saigon Café** is a little bigger, a little brighter, and a little cleaner. However, they're missing the funny-guy servers, and the food ranges from average to above average. If you're in South Kihei and really craving Vietnamese, you may like their *pho*, their noodle dishes, and their lemonade. The catfish in a clay pot is savory, but that's all it is — chunks of catfish. Watch out for bones. They feature big portions at decent prices.

Address: 1280 S. Kihei Rd., Kihei, South Maui
Location: Azeka Makai Marketplace
Meals: Lunch, Dinner
Hours: Daily 10am-9:30pm
Parking: Lot
Phone: 808-875-2088
Website: www.mauivietnameserestaurant.com

$ $

Wailuku Coffee Company *(American)*

The dark paneling, brick walls, and wrought iron café tables and chairs at **Wailuku Coffee Company** are decidedly un-Maui, but the tattooed waitresses and laid back vibe is. The art on the walls is all made by locals, and usually priced to sell.

At one time, this tiny bohemian enclave hosted brilliant entertainment on a tiny corner stage — everything from woo-woo New Agers chanting Sanskrit, soul singers belting out the blues to stomps and whistles, and belly dancers to hopeful, crooning singer songwriters. Wailuku's business set came for high-brow wines and cheese platters, lovingly chosen by Marc Aurel, the original owner. A few years ago, Aurel had to leave Maui quite suddenly. He turned the café over to a *hui* — the Hawaiian word for "community" — comprised of his most savvy waitresses. They kept the business going with barely a hitch — except that as the economy declined, so did the pau hana (after work) revelry. Before long, the fabulous wine bar and rowdy open mic nights were things of the past. Sniff, sniff.

The default owners decided to re-brand and re-open the business, which now mainly caters to Wailuku's lawyers, social workers and shop owners on their way to work or on their lunch break. If you happen to be in Wailuku at breakfast, the baristas make decent coffee and espresso. The café markets its own brand of beans, some of which are sourced here on Maui and roasted by the island's best: Maui Oma Coffee. For lunch, you can build your own sandwich from a reasonably diverse assortment of breads, meats, cheeses, and veggies.

Hopefully Wailuku's continued attempts at revitalization will prove successful, and this little spot will re-emerge as the gypsy flower it once was.

Address: 26 N. Market St., Wailuku, HI 96793
Location: On the same block as the Iao Theater
Meals: Breakfast, Lunch, Dinner
Hours: M-Fri 7am-5pm, Sat-Sun 8am-2pm
Parking: Street
Phone: 808-495-0259

Whole Foods *(Organic/Health Food Store)*

Speculation that Maui residents would not embrace the mainland grocery store **Whole Foods** proved unfounded within a week of their opening in early 2010. The convenient Kahului location — just around the bend from **Costco** and other big box stores — means people from all over the island shop here, and it's busy all day long. While **Whole Foods** is often considered expensive on the mainland, our extraordinarily high food costs here make those prices look average. It's not much more expensive to get your groceries here than it is at any other big grocery store — and sometimes even more cost effective. We can't help but very much appreciate the upscale shopping environment and the exceptional customer service. From the person stocking the dairy section to the fishmongers, butchers, bakers and cashiers,

Whole Foods *(continued)*

you get friendly, helpful, knowledgeable attention. They believe in their product, and it shows. So do we — we include *Whole Foods* in our weekly shopping trips.

The selection for grocery items is small — this is not one of their Emporiums — but select, and there are many gourmet items in stock. You can often get lovely local fresh fish — beautiful whole opakapaka and mahi mahi have been seen resting on an ice bed — but also some delicacies from farther afield. They're premium quality (and attendant premium price). The butchers are the best on Maui, and we are always finding something wonderful in their cases. If you have a grill at your condo, the marinated half chickens are often on sale and make a very tasty meal (we like the tequila lime preparation, but all of them are good). The produce, of course, is beautiful and well-tended and you'll find lots of local choices. The bakery offers decent breads and desserts, but we haven't found anything we crave later, especially at these prices. The cheese mongers are knowledgeable and will cut your selection to the size you need, no matter how small. The wine selection is small, but there are many good choices, and the same is true for beer. The deli has beautiful cold cuts and they can slice them as thin as you need (we like to see through ours).

The salad bar is typically fresh and tasty. The hot bars have a lot of delicious items, including fried chicken that James just adores, plus pretty good soups. The pizza needs some work (flavor in that sauce?) but the sandwiches are hearty. We like the hui chicken here, and also the offerings from the smoker. Vegetarians, of course, love the selections, including the many salads and casseroles in the deli section. We get sushi and Asian foods elsewhere.

The candies-by-the-pound section has chocolate covered toffee almonds (dusted with powdered sugar) that are so addictive we hesitate to include them in this review. They're too often sold out as it is — and they are the perfect thing to buy for a little mid-movie (or midnight) pick-me-up.

This is the best place for breakfast in Kahului, and the line starts well before the store opens. Well-priced breakfast selections and very good coffee are certainly the draw — but so is the fact that they stock their salad and hot bars this early, so workers can get their lunch for later.

There's a small, rather loud, eating area in the store, but many more tables outside. The view — the Maui Mall parking lot — isn't fantastic, but it's clean and comfortable.

Address: 70 Kaahumanu Ave., Kahului, Central Maui
Location: Lot
Meals: Breakfast, Lunch, Dinner
Hours: Daily 8am-9pm
Parking: Lot
Phone: 808-872-3310
Website: www.wholefoodsmarket.com/stores/maui

Top Maui Tips

We write this book as if we were writing a letter to good friends. Perhaps because of our friendly writing style, readers think we know the answers to all questions about Maui — whether they're about what kind of fish to order or where the sun sets or which snorkel trip is best. We always try to help out with complete and useful answers. But answering the same question five times in one week is not only time-consuming, it's inefficient — which is why we're dedicating this section of the guide to our Top Maui Tips.

These are the answers to the Most Important Frequently Asked Questions about Maui we get from readers like you. We hope you find our answers useful; if we save you even a little time and frustration, then we've done our job. If you have any questions that aren't answered here, feel free to send them to editor@TopMauiRestaurants.com and we'll do our best to answer you or point you in the right direction.

Maui Arrival

The vast majority of visitors come in through the airport in Kahului. We've flown in and out of here hundreds of times (James commuted between Washington, DC, and Maui on 72 round trips in the 1990's alone), so we have quite a few tips to share with you.

First, a word about luggage collection. If your flight is coming directly into Maui, your baggage will come with you. If you are getting a connecting flight from another island airport — if, for example, you are flying into Honolulu and switching to a local carrier for the last leg into Maui — your bags might not make it onto your flight. More than once we've checked in to our flight in Honolulu, landed half an hour later in Maui, and waited in vain for our bags to appear on the carousel. *They're probably on the next flight,* the airline personnel shrug. *No problem.* The good news is that we've never had our bags lost — they do show up with the next flight's luggage. The bad news is, of course, that we had to wait for them, when we'd rather be, oh, you know, doing *just about anything else.* If you are prone to high blood pressure, practice your deep breathing — there is nothing to be done but wait, and you will get little satisfaction — or sympathy — from the airline. Thankfully, tighter TSA regulations seem to have reduced the likelihood of this happening.

Depending upon what time you get in, getting your rental car is likely going to take a little while. Some agencies have check-in counters near the baggage area, but for others you'll need to take a shuttle to check-in. Since it can take a while to collect baggage, you might want to send the driver ahead to get the car while waiting. With so many visitors on each flight, the rental car counters can get jam-packed, and this might just give you a jump on the crowds (and a better choice of cars).

Once you're in your car, it takes about half an hour to drive to Kihei/Wailea, and about forty-five minutes to an hour to get out to Lahaina/Ka'anapali/Kapalua. If you're going upcountry or to the North Shore, the trip is typically a little quicker.

If it's still daylight, and you have the time, it's a good idea to stop at Kanaha Beach, which is right behind the car rental agencies. It's a sugar-sand beach with lovely turquoise waves. We like to stop here for a post-plane-ocean-fix. It's worth it to just dip our toes in the water.

Depending upon what time of day you arrive, you might want to stop and get some provisions — most of the best deals can be found in "town" (Kahului) and the resort areas tend to be pricier. You may also be hungry. We have some suggestions for places to stop to eat and/or get some provisions.

Immediately as you leave the airport, turn left to go to ***Costco***, where, if you are a member, you can pick up all sorts of supplies in bulk, from water to suntan lotion to fresh leis to groceries and produce and wine, beer, and spirits. Don't be afraid of picking up suntan lotion in bulk, by the way — the tropical sun is very strong, and you'll probably need more than you think you will.

At the same intersection you'll find Krispy Kreme on your right and Kmart on your left.

Next is the intersection with Hana Highway, where you can turn left to go to Paia, right to go into Kahului and straight to most destinations.

Straight ahead on Dairy Road: *Marco's* is right on this corner. Farther down, you'll find several strip malls with national box stores, plus *Down to Earth*, the all-vegetarian health food store, on the right. You'll find plenty of fast food on Dairy Road, as well as *Amigo's* and the shave ice must-try, *Ululani's* (both are on the right, directly across from McDonald's, just before *Down to Earth*). When you're almost to the Mokulele Highway (or Puunene Ave., depending upon which way you turn), you'll see Wal-Mart tucked back on the left, near the Home Depot.

Left onto Hana Highway: If you turn left onto the Hana Highway, you'll be headed into Paia, home of the fabulous *Mana Foods*. It's only ten minutes away, and, if you're in the mood for food, you can get an ono burger at *Paia Fish Market* or a 'za at *Flatbread*. There are several other good restaurants in Paia, but they might not serve you as quickly as you'd like after a long plane ride.

Right onto Hana Highway: If you turn right onto Hana Highway, you're only two minutes from *Whole Foods*. Just follow the highway as it bends to become Kaahumanu Avenue — the store is on the left just after the bend. You can pick up lovely groceries, produce, wine and beer and, of course, prepared foods. In the same shopping plaza you will find a Long's drugstore — great for alcohol and sundries, snacks, suntan lotion, inexpensive slippers (flip-flops), toothpaste, etc. *Tasaka*

Guri Guri and *Thailand Cuisine* are also here.

Maui closes down pretty early, so if you're getting in late — after 8 or 9pm — you may not be able to take advantage of any of these places by the time you get off the plane, get your bags and get your car. If you must eat, there are fast food joints open, and a 24-hour Denny's on Hana Highway (take your first right after Krispy Kreme, then turn left into the back of their parking lot). Also check reviews that have a plane icon with them — these are also in the area of the airport.

Where to Go for Early Bird Specials or Coupons

Maui is not known for early bird specials. Most of the good to great restaurants offer them only when business is slow, and stop offering them as soon as things pick up again, so it's hard to predict when they'll come up. Three exceptions are *Sansei*, *Cuatro*, and *Ruth's Chris*, all of whom usually offer an early bird of some sort. Check with those restaurants directly for the latest promotions.

There are plenty of early bird specials offered at restaurants we tend to not review ... especially the resort restaurants. So the question, for us, is: how special is that special? Food doesn't taste better when the price goes down. Our bottom line advice is to check with restaurants directly about their current price promotions. You should also check the visitor magazines for current coupons or deals. Many restaurants also list promotions on their websites.

Where to Host a Party

Whether you're planning a romantic dinner for two, a party for twelve to forty, a wedding, or some other special occasion, there are certain restaurants that do parties very well. Some of these are expensive, some are moderate, but all are candidates, depending upon what you're looking for. Please refer to the full reviews for our impressions and contact information.

Bistro Casanova has a small dining area that has French doors, so the space is separate from the rest of the restaurant. There is no view, but it's a pretty restaurant and we enjoy the food and the busy atmosphere.

Café O'Lei in Kihei has a semi-private room, and the Dunes at Maui Lani has a large banquet room. This restaurant is one of the biggest caterers on the island.

Capische? defines elegance for us and has a fabulous view. If you have eight in your party and can do *Il Teatro*, we recommend it. They also are willing to close down the restaurant to the public for private parties.

Cuatro Restaurant is one of our favorites, and we'd host a birthday or wedding rehearsal dinner there in a heartbeat. They will close the restaurant down for you.

David Paul's Island Grill has beautiful food and a beautiful room at the rear of the restaurant that is very private and lovingly appointed. There is no view from back there, but the restaurant is classy and elegant.

Duo has large tables, and you get Four Seasons service.

Flatbread Pizza Company has a private room that is perfect for very casual gatherings. Acoustics can be a little loud.

Gannon's caters to all of the locations at the golf course in Wailea. Heavenly location and great catering. On average, three weddings a day are held here. They also cater to other locations.

Gerard's Restaurant has such lovely personal attention and such good food that we'd go to any special event held here.

Hali'imaile General Store has a big back room that is perfect for large parties.

Humuhumunukunukuapua'a has several wings where large parties can be comfortable, and the setting is lovely.

Lahaina Grill doesn't have a private room, but we've had a table for twelve and they handled it beautifully.

Mama's Fish House is excellent for romantic couples who want to celebrate a special occasion. They can also handle large parties.

Pacific'o has a lovely terrace right on the beach.

Pineapple Grill has several very large tables that seat many people, which is nice when you have a small wedding party.

Plantation House has a large fireplace that is on a slightly elevated level. This area is often used for large parties.

Pulehu has a lovely location and, because it is closed two nights a week, can often accommodate your schedule.

Roy's Bar & Grill can handle large parties (every meal feels like a party there), and is very kid-friendly.

Ruby's is great for a really casual, large get-together. The staff sings to birthday boys and girls.

Sansei has a lot of large tables.

Spago can handle many special occasions and you get that killer view and the excellent service.

Three's has three very separate dining areas, and is particularly good for louder parties — they're one of the few places on Maui that are permitted for music and alcohol consumption until 2am.

Fixed Price Dinners

When business is slow on Maui, nearly every restaurant responds with amazing deals on fixed price dinners. We've eaten four course meals for $39 — unheard of — during the last few years of economic downturn. Ask your server if there are any special deals going, because there just might be. Also check the *Maui News*, *Maui Time*, or *Maui Weekly* for the latest.

Service in Maui Restaurants

We've had dozens of readers just in the last couple of months ask the question "Why is service so bad on Maui??" Despite the almost existential nature of this question (Really … why is it ever bad?), we'll try to answer as best we can.

First of all, it's almost always wonderful in certain restaurants — **Spago**, **Duo**, **Ferraro's** (hmmmm … all at the Four Seasons — is there a pattern here?), **Lahaina Grill**, **Mama's Fish House**, to name a few off the top of our head. Unfortunately, those exceptions may, as they say, prove the rule.

Maui is a dream destination for many. Every year hundreds of new (often young) people move here, eager to taste the good life. Surf, sun, and summer weather all year round — it sounds ideal. And sometimes it proves to be ideal, and they stay. And sometimes, they don't. This rather transient work force makes for slim pickings when restaurants are hiring. Even the most stable-seeming personalities may turn out to be, well, flaky. There's a saying that "Maui either welcomes you with open arms, or she kicks you out." When someone has had enough of the island, they tend to leave. Right away. Like, today. No two week notice — and sometimes not even a courtesy call.

With this relatively unstable work force, many restaurants just can't afford to — or just don't bother to — invest in training. So there's a Catch-22: the employer doesn't invest in the employees, who then don't invest in the employer, etc.

It's also worth pointing out that many people think waiting tables is an easy job to do in between surf sessions. It's entirely possible that in another economy, with a more diverse array of work, they might be doing something very different.

There's a restaurant adage: Customers may come for the food, but they come back for the service. Restaurants that cater mainly to visitors may not worry so much about them coming back. That's why so many of our very favorite restaurants tend to also have good service — they're popular with locals, not just (or in some cases not any) visitors.

Food Trucks to Visit

All over the mainland — and now even on Oahu — there's a food truck revolution. We like to say that Maui is ten years behind the times when it comes to technology (we just got truly high speed internet at our house a month before publication) — and the same is true for many food trends. We have a few decent chefs who've thrown their hat into the ring, but for the most part, Maui's mobile fare is sub-par.

For example, one of the first and most prominent trucks to appear is **Geste Shrimp,** a white truck that parks at Kahului Harbor, Tuesday through Saturday. Between 10:30 am and 5:30pm you can get a heaping plate of twelve shrimp, rice, and macaroni salad mixed with crab for $12. Many people love this place, but we have a couple of problems with it.

First, the shrimp aren't cleaned well.

Second, we just don't find the preparations — way heavy on the margarine — very inviting. (But really, did we have to continue after #1?)

Here are some trucks we feel *are* worth hunting down:

The **Outrigger Pizza Company** carts around a wood-burning oven on a trailer. Brilliant! They create eight gourmet pizzas, including a sumptuous lilikoi (passion fruit) pork pie and a lovely pesto pie. Crusts are crispy with a fine chew and a three-cheese blend. The 9-10 inch pies are $10 apiece. You won't want to share. Amazingly, your made-to-order pizza takes only 90 seconds to bake in the 800-degree oven, so you don't have to wait long — except that there's usually a line to order. Tuesdays and Fridays, the oven is parked at the Azeka Plaza in Kihei, Monday and Thursday they're in Lahaina on Lahainaluna Road, and on Wednesdays they're up in Kula at Long's. We've also caught them in Makawao during the "Third Friday" street fair and at the Saturday Swap Meet in Kahului. Check www.outriggerpizzas.com for updates to their schedule, or call 808-870-7133.

Amigo's Express, the mobile version of our favorite Mexican restaurant, has a colorful, bamboo-paneled truck on the corner of Market and Vineyard in Wailuku. Many of their delicious dishes can be purchased through the window and eaten at a picnic bench under the shade of a massive Banyan tree. Two dollar tacos? Heck, yes! It's open on Monday, Thursday, and Friday from 10am to 8:30pm and Saturday from 10 am to 4pm.

Jawz Tacos started as a lone truck topped with a shark fin, and now includes two trucks and a sit-down restaurant (see the review). You can catch the mobile restaurants every day from 10am-4:30pm near Makena State Beach Park. One is parked across from the entrance, and one before the big red pu'u (volcanic cinder cone). Both serve decent tacos, smoothies, and shave ice.

Also on the way to Makena State Beach Park, there's **Da Local Banana,** a small, bright green and yellow cart that hawks a sweet we adored in childhood: chocolate-dipped frozen bananas. Made with local, organic apple bananas, these brain-freezing delights hit the spot, especially after a hot, salty day at the beach. The "skinny dipper" is plain chocolate, the "yellow polka dot bikini" is rolled in coconut, and our favorite, the "auto-mac-nut crunch," is heavily sprinkled with macadamia nuts. You can also drink fresh, ice-cold coconut water right out of the nut — waaaay better than the canned kind you get at Asian or health food stores and probably even more rehydrating. Melissa, the owner, keeps unpredictable hours, but she can be found most weekdays at Makena, at the Swap Meet in Kahului on Saturday mornings, and on Market Street in Wailuku for the "First Friday" street fair.

Maui's food trucks aren't savvy enough yet to have Twitter handles for foodies to follow their every move, but we're hoping that a few more foodie entrepreneurs take on the challenge of doing mobile right. It's time.

Note: there are several trucks that dot the Road to Hana. Unfortunately, most eventually get shut down by the County, making it tough to include them in this book. If you find something worth writing about, please drop us a line at editor@topmauirestaurants.com.

Local Fish: What You'll Eat

Many visitors come eager to try the fresh fish Maui is famous for. Too many end up ordering mahi mahi, which is nearly ubiquitous on the mainland, and not unique to these waters. (Not that we have any problem with mahi mahi, of course.)

Here's a little guide to the fish you'll likely find at Maui restaurants.

`ahi (pronounce it ah' hee)

Ahi is the Hawaiian word for yellowfin and big eye, tuna. It's excellent served raw as sashimi, or in poke (see below), but you'll also find it cooked. Usually this fish is served seared, but still very pink inside, which is good; because once it is cooked it tastes like canned tuna. You will find it on just about every restaurant's menu in some form or another.

aku (pronounce it ah' koo)

Aku is the Hawaiian word for skipjack tuna, also called bonito. This fish is similar to ahi in its deep red color, but it tastes more strongly of tuna. It's often served as sashimi, made into poke, or cooked similarly to ahi.

a`u (pronounce it ah' oo)

A`u is blue marlin, the common Pacific billfish. It's also known as kajiki in Japan. When eaten raw — try it in poke if you see it — it is similar to ahi in taste. If cooked, it is more like a swordfish.

mahi mahi
(pronounce it mah' hee mah' hee)

In other parts of the world this is called the dolphin fish (it's not a mammal, don't worry). This is a very popular fish because it is firm, with white, delicate flesh. Good grilled for burgers. It's also great sautéed with a macadamia nut crust, which complements the sweet taste.

moana/o
(pronounce it moh (w)ah' nah/noh)

This is a delicate fish with really firm, white meat. Lovely.

moi (pronounce it moy)

At one time you'd be killed for eating this unless you were royalty — today anyone who can afford it is a king (this is James's favorite fish). Steamed or deep-fried, this delicate white fish is "ono" ("delicious").

onaga (pronounce it oh NAH gah)

Onaga is the Hawaiian word for red snapper, and is a broad term for several varieties found in these waters. Snapper is a bottom fish, found in deep waters, and as such is prized by restaurants for its tender flesh and delicate, fresh taste.

ono (pronounce it oh' noh)

Ono is like a large mackerel and is known as wahoo in the Caribbean. It's an open ocean fish, and one of our favorites. The meat is flaky, white, and delicate. The word "ono" means "delicious" in Hawaiian. Get the picture? Great grilled as a fillet for an "ono burger." If you're new to fish, this is a good place to start.

opah (pronounce it oh' pah)

Opah is an open ocean fish, also called a moonfish. It has a lovely firm white meat, and is considered good luck.

opakapaka
(pronounce it OH' pah kah pah kah

Opakapaka is sooooo delicious! This is the pink ruby snapper, or crimson snapper, found only in our waters. It's delicately flavored and moist, and we love it no matter how the chef chooses to prepare it. Its fishing is regulated by the state, so it is not always on the menu.

We don't like to be spoilsports, especially when it comes to food, but we are compelled to mention that ocean sustainability is becoming an increasing concern both here and around the world. We are fishing some species into extinction — and your dollars are votes. If you want to learn more, please visit the Monterey Bay Aquarium Seafood Watch website, www. SeafoodWatch.org, where you can download information their excellent report and even a regional guide (for your own region, and for ours, which is different from any other part of the US). It will tell you what types of fish are most sustainable right now, and which are less so.

Local Fish: Where to Buy It

We often get asked where to buy good local fish. Our real answer is this: buy local fish out of that truck you see parked on the side of the road with the sign that says "fresh fish, $5 per pound."

Here's the deal with local fish on Maui: most of it is loaded from the boat into the fisherman's truck and driven directly to the chef they think will like it best (or give them the best price). There are fishermen who go out every morning just to fish for restaurants. There are others who do it once in a while when they have a morning off, or when they've gotten a panicked call from a chef the night before. It's rare that any fish is left over — but if it is, they'll sell it to you out of their truck. This happens most often along the Hana Highway, but we've seen people along South Kihei Road and out near Kapalua, too.

If you don't see these guys but still want to try cooking fish at your home or condo, you can get good fish at the following retailers. Most sell fish brought in from the Honolulu fish market (not exactly just–caught, but close).

Costco: best prices, but huge quantities. They almost always have slabs of ahi sashimi, and pretty good poke, plus salmon, rainbow trout, and sometimes shellfish from other waters (scallops, King crab legs) at great prices. *808-877-5248, 540 Haleakala Highway, Kahului.*

Times Supermarket (used to be Star Market): this is the best selection of local fish with the best prices. *808-442-4700, 3350 Lower Honoapiilani Rd., Lahaina; 1310 S. Kihei Rd., Kihei.*

Foodland in Kahului has a good fish section and great poke. *808-877-2808, 90 Kane St., Kahului.*

Foodland Farms in Lahaina has a good fish section, if a little pricey. *808-662-7088, 345 Keawe St., Lahaina.*

Eskimo Candy in Kihei occasionally has local fish, and always has fish from Taiwan and Alaska. Spendy prices. *808-879-5686, 2665 Wai Wai Pl., Kihei.*

Fish Market Maui in Honokowai has local fresh fish, spendy prices. *808-665-9895, 3600 Lower Honoapiilani Rd., Lahaina.*

Valley Isle Seafood in Kahului wholesales to restaurants and hotels, but has a small retail operation. Good fish, a little spendy. *808-873-4847, 475 Hukilike Street, Bay D, Kahului*

Whole Foods in Kahului often has a good selection of really fresh local fish caught off Maui's shores.

Tropical Fruits You Should Try

With a yearlong growing season, fresh tropical fruits are always available on Maui. You will certainly enjoy many of these tropical temptations in Maui's restaurants, where they are used in countless ways. But we think you should also savor them all by themselves. Our recommendation is to eat something new every day, starting as soon as you arrive. (If you live here, you might already have two or three of these growing in your yard.)

Start with the most obvious: pineapple, mango, papaya, apple bananas, and avocado. Graduate to the slightly more exotic strawberry guava, lilikoi (passion fruit), starfruit, and lychee. Then go really wild with dragonfruit, cherimoya, kumquat, and loquat.

In addition to fruits, the Valley Isle produces coconut, sugar cane, coffee, Maui onion, and even (yes!) chocolate. None of these edible plants are native to Hawaii — they hail from China, South East Asia, South America, Africa, and elsewhere. But they've been imported and cultivated over the years, for obvious reason.

The most reliable source for local produce is **Mana Foods** in Paia. Their selection is the cheapest, most diverse, and best quality. They're also free with samples of things you may not have tried before.

You can also find many ripe fruits at the **Maui**

Swap Meet (on Saturdays at the University of Hawaii-Maui Community College in Kahului) and at roadside stands around the island, especially on the Road to Hana. (Although, fair warning: the County has been enforcing new regulations that are shutting these stands down.) Our tip is to have plenty of small bills with you at all times, so you can pick up a fresh delicacy anytime the opportunity presents itself.

Try the following while you're here:

Apple bananas are shorter and stubbier than Cavendish bananas (which are the long, slender types found in most mainland grocery stores). These squat bananas taste tangier, with a slight citrus perfume. Their flesh ranges from white to yellow. Once you're hooked on apple bananas, the usual kind just won't do. They're perfect in pancakes and contribute a sun-dried, caramel flavor to banana bread.

Sweet, golden **mangoes** are the essence of summertime. Nothing compares to devouring one whole and sucking the last bit of sweetness from its stiff, hairy seed. If that description embarrasses you, it probably should. Mango flesh is passion incarnate — and very messy.

The trick to eating a mango is in the cut. Slice lengthwise and all the way down, as near as you can to the pit on each side. (You won't be able to cut through it, so don't try.) Pop the two halves apart, and take out the pit. Next, cut through the flesh in lines lengthwise and crosswise — making a crosshatch in each half. Go as far into the flesh as possible, stopping just short of the skin. Now, pop the skin inside out: Squares of mango will stick up like a scrub brush. Scoop them off with a spoon.

Some eat mango with a squeeze of lime. Others like it picked green and pickled. We like ours right off the tree, with the juice running down our chin. The best mangoes are at **Yee's Fruit Stand** in Kihei on South Kihei Road near the intersection of Piikea.

By the way, while most people can enjoy mangoes, some — like Molly — have to avoid them. If you have an allergy to poison oak — Molly gets it when the wind blows the wrong way — you may also be allergic to the sap of mangoes. The flesh itself is usually not a problem, and neither is the juice. But if Molly touches the skin or the sap, she risks an angry red rash.

Papayas grow year-round at the top of tall, slender trees. The fruit are so heavy, and the stalks so slim, they look almost cartoonish. The best papaya are a dark pinkish orange, and come from Ono Organic Farms in Hana. You can also find this same type from the island of Molokai. (**Mana Foods** carries both.)

To eat papaya, slice the fruit lengthwise into two hourglass halves and scoop out the seeds, which look — disconcertingly — like gray fish eggs. Papayas contain many digestive enzymes and are often used as a meat tenderizer. This is why they become gooey soft and nauseatingly sweet as they ripen. Make sure to eat yours while the flesh is still firm.

When they're ripe, scores of bright yellow **lilikoi**, or **passion fruit**, drop from their dark green vines. About the size and shape of a smallish lemon, they're lip-puckeringly tart. As they start to shrivel and turn brown, they grow sweeter. Slice them in half (carefully, so as not to spill the priceless juice) and slurp up the gloppy jelly — seeds and all. Sweet, tart, and possessing an unmistakable delicate fragrance, lilikoi are prized around the world. Chefs in France import them from South East Asia for use in classic salad dressings, sauces, and desserts. We harvest them from our neighbor's fence (shhhh), strain the juice, and make lip-smacking martinis.

Guava trees grow every five feet alongside the road on the way to Hana. Regular guavas are bright yellow; strawberry guavas have pink skin. Both varieties are super sweet and mushy inside. Pick some while hiking in waterfall territory — suck out the inner flesh, and spit out the multitudinous seeds. They grow year-round.

Lychees have deep maroon, dry, bumpy shells that feel a little like a heavy duty paper. Peel this outer covering off to reveal luscious, translucent, pearly flesh around an almond shaped seed. Make sure you inhale the rosy perfume before devouring the sweet flesh. Spit out the seeds. The delicate fruit is used to flavor cocktails, sorbets, and shave ice. Late summer is their season.

The **dragonfruit** is well named. The softball-sized, fleshy, pink-and-green fringed fruit looks like it just might be a dragon's favorite snack. Slice it open to find brilliant fuchsia meat studded with black seeds. (Some varieties are snow white inside.) With looks like this, you might expect a wild and assertive flavor — but it turns out to have a subtle, sweet, kiwi-like taste. It's often used in cocktails and sorbets.

Dragonfruit grows on an opportunistic cactus vine that's found creeping over fences and fallen logs all over Maui — but for the *fruit* to develop, the cacti's giant, night-blooming flower

has to be hand-pollinated. Its short-lived harvest occurs in late spring or summer.

Chocolate, in its raw cacao form, grows at Ono Organic Farms in Hana. You can tour the farm and sample their chocolate — both the raw bean and a homemade confection. *808-248-7779, www.onofarms.com*

Great Coffee

Getting local coffee while you're here is a must-do. While most coffee beans are grown on the Big Island — the most famous, of course, is Kona — some are grown right here on Maui.

MauiGrown Coffee is responsible for growing **Maui Mokka™** beans on a five hundred acre farm just above Ka'anapali. This is a lovely, dark, chocolate-flavored bean that has hints of red wine and currants. You can get a cup at their Company Store in Lahaina (next to the smokestack), but you can also find this bean in blends at *Maui Coffee Roasters* and **Maui Oma** (see below). Another local bean we look for in blends is **Red Catuai**, which is also grown in Ka'anapali.

You can also check out the coffee grown on Haleakala by **O'o Farms** (see the Foodie Tours tip) by visiting the farm, or going to *Aina Gourmet Market*.

The beans are important, of course, but the roast is, too — in fact, it matters a *great deal*. The best roaster is **Maui Oma**, which has an impossibly hard-to-find facility on Alamaha Street in Kahului. Their roasts are not sold in retail stores, so if you want their coffee, you will either have to visit during their limited hours (call first) or buy online (they ship to the mainland). If you're sitting at a restaurant enjoying a cup of coffee, it's likely it came from this roaster. They keep detailed records of each restaurant's blend — so if you fall in love, you'll always be able to get your own fix. They also do gift labels on their bags. Check out the Maui Oma's Choice blend, our favorite. Go to www.HawaiiCoffee.net, or call them to see if you can stop by. 808-871-8664.

While we like **Maui Coffee Roasters** as a restaurant, we do not particularly recommend their roast. However, if you're there for a meal, you might as well get a cup — and if you like it, they sell it in their very convenient retail area. You can also get it at **Costco** in a two pound bag.

If you're craving a cup of coffee on the way to or from Kahului, the best to-go brew is found at **Akamai Coffee** in Kahului. Located in the Home Depot parking lot, it caters mostly to contractors — but also java junkies in the know.

Great Sunday Brunch

You can get a wonderful value by taking advantage of Sunday brunches. Some even feature champagne (usually these are around $50 per person). These places also all do big, beautiful holiday meals and brunches at Thanksgiving, Christmas, New Years, Easter, Mother's Day, and so forth (holiday brunches are usually priced at $75 - $100 per person).

Here are our favorites, but call for details and reservations:

• **Makena Golf Resort** (used to be the Maui Prince) has a good Sunday champagne brunch. They also have done a very good Japanese buffet in the past. 808-875-5888.

• **The Grand Wailea's** brunch is a favorite for the killer view and excellent malasadas. Champagne is included. 808-888-6100.

• **Duo at the Four Seasons** has an excellent daily breakfast and Sunday brunch buffet. 808-874-8000.

• **The Ritz Carlton in Kapalua** kills us at holidays with their over the top champagne brunches. 808-669-6200.

• **Ka'anapali Beach Hotel** runs a Sunday brunch that keeps locals very happy — the brunch with the most local food. Great waffles … and champagne is included. 808-661-0011

Local Food, Defined

There is a difference between Hawaiian food — which has been on these islands for at least a thousand years — and Local food, which is a response to Hawaii's more recent history.

Because of its plantation history, Hawaii is a cultural melting pot. Over the years plantations imported workers from places as far flung as Portugal, Japan, China, Korea, and the Philippines to work in the fields. As people from these cultures worked side by side, they began to get to know each other. As anyone who went to grade school can tell you, food is a universal language, and food was certainly spoken in those plantation fields.

At lunchtime, people shared. The Chinese brought noodle dishes, Japanese brought teriyaki and rice, and Filipinos brought adobo. The Koreans brought kalbi ribs, the Portuguese offered brick-oven baked sweet bread, and the Hawaiians contributed kalua pig. The "mixed plate" that resulted is still Hawaii's most popular lunch.

Plate lunch entrées can include anything from chicken teriyaki or katsu to chopped steak. Whatever your main dish, your sides will include "two scoops" rice and "one scoop" macaroni salad, heavy on the mayonnaise. It's not unheard of to be served spaghetti with a side of rice here in Hawaii.

The best Local food is made fresh to order and can be found at **Sam Sato's**, **Da Kitchen**, **Aloha Mixed Plate**, and **L&L Barbecue** (see reviews). You could also try Honokowai Okazuya, *3600 Lower Honoapiilani Rd., Lahaina, 808-665-0512*

The best take-out options include **Ichiban Okazuya** and Takamiya Market in Wailuku. *359 N Market St., Wailuku, 808-244-3404* www.takamiyamarket.com

In addition to plate lunches, some quintessentially "local" foods you might want to try while you are here include...

Loco Moco

The loco moco is a high-carbohydrate, high-protein dish that was invented in the middle of the last century to help teenage surfers get a fast breakfast. It does look like a growing boy's dream meal: a mountain of steamed rice with a fried egg on top, a hamburger patty on top of that, and brown gravy smothering everything. You can get it anywhere local food is sold, at roadside stands, and even McDonald's. We have

a friend who grew up on Maui who always orders this and it's impressive to watch him systematically put it away.

Saimin (pronounce it sigh-min)

Saimin is simple, warming comfort food. Inexpensive and filling, it's a noodle and broth soup that can be eaten for breakfast, lunch, dinner, and any time in between. When saimin is made from scratch (rather than from a powdered mix with frozen or dried noodles), it is called ramen.

Thin white noodles float in a clear broth (dashi) with green onions and fish cakes (kamaboko). (Yes, that artificial-pink-and-white disc floating in your soup is made from pureed and pounded fish.) Usually char siu (pork) is added, as well as chicken, shrimp, oxtail, wontons, or whatever other protein is on hand. Saimin and ramen connoisseurs argue over what makes the best dashi. It should be flavorful, with just the right viscosity. Various seaweeds, shrimp flakes, and bonito are employed in the quest for the most delicious version. Often, an egg is cracked into the soup just before serving, to add richness.

Saimin is served extraordinarily hot, so you use chopsticks to eat the ingredients, and then, when the soup has cooled a little, drink the broth directly from the bowl. The best noodles are homemade and retain their firmness even after steeping in the broth for a bit. You can get saimin just about anywhere. You can also buy seasoning packets and noodles to make later at home.

Our top picks for saimin: the Star Ramen at **Star Noodle**, saimin or dry mein at **Sam Sato's**, and the gourmet version of ramen at *Sansei*, which comes with Dungeness crab and truffled broth.

SPAM

People in Hawaii eat more SPAM than most places (the Philippines and Guam come close). The meat was introduced during WWII as part of the rations given to the local population, and it caught on wildly. We speculate that it's because salt has always been an important (and sometimes the only) flavoring for island cookery, so the salty pork product is familiar, satisfying, inexpensive, and easy to stack in the cupboard.

A few years ago SPAM's maker sponsored a contest for which the grand prize included a year's supply of SPAM — but excluded Hawaii residents from the winner's circle. Boy, was that a mistake, one that they quickly corrected.

If you have never had SPAM and are ready to try it as part of your culinary education, try SPAM musubi, which is basically nigiri made with SPAM: a finger-sized block of seasoned rice, a thin slice of SPAM on top, and the entire thing wrapped with nori seaweed. You can get it at most grocery stores and convenience stores. Many island gas stations stock SPAM musubi near their cash registers.

Hawaiian Food, Defined

Would you believe that pineapple — the most quintessential symbol of Hawaiian hospitality — is not native to the islands? They're from Brazil!! Given that, you'll understand why genuine Hawaiian food does not generally feature pineapples. No pineapples, no burgers with pineapple slices, no pizza with pineapple slices. In fact, traditional Hawaiian food is pretty simple: starches, proteins, and vegetables. Where Local food is high in simple carbs and saturated fat, Hawaiian food is typically low in both.

The ancient Hawaiians fished, of course. In addition to the many saltwater fish they caught in their nets and cultivated in their sophisticated fishponds, they also harvested shrimp, squid, limpet, crab, and other seafood. They supplemented this with wild birds (the ones they found here) and chickens and pigs (which they brought with them in their voyaging canoes).

These were some of the world's most accomplished farmers. They developed hundreds of varieties of taro and sweet potatoes, and at least forty varieties of bananas, each serving a unique purpose. Breadfruit was yet another staple. They enjoyed coconut and sugar cane, and harvested herbs, ferns, vines, and medicinals from the forests. They used sea salt and surprisingly diverse varieties of limu (seaweed) to flavor their foods.

Where the Meso-Americans had corn, the Hawaiians had taro root, or kalo, which they steamed, baked, and pounded into a sticky, starchy purple paste called Poi. This food was incredibly important, and the key to social graces. Ancient Hawaiians revered the taro plant as their elder brother, so it's treated with deference. Before eating Poi, put a smile on your face and forgive anyone you have disagreements with.

To sample some of the Islands' indigenous eats, try the Hawaiian plates at *Aloha Mixed Plate* or *Da Kitchen* (see restaurant reviews). On

Saturdays only, Surfside Spirits & Deli serves a Hawaiian feast with homemade Poi. *1993 S Kihei Rd # 3 Kihei, 808-879-1385*

Of course, the best way to enjoy Hawaiian food is at a lu'au, a traditional celebration with hula, music, and more food than anyone could possibly eat. The only two we recommend are **Feast at Lele** and **Old Lahaina Lu'au**, both of which are discussed separately.

When you go to a lu'au, you will encounter some or all of the following:

Lau Lau (pronounce it lou lou, it rhymes with how how)

Lau lau is a method of cooking meat or fish. Traditionally, fish and pork were folded into a pocket of tender taro leaves. This tasty parcel was then wrapped in ti leaves and placed in an imu (an underground oven, kind of like a barbecue pit). Hot rocks were placed on the lau lau, and then covered in broad banana leaves to support the dirt that buried the oven until the lau lau was ready, a few hours later.

Today, you'll find lau lau contains pork, chicken, or beef, and often salted butterfish to bring flavor and a rich texture. There is often a vegetable mix added, and the whole thing is wrapped in taro leaves, then in ti leaves, and steamed in a pressure cooker. When you eat the dish, you cut right through the leaves to get to the tender fillings. We sometimes add a little salt. Don't eat the outer ti leaves — they are inedible and only used to cook the dish. But definitely eat the taro leaves.

Kalua Pork or Pig (pronounce it kah lu ah)

This smoky, tender pork dish is extremely popular. The traditional way of making it is in an imu, as described above. The smoke in the oven flavors the pork, and the meat falls off the bone in shredded chunks. It is seasoned with sea salt; delicious. It's often served with a sweet barbecue sauce — mango- or pineapple-flavored — to balance the salt and smoke flavors.

Poke (pronounce it po kay)

Poke is one of our favorite Hawaiian dishes. The ancients used to skin and gut fresh fish, slice the meat into filets, and press them with salt and seaweed. Today, poke refers to just about any raw fish cubed and mixed with seaweed, salt, chopped onion and chili. Bright red sashimi grade ahi is the most popular, tossed with soy sauce, sesame oil, and inamona, a traditional Hawaiian relish made of roasted, mashed kukui nuts. Delicious. Poke can also be made with tako (octopus), crab, mussels, and other fish. It is dressed with tobiko, tomatoes, and even kim chee. One creative fishmonger invented "California Roll" poke with imitation crab and avocado. Find excellent poke at Foodland in Kihei, Pukalani, or Lahaina — our favorite style as of late is the "Flying Hawaiian." You can also get good poke at Takamiya Market in Wailuku (359 N Market St., Wailuku, 808-244-3404. www.takamiyamarket.com), and at Safeway.

Limu (pronounce it lee moo)

Most people have eaten seaweed, or Limu, whether they know it or not. It's often used as a thickening agent in toothpastes and gels. In Hawaii, children start snacking on seaweed as soon as their teeth can tear through a salted sheet of Japanese nori — the roasted seaweed used to wrap nigiri sushi. Ogo is another Japanese seaweed that's popular here. Crunchy, red, and slightly salty, it's a key ingredient in Poke.

The waters surrounding the Hawaiian Islands are flush with many species of edible marine plants, or Limu. Ancient Hawaiians were akamai (smart) enough to cultivate the Limu species they liked best. They used them to make gravies for their meat and fish, as garnishes, snacks, medicines, and even as a lei! Lipoa Street in Kihei is named for a golden type of seaweed that tastes of honey and straw. Limu kohu is like saffron in that it smells metallic and adds an unmistakable quality to any dish it's cooked with. Wawaeiole (va-vy-ee-o-lay) and sea lettuce are soft seaweeds, great for adding to salads.

These authentic tastes of old Hawaii are rare nowadays, but you can still find them in the chill cases at Takamiya Market in Wailuku. (359 N Market St., Wailuku, 808-244-3404. www.takamiyamarket.com)

Lomi Lomi Salmon
(pronounce it low me low me)

Salmon is not native to Hawaii. It's a cold-water fish — and we do not have any cold water here. However, once salmon started showing up in Hawaii markets, it was love at first taste. Salmon is diced and salted, and then mixed by hand with tomatoes, crushed ice, and green onions in a massaging, kneading motion. (Lomi means to massage.) Lomi Lomi Salmon

is served at nearly every modern lu'au, even though it is not truly a local fish, or an ancient dish.

Sweet Potato, or U'ala
(pronounce ooh ah lah)

Sure, you've had sweet potatoes before. But when was the last time you ate one so purple it looked like play dough? Mashed with coconut milk, these gem-like spuds are so delicious they're often served as dessert, in pie or pudding-like cubes called kulolo (koo-low-low).

Poi (pronounce it poy)

To make their traditional staple, Hawaiians cook the heavy taro root by baking it or steaming it. Then they mash it until it is completely demolished. The smooth, richly gooey paste is purple and absolutely beautiful. It's an acquired taste, but worth trying, and once you get over the absolutely weird texture (if you were a paste eater in elementary school, you won't think it's so weird), the flavor can be quite delicate and subtle. Remember, Hawaiians regard poi as a sacred food. So if you're having an argument with your spouse, don't reach for the calabash (poi bowl). It's best to sample poi with a forkful of lomi lomi salmon. The sour poi and salty fish go together well.

Haupia (pronounce it how pee ah)

Haupia is a coconut dessert that is called a pudding, but we think it's closer to a gelatin. It couldn't be a simpler dessert: coconut milk is heated and mixed with arrowroot until it thickens, and then is poured into a pan to firm up in the refrigerator. Many people use cornstarch as the thickener, and while we understand that choice from a cost perspective, we vastly prefer those made with arrowroot. Arrowroot is more neutral in flavor and lets the delicate, flowery coconut come through. It also makes the pudding shinier.

Hawaiian Regional Cuisine, Defined

It is probably clear to you that Hawaiian food has always featured desperately fresh ingredients ... but it's generally either salty or on the bland side, and the textures can be odd to visitors. Local food, on the other hand, tends to be heavy, greasy, and *super* salty.

In the beginning years of Hawaii's visitor industry, restaurants weren't much to write home about. They stocked their larders with produce shipped in from the mainland: limp veggies, jetlagged meats, fruits picked far before their prime. You can imagine the results.

In the late eighties a group of young chefs who loved Hawaii's unique flavors, fresh fish, island produce, and melting pot ethic revolted against this misery. They banded together in order to form partnerships with island farmers, ranchers, and fishermen. Using ripe, homegrown ingredients, they cooked up something new called Hawaiian Regional Cuisine.

Twelve is a significant number in many cultures, certainly in ours, and in our more romantic moments we like to call this group of chefs the Hawaiian Apostles of Food. The twelve chefs were:

Sam Choy (Sam Choy's)

Roger Dikon (formerly of Maui Prince Hotel)

Mark Ellman (*Honu*, *Mala*, *Penne Pasta*, *Maui Tacos*, the former Avalon)

Amy Ferguson Ota (formerly Hotel Hana Maui)

Beverly Gannon (*Hali'imaile General Store*, *Joe's*, *Gannon's*)

Jean-Marie Josselin (Josselin's Bar & Grill, formerly A Pacific Café)

George Mavrothalassitis (Chef Mavro)

Peter Merriman (*Merriman's Kapalua*, *Hula Grill*)

Philippe Padovani (Padovani's Grill, Padovani's Chocolates)

Gary Strehl (formerly of Hawaii Prince Hotel)

Alan Wong (Alan Wong's, Pineapple Room, Alan Wong's Tokyo — and, in early 2012, a new restaurant at the Grand Wailea!)

Roy Yamaguchi (*Roy's Bar & Grill* worldwide).

The majority of these paradigm-shifting chefs hailed from Maui. So don't let anyone tell you that all the culinary fireworks happen in Honolulu!

We'd like to take a moment now to say thank you to these twelve pioneers, who moved Hawaiian food away from pineapple on pizza and frozen food warmed up to a fusion cuisine that applies European sauces and cooking techniques to local ingredients. The result is beautiful, fanciful, delicious food that has people all over the world moaning and rolling their eyes with delight.

We'd also like to say thank you to the chefs

who came after them and continue to develop Hawaii as a base for world-class cuisine. There is some debate about how Hawaiian Regional Cuisine differs from Pacific Rim, which came a little later, but we're of the mind that Pacific Rim cuisine is not just about Hawaii — it's also about Asia, Indonesia, Polynesia, South America, and California (any food that comes from the rim of the Pacific Ocean).

Whatever you call it, the best food in Hawaii's restaurants crosses boundaries, plays with the senses (taste and vision and touch and smell and even, at times, sound), is colorful, surprising, and simply scrumptious. Unlike other cuisines, with their long histories and firm rules, the fusion cuisine on the islands continues to evolve and grow.

Where to Get Groceries, Beer, & Wine

If you're staying in a condo or vacation rental during your stay on Maui, you'll want to stock the fridge. We'll share our own favorite shopping spots with you. There are many more, but these are the places we go first for the best prices and the best selection.

Be prepared for sticker shock, though. A gallon of milk can run you as high as $8, and even a tin of sardines will be $.50-$1 more than you are used to paying back home. Food prices contribute to the overall high cost of living here. You'll do best by shopping in more than one place to get the best deals.

Ah Fook's Super Market

Ah Fook's is a small Asian market in Kahu-lui where you can find everything you didn't know you needed. A good place to browse even if you're not planning on buying anything. This is where you can local noodles and sausages and fish — pricey, but interesting. *65 W Kaahumanu Ave., Kahului, (808) 877-3308*

Costco

Locals buy a lot of groceries here. **Costco** stocks fresh local produce in season year-round, and local coffee from **Maui Coffee Roasters**, too. With a convenient location right next to the airport, we highly recommend a stop here to stock up on everything from bottled water to local salad greens. They have a good selection of wine, beer, and spirits, and a killer chocolate/macadamia nut treat section. Just remember to bring your membership card with you. *Directions from the airport: As you exit the airport, turn left at the first light onto Haleakala Highway, and then right into the Costco parking lot. 540 Haleakala Highway, Kahului.*

Foodland

Foodland locations are typically much smaller than Safeway, but they're good local grocery stores. We like their bakery line, *Tutu's*, especially for hot dog/hamburger rolls. Prepared sandwich bar, fried chicken, and sushi are all pretty good for supermarket food. We like their poke very much. We also think they have a pretty good wine buyer, and carry a good line of beer and spirits. *90 Kane St., Kahului; Kihei Town Ctr., Kihei; 878 Front Street, Lahaina.*

Foodland Farms

This is a Foodland-owned and operated full-service grocery store that focuses on natural and whole foods. They still have plenty of chips and sodas, however, and a good wine selection. Their prices are high, but we like shopping here if we're on the West Side. *335 Keawe St., Lahaina*

Guava, Gouda and Caviar

This store was known as Who Cut the Cheese in its former location, but changed its name when they moved up to Wailea. We go for the wine selection, but mostly the cheese selection, hand-cut to your specifications. These ladies love their work. *Wailea Gateway Center, Wailea*

Hawaii Liquor Superstore

This big liquor store stocks everything we can think of when we think cocktails: syrups, mixes, and all the spirits, plus wine and beer; and everything at good prices. They have the largest selection of wine on the island. *Maui Marketplace, Dairy Road, Kahului, 808-877-8778*

Long's Drug Store

Buy your wine and beer here! Believe it or not, this we-stock-a-little-of-everything drug store has the best selection, some of the most knowledgeable buyers, and the best prices on the island outside of Costco. Also get your Maui Cattle Company steaks here. *100 E Kaahumanu Ave Kahului; 1215 South Kihei Road, Kihei; 1221 Honoapiilani Hwy., Lahaina.*

Mana Foods

We love this health food store in Paia for everything from skin care products to local produce. The owner works hard to keep prices low on everything. See the review in the restaurant section. *Mana Foods, Baldwin Ave., Paia*

Maui Prime

Maui Prime is a wholesaler to many of the best restaurants, but they also have a very good retail outlet. Cheese, olives, fresh local eggs, and a good meat and fish section, as well as many gourmet grocery items and a careful selection of wine. *808.661.4912, 142 Kupuohi St., Lahaina*

Maui Swap Meet

This farmer's market/crafts fair is a Saturday ritual for us. Go early for the best produce, and try all the exotic treats. Make a point of stopping at the **Ono Organic Farms** stand, with its fresh Hana produce. If you like to cook, this is a must. Plenty of souvenirs, too. *At University of Hawaii-Maui Community College, Kahului.*

Safeway

Safeway is the best all-around standard grocery store. Their weekly sales start on Wednesdays. Decent prices on beer and wine. If you have a Safeway club card, you'll get the same special deals you get at home (our sale prices aren't quite as good a deal as yours probably are). Note to Canadians: yes, your card works here. *170 E Kamehameha Ave, Kahului; 277 Pi'ikea Ave, Kihei; 1221 Honoapiilani Hwy, Lahaina.*

Takamiya Market

Takamiya Market in Wailuku has lots of local and Hawaiian food to-go. We don't love their food, particularly, but it's one of the only places to get limu, or seaweed, and for that reason, we include it. *359 N Market St., Wailuku, 808-244-3404. www.takamiyamarket.com*

Times Supermarket

The Times Supermarket chain of grocery stores has a decent natural foods selection, plus a good local fish section. *70 E Kaahumanu Ave, Kahului; 1310 South Kihei Road, Kihei.*

Wailea Wine

Not just a very good collection of wine, also gourmet foods and pantry items, beer, liquor and cigars. *161 Wailea Ike Place, Wailea; 808-879-0555*

Wine Corner

The Wine Corner has very knowledgeable staff and careful selections. *149 Hana Hwy., Paia, 808-579-8904*

Whole Foods Market

We shop at **Whole Foods** for just about everything, including meat, fish, produce, and grocery items. They also have the best price on James's favorite gin, Hendricks. *Maui Mall, Kahului*

A Word on Beef and Chicken

Maui Cattle Company grazes their cows on the slopes of Haleakala, so the beef is usually not frozen before you get it. It also tastes amazingly rich and complex, although the butchering leaves something to be desired. (We need a good butcher here. Are you a good butcher? Do you want to live on Maui?) You can buy it at Long's Drug Stores. If you prefer, **Costco** and Safeway have the best quality and prices on the island for beef, chicken, and other meat. The USDA Prime cuts of beef that are sold at **Costco** are some of the best steaks we've had in or out of restaurants. Mary's chicken, available at **Whole Foods**, has stolen our hearts.

Where to Get Great Produce

Our favorite place to buy produce is the **Maui Swap Meet** at University of Hawaii-Maui Community College on Saturdays in Kahului, from 6am-1pm.

There are smaller farmer's markets all over the island, too. Pick up a copy of *Edible Islands* (this magazine is in racks all over the island, especially health food stores) to get a current listing of markets. In the meantime, check these out:

In Central Maui, check out the Queen Kaahumanu Center's market in Kahului on Tuesdays, Wednesdays, and Fridays. There is also a good market at Maui Mall on Tuesdays, Wednesdays, and Fridays.

In West Maui, check out the market in Honokowai across from Honokowai Park. They sell on Mondays, Wednesdays, and Fridays.

In South Maui, there's a market on South Kihei Road, in the Suda Store parking lot on every weekday. Also, be sure to check out the Lipoa St. Market on Saturday mornings, but get there early — things sell out fast.

Upcountry, you can find a market in the morning on Saturdays at the Eddie Tam Center on Makawao Avenue in Makawao.

In Hana there's a market on Saturdays across from Hasegawa General Store, and the Hana

Fresh market is open at the Hana Medical Center on Mondays, Thursdays, and Saturdays.

Mana Foods in Paia has a consistently excellent selection of local produce at prices that usually beat everyone else's.

Other natural food stores with good produce sections are **Hawaiian Moons** in Kihei, and **Down to Earth** in Kahului (both are reviewed in the Guide). **Whole Foods** in Kahului has a fantastic selection. We also go to **Costco** for local tomatoes, local Kula greens, and papayas and mangos in season, as well as organic produce from the mainland.

Omiyage: Food Gifts for Those Poor People You Left Behind

Once you've stuffed your belly, it's time to stuff your suitcase. What delicious, island-made morsels will you dole out to your luckiest friends back home?

Hawaii has adopted the Japanese custom of giving omiyage, or edible souvenirs, as gifts. Each island has its most coveted omiyage. If kama'aina ("child of the land" — someone who grew up here) traveling inter-island want a ride home from the airport, they best not return without the signature treat. It's normal to see aunties toting three boxes of Krispy Kreme donuts or **Komoda** cream puffs on flights from Maui to Oahu.

Most perishables won't survive mainland flights, but there are plenty of goodies that will. **Maui Coffee Roasters** (444 Hana Hwy., Kahului, 808-877-2877) on the way to Kahului Airport sells whole macadamia nuts submerged in dark chocolate. Irresistible. Better hide these in checked baggage; they won't survive long if you can reach them during your flight.

Topped with bright aloha print bonnets, **Jeff's Jams and Jellies** (sold at the Swap Meet, **Ono Gelato**, and www.jeffsjamsandjellies.com) offer a portable taste of the Islands. Sweet lilikoi and guava butters, mango chutney, and Kula strawberry jam are made with simple, entirely pronounceable ingredients.

Kona coffee may be touted worldwide, but Maui-grown beans have been rising in the ranks. At recent cupping contests, the Valley Isle has stolen the laurels from its neighbor. We recommend **MauiGrown Mokka and Red Catuai** — both exceptional coffees. The Maui Mokka is a rare 1,000-year-old variety that translates in the cup as rich, smooth, and chocolaty. Red Catuai is aromatic and bold. (MauiGrown storefront 277 Lahainaluna Road, Lahaina 808-661-2728 www.mauigrowncoffee.com) You can also get these in blends at **Maui Oma** — see the coffee Tip for other ideas.

Long's Drugs (locations in Kihei, Kahului, and Pukalani) is a one-stop-shop for foodie gifts. You'll find a wide selection of macadamia nuts — everything from honey roasted to Maui onion and garlic. Call us purists; we prefer plain, dry roasted. But we'll toss purity to the wind for a jar of Mele Macs — milk chocolate and toffee covered balls of mac nut magic. Mac Farms honey roasted macadamia nuts are also fantastic. (We like just about any flavor they make.) The dry goods aisle has other treats, too: taro pancake mix and lilikoi salad dressing. If Asian condiments are hard to find back home, stock up on dried seaweed, wasabi, and furikake (sushi spice) shakers. Award adventurous eaters with a sampling of "crack seed," mouth-puckering candy made from various pickled fruits and liberally dusted in li hing mui powder. Some will love it; others will cry "gag" gift.

Manju (a Japanese pastry filled with adzuki bean paste) is among the most popular local omiyage. **Home Maid Bakery** (1005 Lower Main St., Wailuku 808-244-7015) sells several flavors of unusually crispy manju, including coconut and purple sweet potato. They're like miniature pies, sold in boxes of five. We prefer the humble baked manju at **Sam Sato's** (1750 Wili Pa Loop, Wailuku 808-244-7124) filled with sweet lima bean paste. If that sounds weird, give it a try. They're only 75 cents apiece.

Marketed from here to Timbuktu, Maui Gold® pineapple happens to live up to the hype. When the Maui Land & Pineapple Company — who'd been in the business of growing the prickly fruit for 100-plus years — closed up their farm, Hali'imaile Pineapple Company took over their cherished crop. This sun-ripened, sweet, low-acid pineapple is great fresh or grilled.

Thanks to the introduction of the pesky fruit fly decades ago, all fruits and vegetables have to pass agricultural inspection before leaving Hawaii. It can't be done on the fly; you need to purchase airport-ready fruits (including pineapples) in advance. Get yours at **TakeHomeMaui** (121 Dickenson St., Lahaina 808-661-8067 www.takehomemaui) or, for considerably more moolah, in the **Kahului Airport lobby**.

While technically not edible, several locally made soaps smell good enough to eat. **Kula**

Herbs soap bars are wrapped in handmade paper and sold in several sizes. (**Mana Foods**, **Ono Gelato**, and online at http://kulaherbs.com/)

Foodie Tours

Several farms open their doors to visitors. Here are a few of our favorite ways to spend our time.

Surfing Goat Dairy is a working goat farm that produces delicious, award-winning cheese. We highly recommend stopping by and sampling the cheese or taking one of their tours (ever milked a goat?). The goats play on surfboards (for real) and it's a dry, dusty, but pungent and tasteful stop. 808-878-2870, www.surfinggoatdairy.com

Ono Organic Farms grows some pretty exotic fruit, which is all organic, and all handpicked. The farm is beautiful, and our favorite episode of Wolfgang Puck's old cooking show featured Wolfgang visiting with owner Chuck Boerner. They give thirty minute tours of the farm, but call for details. If you're driving to Hana, this is a must stop. 808-248-7779, www.onofarms.com

Tedeschi Winery is up in Kula, in a historic building that is peaceful and lovely to visit. We like the free tour of the grounds, and if you try the wines, the pineapple sparkling wine is interesting. 877-878-6058, www.mauiwine.com

We really like going up to Kula to **Ali'i Kula Lavender Farm**. This serene, delicious-smelling working farm grows over 45 varieties of lavender and makes several soaps, potpourri, and other lavender-themed products. You can walk through the grounds yourself, or take a tour. The view is stunning. 808-878-3004, www.aliikulalavender.com

One of our favorite Maui chefs, James Mc-Donald of *I'o*, *Pacific'o*, and the lu'au Feast at Lele established this organic farm in Kula, **O'O Farm**, specifically to grow fresh produce for his restaurants. You can take a tour that includes a picnic lunch made from what you pick. Delicious. 808-667-4341, www.oofarm.com

Local foodie Jeannie Wenger owns **Maui Culinary Tours**. She'll take you on a driving tour of local farms and then arrange a three course dinner at one of her favorite restaurants. 808-283-5924, www.mauiculinarytours.com

Where to Catch a Movie

If you want to get away from the tropical beauty for a while there are several movie theaters that show the most popular offerings: two in Lahaina, two in Kahului, and one in Kihei. You can find the listings in the *Maui News*, *Maui Time*, or *Maui Weekly*.

But if you like seeing art films, documentaries, and independent movies in a beautiful space, go to the **Maui Arts and Cultural Center** (MACC) and catch a movie from the **Maui Film Festival** (MFF). If you're here in December, check out their First Light Festival, which shows all the films Festival Director Barrie Rivers believes will win Oscar Awards. If you're here in June, make a point of attending the weeklong, star-studded, foodie-fabulous **Maui Film Festival** — our favorite event of the year. While they show films all over the is-

land, the most unusual — and best — venue is the Celestial Cinema, a giant outdoor movie theater with a gigantic screen and state of the art sound (honest, it's miraculous that they can make outdoor sound systems this good). There is nothing like sitting outside on a Maui summer night and watching a beautiful film. Every evening begins with a short tour of the stars with Maui's resident philosopher-astronomer, Harriet Witt. She's a lovely soul with a cosmic passion for the skies, and her presentation alone is worth the price of admission. Don't miss the Taste of Wailea, or the opening night event — if tickets are available — which is often held at *Capische?* Check out the Maui Film Festival's schedule at www.mauifilmfestival.com.

Maui Nightlife

Is there nightlife on Maui? Absolutely! Just about every Saturday night we turn on the lights on our back lanai (porch) and watch the geckos hanging out on the ceiling commit unspeakable acts of violence against various hapless insects. Sometimes they even … "dance" … with each other.

It's true that the nightlife on Maui is pretty sedate, especially in contrast to Honolulu's scene. Places to dance open and close fairly rapidly, so it's best to check out the local papers for listings. The *Maui Time* is especially useful. Your concierge will also have some ideas, as well. You will be able to see plenty of live music, however, and those listings will be in any of the newspapers and posted everywhere flyers are located.

Shows Worth Seeing

There may not be clubs on Maui, but there are some entertainments that may draw you in. In addition to the only two lu'aus we've ever recommended — *Old Lahaina Lu'au* and *Feast at Lele* — *'Ulalena* is amazing. We know of no better way to understand how Hawaiians feel about Hawaii than to see this show. Kids love it, especially the part when Pele, the volcano goddess, erupts. They also have dinner-and-a-show deals with some of our favorite Lahaina restaurants. Toll free number is 808-856-7958, www.ulalena.com

We also love **Warren and Annabelle's**, the incredibly funny magic show that is harder to get into than you might think. The close up magic performed in this intimate theater is nothing short of astonishing. Be prepared to laugh, a lot. That's all we're saying — it's too fun to give away more. Over twenty-one only. 808-667-6244, www.warrenandannabelles.com

If you like circus, you will definitely get a kick out of **Cirque Polynesia** at the Hyatt in Ka'anapali. We hold our breath through a couple of death-defying acts. The stage construction is less-than-professional, but the acts are definitely the real deal. A fun evening that is great for kids as well as adults. 808-667-4540, www.cirquepolynesia.com

The **Maui Arts and Cultural Center** in Kahului is a great place to see world-class concerts and wonderful gallery exhibitions. To find out what they're doing when you're here, check out their schedule on line or pick up their calendar at activity booths. 808-242-7469, www.mauiarts.org

Maui Onstage at the Iao Theater in Wailuku puts on several musicals and plays every year. This is good community theater in a beautiful Mission style theater that was built in 1928 (and is finally air-conditioned). 808-244-8680, www.mauionstage.com

Traffic Tips

We're pretty funny about traffic on Maui. Whether we grew up here, come from big cities with lots of traffic, or small towns with one stoplight, people who live on Maui think that traffic here is Just Awful. Why, it can take us a whole thirty minutes to drive from our home in Kihei to the Home Depot in Kahului! How inconvenient! (It used to take Molly that long to cross New York City's midtown on the bus — on a good day — and don't even get James started on the Capital Beltway.)

We get remarkably complacent in our little corners of the island. It's entirely possible that someone who lives and works on the West Side (Lahaina, Ka'anapali, etc.) hasn't visited South Maui in over a year. When we go to dinner on the west side and servers find out we're from Kihei, they marvel that we were willing to drive *so far.*

How far is it? Maybe forty-five minutes or an hour, tops.

So when we complain about traffic, we might really be complaining about driving. The relaxed lifestyle can lead to a particular Maui-style *inertia.*

Given all of the above it's also true that you will see a marked increase in the number of cars on the road during the mornings and in the evenings. You're not likely to be terribly *slowed down* by them, but you will need to pay more attention while you drive.

Because there is generally one road to any part of the island, when an accident occurs or something happens to close the road, travel can go from slow to nonexistent.

Many visitors are so struck by the gorgeous, ever-changing scenery that they drive as if they were a little drunk, which is another reason why traffic can be slow.

And when it's whale season, *fuhgeddaboudit*. Everyone's distracted when giant mammals throw themselves into the air and make gigantic splashes.

Our advice is to remind yourself that you're driving a dangerous vehicle, fasten your seat belt (both seat belts and child restraints are required by law in Hawaii), and make sure you pay attention to the speed limit, which changes quite often on our roads.

We also recommend never, ever leaving anything of value in your car, because break-ins and theft can be a problem. When we drive to Hana, we tend to keep our car messy so that it looks local, and we make sure that any maps or guidebook-looking books come with us when we leave the car. We even have friends who leave their doors unlocked so that it is easy for someone to find out there's nothing of value in the car. This mitigates the risk of a smashed window. We don't leave valuables in the trunk, either, because it's just too easy these days to get in through the backseat.

The Road to Hana

Every once in a while a reader asks us if the Road to Hana "is really worth it." Argghhh!!!

This is one of the hardest questions to answer. We know it's worth it for *us*, but we also know people who felt it was a waste of time on their vacation. If you hate long, twisty roads on the mainland, or if you get carsick, or if you just aren't that interested in a beautiful scene that changes with every mile, it may not be for you.

If, on the other hand, gorgeous waterfalls, beautiful pools, endless ocean vistas, incredibly lush rainforests, and soaring mountain peaks sound like fun, you want to drive the Road. If you do go, we have some things for you to keep in mind.

Here's what it's like for the driver on The Road to Hana: You drive a car you don't know that well for several hours (two if you don't stop) at 20 miles per hour around endless hairpin curves. Your hands clench the wheel (whether you want them to or not) because you keep getting surprised by what's around the next bend.

Everyone else in the car oooooohs and ahhhhhs and exclaims "Look at that!"

You miss whatever they saw, and are surprised by how fast that car is coming from the other direction on the one lane bridge.

There are two ways to mitigate the fatigue the driver inevitably feels after a while. You can switch driving responsibilities with someone else, so that no one gets too tired and no one misses all the beauty, or you can go on a tour and let someone else do all the driving. We recommend **Valley Isle Excursions**, 808-661-8687. (Valley Isle is a sponsor for this edition of *Top Maui Restaurants*, and we love their tour, which takes you all the way around the volcano).

If you drive yourself, of course, you get full control and can stop as often as you like — which we also love. If this is your choice, you must get the brand new CD travel guide to Hana: **Experiencing the Road to Hana … and Beyond!** We have all of the CD guides, and this is the only one we don't want to throw out the window. In fact, we've listened to it at home (this is true) … because the music is so great. OK, enough, you'll read about it in detail in a little bit — they're a sponsor of ours.

Stopping along the Road to gawk at the beauty is good, because once you get to Hana, you might wonder what the fuss is about — it's a little fishing village, and not much is happening (and they like it that way). If you stay in Hana, you'll find that a *lot* happens here, but it's mostly internal. When we're here for more than twenty-four hours, something inside starts to unwind, and we relax more deeply than we do anywhere else.

Most people, however, are not staying. If you are one of those, budget at least eight hours to drive to Hana and then back. If you decide to keep going "all the way around" Haleakala — which we recommend — you are going to take at least eight hours. This includes plenty of stopping, but a fairly measured pace. It can take as long as twelve hours to do it at a leisurely pace.

There are only a couple of places to eat in Hana, none of which we particularly recommend … so we highly recommend packing a picnic lunch and road snacks to eat in the car. We like to pack a cooler with plenty of water and caffeinated drinks, leave very early (at around 7am), stop in Paia for breakfast, and be on the Road by 8am. This puts us at the head of the long lines of cars and gives us plenty of time to meander and stop wherever we want to.

There are several little roadside stands along the Road, and several farms. The following is a list of some of our favorite places to stop that are reliably open:

Ono Organic Farms is a must stop, as we described above. 808-248-7779, www.ono-farms.com

Our beautiful friends Krista and Ian own a tropical flower farm in Hana. Make a point of stopping at **Hana Tropicals** to visit their orchid house, ask your tropical flower questions, and take a tour of the pesticide-free farm. They also have a sacred labyrinth that you can use for a walking meditation to work the kinks out from the road. They ship their flowers anywhere, and their bouquets are spectacular. They offer sterling customer service. 808-248-7533, www.hanatropicals.com

The **Hana Coast Gallery** is just next to the Hotel Hana-Maui and is one of our favorite places to view art on Maui. It's a very particular collection of the absolute cream of the crop of local artists. If you love art, it's a must-do. While you're there, get a drink in the hotel's gracious lobby and look at Hana's beautiful harbor. 808-248-8636, www.hanacoast.com

Kahanu Gardens is a National Tropical Botanical Garden located in Hana, and if they're open when you visit, we highly recommend stopping in and walking the gardens. The largest heiau in Polynesia is located here. This massive lava-rock structure is an ancient place of worship known as Pi`ilanihale. 808-248-8912 www.ntbg.org

Haleakala Crater

Another impossible question to answer is "should I go to Haleakala for sunrise?" If you go on a morning when the sunrise is perfect — the clouds perfectly encircle the mountain just below the crater, and the sunlight comes up through them and creates a stunning ocean of rainbows below you — it's definitely worth it.

If you go on a morning when there are no clouds, well, it's still very pretty, but not you might think *what's the big deal?*

Of course, you can never predict nature, so if you get the intuitive feeling that yes, you should venture up the mountain, we recommend going on your first full day, or your second, when you are still on mainland time. It will be easier to wake up early enough to drive up the mountain — which can take at least two hours from our home in Kihei. We'd leave at least two and a half hours to drive there from Ka'anapali.

Sunrise does not wait for you, so make sure you are there at least thirty to forty-five minutes before the show. If sunrise is at 5:30am, we would leave Kihei by 3:00am at the latest. You can call the National Weather Service at 866-

944-5025 for sunrise time and the weather forecast at the summit.

We always bring plenty of layers and gloves and scarves and hats, because it's very cold up there at 10,000 feet. We often leave the extra clothes off at first, and then add layers as we get higher in altitude. Even with our down parkas we can get cold (but we're acclimated to the tropics). You might even want to take the comforter off the bed!

Bring a few snacks to tide you over before breakfast. After sunrise, you can grab breakfast at **La Provence** or **Kula Lodge**, or wait to get down to Paia and go to **Moana Bakery and Café**, our personal favorite for this trip.

If sunrise is just too early for you, you might consider catching a sunset, instead. It's not as dramatic, because the western cloud cover is not as likely to give that stained window effect as it does in the east. However, it's still a beautiful place to watch the sun go down. If it's a full moon (or the day before) you can watch the full moon rise in the east while the sun sets in the west. Heavenly.

West Maui Mountains

Despite the beauty it offers, the road that winds around the West Maui Mountains scares us way more than the Road to Hana does. It's truly one way, and built for mountain goats, not cars. But it's breathtaking, too. *Julia's Best Banana Bread* is out there, as well as our *favorite* artist gallery, **Turnbull Studios**.

Steve and Christine are friends of ours, and they live and work at the studio. In addition to their own sculpture, you can find many other local Maui artists' work for sale, and several smaller items that make precious souvenirs. This and the Hana Coast Gallery (where you can also see Christine's work) are two very special places for anyone who loves art. If you don't want to drive all the way around the West Maui Mountains from Kapalua, you can take the road from the other direction, Wailuku, and the studio is only twenty minutes from town. They also opened a second gallery, **Turnbull Fine Art,** in Paia, which you don't have a single excuse for not visiting. *Turnbull Studios, Gallery and Sculpture Garden, 5030 Kahekili Hwy., Wailuku,* 808-244-0101, www.turnbullstudios. org; *Turnbull Fine Art, 137 Hana Highway, Paia,* 808-579-9385, www.turnbullfineart.com

Daytrip to Lana'i? Yes!

Lana'i is where we chose to get married, and where we go, at least three times a year, to get away from the hustle and bustle of Maui. (We have to go *somewhere* for vacation!) We adore Lana'i. The island is beautiful in a completely different way from Maui, and there is nothing to "do" so we relax really deeply there.

The Four Seasons runs two resorts on Maui — both are stunning. **Manele Bay** sits on a picture-perfect cove that is home to pods of dolphins. Set high above the bay, but just a five minute walk to the sparkling beach, this resort is a dream. The cavernous lobby is painted with floor to ceiling murals of a Chinese wedding festival, and we can sit there for hours, just watching the dolphins and the light play.

The **Lodge at Koele** is more sedate. A much more rustic decor is in force: dark wood, two mammoth fireplaces (that are lit each evening — it's a little chilly at this elevation), and lovely floral patterns on the walls. After years of going over, we actually prefer it to Manele Bay. It's quieter and our relaxation is nearly overwhelming. This is also where you will find one of the best kitchens in the county. Everything is home-made — sausages, lemon curd, pastries — everything. Every afternoon they have a high tea menu in their bar that is filled with so many delicious little pastries and finger sandwiches that even just writing about it makes us want to call over for a reservation. And dinner in their formal restaurant, The Dining Room, is top notch. (Order the Grand Marnier soufflé for dessert, by the way.) Service on Lana'i is very good. It is Four Seasons, true. But it's also a much smaller place — most of the people who work here have lived here for a long time. The workforce is less transient.

But you don't have to stay at the Four Seasons to enjoy Lana'i. There's the less expensive (but not inexpensive) **Hotel Lana'i,** for one. You can also just go over for a day. You can take a very early ferry out, hang out on the beach just a short walk from the ferry dock, have lunch at the hotel (or bring it with you), and get back on a ferry in the afternoon. Call **Expeditions Ferry** for ferry tickets (passenger only, no cars): 808-661-3756 or www.go-lanai.com.

The Four Seasons resorts run a shuttle between the beachside Manele Bay resort and the pine-tree-ringed Lodge at Koele resort, with a stop in quaint Lana'i City. Resort guests have access to the shuttle as part of their transportation fee, but you can also get a pass if you are not a guest. Call the Four Seasons Resorts directly for the details: 808-565-2000.

Moving to Maui

Most people who visit Maui have the passing thought "It would be so great to live here." And it is. But living here is not like being on vacation all the time. You're far away from friends and family, and the cost of living is very high (unless you're from places like New York City, in which case you won't think it's all *that* expensive).

Everyone we know who moved to Maui from somewhere else ultimately did it because they *knew* they were supposed to.

Be prepared for anyone who lives here to roll their eyes a little when you express your desire, and don't take it personally. So many people say it, and so few do it, that we on Maui take a "wait and see" approach. Until you have actually moved here, you might not find a job or a place to live, for example. It's like you have to prove that you're here before Maui opens her arms.

Now, it's a little different for retirees. And it's also different for people with special skills that are needed on the island. If you're really serious about moving to Maui, we recommend you ask plenty of locals when they got here, how they got here, and why they came. Also ask, *"Why do you live here?"* rather than stating *"It must be great to live here."* We can't argue with the fact that it is a great place to live, but why we stay is a little different for everyone.

If you are serious, we recommend speaking to one of the two realtors who sponsor this edition of ***Top Maui Restaurants***. Both are personal friends, and Josh is James's golf buddy. We trust both to steer you right and neither play games.

If you have a pet and want to find out what's involved in bringing them to Maui, call our vet and dear friend, **Dr. Demian Dressler**. His hospital, **South Shore Veterinary Care**, has a wonderful service that we recommend any pet lover moving to Maui use. They'll coordinate every detail of your pet's move with the state's vaccination and quarantine inspectors (we don't have rabies here, so the state makes you jump through some hoops to prove that your pet isn't infected). A vet tech will even meet your pet as they leave the plane so they aren't alone while the state inspects their papers. It's a great service and helps you to avoid the ninety day quarantine. 808-874-3422, www.vetinki-hei.com.

Our Sponsors

It may seem strange that we have local Maui businesses sponsoring *Top Maui Restaurants*, but it's a lot less strange than you might think. First, a little about the economics of food journalism: most dining reviews are written for magazines and newspapers, which make money by taking advertising. Bloggers make money from advertising, as do online peer-review travel websites.

You may or may not know this, but a shocking amount of travel writing is actually comped by the establishments featured — in other words, the restaurant or hotel gave the writer free meals and accommodations.

(We don't understand this. If we don't share your pain at having to pay $120 for a bad meal, how can we possibly review it? No restaurant can influence our review, because we don't take restaurant advertising.)

We don't take sponsorships from just anybody, either. Our reputation is on the line when we endorse other businesses. To underwrite *Top Maui Restaurants*, sponsors have to offer services or products that are of superior quality, and relevant and useful to you. We have to have had personal experience with the sponsor, and they have to have a sterling reputation.

Obviously we can't take advertising from restaurants, not even from restaurants we love. It's too much of a conflict of interest, and even if we could be sure the advertising relationship wouldn't influence our review, we don't want even the *appearance* of a biased review.

Every sponsor shares a few things in common. First, they appreciate the value this book delivers. Second, they love food — whether they eat at the most expensive restaurants or the least. (It is funny how many quizzed us about our methods and our favorite restaurants — or even read the book cover to cover — before they decided we were telling the unvarnished truth about Maui restaurants.)

Third, they consider our readers the cream of the crop of Maui visitors. If you care enough about your vacation to plan your meals, and know that just relying on Internet reviews or concierge recommendations can get you into trouble, you will appreciate the high quality our sponsors deliver.

As you read what we have to say about these businesses, keep in mind that we have hand-selected these for *you*. Just like we don't want you to waste your time or money at bad restaurants, we don't want you to waste it on anything else. We have had many requests over the years for advertising (mostly from restaurants), but when we started accepting sponsorships with the 2010 edition, we only took businesses worthy of your vacation dollars.

Please support our sponsors, because they support us — and let them know that you found them in *Top Maui Restaurants.*

Leave the Driving to Valley Isle Excursions

For some, the twisty Road to Hana is a delightful jaunt, while for others, the 600 hairpin turns make it more like a never-ending odyssey. If you fall into the latter category, call **Valley Isle Excursions**. Enthusiastic readers first alerted us to their service several years ago, and after getting to know the owners and taking their tour, we've discovered their secret: the Aloha spirit is built into every aspect of their business.

You'll journey the full circle of Haleakala starting from Paia along the Hana Highway all the way to the fishing village of Hana, but also even further, to the darling little church in Kipahulu where Charles Lindbergh is buried, through the dramatic, windswept gorges in Kaupo and up to the eucalyptus-scented heights of Kula. The vans are small (holding only twelve) but also tall: the plate glass windows stretch from your waist to well over your head. The seats are wide and comfy, and a cooler in the back totes snacks and drinks. Lunch is

fresh and tasty and is served in Hana itself, and if you're lucky a village friend will provide entertainment.

All of that is wonderful; but what is *really* special about Valley Isle Excursions is the people behind the wheel. Each driver is a certified tour guide, and each had to undergo a rigorous two months of training before they could give their own tour. But that's only the beginning. They don't work off a script: instead, they use their own passions and interests to inform their tour. It doesn't get stale, either: even if you tour with the same person twice, you don't hear the same stories over and over again. Where the owners found so many spectacular personalities to usher us through eight hour tours in an enclosed space is a mystery, but it works for us, and it will work for you. With door-to-door (or very close) transportation, we couldn't ask for better service or value. Call Valley Isle Excursions and mention this ad for specials: **808–661–TOUR**. You can also visit their website: **www.TourMaui.com**

If You're Driving to Hana, You Need This CD Guide

"Which CD guide gives the best tour when we drive ourselves to Hana?" our readers have often asked. "None!" we used to insist, "Nothing captures the majesty and the breathtaking experience like your own senses do! Just open the windows and immerse yourself!"

After using the extraordinary R2H CD guide, **"Experiencing the Road to Hana … and Beyond!"** we've changed our minds.

This is the one guide you should get if you are making the drive to Hana and around Haleakala. The narrative is delivered in a friendly, almost intimate manner and is downright intuitive: precisely as a question occurs to us, we hear the answer on the guide.

And the music! Scored by folks in Hollywood who create soundtracks for major motion pictures, this is not just a handful of favorite tracks from local musicians, but a combination of traditional and contemporary mellow Hawaiian music blended with gorgeous, soaring orchestral sections.

The beauty of the Road to Hana still catches us by surprise, and still prompts the questions

"could this be real, or is it a movie set??" Combine that with listening to this guide and you get an almost unbearably romantic, emotional event.

We've driven the Road many times, but after using this guide and the accompanying itinerary, we have experienced it in a different way and found some spots we didn't know about.

We're also impressed with — and thankful for — the guide's respect for local culture and property. You will find *real* Hawaii adventure without crossing private property or bumbling into sacred areas that should remain sacrosanct.

Put simply: we adore this guide. A must-have if you are driving yourself, it's available in a downloadable MP3 format (with a PDF map), but we highly recommend getting the physical CD because it is more convenient for your rental car and comes with excellent tips, one-and-two-day itineraries, and a superb map.

To get a taste, watch the video and listen to samples at **www. theR2H.com**, where you can also place an order or find out where to buy the CD on

Maui.

Historic Sky Adventures at the Edge of the Forest: Piiholo Ranch Zipline

Whether you're an old hand at ziplining — flying through the air like a movie action hero while securely anchored to the strongest of cables — or a rank beginner, we say this: don't think about it a minute longer. Just *book* your adventure at Piiholo Ranch Zipline. This course, which includes the longest side-by-side zipline in the state of Hawaii — over half a mile — is A.M.A.Z.I.N.G.

Of course, it would be. It's owned and run by the Baldwin family (as in Baldwin High School, Baldwin Avenue, Baldwin Museum, Baldwin Beach, Alexander & Baldwin Sugar Museum)... let's just say that this seventh-generation ranch family has a most spectacular and special connection to the land. Whether you take their four-line or five-line tours, explore the aerial bridges in their newest Canopy Tour, or just walk along, you won't find this combination of adrenaline-pumping adventure, Maui history, and eco-friendly tour of Maui's lush natural beauty anywhere else.

The ranch is in Makawao, which means "edge of the forest," and climbs up Haleakala's lush, verdant, rainforest. As you zip along at speeds up to 40 miles per hour, you get 360-degree views of the volcano's summit, the deep blue ocean below (including the big waves on the North Shore in season), and the imposing, jagged West Maui Mountains. Below are precious tropical forests (including endangered koa trees), ravines so lush you'll wonder how you could cross them any other way (you can't) and the work-ing cattle ranch. You might even catch a glimpse of patriarch Peter Baldwin tending his herd of Corriente cattle. (If he's not there he's probably competing in a rodeo somewhere — being in his 70's doesn't seem to slow him down.)

Safe and fun for everyone — children as young as eight can do the courses — and flexible enough to accommodate the more timid members of your group as well as the lion-hearted, checking ziplining off your bucket list at Piiholo Ranch Zipline is a must-do Maui activity. Their tours are small and very popular, so book ASAP: **808-572-1717** or **www.PiiholoZipline.com**. Tell them James and Molly of Top Maui Restaurants sent you to get **$20 off per couple**!

See the Quirky Goats, Eat the Delicious Cheese at Surfing Goat Dairy

Early in our relationship James took Molly to **Surfing Goat Dairy** for a piece of lilikoi quark cheesecake. Quark is a fresh cheese that makes a cake very similar to cheesecake, but lighter and a little wobblier in texture. Molly had never had it, and the combination of the tangy goat's cheese with the light, sweet-tart passion fruit (lilikoi) set her into a kind of reverie. James didn't want to disturb her pleasure by asking for a bite — he just bought another piece. They had a lovely little picnic at the farm, surrounded by the sounds of goats playing (literally) on surfboards and the cheese-making equipment going full steam.

While kids love visiting the goats at Surfing Goat Dairy, we think that foodies of all ages must make a point of stopping in. For a mere $7 you can get a twenty minute guided walking tour of the farm, and for $12 you can register for their Evening Chores tour (which includes hand–milking a goat). We like the milking, but we also recommend the "Grand Tour" which is every few weeks and includes watching the cheese getting made (and lots of samples).

Surfing Goat Dairy is not just a "local" dairy making "good" cheese; **it's won seventeen national awards from the American Cheese Society and the American Dairy Goat Association**. On our shopping list for holiday and birthday indulgences: Rolling Green, the award-winning chevre made with fresh garlic and chives. Call **808–878–2870** or visit **www.SurfingGoatDairy.com** to find out when you can visit the goats.

Choice Snorkeling at Molokini on the Lani Kai

There are dozens of boats that will take you on a snorkel cruise to Molokini, Coral Gardens, or one of the many "Turtle Towns," but we recommend the **Lani Kai**, for several reasons.

The boat itself is a powerful catamaran that holds only sixty-nine passengers, which means smaller groups and more personal attention and instruction from the crew, which is important: on our last snorkel we saw a crew member get in the water and swim alongside a novice snorkeler until she was absolutely comfortable. Even better for us old hands, if you know what you're doing, they leave you alone to enjoy yourself.

They don't "narrate" the cruise too much, which we like, but are also available for questions, which we like even more.

Each snorkel boat's license specifies exactly where they can anchor at Molokini Crater, and some spots are better than others. The Lani Kai gets a sweet spot really close to the inner wall of the crater, which means the water is almost always clear and you don't have to wander too far to see the wildlife.

The SNUBA instruction is thorough and fun, and the included sandwiches and salads are good quality. Drinks, including mai tais (the best we've had on a snorkel boat) and beer are also part of the deal, and if you're here during whale season, you'll likely see more than one as you cross to Molokini.

We've even chartered the Lani Kai to take us and sixty of our friends on a sunset cruise to

entertainment. Here they are.

Old Lahaina Lu'au: Authentic and Wildly Entertaining

If you want to go to a *real* lu'au — as real a lu'au as you'll get without becoming close to a local family and getting an invitation to a feast at the beach or in the backyard — **Old Lahaina Lu'au** is a must-do. And hey, it's on the beach in Lahaina!

The grounds are glorious and meticulously tended, and we love wandering them before the evening begins (so check in as early as you can). You'll receive your first tropical libation of the evening along with your lei greeting from one of the welcoming dancers. Don't drink too fast — they're stronger than they taste, and you can always get another one later (all drinks are included in the ticket price). The sunset over Lahaina Harbor is like a postcard, but turn your eyes away long enough to see the imu — the traditional Hawaiian barbecue pit — when they remove the pig that's been roasting in preparation for the night's feast.

You will know the evening has begun in earnest when the show starts. The meal is served by a giant buffet, which means each table goes up, one at a time, to pile their plates. Do not in the least worry about being hungry — the bread will keep your stomach happy while the singers and dancers distract your eyes and mind. Even

celebrate James's fortieth birthday. An excellent value if you're in the mood for a snorkel trip; call **808-244-1979** or visit **www.MauiSnorkeling.com**, and make sure to mention *Top Maui Restaurants* or James and Molly when you do.

The Only Lu'aus We Recommend

We're constantly asked if a lu'au is really worth going to … probably because even the most inexperienced of travelers recognizes the tourist-trap potential inherent in such a "real Hawaiian" experience. For years we've recommended — and highly rated — two lu'aus (and only these two). They're both independent of a resort and serve authentic, well-executed meals. They're very different from each other, but we enjoy each one tremendously and give both our unqualified thumbs up for both the food and the

the most cynical of our friends have melted at the heart-filled production, which combines a little bit of history with a whole lot of hula and fantastic music. The choreography and the dancing is stunning — if you took the free hula lessons earlier in the evening, you'll probably sigh in empathy, knowing just how very hard it is to create this most sacred dance this beautifully.

The food itself is a gorge-fest for Hawaiian cuisine. The kalua pig — the one you just saw lifted out of the ground — is a must-try: sweet, smoky, and tangy with their barbecue sauce. Other authentic and well-executed dishes include the salty and tender lomi lomi salmon, hui (soy-glazed) chicken, and the tender, fresh pohole fern salad. The silky poi is a must-try, and if you've never had it, a server will show you how to eat it.

Old Lahaina Lu'au is booked months ahead of time during high seasons, so make your reservations now by calling **808-667-0553** or visiting **www.OldLahainaLuau.com**, and make sure you mention us when you book. We've also gotten a last minute reserva-

tion by stopping by the same day to see if there's a cancellation.

Feast at Lele: A Foodie's Dream Lu'au

One of our very favorite chefs, James McDonald of **Pacific'o** and **I'o**, provides the food for **Feast at Lele**, making this a culinary adventure you will not get anywhere else in the state. Meanwhile, the evening's entertainment is provided by the owners of Old Lahaina Lu'au, so even though the food is different than what you'll find at that more traditional venue, you still have an incredibly authentic cultural experience. (In fact, the food contributes to the authenticity — but more on that in a minute.)

The departure from the traditional begins with the seating arrangements. You get your own table, which immediately transforms the evening into an exotic, unbearably romantic dinner theater. The beach and Lahaina harbor view at sunset is spectacular, and both the waves and the sand are used as props during the show.

The entertainment begins almost immediately ... as do

the drinks. The bartenders at **I'o** (next door) are creative and confident, and the tropical (and not-so) creations they have contributed to this menu are mind-bending (get transportation). The beer and wine list are similarly lovely.

Feast at Lele is like a wildly entertaining history and culture lesson served in five courses, each of which represents one of the four regions that contribute to Hawaii's lu'au traditions: Hawaii, New Zealand, Tahiti, and Samoa. Traditional delicacies from each are served in simple, unpretentious preparations, giving you a true insider perspective on the culture under consideration. (Because really, what could give you more information about a culture than eating their food?) Chef James insists on the same meticulously fresh, organic ingredients he uses elsewhere, including all that amazing produce from his organic farm, O'o.

The entertainment matches the courses: when you're eating Tahitian you're also watching a mesmerizing, grass-skirted Tahitian number. The fifth course — if you

have room — is dessert and fire dancing (with a little comedy).

To book your table — the venue is intimate and reservations fill very quickly — call **808-667-5353** or visit **www.FeastAtLele.com**, and make sure you tell them that we sent you.

Maui's Best Massage Really Is

Little known fact: Molly was a massage therapist in her former life in New York City, and she absolutely hates — *hates* — paying for an average massage. After just one at-home appointment with Sam Molitas — who recently moved to Maui from the Big Island — she breathed a sigh of relief. Maybe it's his years of training, or his wide range of experience (Chicago's New School to Esalen to exclusive Hawaiian resort spas), or maybe it's just that he has what massage therapists call "great hands" ... whatever the reason, we finally have someone she can depend upon to straighten her out when she's tied up in knots.

Even if Sam isn't available when you call **Maui's Best Massage** — the outcall massage therapy practice he runs — you can be sure that he hand-picked the therapist you book. This is important, because the only profession more popular than Realtor on Maui is Massage Therapist ... and they are not all created equally. Sam's therapists have trained in and worked in the best resorts, and they share his compassion and skill. And best of all, they come to *you*, so after your massage you can rest, or even nap. Whether you are looking for a rejuvenating and relaxing Swedish massage, the relentlessly soulful lomi lomi (the Hawaiian massage that feels like ocean waves repeatedly cleansing you inside and out),

structural work like deep tissue massage, or a combination of techniques, you can be sure that Sam is sending you the right person.

Attitude plays a tremendous role in great massages. If the therapist is distracted or upset or sees it as "just a job," your experience can suffer. That's why two people can each pay hundreds of dollars at a high end facility and one will feel blissed out and the other will just feel lighter (in the wallet). Sam's discernment in choosing his therapists, and his insistence that they come to you, is key. Maui's Best Massage ... really is. They book fast, so if you are visiting, make your appointment as soon as you know where you will be staying — and if you live on Maui, don't delay. Tell them Molly sent you and you deserve the *best*: **808-426-7418**, or **www.MauisBest-Massage.com**.

The Ride of Your Life with Ocean Riders

The first time we went out with **Ocean Riders** was a Tuesday, and we felt a little resistant to taking *an entire day off in the middle of the week* just to tour Lana'i's (admittedly breathtaking) coast on a small snorkel boat. Could this really be worth it? (Yeah, we are card-carrying work-aholics.) Five minutes into the trip all was forgotten; it's hard to think about — much less worry about — much of *anything* when you're riding the waves with this crew.

Ocean Riders is serious about their business, which is to provide you with an unforgettable, thrilling and fun day circumnavigating Lana'i. They use a serious boat: a rigid hull inflatable (H.B.I.), the same type the Coast Guard uses for search and rescue. When the captain opens her up, she *barely* skims the surface of the wa-

ter — you feel like you're flying — and she can stop on a *dime*. Her thick hull can take a tremendous pounding, which means the open ocean waters on the back side of Lana'i don't get the best of her. (Some boats have to turn around if the surf is high, but Ocean Riders always shows you the whole island.) When Captain Patty, a petite, calm, confident and skilled captain who has been working these waters for decades, decides to give you a thrill, hold on to your hat ... and your wife.

In between carving giant wakes into the ocean and zooming so close to the cliffs that you will be forgiven for covering your eyes, you'll indulge in peaceful snorkeling at isolated spots unlike any you'll find on Maui. These stops are not timed: they end when everyone is back in the boat (and there are only 18 of you, so there is plenty of instruction if you need it). Along the way you will glimpse ali'i (royal) burial caves and cruise weirdly colorful sea caves that almost shimmer with their ancient, sacred vibes.

Everything about this excursion earns an A+, from the

equipment to the crew's competence and knowledge of local lore to the itinerary itself. It's well worth every penny, and one of the very best tours on Maui. Their trips book fast, so call **808-661-3586** now and tell them we sent you. Also see their website: **www. MauiOceanRiders.com**

Really Great Realtors

The Maui real estate market features everything from studio condos to beachfront estates worth tens of millions, which is why you can't throw a stone on Maui without hitting a Realtor. If you even *hint* that you are thinking about buying or selling a home on this island, they will swarm like ants in a sugar bowl. And if you're serious, you'll want a personal recommendation to help you choose a real estate professional. We have two people we recommend, both of whom we like, trust and respect.

Wailea Makena Expert: Josh Jerman

Josh Jerman closed on a property an average of every ten days in 2011, making him one of a select few

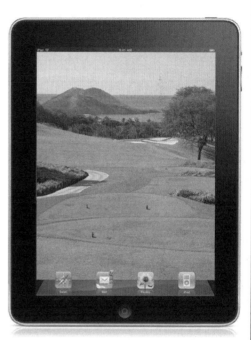

top-producing Maui Realtors. He works from dawn to dusk, except for every other Thursday afternoon when he meets James for golf (having already put in a full eight hours). Discipline and an old-fashioned work ethic aren't the only reasons Josh wins industry awards and attracts exclusive clients. Insightful and generous, he is a great guy who embodies "aloha." He grew up on Maui, and established a foundation which to date has awarded more than $25,000 in college scholarships to Maui high school seniors. Josh is actively involved with many community groups and serves on the Board of Directors for the Realtors Association of Maui.

Josh truly **is** *awesome*. We're not the only ones who think so: in 2005, *Pacific Business News* asked an independent panel to pick their "Forty under Forty" Hawaii leaders. Josh was only 27 years old at the time, but made the list — honored for his community-minded spirit, people skills and high business acumen. Right on!

Josh hangs his real estate license with The Wailea Group, and is an expert in the luscious Wailea and Makena district (but is also available for other areas of Maui).

Whether you are a buyer or seller, he will negotiate the best value for you. He's not high pressure (that niche is occupied by others). Instead, he gets to know you over time, engages in intelligent conversations about meaningful subjects punctuated by fun (and sometimes hilarious) outbursts. It can take years to find the right buyer for these gem-like homes, so it's lucky for you he has the patience of Solomon. Warning: you may find you have a friend you would do anything for, because you know he would do anything for you (we did).

Josh handles everything from the first phone call to getting the keys to the house — a rare trait in real estate professionals. He has a top-notch team to support him 24/7 and he practically redefines "exceptional customer service."

Call Josh on his cell at **808-283-2222** or visit his website **www.JoshJerman.com** to start your conversation (and don't forget to tell him we sent you). Also, download his new app for your smartphone: it's the first of its kind for the Maui real estate market. It uses GPS to show you all available properties in the immediate area. Awesome.

She Keeps Going Until You're Home: Debbie Guimond

Debbie Guimond is like the Energizer Bunny: if you're her real estate client, she keeps going and going and going and going until you find your perfect Maui home. We love Debbie not just for her outgoing, upbeat personality, but also for her friendly, pleasant determination. Whether showing you a potential place or negotiating the closing, she's a straight talker and doesn't play around ... although we think she might be a Kenny Rogers fan, because she knows when to hold, when to fold, and when to, if necessary, walk away (because in Maui, there's always another dream place to see).

Maybe this cheerful, pragmatic, "get her done" attitude comes from the twenty-three years Debbie spent as a nurse before she switched careers. She is tirelessly dedicated to her clients, listens closely, and has a real talent for hearing what you're not quite able to articulate yourself. She's almost a professional matchmaker — between you and your perfect place. Her pursuit

of your Maui address translates into excellent customer service. She isn't satisfied unless you are 100%, completely, fulfilled.

Personality only gets you so far; luckily, Debbie is something of a techie, which means that she is constantly leveraging the newest technology to make her job — and your buying or selling experience — quicker and more streamlined. She's also moved fifty-two — fifty-two! — times in her lifetime, living in every corner of this country, which means she knows exactly how much effort and time it takes to uproot and establish a new place.

Debbie has finally found her roots in Maui — it's the only place she's ever lived that really feels like home, and she loves it with the passion and commitment of the converted. After being here for eight years she knows the island's market from Haleakala to Kapalua and back again; combine that knowledge with the expertise of her network of reliable real estate professionals and you get a Realtor ready, willing and able to help. Whether you're buying or selling, interested in a vacation rental, a condo, or a home, Debbie has tons of information on her website: **www.RealEstateSalesMaui.com**. Go there now to stop dreaming and start looking for your very own Maui street address. She's a fantastic Maui connection — make sure you mention us when you talk to her.

The Best Stylists on Maui: Salon 253

You know your hair stylist is good when complete strangers stop you to ask "Who cuts your hair?" This used to happen to Molly all the time when she lived in New York, and now, here, too — ever since she started visiting **Salon 253** in Wailuku.

This stylish little hair emporium hidden down a side street is an oasis of real talent, and if you have any hair need — whatsoever — you should book an appointment (now — they book weeks ahead). The owners, best friends Adiel and Nicole, each already had a "full book" of customers who followed them to their brand-new business in mid-2011. Within weeks, Salon 253 became known as the hippest place to get pretty on Maui. Men (including James) are comfortable here, and even children love these fun, upbeat women.

In addition to any kind of service you can think of — cuts, color, hot oil treatments, blow-outs — they have fantastic bridal services. They are always up-to-date on the latest trends, are experts at figuring out what will complement your face and personality — and Adiel's styles and up-dos have been featured in bridal expos and in island bridal magazines.

Whether you need a special occasion up-do, color, or just a good wash and blow-out before you go out for a romantic evening, call them at **808-270-2759**. Or better yet, book online at **www.Salon253Maui.com**. Make sure you tell them we sent you for **10% off services** ... and be prepared to laugh once you're there. Fun is served, right along with the complimentary espresso drinks.

Top Maui Restaurants

If your blood sugar is low, or if you're a bottom-line kind of reader, you may not want to *read all those words* in our reviews. The articles and listings in this section of *Top Maui Restaurants* are designed to help you get the information you need quickly.

The first article addresses **food cravings**. Whether you're in the mood for sushi, sweets, or steak, you will find our top picks for as many types of foods as we can think of.

Next, you'll find our favorite restaurants listed by island **location**. No matter where on Maui you end up, you'll know where we would eat in that area.

Finally, you'll find a listing of our very favorite restaurants by **value** — the very best from $ to $$$$. These are the places where we're happy spending money.

Remember, we only list the places we would patronize even if we didn't have to review them. These are the real *Top Maui Restaurants.*

The last list is every restaurant in this book, ranked by their individual **ratings**.

Finally, at the end of this section you will find a comprehensive **Index** that lists as many keywords as we could find. So if you're looking for something or someone or somewhere, look there.

Enjoy!

When You're Craving…

Sometimes you just need a good piece of cake. Or a steak. Or a quivery pile of sashimi. Or … or … or…

When you're grabbed by a food-related desire, check this listing to see where we would go, if we were craving such a thing.

This is not a comprehensive list. There are often many more restaurants that you *could* visit for dishes in each category. But after years of telling you *all* the restaurants that serve each food, we've realized that you really only want our best recommendations. We even include some categories just to tell you that we *don't* have a recommendation.

Baked Goods & Pastries

Aina Gourmet Market in Ka'anapali has good bagels, cupcakes, and several other good options. Glad they're on the West Side. 130 Kai Malina Pkwy, Ka'anapali, 808-662-2832

Anthony's Coffee Co. is always good for a muffin break. 90 Hana Highway, Paia, 808-579-8340

La Provence is way the heck up the mountain, and the pastries sell out early. But they are perfect. 3158 Lower Kula Road, Kula, 808-878-1313

Leoda's Kitchen and Pie Shop in Olowalu threatens to waylay us each time we drive in or out of Lahaina for those dessert pies and very good bread. 820 Olowalu Village Rd., Lahaina, 808-662-3600

Mana Foods in Paia has wonderful vegan pastries. 49 Baldwin Ave., 808-579-8078

Also in Paia, you'll find **Moana Bakery &**

Café, which has great apple strudel. 71 Baldwin Ave., 808-579-9999

When the **Maui Bake Shop** re-opened in Wailuku, we were thrilled to have access once again to these fantastic pastries. 2092 West Vineyard St., Wailuku, 808-242-0064

Ono Gelato stores in Lahaina and Kihei both have excellent pastries and sweets. 815 Front St., Lahaina, 808-495-0203, or 1280 S. Kihei Rd., Kihei, 808-495-0287

Rodeo General Store in Makawao, and now in Kihei for chocolate cake. 3661 Baldwin Ave., Makawao, 808-572-1868; and 1847 S. Kihei Rd., Kihei, 808-633-4990

Sam Sato's in Wailuku for manju and turnovers. 1750 Wili Pa Loop, Wailuku, 808-244-7124

T. Komoda Store and Bakery in Makawao for their malasadas (if fresh), and stick donuts. 3674 Baldwin Ave., Makawao, 808-572-7261

Barbecue

Beach Bums Bar & Grill has lovely smoked barbecue. 300 Ma'alaea Rd., Ma'alaea, 808-243-2286

Fat Daddy's Smokehouse in Kihei has great brisket and pulled pork. 1913 S. Kihei Rd., Kihei, 808-879-8711

Honolua Store in Kapalua has a good selection of grilled items. 900 Office Road, Kapalua, 808-665-9105

Isana Restaurant for tabletop Korean bbq. 515 S. Kihei Rd., Kihei, 808-874-5700

There's also a **Famous Dave's BBQ** in Lahaina, if you are familiar with this national chain.

Boxed Lunch/Picnic for the Road to Hana

Anthony's Coffee Co. is open really early and does a nice lunch. 90 Hana Highway, Paia, 808-579-8340

Café Mambo and Picnics, 30 Baldwin Rd., Paia, 808-579-8021

CJ's Deli & Diner is a good option if you're on the West side. 2580 Keka'a Dr., Ka'anapali, 808-667-0968

Breakfast or Brunch

Aina Gourmet Market has good bagels and other breakfast items. 130 Kai Malina Pkwy, Ka'anapali, 808-662-2832

Anthony's Coffee Co. is a good choice for breakfast. 90 Hana Highway, Paia, 808-579-8340

Café @ La Plage does pretty nice bagels and excellent coffee. 2395 S. Kihei Rd., Kihei, 808-875-7668

Colleen's in Haiku has a satisfying breakfast and good coffee. 810 Haiku Rd., Haiku, 808-575-9211

Duo at the Four Seasons has a great breakfast buffet every day, and really goes all out on holidays like Mother's Day and Easter. 3900 Wailea Alanui, Wailea, 808-874-8000

Five Palms Restaurant in the mornings is beautiful and the food is good. Special brunches on Easter and Mother's Day are really nice and include champagne! 2960 S. Kihei Rd., Kihei, 808-879-2607, and 1450 Front St., Lahaina, 808-661-0937

Grandma's Coffeehouse in Keokea — way up on Haleakala — has a nice breakfast, especially with live music on Sundays. 153 Kula Hwy, 808-375-7853

Honolua Store in Kapalua has inexpensive and tasty breakfast items. 900 Office Road, Kapalua, 808-665-9105

La Provence in Kula ... yummm ... 3158 Lower Kula Rd., Kula, 808-878-1313

Lahaina Coolers does a nice breakfast. 180 Dickenson St., Lahaina, 808-661-7082

Longhi's has nice breakfasts, with good coffee. 3750 Wailea Alanui Dr., Wailea, 808-891-8883, and 888 Front St., Lahaina, 808-667-2288

Mala's weekend brunches are well-worth a

stop. 1307 Front St., Lahaina, 808-667-9394

Marco's Grill & Deli serves no-nonsense and reasonably-priced diner breakfasts. 444 Hana Highway, Kahului, 808-877-4446

We love heading to **Maui Bake Shop** for breakfast before a hike. A lovely meal, every time. 2092 West Vineyard St., Wailuku, 808-242-0064

Moana Bakery & Café is our favorite place in Paia for breakfast. 71 Baldwin Ave., 808-579-9999

North Shore Café in Haiku is an inexpensive, great little breakfast spot. 824 Kokomo Road, Haiku, 808-575-2770

Ruby's has reliable and tasty breakfast fare in Kahului. 275 W. Kaahumanu Ave., Kahului, 808-248-7829

Sea House in Napili has our favorite breakfast fare on the West side. 5900 Lower Honoapiilani Rd., Napili, 808-669-1500

Three's Bar & Grill in Kihei has good Benedicts and excellent coffee. 1945 S. Kihei Rd., Kihei, 808-879-3133

Whole Foods in Kahului has good breakfast fare, and excellent coffee. 70 Kaahumanu Ave., Kahului, 808-872-3310

Burgers

Café Mambo has a good burger — especially at Happy Hour prices. 30 Baldwin Ave., Paia, 808-579-8021

Café O'Lei always has a decent burger with fresh toppings on the menu. 2439 S. Kihei Rd., Kihei, 808-891-1368, 62 N. Market St., Wailuku, 808-891-1368, and 1333 Maui Lani Parkway, Kahului, 808-877-0073

Colleen's has a big juicy burger. 810 Haiku Rd., Haiku, 808-575-9211

Cool Cat Café is known for their burgers and if you're on the relative food wasteland that is Front Street, they're your best bet. 658 Front St., Lahaina, 808-667-0908

The burgers off the grill in **Honolua Store** are satisfying. 900 Office Road, Kapalua, 808-665-9105

The burgers at **Five Palms Restaurant** are go-to lunches for us when we're craving one in Kihei. 2960 S. Kihei Rd., Kihei, 808-879-2607, and 1450 Front St., Lahaina, 808-661-0937

Leoda's Kitchen and Pie Shop has huge burgers with fresh toppings, including several cheeses. 820 Olowalu Village Rd., Lahaina, 808-662-3600

Longhi's burger is generously portioned and grilled perfectly. They often have it on lunch special, too. 3750 Wailea Alanui Dr., Wailea, 808-891-8883, and 888 Front St., Lahaina, 808-667-2288

It feels a little silly to order a burger at **Mala** ... but if you're in the mood and nothing else is tempting you (how could that be true?), this is a great burger. 1307 Front St., Lahaina, 808-667-9394, 3700 Wailea Alanui Drive, Wailea, 808-879-1922

Maui Brewing Company sliders are really yummy. 4405 Honoapiilani Hwy, Kahana, 808-669-3474

Ruby's has good burgers. We're particularly fond of their sliders. 275 W. Kaahumanu Ave., Kahului, 808-248-7829

Teddy's Bigger Burgers has brought really fantastic burgers to Maui. Thanks, guys. 335 Keawe St., Lahaina, 808-661-9111

'Umalu is probably your best bet for a good burger in Ka'anapali. 200 Nohea Kai Dr., Ka'anapali, 808-661-1234

Cheese

Guava, Gouda and Caviar, formerly known as Who Cut the Cheese? has a lovely assortment of cheeses. They are not reviewed in this edition for their food, but we certainly recommend stopping in if you have a hankering. Wailea Gateway Center, Wailea, 808-874-3930

Surfing Goat Dairy has an amazing selection of cheeses in their store — and they ship to you at home, too. 3651 Omaopio Rd., Kula, 808-878-2870

The cheese buyer at **Whole Foods** knows their stuff, and so do the cheese mongers. 70 Kaahumanu Ave., Kahului, 808-872-3310

Chinese

When our favorite Chinese restaurant, East Ocean, announced they were closing just before we finalized this edition of *Top Maui Restaurants*, we finally bought a really good, carbon steel wok.

Coffee/Espresso

Please see the Tip about coffee in the **Top Maui Tips** section about where to buy coffee. Also, these places offer a good cuppa when you're craving coffee:

Anthony's Coffee Co., 90 Hana Highway, Paia, 808-579-8340

Café @ La Plage, 2395 S. Kihei Rd., Kihei, 808-875-7668

Café Mambo and Picnics, 30 Baldwin Rd., Paia, 808-579-8021

Grandma's Coffeehouse, 153 Kula Hwy, 808-375-7853

La Provence, 3158 Lower Kula Road, Kula, 808-878-1313

Maui Bake Shop, 2092 West Vineyard St., Wailuku, 808-242-0064

Moana Bakery & Café, 71 Baldwin Ave., 808-579-9999

Whole Foods, 70 Kaahumanu Ave., Kahului, 808-872-3310

Crepes

Bistro Casanova has nice savory and sweet crepes available all day long. 33 Lono Ave., Kahului, 808-873-3650

Café Des Amis has nice crepes, including a sugar-and-lime version that we really like. 42 Baldwin Ave., Paia, 808-579-6323

Fajitas

Unfortunately, no one does really *fantastic* fajitas on Maui — not even our favorite Mexican joint, **Amigo's**. On the other hand …

… The duck fajitas at **Café Mambo** must be eaten at least once every fiscal quarter. 30 Baldwin Rd., Paia, 808-579-8021

French/Bistro

Bistro Casanova has good bistro dishes, including wonderful steaks and frites. 33 Lono Ave., Kahului, 808-873-3650

Gerard's is lovely. 174 Lahainaluna Rd., Lahaina, 808-661-8939

German

Brigit & Bernard's Garden Café is a lovely little biergarten with a really good Octoberfest. 335 Hoohana St., Kahului, 808-877-6000

Happy Hour

A good Happy Hour features killer drinks and killer pupus at special prices. Here are our favorite places for Happy Hour as of publication. Please call for current times.

Bistro Casanova has a very nice Happy Hour. 33 Lono Ave., Kahului, 808-873-3650

Café Mambo and Picnics has a good Happy Hour, and everyone knows it. 30 Baldwin Rd., Paia, 808-579-8021

Dog & Duck is a good little pub with a good little Happy Hour. 1913 S. Kihei Rd., Kihei, 808-875-9669

Capische? kills us with their new Happy Hour. See the review for details — or just get up there. 555 Kaukahi St., Wailea, 808-879-2224

We are at the **Five Palms** Happy Hour at least twice a month. Good appetizers and drink specials, great view. 2960 S. Kihei Rd., Kihei, 808-879-2607, and 1450 Front St., Lahaina, 808-661-0937

We like the drinks at **Mai Tai Lounge**, especially at Happy Hour prices. 839 Front St., Lahaina, 808-661-5288

Mala's Happy Hour makes us very happy, indeed. Both locations have great bartenders, and you get turtles in Lahaina. 1307 Front St., Lahaina, 808-667-9394, 3700 Wailea Alanui Drive, Wailea, 808-879-1922

Heading to **Maui Brewing Company** for Happy Hour is a no-brainer. 4405 Honoapiilani Hwy, Kahana, 808-669-3474

Milagros in Paia has fantastic margaritas and great people watching at Happy Hour. 3 Baldwin Ave., Paia, 808-579-8755

Pacific'o at Happy Hour is lovely lovely lovely. 505 Front St., Lahaina, 808-667-4341

Tommy Bahama's Tropical Café has a great Happy Hour — too bad it's only at the bar. But well worth it. 3750 Wailea Alanui Drive

Hawaiian Regional Cuisine/ Pacific Rim

You really should visit one of these restaurants (at least) once (at least). Most are spendy, but all are worth it for the food.

The Banyan Tree in Kapalua is amazing for high end food. 1 Ritz-Carlton Drive, Kapalua, 808-669-6200

Café O'Lei is reliable for good food at really reasonable prices. 2439 S. Kihei Rd., Kihei, 808-891-1368, 62 N. Market St., Wailuku, 808-891-1368, and 1333 Maui Lani Parkway, Kahului, 808-877-0073

David Paul's Island Grill has fabulous food. 900 Front St., Lahaina, 808-662-3000

Honu wants you to think East Coast ... but there are plenty of Pacific Rim preparations here. 1295 Front St., Lahaina, 808-667-9390

Lahaina Grill in consistently great. 127 Lahainaluna Rd., Lahaina, 808-667-5117

Mala is one our favorite restaurants on the island. 1307 Front St., Lahaina, 808-667-9394, 3700 Wailea Alanui Drive, Wailea, 808-879-1922

Mama's is the most Hawaiian of restaurants — and has delicious Polynesian food. 799 Poho Place, Paia, 808-579-8488

Pacific'o is always great'o. 505 Front St., Lahaina, 808-667-4341

Pineapple Grill is a great choice for excellent dishes in this cuisine. 200 Kapalua Dr., Kapalua 808-669-9600

Roy's is still a fantastic classic. Make sure you call to see if they're in their new digs! January 2012: 4405 Honoapiilani Hwy., Kahana; after January 2012: 2290 Ka'anapali Pkwy, Ka'anapali, 808-669-6999

Sansei Delicious, and lots of price promotions (for early birds and night owls). 1881 S. Kihei Rd., Kihei, 808-879-0004, and 600 Office Rd., Kapalua, 808-669-6286

Spago is one of our favorite restaurants. 3900 Wailea Alanui Dr., Wailea, 808-874-8000

Healthy/Organic/Local Ingredients

These restaurants and/or health food stores have a relentless commitment to fresh, local, organic food that doesn't get in the way of flavor or satisfaction.

Aina Gourmet Market, 130 Kai Malina Pkwy, Ka'anapali, 808-662-2832

Alive & Well has good takeout and excellent supplement advice. 340 Hana Hwy., Kahului, 808-877-4950

The Banyan Tree makes fantastic food out of top-notch ingredients. 1 Ritz-Carlton Drive, Kapalua, 808-669-6200

Capische? Delish. 555 Kaukahi St., Wailea, 808-879-2224

Coconut's Fish Café: We love *Coconut's* for their excellent food, and we appreciate that they work hard to cut the fat and increase the freshness in their preparations. 1279 S. Kihei Rd., Kihei, 808-875-9979

David Paul's Island Grill focuses on local

and always flavorful. 900 Front St., Lahaina, 808-662-3000

Flatbread Pizza Company: This is great pizza made from mostly local, unique produce. Delicious and Maui-centric. 89 Hana Hwy., Paia, 808-579-8989

Fresh Mint is crazy delicious. And vegan. 115 Baldwin Ave., Paia, 808-579-9144

Honu, sister to **Mala**, features fresh and local foods (with some exceptions). 1295 Front St., Lahaina, 808-667-9390

I'o If you have your own certified-organic farm and your fish comes from the beach outside ... what more could you want for local, organic, fresh? 505 Front St., Lahaina, 808-661-8422

Joy's Place Delicious and inexpensive (for the quality) sandwiches! 1993 S. Kihei Rd., Kihei, 808-879-9258

Mala is known for its local focus and delicious food. 1307 Front St., Lahaina, 808-667-9394, 3700 Wailea Alanui Drive, Wailea, 808-879-1922

Mama's lists the provenance of just about every ingredient used in their delicious recipes. 799 Poho Place, Paia, 808-579-8488

Mana Foods You can always find something here to love. 49 Baldwin Ave., Paia, 808-579-8078

Pacific'o: *I'o*, dit-to. 505 Front St., Lahaina, 808-667-4341

Pineapple Grill is lovely and fresh and decadent. 200 Kapalua Dr., Kapalua 808-669-9600

Spago loves local ingredients, even though it's a chain. 3900 Wailea Alanui Dr., Wailea, 808-874-8000

Whole Foods knows where everything comes from and how it was raised and you can find lots of local items. 70 Kaahumanu Ave., Kahului, 808-872-3310

Ice Cream/Frozen Treats

Ono Gelato is decadent and addictive. 115 Hana Highway, Paia, 808-579-9201; 815 Front St., Lahaina, 808-495-0203; or 1280 S. Kihei Rd., Kihei, 808-495-0287

Tasaka Guri Guri You will not find this treat anywhere else on the planet. 70 E. Kaahumanu Ave., Kahului, 808-871-4513

Ululani's Hawaiian Shave Ice If you don't stop here at least once, we don't love you anymore. 819 Front Street, Lahaina, 360-606-2745; 790 Front Street, Lahaina, 360-606-2745; 333 Dairy Road, Kahului, 360-606-2745

Indian

Thank you to **Monsoon India** for very good Indian food. 760 S. Kihei Rd., Kihei 808-875-6666

Italian

Pizza recommendations are listed separately.

Antonio's has some good dishes on offer. 1215 S. Kihei Rd., Kihei, 808-875-8800

Aroma D'Italia Ristorante has good basic

Italian-American food. Reliable. 1881 S. Kihei Rd., Kihei, 808-879-0133

Capische? Cue the harp strings — this is our favorite restaurant! 555 Kaukahi St., Wailea, 808-879-2224

Ferraro's Bar e Ristorante Stunning setting, sterling service, very good. Four Seasons Resort, 3900 Wailea Alanui Dr., Wailea, 808-874-8000

Marco's Grill & Deli has some very good pasta dishes. 444 Hana Hwy, Kahului, 808-877-4446

Penne Pasta Good Italian food in Lahaina at reasonable prices. 180 Dickenson St., Lahaina, 808-661-6633

Japanese

See sushi listings for sushi recommendations.

Ichiban Okazuya is a great little to-go place in Wailuku. 2133 Kaohu St., Wailuku, 808-244-7276

Izakaya Matsu is a tiny little tavern that offers small plates of reasonably priced (for Maui) Japanese food. 1280 S. Kihei Rd., Kihei, 808-874-0990

Kai Wailea is spendy, but the food is good. 3750 Wailea Alanui Dr., Wailea, 808-875-1955

Kobe is fun for teppanyaki fans. 136 Dickenson St., Lahaina, 808-667-5555

Sansei Fun and extravagant versions of classic Japanese dishes. 1881 S. Kihei Rd., Kihei, 808-879-0004, and 600 Office Rd., Kapalua, 808-669-6286

Sam Sato's in Wailuku has good noodles. 1750 Wili Pa Loop, Wailuku, 808-244-7124

Star Noodle has tasty and inexpensive dishes. 286 Kupuohi St., Lahaina, 808-667-5400

Korean

Isana is good tabletop Korean. 515 S. Kihei Rd., Kihei, 808-874-5700

Latin American Fusion

Cuatro Restaurant is yummy. Don't miss the won ton sushi pupu. 1881 S. Kihei Rd., Kihei, 808-879-1110

Local/Plate Lunch

Aloha Mixed Plate has good plate lunch and amazing views. 1285 Front St., Lahaina, 808-661-3322

Café O'Lei is reliable for good food and has eminently reasonable plate lunch specials. 2439 S. Kihei Rd., Kihei, 808-891-1368, 62 N. Market St., Wailuku, 808-891-1368, and 1333 Maui Lani Parkway, Kahului, 808-877-0073

Da Kitchen is da place. 425 Koloa St, Kahului, 808-871-7782; 2439 S. Kihei Rd, Kihei, 808-875-7782; and 658 Front St., Lahaina, 808-661-4900

Eskimo Candy has good poke and some good plate lunch. 2665 Wai Wai Place, Kihei, 808-879-5686

Honolua Store in Kapalua has good plate

lunch. 900 Office Road, Kapalua, 808-665-9105

Leoda's Kitchen and Pie Shop has good — if a little pricey — options for local food. 820 Olowalu Village Rd., Lahaina, 808-662-3600

Sam Sato's in Wailuku. 1750 Wili Pa Loop, Wailuku, 808-244-7124

Star Noodle is our favorite place for tasty local dishes - not strictly plate lunch, but definitely local in its ethic. 286 Kupuohi St., Lahaina, 808-667-5400

Lu'aus

We've only ever recommended two lu'aus — even before they sponsored this edition. The food, show and overall experience are worth the ticket price.

Feast at Lele 505 Front St., Lahaina, 808-667-5353

Old Lahaina Lu'au 1251 Front Street, Lahaina, 808-667-1998

Mexican/ Tex-Mex

Amigo's has three locations, and they're all giving you good Mexican food. Shrimp diabla. 41 E. Lipoa St., Kihei, 808-879-9952; 333 Dairy Rd., Kahului, 808-872-9525; and 658 Front St., Wharf Cinema Center, Lahaina, 808-661-0210

Cilantro has delicious and authentic dishes prepared with plenty of love. 170 Papalaua St., Lahaina, 808-667-5444

Milagros Food Co. Milagros has good food and excellent margaritas. 3 Baldwin Ave., Paia, 808-579-8755

Mediterranean

Pita Paradise has scrumptious pitas, a lovely hummus platter, and gracious service. 1913 S. Kihei Rd., Kihei, 808-875-7679; and 10 Wailea Gateway Place, Kihei (Wailea), 808-879-7177

Pizza

We like the pizzas at **Ferraro's**. Four Seasons Resort, 3900 Wailea Alanui Dr., Wailea, 808-874-8000

Flatbread Pizza Company makes excellent, thin-but-chewy-crusted flatbreads. 89 Hana Hwy., Paia, 808-579-8989

Prepared Foods

When we need to just pick up some food to go, we head to one of these places:

Aina Gourmet Market, 130 Kai Malina Pkwy, Ka'anapali, 808-662-2832

Alive & Well, 340 Hana Hwy., Kahului, 808-877-4950

Honolua Store 900 Office Rd., Kapalua, 808-665-9105

Ichiban Okazuya, 2133 Kaohu St., Wailuku, 808-244-7276

Mana Foods 49 Baldwin Ave., Paia, 808-579-8078

Rodeo General Store, 3661 Baldwin Ave., Makawao, 808-572-1868; and 1847 S. Kihei Rd., Kihei, 808-633-4990

Whole Foods, 70 Kaahumanu Ave., Kahului, 808-872-3310

Sandwiches

Sometimes you just want a good sandwich. Here are our favorite places.

Aina Gourmet Market, 130 Kai Malina Pkwy, Ka'anapali, 808-662-2832

Café @ La Plage, 2395 S. Kihei Rd., Kihei, 808-875-7668

Café O'Lei is always reliable. 2439 S. Kihei Rd., Kihei, 808-891-1368, 62 N. Market St., Wailuku, 808-891-1368, and 1333 Maui Lani Parkway, Kahului, 808-877-0073

Coconut's Fish Café: Their steak sandwich kills, as do their fish burgers. 1279 S. Kihei Rd., Kihei, 808-875-9979

Honolua Store, 900 Office Rd., Kapalua, 808-665-9105

Joy's Place, 1993 S. Kihei Rd., Kihei, 808-879-9258

Main Street Bistro, 2051 Main St., Wailuku, 808-244-6816

Paia Fish Market for their ono burgers. 100 Hana Hwy, Paia, 808-579-8030

Pita Paradise pitas are our idea of the perfect sandwich. 1913 S. Kihei Rd., Kihei, 808-875-7679; and 10 Wailea Gateway Place, Kihei (Wailea), 808-879-7177

Seafood

Whether you're looking for a really good fish taco or the fanciest wok-fried moi presentation, this is where we would go, were we you:

The Banyan Tree in Kapalua has excellent fish dishes. 1 Ritz-Carlton Drive, Kapalua, 808-669-6200

Bubba Gump Shrimp Co. Their shrimp is really good, and if you're in Lahaina and in the mood for something fried and family-friendly, this is a good choice. 889 Front St. Lahaina, 808-661-3111

Café O'Lei is always reliable. 2439 S. Kihei Rd., Kihei, 808-891-1368, 62 N. Market St., Wailuku, 808-891-1368, and 1333 Maui Lani Parkway, Kahului, 808-877-0073

We never regret ordering the fish at **Capische?** 555 Kaukahi St., Wailea, 808-879-2224

Coconut's Fish Café: Yummy fish burgers and fish tacos. 1279 S. Kihei Rd., Kihei, 808-875-9979

Cuatro Restaurant has excellent fish preparations. 1881 S. Kihei Rd., Kihei, 808-879-1110

David Paul's Island Grill always has killer fish dishes. 900 Front St., Lahaina, 808-662-3000

Honu is reminiscent of an East Coast fish shack... but so much more. 1295 Front St., Lahaina, 808-667-9390

I'o offers perfectly cooked, desperately fresh fish. 505 Front St., Lahaina, 808-661-8422

Japengo has wonderful fish dishes. 200 Nohea Kai Dr., Ka'anapali, 808-667-4796

Lahaina Grill is known for its bold, fresh preparations. 127 Lahainaluna Rd., Lahaina, 808-667-5117

Mala is incredible. 1307 Front St., Lahaina, 808-667-9394, 3700 Wailea Alanui Drive, Wailea, 808-879-1922

Mama's has amazing fish dishes. 799 Poho Place, Paia, 808-579-8488

Pacific'o has fabulous choices. 505 Front St., Lahaina, 808-667-4341

Paia Fish Market for their ono burgers. 100 Hana Hwy, Paia, 808-579-8030

Pineapple Grill is a great choice for when you're craving fish. 200 Kapalua Dr., Kapalua 808-669-9600

Roy's pistachio-encrusted ahi is delicious, among many others. January 2012: 4405 Honoapiilani Hwy., Kahana; after January 2012: 2290 Ka'anapali Pkwy, Ka'anapali, 808-669-6999

Sansei Great fish preparations. 1881 S. Kihei Rd., Kihei, 808-879-0004, and 600 Office Rd., Kapalua, 808-669-6286

Spago is one of our favorite restaurants, and James orders their wok-fried moi whenever they have it. 3900 Wailea Alanui Dr., Wailea, 808-874-8000

Shave Ice

Ululani's Hawaiian Shave Ice is the only shave ice joint we recommend. Thank good-ness they've expanded beyond their original location — and may even open in South Maui in 2012! 819 Front Street, Lahaina, 360-606-2745; 790 Front Street, Lahaina, 360-606-2745; 333 Dairy Road, Kahului, 360-606-2745

Steak

A good steak dinner is one of the great joys in life. Here's where you can get a very good steak.

The Banyan Tree, 1 Ritz-Carlton Drive, Kapalua, 808-669-6200

Bistro Casanova, 33 Lono Ave., Kahului, 808-873-3650

Capische? 555 Kaukahi St., Wailea, 808-879-2224

David Paul's Island Grill, 900 Front St., Lahaina, 808-662-3000

Duo, 3900 Wailea Alanui, Wailea, 808-874-8000

Gerard's, 174 Lahainaluna Rd., Lahaina, 808-661-8939

I'o, 505 Front St., Lahaina, 808-661-8422

Lahaina Grill does, too. 127 Lahainaluna Rd., Lahaina, 808-667-5117

Makawao Steak House, especially for the prime rib. 3612 Baldwin Ave., Makawao, 808-572-8711

Mala, 1307 Front St., Lahaina, 808-667-9394, 3700 Wailea Alanui Drive, Wailea, 808-879-1922

Mama's, 799 Poho Place, Paia, 808-579-8488

Pacific'o, 505 Front St., Lahaina, 808-667-4341

Pineapple Grill, 200 Kapalua Dr., Kapalua 808-669-9600

Roy's, January 2012: 4405 Honoapiilani Hwy., Kahana; after January 2012: 2290 Ka'anapali Pkwy, Ka'anapali, 808-669-6999

Ruth's Chris Steak House, Address: 3750 Wailea Alanui Dr., Wailea, 808-874-8880; and 900 Front St., Lahaina, 808-661-8815

Spago, 3900 Wailea Alanui Dr., Wailea, 808-874-8000

Sushi

Some of these places offer authentic sushi, and others do big extravagant rolls... and all are places we head to when we need a sushi fix.

Cane and Taro has many of our favorite **Sansei** rolls, but you don't have to leave Ka'anapali. 2435 Ka'anapali Pkwy, Ka'anapali, 808-662-0668

Japengo has extravagant rolls and amazing sashimi. 200 Nohea Kai Dr., Ka'anapali, 808-667-4796

Kai Wailea has good sushi. 3750 Wailea Alanui Dr., Wailea, 808-875-1955

Koiso Sushi Bar is our favorite place to get authentic sushi from a true sushi master. 2395 S. Kihei Rd., Kihei, 808-875-8258

Sansei Very good sushi, including wild "third-generation" rolls. 1881 S. Kihei Rd., Kihei, 808-879-0004, and 600 Office Rd., Kapalua, 808-669-6286

Sushi Paradise has very delicious and authentic sushi. 1215 S. Kihei Rd., Kihei, 808-879-3751

Thai

Thai food is delicious, and we're lucky to have a couple of good restaurants on Maui.

Thai Chef in Lahaina is a hole in the wall and BYOB, but delicious. 878 Front St., Lahaina, 808-667-2814

We visit **Thailand Cuisine** at least once a month. 70 E. Ka'ahumanu Ave., Kahului, 808-873-0225; and 1819 S. Kihei Rd., Kihei, 808-875-0839

Vegetarian

The only real vegetarian restaurant on Maui is **Fresh Mint**. But several other restaurants make an effort to feed herbivores well. Some of these restaurants have a separate menu for veggies, while others have chefs who love a challenge and can make you something wonderful from the day's freshest ingredients. All make our veggie friends happy.

A Saigon Café 1792 Main St, Wailuku, 808-243-9560

Alive & Well 340 Hana Hwy., Kahului, 808-877-4950

Antonio's 1215 S. Kihei Rd., Kihei, 808-875-8800

The Banyan Tree 1 Ritz-Carlton Drive, Kapalua, 808-669-6200

Bistro Casanova 33 Lono Ave, Kahului, 808-873-3650

Café Des Amis 42 Baldwin Ave., Paia, 808-579-6323

Café Mambo and Picnics 30 Baldwin Ave., Paia, 808-579-8021

Down to Earth 305 Dairy Rd, Kahului, 808-877-2661

Flatbread Pizza Company 89 Hana Hwy., Paia, 808-579-8989

Fresh Mint 115 Baldwin Ave., Paia, 808-579-9144

Hawaiian Moons Natural Foods 2411 S. Kihei Rd., Kihei, 808-875-4356

Honu 1295 Front St., Lahaina, 808-667-9390**'O** 505 Front St., Lahaina, 808-661-8422

Joy's Place 1993 S. Kihei Rd., Kihei, 808-879-9258

Lahaina Grill 127 Lahainaluna Rd., Lahaina, 808-667-5117

Mala, 1307 Front St., Lahaina, 808-667-9394, 3700 Wailea Alanui Drive, Wailea, 808-879-1922

Mana Foods 49 Baldwin Ave., Paia, 808-579-8078

Milagros Food Co. 3 Baldwin Ave., Paia, 808-579-8755

Moana Bakery & Café 71 Baldwin Ave., Paia, 808-579-9999

Monsoon India 760 S. Kihei Rd., Kihei, 808-875 6666

Pacific'o 505 Front St., Lahaina, 808-667-4341

Pita Paradise 1913 S. Kihei Rd., Kihei, 808-875-7679

Sansei Seafood Restaurant & Sushi Bar. 1881 S. Kihei Rd., Kihei, 808-879-0004; and 600 Office Rd., Kapalua, 808-669-6286

Spago 3900 Wailea Alanui Dr., Wailea, 808-874-8000

Thai Chef 878 Front St., Lahaina, 808-667-2814

Thailand Cuisine 70 E. Ka'ahumanu Ave., Kahului, 808-873-0225; and 1819 S. Kihei Rd., Kihei, 808-875-0839

Vietnamese

A Saigon Café is one of our favorite restaurants. Excellent, fresh Vietnamese. Decor? Not so much... 1792 Main St, Wailuku, 808-243-9560

Ba-Le Sandwiches offers inexpensive food that's pretty tasty — and quick. 1221 Honoapiilani Highway, Lahaina, 808-661-5566; 270 Dairy Rd., Kahului, 808-877-2400; 247 Pi'ikea Ave., Kihei, 808-875-6400; and 1824 Oihana St., Wailuku, 808-249-8833

Fresh Mint Vegan Vietnamese. Even carnivores love this food. 115 Baldwin Ave., Paia, 808-579-9144

Favorite Restaurants by Location

Sometimes you are caught feeling a little peckish in an unfamiliar area. Here's a list of the places we would visit.

Central Maui (Kahului, Wailuku, Ma'alaea)

Central Maui is home to many permanent Maui residents, and there aren't many visitor activities here ... so the restaurants tend to be less expensive. Our favorites in this area are:

Kahului

Amigo's *(Mexican)* 333 Dairy Rd., Kahului, 808-872-9525

Bistro Casanova *(Mediterranean/Italian)* 33 Lono Ave, Kahului, 808-873-3650

Brigit & Bernard's Garden Café *(German)* 335 Hoohana St., Kahului, 808-877-6000

Café O'Lei *(Local/Pacific Rim)* 1333 Maui Lani Parkway, Kahului, 808-877-0073

Ruby's *(American)* 275 W. Ka'ahumanu Ave., Kahului, 808-248-7829

Tasaka Guri Guri *(Guri Guri)* 70 E. Kaahumanu Ave., Kahului, 808-871-4513

Thailand Cuisine *(Thai)* 70 E. Ka'ahumanu Ave., Kahului, 808-873-0225

Ululani's Hawaiian Shave Ice, 333 Dairy Road, Kahului, 360-606-2745

Whole Foods *(Healthy/Organics)* 70 Kaahumanu Ave., Kahului, 808-872-3310

Ma'alaea

Beach Bums Bar & Grill *(American/Barbecue)* 300 Ma'alaea Rd., Ma'alaea, 808-243-2286

Wailuku

A Saigon Café *(Vietnamese)* 1792 Main St, Wailuku, 808-243-9560

Café O'Lei *(Local/Pacific Rim)* 62 N. Market St., Wailuku, 808-891-1368

Ichiban Okazuya *(Japanese)* 2133 Kaohu St., Wailuku, 808-244-7276

Maui Bake Shop *(Bakery, Deli)* 2092 W. Vineyard St., Wailuku, 808-242-0064

Sam Sato's *(Japanese)* 1750 Wili Pa Loop, Wailuku, 808-244-7124

North Shore (Paia)

The north shore — specifically, Paia — is home to Maui's counter-culture, and they demand high quality ingredients and low prices. Visitors come through on their way to Hana (and to shop in the not-dirt-cheap boutiques) so it gets busy and parking is terrible. But there are some really good restaurants here, including:

Anthony's Coffee Co. *(Coffeehouse)* 90 Hana Highway, Paia, 808-579-8340

Café Des Amis *(Mediterranean/Indian)* 42 Baldwin Ave., Paia, 808-579-6323

Café Mambo and Picnics *(Mediterranean)* 30 Baldwin Ave., Paia, 808-579-8021

Flatbread Pizza Company *(Pizza)* 89 Hana Hwy., Paia, 808-579-8989

Fresh Mint *(Vegan/Vietnamese)* 115 Baldwin Ave., Paia, 808-579-9144

Mama's Fish House *(Pacific Rim)* 799 Poho Pl., Paia, 808-579-8488

Mana Foods *(Organic/Vegan)* 49 Baldwin Ave., Paia, 808-579-8078

Milagros Food Co. *(Mexican)* 3 Baldwin Ave., Paia, 808-579-8755

Moana Bakery & Café 71 Baldwin Ave., Paia, 808-579-9999

Ono Gelato *(Gelato/Ice Cream)* 115 Hana Hwy, Paia, 808-579-9201

Paia Fish Market *(American)* (For ono burgers) 100 Hana Hwy., Paia, 808-579-8030

South Maui (Kihei, Wailea)

South Maui is home to the fastest growing population of permanent Maui resident, but also hundreds of condos and vacation rentals, as well as some of the most exclusive resorts on the island. There are restaurants in every price range here. Our favorites are:

Kihei

Amigo's *(Mexican)* 41 E. Lipoa St., Kihei, 808-879-9952

Café @ La Plage *(coffeehouse)* 2395 S. Kihei Rd., Kihei, 808-875-7668

Café O'Lei *(Pacific Rim/American)* 2439 S. Kihei Rd., Kihei, 808-891-1368

Coconut's Fish Café *(American)* 1279 S. Kihei Rd., Kihei, 808-875-9979

Cuatro Restaurant *(Latin/Asian Fusion)* 1881 S. Kihei Rd., Kihei, 808-879-1110

Dog & Duck *(Pub)* 1913 S. Kihei Rd., Kihei, 808-875-9669

Duo *(American)* 3900 Wailea Alanui, Wailea, 808-874-8000

Fat Daddy's Smokehouse *(American/Barbecue)* 1913 S. Kihei Rd., Kihei, 808-879-8711

Five Palms Restaurant *(American/Pacific Rim)* 2960 S. Kihei Rd., Kihei, 808-879-2607

Izakaya Matsu *(Japanese)* 1280 S. Kihei Rd., Kihei, 808-874-0990

Joy's Place *(Vegetarian/American)* 1993 S. Kihei Rd., Kihei, 808-879-9258

Koiso Sushi Bar 2395 S. Kihei Rd., Kihei, 808-875-8258

Monsoon India *(Indian)* 760 S. Kihei Rd., Kihei, 808-875 6666

Ono Gelato *(gelato)* 1280 S. Kihei Rd., Kihei, 808-495-0287

Pita Paradise *(Mediterranean)* 1913 S. Kihei Rd., Kihei, 808-875-7679

Rodeo General Store, *(Deli, Prepared Foods)* 1847 S. Kihei Rd., Kihei, 808-633-4990

Sansei Seafood Restaurant & Sushi Bar *(Sushi/Pacific Rim)* 1881 S. Kihei Rd., Kihei, 808-879-0004

Thailand Cuisine *(Thai)* 1819 S. Kihei Rd., Kihei, 808-875-0839

Wailea

Capische? *(Italian)* 555 Kaukahi St., Wailea, 808-879-2224

Ferraro's Bar e Ristorante *(Italian)* 3900 Wailea Alanui Dr., Wailea, 808-874-8000

Pita Paradise *(Mediterranean)* 10 Wailea Gateway Place, Kihei (Wailea), 808-879-7177

Ruth's Chris Steak House *(American)* 3750 Wailea Alanui Dr., Wailea, 808-874-8880

Spago *(Pacific Rim)* 3900 Wailea Alanui Dr., Wailea, 808-874-8000

Tommy Bahama's Tropical Café *(American)* 3750 Wailea Alanui Dr., Wailea, 808-875-9983

Upcountry (Haiku, Kula, Makawao, Pukalani)

Upcountry is lovely, but there are only a handful of restaurants. Several are worth a stop-in. Here are our recommendations.

Haiku

Colleen's *(American/Pacific Rim)* 810 Haiku Rd., Haiku, 808-575-9211

North Shore Café *(Local/Breakfast)* 824 Kokomo Road, Haiku, 808-575-2770

Kula

Grandma's Coffeehouse *(Coffeehouse)* 153 Kula Hwy, Kula, 808-375-7853

La Provence *(French)* 3158 Lower Kula Rd., Kula, 808-878-1313

Makawao

Casanova *(Italian)* 1188 Makawao Ave., Makawao, 808-572-0220

Makawao Steak House *(Steakhouse)* 3612 Baldwin Ave., Makawao, 808-572-8711

Rodeo General Store, *(Deli/Prepared Foods)* 3661 Baldwin Ave., Makawao, 808-572-1868

T. Komoda Store and Bakery *(Bakery)* 3674 Baldwin Ave., Makawao, 808-572-7261

West Maui (Ka'anapali, Kahana, Kapalua, Lahaina, Napili, Olowalu)

West Maui has plenty of permanent residents, but there is no denying that it is tourist central. There are many restaurants ... but the ones we think are reliably worth your time and dollars are:

Ka'anapali

Aina Gourmet Market *(Deli, Prepared Foods)* 130 Kai Malina Pkwy, Ka'anapali, 808-662-2832

Japengo *(Sushi, Pacific Rim)* 200 Nohea Kai Dr., Ka'anapali, 808-667-4796

Roy's Bar & Grill *(Pacific Rim)* (after January 2012) 2290 Ka'anapali Pkwy, Ka'anapali, 808-669-6999

'Umalu *(Pacific Rim/American)* 200 Nohea Kai Dr., Ka'anapali, 808-661-1234

Kahana

Maui Brewing Company Brew Pub *(American)* 4405 Honoapiilani Hwy, Kahana, 808-669-3474

Roy's Bar & Grill *(Pacific Rim)* (until January 2012, when they move to a new location in Ka'anapali) 4405 Honoapiilani Hwy., Kahana, 808-669-6999

Kapalua

The Banyan Tree *(Pacific Rim)* 1 Ritz-Carlton Drive, Kapalua, 808-669-6200

Honolua Store *(American/Local/Plate Lunch)* 900 Office Rd., Kapalua, 808-665-9105

Pineapple Grill *(Pacific Rim)* 200 Kapalua Dr., Kapalua, 808-669-9600

Sansei Seafood Restaurant & Sushi Bar *(Sushi/Pacific Rim)* 600 Office Rd., Kapalua, 808-669-6286

Lahaina

Aloha Mixed Plate *(Local/Plate Lunch)* 1285 Front St., Lahaina, 808-661-3322

Amigo's *(Mexican)* 658 Front St., Wharf Cinema Center, Lahaina, 808-661-0210

Cilantro *(Mexican)* 170 Papalaua St., Lahaina, 808-667-5444

David Paul's Island Grill *(Pacific Rim)* 900 Front St., Lahaina, 808-662-3000

Gerard's Restaurant *(French)* 174 Lahainaluna Rd., Lahaina, 808-661-8939

Honu, *(Seafood/Pacific Rim)* 1295 Front St., Lahaina, 808-667-9390

I'o *(American/Pacific Rim)* 505 Front St., Lahaina, 808-661-8422

Kobe *(Japanese Steakhouse)* 136 Dickenson St., Lahaina, 808-667-5555

Lahaina Grill *(Pacific Rim)* 127 Lahainaluna Rd., Lahaina, 808-667-5117

Mala *(Pacific Rim)* 1307 Front St., Lahaina, 808-667-9394

Ono Gelato *(Gelato)* 815 Front St., Lahaina, 808-495-0203

Pacific'o *(Pacific Rim)* 505 Front St., Lahaina, 808-667-4341

Penne Pasta *(Italian)* 180 Dickenson St., Lahaina, 808-661-6633

Ruth's Chris Steak House *(American)* 900 Front St., Lahaina, 808-661-8815

Star Noodle *(Local/Japanese/Pacific Rim)* 286 Kupuohi St., Lahaina, 808-667-5400

Teddy's Bigger Burgers *(American)* 335 Keawe St., Lahaina, 808-661-9111

Thai Chef *(Thai)* 878 Front St., Lahaina, 808-667-2814

Ululani's Hawaiian Shave Ice *(Shave Ice)* 819 Front Street, Lahaina, and 790 Front Street, Lahaina, 360-606-2745

Napili

Sea House Restaurant *(American/Pacific Rim)* (breakfast only) 5900 Lower Honoapiilani Rd, Napili, 808-669-1500

Olowalu

Leoda's Kitchen and Pie Shop *(Local, Pacific Rim, Bakery)* 820 Olowalu Village Rd., Lahaina, 808-662-3600

Favorite Restaurants in Every Price Range

Here are our favorite restaurants in each price range ($-$$$$), grouped by location. These are the restaurants that give you a good value. Please read the reviews for all of thoughts on each of these restaurants.

$ Inexpensive: Average Entree is $10 & Under

$ in Central Maui

Amigo's *(Mexican)* 333 Dairy Rd., Kahului, 808-872-9525

Ichiban Okazuya (Japanese) 2133 Kaohu St., Wailuku, 808-244-7276

Maui Bake Shop *(Bakery, Deli)* 2092 W. Vineyard St., Wailuku, 808-242-0064

Tasaka Guri Guri *(Guri Guri)* 70 E. Ka'ahumanu Ave., Kahului, 808-871-4513

Sam Sato's *(Japanese)* 1750 Wili Pa Loop, Wailuku, 808-244-7124

Ululani's Hawaiian Shave Ice, 333 Dairy Road, Kahului, 360-606-2745

Whole Foods (Healthy/Organics) 70 Kaahumanu Ave., Kahului, 808-872-3310

$ in North Shore

Anthony's Coffee Co. *(Coffeehouse)* 90 Hana Highway, Paia, 808-579-8340

Café Des Amis *(Mediterranean/Indian)* 42 Baldwin Ave., Paia, 808-579-6323

Mana Foods *(Organic/Vegan)* 49 Baldwin Ave., Paia, 808-579-8078

Ono Gelato *(Gelato/Ice Cream)* 115 Hana Hwy, Paia, 808-579-9201

Paia Fish Market 100 Hana Hwy., Paia, 808-579-8030

$ in South Maui

Amigo's *(Mexican)* 41 E. Lipoa St., Kihei, 808-879-9952

Café @ La Plage *(American)* 2395 S. Kihei Rd., Kihei, 808-875-7668

Joy's Place *(Vegetarian/American)* 1993 S. Kihei Rd., Kihei, 808-879-9258

Ono Gelato *(gelato)* 1280 S. Kihei Rd., Kihei, 808-495-0287

Rodeo General Store, *(Deli, Prepared Foods)* 1847 S. Kihei Rd., Kihei, 808-633-4990

$ Upcountry

Grandma's Coffeehouse *(Coffeehouse)* 153 Kula Hwy, Kula, 808-375-7853

North Shore Café *(Local/Breakfast)* 824 Kokomo Road, Haiku, 808-575-2770

Rodeo General Store, *(Deli/Prepared Foods)* 3661 Baldwin Ave., Makawao, 808-572-1868

T. Komoda Store and Bakery *(Bakery)* 3674 Baldwin Ave., Makawao, 808-572-7261

$ in West Maui

Aina Gourmet Market *(Deli, Prepared Foods)* 130 Kai Malina Pkwy, Ka'anapali, 808-662-2832

Aloha Mixed Plate *(Local/Plate Lunch)* 1285 Front St., Lahaina, 808-661-3322

Amigo's *(Mexican)* 658 Front St., Wharf Cinema Center, Lahaina, 808-661-0210

Cilantro *(Mexican)* 170 Papalaua St., Lahaina, 808-667-5444

Honolua Store *(American/Local/Plate Lunch)* 900 Office Rd., Kapalua, 808-665-9105

Ono Gelato *(Gelato)* 815 Front St., Lahaina, 808-495-0203

Ululani's Hawaiian Shave Ice *(Shave Ice)* 819 Front Street, Lahaina, and 790 Front Street, Lahaina, 360-606-2745

$$ Moderate: Average Entree is $20 & Under

$$ in Central Maui

A Saigon Café *(Vietnamese)* 1792 Main St, Wailuku, 808-243-9560

Beach Bums Bar & Grill *(American/Barbecue)* 300 Ma'alaea Rd., Ma'alaea, 808-243-2286

Brigit & Bernard's Garden Café *(German)* 335 Hoohana St., Kahului, 808-877-6000

Café O'Lei *(Local/Pacific Rim)* 1333 Maui Lani Parkway, Kahului, 808-877-0073; and 62 N. Market St., Wailuku, 808-891-1368

Ruby's *(American)* 275 W. Ka'ahumanu Ave., Kahului, 808-248-7829

Thailand Cuisine *(Thai)* 70 E. Ka'ahumanu Ave., Kahului, 808-873-0225

$$ in North Shore

Café Mambo and Picnics *(Mediterranean)* 30 Baldwin Ave., Paia, 808-579-8021

Flatbread Pizza Company *(Pizza)* 89 Hana Hwy., Paia, 808-579-8989

Fresh Mint *(Vegan/Vietnamese)* 115 Baldwin Ave., Paia, 808-579-9144

Milagros Food Co. *(Mexican)* 3 Baldwin Ave., Paia, 808-579-8755

Moana Bakery & Café 71 Baldwin Ave., Paia, 808-579-9999

$$ in South Maui

Café O'Lei *(Pacific Rim/American)* 2439 S. Kihei Rd., Kihei, 808-891-1368

Coconut's Fish Café *(American)* 1279 S. Kihei Rd., Kihei, 808-875-9979

Dog & Duck *(Pub)* 1913 S. Kihei Rd., Kihei, 808-875-9669

Fat Daddy's Smokehouse *(American/Barbecue)* 1913 S. Kihei Rd., Kihei, 808-879-8711

Izakaya Matsu *(Japanese)* 1280 S. Kihei Rd., Kihei, 808-874-0990

Koiso Sushi Bar 2395 S. Kihei Rd., Kihei, 808-875-8258

Monsoon India *(Indian)* 760 S. Kihei Rd., Kihei, 808-875 6666

Pita Paradise *(Mediterranean)* 1913 S. Kihei Rd., Kihei, 808-875-7679; and 10 Wailea Gateway Place, Kihei (Wailea), 808-879-7177

Thailand Cuisine *(Thai)* 1819 S. Kihei Rd., Kihei, 808-875-0839

$$ Upcountry

Casanova *(Italian)* 1188 Makawao Ave., Makawao, 808-572-0220

Colleen's *(American/Pacific Rim)* 810 Haiku Rd., Haiku, 808-575-9211

La Provence *(French)* 3158 Lower Kula Rd., Kula, 808-878-1313

$$ in West Maui

Leoda's Kitchen and Pie Shop *(Local, Pacific Rim, Bakery)* 820 Olowalu Village Rd., Lahaina, 808-662-3600

Maui Brewing Company Brew Pub *(American)* 4405 Honoapiilani Hwy, Kahana, 808-669-3474

Penne Pasta *(Italian)* 180 Dickenson St., Lahaina, 808-661-6633

Sea House Restaurant *(American/Pacific Rim)* (breakfast only) 5900 Lower Honoapiilani Rd, Napili, 808-669-1500

Star Noodle *(Local/Japanese/Pacific Rim)* 286 Kupuohi St., Lahaina, 808-667-5400

Teddy's Bigger Burgers *(American)* 335 Keawe St., Lahaina, 808-661-9111

Thai Chef *(Thai)* 878 Front St., Lahaina, 808-667-2814

$$$ Expensive: Average Entree is $35 & Under

$$$ in Central Maui

Bistro Casanova *(Mediterranean/Italian)* 33 Lono Ave, Kahului, 808-873-3650

$$$ in North Shore (none)

$$$ in South Maui

Cuatro Restaurant *(Latin/Asian Fusion)* 1881 S. Kihei Rd., Kihei, 808-879-1110

Five Palms Restaurant *(American/Pacific Rim)* 2960 S. Kihei Rd., Kihei, 808-879-2607

Ruth's Chris Steak House *(American)* 3750 Wailea Alanui Dr., Wailea, 808-874-8880

Sansei Seafood Restaurant & Sushi Bar *(Sushi/Pacific Rim)* 1881 S. Kihei Rd., Kihei, 808-879-0004

Tommy Bahama's Tropical Café *(American)* 3750 Wailea Alanui Dr., Wailea, 808-875-9983

$$$ Upcountry

Makawao Steak House *(Steakhouse)* 3612 Baldwin Ave., Makawao, 808-572-8711

$$$ in West Maui

David Paul's Island Grill *(Pacific Rim)* 900 Front St., Lahaina, 808-662-3000

Honu, *(Seafood/Pacific Rim)* 1295 Front St., Lahaina, 808-667-9390

Japengo *(Sushi, Pacific Rim)* 200 Nohea Kai Dr., Ka'anapali, 808-667-4796

Kobe *(Japanese Steakhouse)* 136 Dickenson St., Lahaina, 808-667-5555

Mala *(Pacific Rim)* 1307 Front St., Lahaina, 808-667-9394

Roy's Bar & Grill *(Pacific Rim)* (after January 2012) 2290 Ka'anapali Pkwy, Ka'anapali, 808-669-6999

Ruth's Chris Steak House *(American)* 900 Front St., Lahaina, 808-661-8815

Sansei Seafood Restaurant & Sushi Bar *(Sushi/Pacific Rim)* 600 Office Rd., Kapalua, 808-669-6286

'Umalu *(Pacific Rim/American)* 200 Nohea Kai Dr., Ka'anapali, 808-661-1234

$$$$ Very Expensive: Average Entree is $35 & Up

$$$$ in Central Maui (none)

$$$$ in North Shore

Mama's Fish House *(Pacific Rim)* 799 Poho Pl., Paia, 808-579-8488

$$$$ in South Maui

Capische? *(Italian)* 555 Kaukahi St., Wailea, 808-879-2224

Duo *(American)* 3900 Wailea Alanui, Wailea, 808-874-8000

Ferraro's Bar e Ristorante *(Italian)* 3900 Wailea Alanui Dr., Wailea, 808-874-8000

Spago *(Pacific Rim)* 3900 Wailea Alanui Dr., Wailea, 808-874-8000

$$$$ Upcountry (none)

$$$$ in West Maui

The Banyan Tree *(Pacific Rim)* 1 Ritz-Carlton Drive, Kapalua, 808-669-6200

Gerard's Restaurant *(French)* 174 Lahainaluna Rd., Lahaina, 808-661-8939

I'o *(American/Pacific Rim)* 505 Front St., Lahaina, 808-661-8422

Lahaina Grill 127 Lahainaluna Rd., Lahaina, 808-667-5117

Pacific'o *(Pacific Rim)* 505 Front St., Lahaina, 808-667-4341

Pineapple Grill *(Pacific Rim)* 200 Kapalua Dr., Kapalua, 808-669-9600

Restaurants Listed by Ratings

Food Ratings

The Banyan Tree
Capische?
Cuatro Restaurant
Flatbread Pizza Company

Gerard's Restaurant
Koiso Sushi Bar
Roy's Bar & Grill
Sansei Seafood
   Restaurant & Sushi Bar

Spago
Thailand Cuisine
Ululani's Hawaiian
   Shave Ice

Duo
Honu Seafood & Pizza

Ono Gelato
Pacific'o

Tommy Bahama's
   Tropical Café

A Saigon Café
Aina Gourmet Market
Amigo's
Beach Bums Bar & Grill
Bistro Casanova
Brigit & Bernard's
   Garden Café
Café Mambo and Picnics
Casanova
Cilantro
Coconut's Fish Café
Colleen's
David Paul's Island Grill
Ferraro's Bar e Ristorante
Fresh Mint

Humuhumunu-
   kunukuapua'a
Ichiban Okazuya
Japengo
Joy's Place
La Provence
Lahaina Grill
Leoda's Kitchen and Pie
   Shop
Main Street Bistro
Mala Ocean Tavern
Mala Wailea
Mama's Fish House
Maui Bake Shop & Deli
Moana Bakery & Café
Monsoon India

Pineapple Grill
Pita Paradise
Rodeo General Store
Ruby's
Ruth's Chris Steak
   House
Sea House Restaurant
Star Noodle
Sushi Paradise
T. Komoda Store and
   Bakery
Teddy's Bigger Burgers
Thai Chef
Tropica
'Umalu
Whole Foods

Aroma D'Italia Ristorante
Ba-Le Sandwiches
Café Des Amis
Café O'Lei
Cane and Taro

Cinnamon Roll Fair
Izakaya Matsu
Joe's Bar & Grill
Kai Wailea
Longhi's
Mana Foods

Marco's Grill & Deli
Maui Brewing Company Brew Pub
Paia Fish Market
Pulehu, an Italian Grill

---

808 Deli
Alive & Well
Aloha Mixed Plate
Anthony's Coffee Co.
Antonio's
Big Wave Café
Bistro Molokini
Blue Moon
Bubba Gump Shrimp Co.
Buzz's Wharf
Café @ la Plage
Castaway Café
Cheeseburger in Paradise
Cheeseburger Island Style
China Boat
China Bowl & Asian Cuisine
CJ's Deli & Diner
Cool Cat Café
Costco
Da Kitchen
Dog & Duck
Dollie's Gourmet Pizza
Down to Earth
Dragon Dragon Chinese Restaurant

Eskimo Candy
Fat Boy Burger
Fat Daddy's Smokehouse
Five Palms Restaurant
Fred's Mexican Café
Gannon's
Gazebo Restaurant
Giannotto's Pizzeria
Grandma's Coffeehouse
Hali'imaile General Store
Hawaiian Moons Natural Foods
Honolua Store
Hula Grill
I'o
Isana Restaurant
Jawz Tacos
Julia's Best Banana Bread
Kihei Caffe
Kimo's
Kobe
Kula Lodge Restaurant
L&L Hawaiian Barbecue
Lahaina Coolers
Lahaina Pizza Company
Leilani's on the Beach
Lulu's

Lulu's Lahaina Surf Club
Makawao Steak House
Makawao Sushi & Deli
Mama's Ribs & Rotisserie
Market Fresh Bistro
Maui Coffee Roasters
Maui Culinary Academy Food Court and "Class Act"
Maui Tacos
Maui Thai
Merriman's Kapalua
Milagros Food Co.
Mixed Plate
Moose McGillycuddy's
Mulligans on the Blue
Nikki's Pizza
North Shore Café
Ocean's Beach Bar & Grill
Penne Pasta
Pizza Madness
The Plantation House Restaurant
Polli's Mexican Restaurant
Sam Sato's

Shaka Pizza	Stella Blues Café	Three's Bar & Grill
Son'z at Swan Court	Taqueria Cruz	Vietnamese Cuisine
South Shore Tiki Lounge	Tasaka Guri Guri	Wailuku Coffee Company

| Bangkok Cuisine | Matteo's Pizzeria | Nick's Fishmarket |
| Duke's | MonkeyPod Kitchen by Merriman | |

| 808 Bistro | Mai Tai Lounge | Sunrise Café |
| Charley's Restaurant & Saloon | Sarento's on the Beach | Tasty Crust |

| Betty's Beach Café | Cary & Eddie's Hideaway Buffet |

Ambience Ratings

Capische?
David Paul's Island Grill
Duke's
Ferraro's Bar e Ristorante
Gannon's
Gazebo Restaurant

Hula Grill
Humuhumunu-kunukuapua'a
Kula Lodge Restaurant
Leilani's on the Beach
Mama's Fish House
Merriman's Kapalua

Nick's Fishmarket
The Plantation House Restaurant
Sarento's on the Beach
Son'z at Swan Court
Spago

Aloha Mixed Plate
Five Palms Restaurant

Honu Seafood & Pizza
Longhi's

808 Bistro
The Banyan Tree
Betty's Beach Café
Bistro Casanova
Bistro Molokini
Bubba Gump Shrimp Co.
Buzz's Wharf
Café Des Amis
Café O'Lei
Castaway Café
Cheeseburger in Paradise
Cheeseburger Island Style
Cool Cat Café
Cuatro Restaurant
Duo
Gerard's Restaurant
Hali'imaile General Store

I'o
Japengo
Joe's Bar & Grill
Julia's Best Banana Bread
Kimo's
La Provence
Lahaina Grill
Lahaina Pizza Company
Leoda's Kitchen and Pie Shop
Mai Tai Lounge
Makawao Steak House
Mala Ocean Tavern
MonkeyPod Kitchen by Merriman
Monsoon India
Mulligans on the Blue
Ocean's Beach Bar & Grill

Pacific'o
Penne Pasta
Pineapple Grill
Pita Paradise
Pizza Madness
Pulehu, an Italian Grill
Roy's Bar & Grill
Ruth's Chris Steak House
Sansei Seafood Restaurant & Sushi Bar
Sea House Restaurant
Star Noodle
Thailand Cuisine
Tommy Bahama's Tropical Café
'Umalu
Wailuku Coffee Company

Aroma D'Italia Ristorante
Colleen's

Dragon Dragon Chinese Restaurant
Honolua Store

Moose McGillycuddy's

Aina Gourmet Market
Anthony's Coffee Co.
Beach Bums Bar & Grill
Big Wave Café
Brigit & Bernard's Garden Café
Café @ la Plage
Café Mambo and Picnics
Cane and Taro

Cary & Eddie's Hideaway Buffet
Casanova
Charley's Restaurant & Saloon
China Boat
China Bowl & Asian Cuisine
Cilantro
CJ's Deli & Diner

Coconut's Fish Café
Dollie's Gourmet Pizza
Fat Boy Burger
Fat Daddy's Smokehouse
Flatbread Pizza Company
Fred's Mexican Café
Grandma's Coffeehouse
Isana Restaurant
Jawz Tacos

Kai Wailea
Kihei Caffe
Kobe
Lahaina Coolers
Lulu's
Lulu's Lahaina Surf Club
Main Street Bistro
Makawao Sushi & Deli
Mala Wailea
Marco's Grill & Deli
Market Fresh Bistro
Matteo's Pizzeria
Maui Bake Shop & Deli
Maui Brewing Company Brew Pub

Maui Coffee Roasters
Maui Culinary Academy Food Court and "Class Act"
Maui Tacos
Maui Thai
Milagros Food Co.
Moana Bakery & Café
North Shore Café
Ono Gelato
Paia Fish Market
Polli's Mexican Restaurant
Rodeo General Store
Ruby's

Sam Sato's
Shaka Pizza
South Shore Tiki Lounge
Stella Blues Café
Sunrise Café
Sushi Paradise
Teddy's Bigger Burgers
Three's Bar & Grill
Tropica
Ululani's Hawaiian Shave Ice
Vietnamese Cuisine
Whole Foods

Antonio's

Blue Moon

808 Deli
A Saigon Café
Alive & Well
Amigo's
Ba-Le Sandwiches
Bangkok Cuisine
Cinnamon Roll Fair
Costco
Da Kitchen
Dog & Duck
Down to Earth

Eskimo Candy
Fresh Mint
Giannotto's Pizzeria
Hawaiian Moons Natural Foods
Ichiban Okazuya
Izakaya Matsu
Joy's Place
Koiso Sushi Bar
L&L Hawaiian Barbecue

Mama's Ribs & Rotisserie
Mana Foods
Mixed Plate
Nikki's Pizza
T. Komoda Store and Bakery
Taqueria Cruz
Tasaka Guri Guri
Tasty Crust
Thai Chef

Service Ratings

Duo
Ferraro's Bar e Ristorante
Gerard's Restaurant

Lahaina Grill
Spago

Ululani's Hawaiian Shave Ice
Whole Foods

---

808 Bistro
A Saigon Café
Alive & Well
Amigo's
Aroma D'Italia Ristorante
The Banyan Tree
Bubba Gump Shrimp Co.
Café @ la Plage
Café O'Lei
Capische?
Casanova
Cilantro
Coconut's Fish Café
Cool Cat Café

Cuatro Restaurant
Dog & Duck
Giannotto's Pizzeria
Grandma's Coffeehouse
Hali'imaile General Store
Joe's Bar & Grill
Joy's Place
Kobe
Koiso Sushi Bar
Lahaina Coolers
Main Street Bistro
Mala Ocean Tavern
Mala Wailea
Mama's Fish House
Maui Bake Shop & Deli
Ono Gelato

Pita Paradise
Roy's Bar & Grill
Ruby's
Ruth's Chris Steak House
Sam Sato's
Sansei Seafood Restaurant & Sushi Bar
Sea House Restaurant
Star Noodle
Teddy's Bigger Burgers
Thailand Cuisine
Tommy Bahama's Tropical Café
Wailuku Coffee Company

Jawz Tacos
Leoda's Kitchen and Pie Shop

Pacific'o
Pulehu, an Italian Grill

---

808 Deli
Aina Gourmet Market
Anthony's Coffee Co.
Antonio's
Ba-Le Sandwiches
Beach Bums Bar & Grill

Betty's Beach Café
Big Wave Café
Bistro Molokini
Blue Moon
Brigit & Bernard's Garden Café
Buzz's Wharf

Café Mambo and Picnics
Cane and Taro
Charley's Restaurant & Saloon
China Boat
China Bowl & Asian Cuisine

Cinnamon Roll Fair
CJ's Deli & Diner
Colleen's
Costco
Da Kitchen
David Paul's Island Grill
Dragon Dragon Chinese
 Restaurant
Duke's
Eskimo Candy
Fat Boy Burger
Fat Daddy's Smokehouse
Five Palms Restaurant
Flatbread Pizza Company
Fred's Mexican Café
Gannon's
Gazebo Restaurant
Hawaiian Moons Natural
 Foods
Honolua Store
Honu Seafood & Pizza
Hula Grill
Humuhumunu-
 kunukuapua'a
Ichiban Okazuya
I'o
Isana Restaurant

Izakaya Matsu
Japengo
Julia's Best Banana Bread
Kai Wailea
Kihei Caffe
Kimo's
Kula Lodge Restaurant
Lahaina Pizza Company
Leilani's on the Beach
Longhi's
Mai Tai Lounge
Makawao Steak House
Mana Foods
Marco's Grill & Deli
Market Fresh Bistro
Matteo's Pizzeria
Maui Brewing Company
 Brew Pub
Maui Coffee Roasters
Maui Tacos
Maui Thai
Merriman's Kapalua
Milagros Food Co.
Mixed Plate
MonkeyPod Kitchen by
 Merriman
Monsoon India

Nick's Fishmarket
Nikki's Pizza
North Shore Café
Paia Fish Market
Penne Pasta
Pineapple Grill
Pizza Madness
The Plantation House
 Restaurant
Polli's Mexican
 Restaurant
Rodeo General Store
Sarento's on the Beach
Shaka Pizza
Son'z at Swan Court
South Shore Tiki Lounge
Stella Blues Café
Sushi Paradise
T. Komoda Store and
 Bakery
Tasaka Guri Guri
Thai Chef
Three's Bar & Grill
Tropica
'Umalu
Vietnamese Cuisine

Aloha Mixed Plate

Taqueria Cruz

Bangkok Cuisine
Bistro Casanova
Café Des Amis
Cary & Eddie's Hideaway
    Buffet
Castaway Café
Cheeseburger in Paradise
Cheeseburger Island
    Style

Dollie's Gourmet Pizza
Down to Earth
Fresh Mint
L&L Hawaiian Barbecue
Lulu's
Lulu's Lahaina Surf Club
Makawao Sushi & Deli
Mama's Ribs &
    Rotisserie

Maui Culinary Academy
    Food Court and "Class
    Act"
Moana Bakery & Café
Moose McGillycuddy's
Mulligans on the Blue
Ocean's Beach Bar &
    Grill
Sunrise Café
Tasty Crust

La Provence

Love Ratings

The Banyan Tree
Capische?
Cilantro
Coconut's Fish Café
Cuatro Restaurant
David Paul's Island Grill
Flatbread Pizza Company
Fresh Mint
Gerard's Restaurant

Grandma's Coffeehouse
Honu Seafood & Pizza
Ichiban Okazuya
Joy's Place
Koiso Sushi Bar
Main Street Bistro
Mala Ocean Tavern
Mala Wailea
Maui Brewing Company

Brew Pub
Ono Gelato
Pineapple Grill
Star Noodle
Tasaka Guri Guri
Three's Bar & Grill
Ululani's Hawaiian Shave
    Ice
Whole Foods

Alive & Well
Leoda's Kitchen and Pie
    Shop

Roy's Bar & Grill

808 Deli
A Saigon Café
Aina Gourmet Market
Amigo's
Aroma D'Italia
  Ristorante
Beach Bums Bar & Grill
Bistro Casanova
Brigit & Bernard's
  Garden Café
Buzz's Wharf
Café @ la Plage
Café Des Amis
Café Mambo and Picnics
Café O'Lei
Casanova
Cinnamon Roll Fair
Colleen's
Da Kitchen
Down to Earth
Duo
Fat Daddy's Smokehouse

Ferraro's Bar e Ristorante
Giannotto's Pizzeria
Hali'imaile General Store
Hawaiian Moons Natural
  Foods
Humuhumunu-
  kunukuapua'a
I'o
Julia's Best Banana Bread
Kihei Caffe
La Provence
Lahaina Grill
Mama's Fish House
Mana Foods
Market Fresh Bistro
Maui Bake Shop & Deli
Maui Coffee Roasters
Maui Culinary Academy
  Food Court and "Class
  Act"
Milagros Food Co.
Mixed Plate
Moana Bakery & Café

Monsoon India
Nikki's Pizza
North Shore Café
Pacific'o
Paia Fish Market
Penne Pasta
Pita Paradise
Rodeo General Store
Ruth's Chris Steak
  House
Sam Sato's
Sansei Seafood
  Restaurant & Sushi Bar
Sea House Restaurant
Spago
Taqueria Cruz
Teddy's Bigger Burgers
Thai Chef
Thailand Cuisine
Tommy Bahama's
  Tropical Café
Tropica

Honolua Store

Izakaya Matsu

Japengo

---

808 Bistro
Aloha Mixed Plate
Anthony's Coffee Co.
Antonio's
Ba-Le Sandwiches
Bangkok Cuisine

Bistro Molokini
Bubba Gump Shrimp
  Co.
Cane and Taro
CJ's Deli & Diner
Costco

Dog & Duck
Dollie's Gourmet Pizza
Dragon Dragon Chinese
  Restaurant
Eskimo Candy
Fat Boy Burger

Five Palms Restaurant
Hula Grill
Isana Restaurant
Jawz Tacos
Joe's Bar & Grill
Kai Wailea
Kimo's
Kobe
Kula Lodge Restaurant
L&L Hawaiian Barbecue
Lahaina Coolers
Leilani's on the Beach
Longhi's
Makawao Steak House

Makawao Sushi & Deli
Mama's Ribs & Rotisserie
Marco's Grill & Deli
Matteo's Pizzeria
Maui Tacos
Maui Thai
Merriman's Kapalua
MonkeyPod Kitchen by Merriman
Moose McGillycuddy's
Mulligans on the Blue
Pizza Madness

The Plantation House Restaurant
Pulehu, an Italian Grill
Ruby's
Shaka Pizza
South Shore Tiki Lounge
Stella Blues Café
Sushi Paradise
T. Komoda Store and Bakery
'Umalu
Vietnamese Cuisine
Wailuku Coffee Company

Big Wave Café
Blue Moon
Cary & Eddie's Hideaway Buffet
Castaway Café
Cheeseburger in Paradise
Cheeseburger Island Style
China Boat

China Bowl & Asian Cuisine
Cool Cat Café
Duke's
Gannon's
Gazebo Restaurant
Lahaina Pizza Company
Lulu's
Lulu's Lahaina Surf Club

Mai Tai Lounge
Nick's Fishmarket
Ocean's Beach Bar & Grill
Polli's Mexican Restaurant
Sarento's on the Beach
Son'z at Swan Court
Sunrise Café

Betty's Beach Café
Charley's Restaurant & Saloon

Fred's Mexican Café
Tasty Crust

Value Ratings

Aloha Mixed Plate
Café Des Amis
Da Kitchen
Fat Daddy's Smokehouse
Flatbread Pizza Company
Giannotto's Pizzeria
Honolua Store
Ichiban Okazuya

Jawz Tacos
L&L Hawaiian Barbecue
Mana Foods
Maui Coffee Roasters
Maui Culinary Academy
  Food Court and "Class
  Act"
Nikki's Pizza
North Shore Café

Paia Fish Market
Sam Sato's
Tasaka Guri Guri
Tasty Crust
Thai Chef
Thailand Cuisine
Ululani's Hawaiian Shave
  Ice

Penne Pasta

---

808 Deli
A Saigon Café
Amigo's
Anthony's Coffee Co.
Antonio's
Ba-Le Sandwiches
The Banyan Tree
Bistro Casanova
Café Mambo and Picnics
Café O'Lei
Capische?
Casanova
Castaway Café
Cilantro
CJ's Deli & Diner
Coconut's Fish Café
Colleen's
Cuatro Restaurant

David Paul's Island Grill
Dog & Duck
Down to Earth
Duo
Eskimo Candy
Gerard's Restaurant
Grandma's Coffeehouse
Honu Seafood & Pizza
Humuhumunu-
  kunukuapua'a
I'o
Izakaya Matsu
Julia's Best Banana Bread
Kobe
Koiso Sushi Bar
Lahaina Grill
Leoda's Kitchen and Pie
  Shop

Main Street Bistro
Makawao Steak House
Mala Ocean Tavern
Mala Wailea
Mama's Ribs &
  Rotisserie
Marco's Grill & Deli
Matteo's Pizzeria
Maui Bake Shop & Deli
Maui Brewing Company
  Brew Pub
Maui Tacos
Milagros Food Co.
Mixed Plate
Monsoon India
Ocean's Beach Bar &
  Grill
Ono Gelato

Pacific'o
Pineapple Grill
Pita Paradise
Pizza Madness
The Plantation House
Restaurant
Rodeo General Store
Roy's Bar & Grill

Ruby's
Ruth's Chris Steak
House
Sansei Seafood
Restaurant & Sushi Bar
Sea House Restaurant
South Shore Tiki Lounge
Spago

Star Noodle
Taqueria Cruz
Teddy's Bigger Burgers
Three's Bar & Grill
Wailuku Coffee
Company

Aroma D'Italia
Ristorante
Dragon Dragon Chinese
Restaurant

Five Palms Restaurant
Joe's Bar & Grill
Kihei Caffe
Lulu's

MonkeyPod Kitchen by
Merriman
Tommy Bahama's
Tropical Café

808 Bistro
Alive & Well
Bangkok Cuisine
Beach Bums Bar & Grill
Big Wave Café
Bistro Molokini
Blue Moon
Brigit & Bernard's
Garden Café
Bubba Gump Shrimp
Co.
Buzz's Wharf
Café @ la Plage
Cane and Taro
Cary & Eddie's Hideaway
Buffet
Charley's Restaurant &
Saloon
Cheeseburger in Paradise
Cheeseburger Island

Style
China Boat
China Bowl & Asian
Cuisine
Cinnamon Roll Fair
Cool Cat Café
Dollie's Gourmet Pizza
Duke's
Fat Boy Burger
Ferraro's Bar e Ristorante
Fred's Mexican Café
Fresh Mint
Gannon's
Gazebo Restaurant
Hali'imaile General Store
Hawaiian Moons Natural
Foods
Hula Grill
Isana Restaurant
Japengo

Joy's Place
Kai Wailea
Kimo's
Kula Lodge Restaurant
La Provence
Lahaina Coolers
Lahaina Pizza Company
Leilani's on the Beach
Longhi's
Lulu's Lahaina Surf Club
Mai Tai Lounge
Makawao Sushi & Deli
Mama's Fish House
Market Fresh Bistro
Maui Thai
Merriman's Kapalua
Moana Bakery & Café
Moose McGillycuddy's
Mulligans on the Blue

Nick's Fishmarket	Stella Blues Café	Tropica
Polli's Mexican Restaurant	Sunrise Café	'Umalu
Pulehu, an Italian Grill	Sushi Paradise	Vietnamese Cuisine
Shaka Pizza	T. Komoda Store and Bakery	Whole Foods

Betty's Beach Café	Sarento's on the Beach	Son'z at Swan Court

Overall Ratings

OVERALL: 4.6 out of 5 stars

Capische?	Spago
Gerard's Restaurant	Ululani's

OVERALL: 4.4 out of 5 stars

The Banyan Tree	Thailand Cuisine
Cuatro Restaurant	

OVERALL: 4.3 out of 5 stars

Duo
Roy's Bar & Grill

OVERALL: 4.2 out of 5 stars

David Paul's Island Grill	Honu Seafood & Pizza	Sansei Seafood Restaurant & Sushi Bar
Ferraro's Bar e Ristorante	Lahaina Grill	Star Noodle
Flatbread Pizza Company	Mala Ocean Tavern	

OVERALL: 4.1 out of 5 stars

Coconut's Fish Café
Ono Gelato

OVERALL: **4** out of 5 stars	Cilantro
	Humuhumunu-
	  kunukuapua'a
	Koiso Sushi Bar
	Leoda's Kitchen and Pie
	  Shop
	Main Street Bistro
		Makawao Steak House
		Mala Wailea
		Mama's Fish House
		Pacific'o
		Pineapple Grill
		Pita Paradise
			Ruth's Chris Steak
			  House
			Sea House Restaurant
			Tommy Bahama's
			  Tropical Café
			Whole Foods

OVERALL: **3.9** out of 5 stars	Café O'Lei		
OVERALL: **3.8** out of 5 stars	Grandma's Coffeehouse Ichiban Okazuya	Monsoon India Sam Sato's	Teddy's Bigger Burgers

OVERALL: **3.7** out of 5 stars	Aroma D'Italia
	  Ristorante
	Café Des Amis
		Colleen's
		Maui Brewing Company
		  Brew Pub
			Paia Fish Market
			Penne Pasta

OVERALL: **3.6** out of 5 stars	A Saigon Café
	Aina Gourmet Market
	Aloha Mixed Plate
	Amigo's
	Bistro Casanova
	Café Mambo and Picnics
	Casanova
	Fat Daddy's Smokehouse
	Giannotto's Pizzeria
		Hali'imaile General Store
		Honolua Store
		I'o
		Joe's Bar & Grill
		Joy's Place
		Julia's Best Banana Bread
		Maui Bake Shop & Deli
		Maui Coffee Roasters
		North Shore Café
			The Plantation House
			  Restaurant
			Rodeo General Store
			Ruby's
			Tasaka Guri Guri
			Thai Chef
			Three's Bar & Grill
			Wailuku Coffee
			  Company

OVERALL: **3.5** out of 5 stars	Japengo Jawz Tacos	Mana Foods	

OVERALL:
3.4
out of 5 stars

Beach Bums Bar & Grill
Brigit & Bernard's Garden Café
Bubba Gump Shrimp Co.
Buzz's Wharf
Café @ la Plage
Cane and Taro
Cinnamon Roll Fair

Da Kitchen
Five Palms Restaurant
Hula Grill
Kobe
Kula Lodge Restaurant
Leilani's on the Beach
Maui Culinary Academy Food Court and "Class Act"

Milagros Food Co.
Nikki's Pizza
Pizza Madness
Pulehu, an Italian Grill
Sushi Paradise
Tropica
'Umalu

OVERALL:
3.3
out of 5 stars

Alive & Well
Kihei Caffe

Longhi's
Marco's Grill & Deli

OVERALL:
3.2
out of 5 stars

808 Bistro
808 Deli
Anthony's Coffee Co.
Bistro Molokini
CJ's Deli & Diner
Cool Cat Café
Costco
Dog & Duck

Dragon Dragon Chinese Restaurant
Fresh Mint
Gannon's
Gazebo Restaurant
Izakaya Matsu
Kimo's
La Provence
Lahaina Coolers
Market Fresh Bistro

Maui Tacos
Merriman's Kapalua
Mixed Plate
Moana Bakery & Café
MonkeyPod Kitchen by Merriman
South Shore Tiki Lounge
T. Komoda Store and Bakery

OVERALL:
3.1
out of 5 stars

Antonio's
Ba-Le Sandwiches
Duke's

Kai Wailea
Matteo's Pizzeria
Moose McGillycuddy's

Nick's Fishmarket
Taqueria Cruz

OVERALL:
3
out of 5 stars

Castaway Café
Down to Earth
Eskimo Candy
Fat Boy Burger
Hawaiian Moons Natural Foods

Isana Restaurant
L&L Hawaiian Barbecue
Lahaina Pizza Company
Maui Thai
Mulligans on the Blue

Ocean's Beach Bar & Grill
Shaka Pizza
Son'z at Swan Court
Stella Blues Café
Vietnamese Cuisine

| **OVERALL:** **2.8** out of 5 stars | Big Wave Café
Cheeseburger in Paradise
Cheeseburger Island Style
China Boat | China Bowl & Asian Cuisine
Dollie's Gourmet Pizza
Mai Tai Lounge
Makawao Sushi & Deli | Mama's Ribs & Rotisserie
Polli's Mexican Restaurant
Sarento's on the Beach |

| **OVERALL:** **2.7** out of 5 stars | Blue Moon
Lulu's |

| **OVERALL:** **2.6** out of 5 stars | Fred's Mexican Café
Lulu's Lahaina Surf Club |

| **OVERALL:** **2.5** out of 5 stars | Bangkok Cuisine |

| **OVERALL:** **2.4** out of 5 stars | Charley's Restaurant & Saloon | Sunrise Café
Tasty Crust |

| **OVERALL:** **2.2** out of 5 stars | Betty's Beach Café
Cary & Eddie's Hideaway Buffet |

Index

Thank You!

We appreciate you taking the time to use this guide, and we hope that it has been truly helpful to you. If you want to contact us, do so through our website: www.TopMauiRestaurants.com.

Five Minute Thank You: Review the Reviewers

Readers who like to express themselves, step forward! We so appreciate you taking five minutes to write a review of **Top Maui Restaurants** at your favorite online bookseller. It's word of mouth from readers like you that inspired this book's publication in the first place, and every edition gets better because of you. We appreciate your support.

We May Feel Full ... But Over 10,000 of Our Neighbors on Maui Are Hungry

According to the **Maui Food Bank**, there are over 10,000 people struggling with hunger in Maui County. This is despicable and wrong and bad and horrible, and we wish that we could just STOP IT. It would mean the world to us if you would donate to our favorite charity, the Maui Food Bank. If you are on Maui, look for their donation bins in supermarkets to make a food donation, or make a general donation through their website at any time and from anywhere in the world. We thank you from the bottom of our hearts.

Maui Food Bank
www.MauiFoodBank.com

Register This Book and Get Free Updates!

We want to be able to keep in touch with you throughout the year as we send out updates from our blog, www.MauiRestaurantsBlog.com.

When you register your book with our site, not only will you get **Aloha Fridays**, our (usually) weekly update on the Maui restaurant scene, but we will also send you a special "down-and-dirty" email that lists updates for this edition.

The email will list restaurants that have closed since publication, and also significant new restaurants worth your time and dollars. If our opinion of a restaurant changes significantly, we will tell you, briefly, how and why. We'll also alert you to any new food stands or Maui delicacies we think you should try while you're here. And even if you register your book months before you need to use it, you can still get this latest information by emailing customer support at cs@topmauirestaurants.com. Include the email address you used to register the book, and ask to get the latest update email.

Register your book here:

www.TopMauiRestaurants.com/2012

Made in the USA
San Bernardino, CA
08 November 2012